TRUST MANAGEMENT II

IFIP – The International Federation for Information Processing

IFIP was founded in 1960 under the auspices of UNESCO, following the First World Computer Congress held in Paris the previous year. An umbrella organization for societies working in information processing, IFIP's aim is two-fold: to support information processing within its member countries and to encourage technology transfer to developing nations. As its mission statement clearly states,

> IFIP's mission is to be the leading, truly international, apolitical organization which encourages and assists in the development, exploitation and application of information technology for the benefit of all people.

IFIP is a non-profitmaking organization, run almost solely by 2500 volunteers. It operates through a number of technical committees, which organize events and publications. IFIP's events range from an international congress to local seminars, but the most important are:

• The IFIP World Computer Congress, held every second year;
• Open conferences;
• Working conferences.

The flagship event is the IFIP World Computer Congress, at which both invited and contributed papers are presented. Contributed papers are rigorously refereed and the rejection rate is high.

As with the Congress, participation in the open conferences is open to all and papers may be invited or submitted. Again, submitted papers are stringently refereed.

The working conferences are structured differently. They are usually run by a working group and attendance is small and by invitation only. Their purpose is to create an atmosphere conducive to innovation and development. Refereeing is less rigorous and papers are subjected to extensive group discussion.

Publications arising from IFIP events vary. The papers presented at the IFIP World Computer Congress and at open conferences are published as conference proceedings, while the results of the working conferences are often published as collections of selected and edited papers.

Any national society whose primary activity is in information may apply to become a full member of IFIP, although full membership is restricted to one society per country. Full members are entitled to vote at the annual General Assembly, National societies preferring a less committed involvement may apply for associate or corresponding membership. Associate members enjoy the same benefits as full members, but without voting rights. Corresponding members are not represented in IFIP bodies. Affiliated membership is open to non-national societies, and individual and honorary membership schemes are also offered.

TRUST MANAGEMENT II

*Proceedings of IFIPTM 2008: Joint iTrust and
PST Conferences on Privacy, Trust Management
and Security, June 18-20, 2008, Trondheim, Norway*

Edited by
Yücel Karabulut
SAP Research
USA

John Mitchell
Stanford University
USA

Peter Herrmann
Norwegian University of Science and Technology
Norway

Christian Damsgaard Jensen
Technical University of Denmark
Denmark

Trust Management II

Edited by Yücel Karabulut, John Mitchell, Peter Herrmann
and Christian Damsgaard Jensen

p. cm. (IFIP International Federation for Information Processing, a Springer Series
in Computer Science)

ISSN: 1571-5736 / 1861-2288 (Internet)
ISBN: 978-1-4419-3477-2
e-ISBN: 978-0-387-09428-1

Printed on acid-free paper

Printed in the United States of America.

9 8 7 6 5 4 3 2 1

springer.com

Preface

This volume contains the proceedings of the IFIPTM 2008, the Joint iTrust and PST Conferences on Privacy, Trust Management and Security, held in Trondheim, Norway from June 18 to June 20, 2008.

IFIPTM 2008 provides a truly global platform for the reporting of research, development, policy and practice in the interdependent areas of Privacy, Security, and Trust. Following the traditions inherited from the highly successful iTrust and PST conference series, IFIPTM 2008 focuses on trust, privacy and security from multidisciplinary perspectives. The conference is an arena for discussion about relevant problems from both research and practice in the areas of academia, business, and government.

IFIPTM 2008 is an open IFIP conference, which only accepts contributed papers, so all papers in these proceedings have passed strict peer review. The program of the conference features both theoretical research papers and reports of real world case studies. IFIPTM 2008 received 62 submissions. The program committee selected 22 papers for presentation and inclusion in the proceedings. In addition, the program and the proceedings include 3 demo descriptions.

The highlights of IFIPTM 2008 include invited talks and tutorials by industrial and academic experts in the fields of trust management, privacy and security, including Jon Bing and Michael Steiner.

Running of an international conference requires an immense effort from all parties involved. We would like to thank the program committee members and several other external referees for having provided timely and in-depth reviews of the submitted papers. In particular, we appreciate the logistics support provided by the Norwegian University of Science and Technology (NTNU).

We are grateful to the Norwegian University of Science and Technology (NTNU), the Research Council of Norway (NFR) and SAP Research for their financial support for IFIPTM 2008.

We hope you enjoy the proceedings and the conference.

June 2008   Yücel Karabulut
                                                                                   John Mitchell
                                                                                   Peter Herrmann
                                                                      Christian Damsgaard Jensen

Organization

Executive Committee

General Chairs

Peter Herrmann
Christian Damsgaard Jensen

Program Chairs

Yücel Karabulut
John Mitchell

Workshop and Tutorial Chairs

Elisa Bertino
Dan Lin

Demonstration Chair

Audun Jøsang

Local Organization Chair

Frank Alexander Kraemer

Program Committee

Tuomas Aura
Adrian Baldwin
Matt Bishop
Anupam Datta
Mourad Debbai
Theo Dimitrakos
Dag Elgesem
Sandro Etalle
Rino Falcone
Ali Ghorbani
Valérie Issarny
Sushil Jajodia
Dawn Jutla
Günther Karjoth
Angelos Keromytis
Dogan Kesdogan
Larry Korba
Larry Koved
Mark Kramer
Ninghui Li
Stephane Lo Presti
Javier Lopez
Stephen Marsh
Fabio Martinelli
Fabio Massacci
Deborah McGuinnes
Ali Miri
Mogens Nielsen
Babak Sadighi
Pierangela Samarati
Ravi Sandhu
Kent Seamons
Jean-Marc Seigneur
Vitaly Shmatikov
Jessica Staddon
Ketil Stølen
Vipin Swarup
Sotirios Terzis
David Townsend
Julien Vayssiere
Javier Garcia Villalba
William H. Winsborough
Marianne Winslett

External Reviewers

Adam Barth
Matthew Burnside
Roberto Speicys Cardoso
Marcin Czenko
Heidi Dahl
Sabrina De Capitani di Vimercati
Jeroen Doumen
Tariq Ehsan Elahi
Deepak Garg
Ragib Hasan
Maritza Jonhson
Adam Lee
Soumyadeb Mitra
Marinella Petrocchi
Atle Refsdal
Ludwig Seitz
Bjørnar Solhaug
Emmanuele Zambon

Table of Contents

Full Papers

Demonstration Overviews

Trust Management in P2P Systems Using Standard TuLiP

Marcin Czenko, Jeroen Doumen, and Sandro Etalle

Abstract In this paper we introduce Standard TuLiP - a new logic based Trust Management system. In Standard TuLiP, security decisions are based on security credentials, which can be issued by different entities and stored at different locations. Standard TuLiP directly supports the distributed credential storage by providing a sound and complete Lookup and Inference AlgoRithm (LIAR). In this paper we focus on (a) the language of Standard TuLiP and (b) on the practical considerations which arise when deploying the system. These include credential encoding, system architecture, system components and their functionality, and also the usability issues.

1 Introduction

In the context of the I-Share project [7] we are developing a security infrastructure for secure content sharing in P2P networks, and for secure internet TV. The underlying idea is that users of a P2P system organise themselves in so-called virtual communities [10] sharing tastes, interests, or business objectives. These virtual communities need a highly decentralised yet fine-grained policy enforcement system to protect data from undesired disclosure. Traditional approaches based on access control are not adequate as they expect that the system entities can be statically

Marcin Czenko
Department of Computer Science
University of Twente, The Netherlands, e-mail: marcin.czenko@utwente.nl

Jeroen Doumen
Department of Computer Science
University of Twente, The Netherlands, e-mail: jeroen.doumen@utwente.nl

Sandro Etalle
Eindhoven University of Technology and
University of Twente, The Netherlands, e-mail: s.etalle@tue.nl

Please use the following format when citing this chapter:

Czenko, M., Doumen, J. and Etalle, S., 2008, in IFIP International Federation for Information Processing, Volume 263; *Trust Management II*; Yücel Karabulut, John Mitchell, Peter Herrmann, Christian Damsgaard Jensen, (Boston: Springer), pp. 1–16.

enumerated and assigned the appropriate privileges in advance. In virtual communities the users often do not know each other and need to have reason to *trust* other peers before taking an action. It was shown [8] that trust is a significant factor in the success of such systems.

The obvious choice was to have a policy specification and enforcement system based on *Trust Management* [4, 5, 12, 15], in which security decisions are based on security *credentials*. In Trust Management a credential represents a permission or a capability assigned by the credential issuer to the credential subject. Credentials can be simple *facts* assigning a specific permission or a *role* to a specific user, or they can express more sophisticated *rules* describing roles of groups of users without enumerating their members. An important feature of Trust Management is that credentials can be issued by different authorities and stored at different locations. The user can access a resource if it can be proven that she has a certain role. This is done by evaluating a chain of credentials.

In the setting of our project, the trust management system has to meet the following (rather common) requirements: First, the policy language should be simple (possibly based on a well-known language), extensible (e.g. by interfacing it with external components, like constraint solvers), it should allow calculations and should be able to express complex policies. Secondly, the underlying architecture should be completely decentralised; in particular, the credential storage should be not only decentralised, but one should be able to determine whether a credential should be stored by the issuer or by some other entity (e.g. the so-called subject of the credential), like in the RT [13] trust management system. Thirdly, the system should enjoy a sound and complete decision algorithm, i.e. an algorithm which - in spite of the decentralised storage of the credentials - will always be able to make the appropriate decision and deliver the correct chain of credentials supporting it, if one exists (more about this later).

Present TM systems do not satisfy all three conditions; RT [13, 12] comes very close by satisfying the second and third requirements, but at the cost of a syntax which is too inflexible for our purposes (see our [6] for a discussion on this). Other systems either do not support decentralised storage or do not enjoy a sound and complete decision algorithm (see the Related Work section for the details).

To meet all requirements, we have developed a new trust management system: Standard TuLiP. Standard TuLiP is based on the theoretical basis laid in Core TuLiP [6], i.e. on the same concept of credential storage system and on a similar decision algorithm (which in turn is inspired by the architecture of RT [13]). But while Core TuLiP is more or less a theoretical exercise based on a very restricted syntax, Standard TuLiP is a full fledged Trust Management system with not only a more flexible syntax, but with the support of a whole distributed infrastructure, with APIs for the specification, the validation and the storage of the credentials, APIs for interrogating the decision procedure and a number of changes w.r.t. Core TuLiP which make it amenable for a practical deployment (to mention one, the choice of including the mode in the credential specification, which allows to reduce dramatically the workload of the lookup algorithm).

In this paper we present the Standard TuLiP system. In particular, we concentrate on the practical issues related to its deployment and use. We start with Sect. 2 where we introduce the XML syntax of Standard TuLiP credentials and policies and how they are represented in the logic programming form. In Sect. 3 we show how we can specify the credential storage by using modes. We introduce the notion of *traceable* credentials in order to guarantee that all required credentials will be found later when needed in a proof. Section 4 deals with the architecture of Standard TuLiP. We introduce basic components, show their functionality and also say how they communicate with each other. In particular we show how credentials are stored and how we find them. Then, in Sect. 5 we show the system from the user perspective: we answer questions like how to write credentials, send queries, and we also discuss the problem of credential and user identifier revocation. We finish the paper with Related Work in Sect. 6 and Conclusions and Future Work in Sect. 7.

2 Policies

Standard TuLiP is a credential-based, role-based Trust Management system. Informally, a credential is a signed statement determining which role can be assigned to an entity. A role can then be further associated with permissions, capabilities, or actions to be performed. For example, the University of Twente may issue a credential saying that *Alice* is a student of it, which directly or indirectly may give Alice a certain set of permissions (like buying a book in an online store at a discount price). Here, the University of Twente is called the *issuer* of the credential, Alice is called its *subject*, and student is the *role name*. A credential is always signed by its issuer, as it is the issuer who has the authority of associating certain rights with the subject. A credential can also contain additional information about the subject. For instance, a student usually has a student number, she belongs to a certain department, etc. This information is stored in the *properties* section of a credential. Standard TuLiP uses XML [21] as a language for credential representation. The use of XML is convenient for several reasons. Firstly, XML is a widely accepted medium for electronic data exchange and is widely supported by many commercial and free tools. Secondly, the use of XML namespaces [22] can help in avoiding name conflicts and facilitates the definition of common vocabulary.

We distinguish two types of credentials: the basic credential, and the conditional credential. The first is just a direct role assignment (e.g. "Alice is a student"), while the latter can express role assignments under some constraints.

Basic credentials. Figure 1 shows the XML encoding of a basic Standard TuLiP credential, which consists of a single *credential* XML element. The *credential* XML element, in turn, contains a single *permission* XML element, which consists of a *role name*, *mode*, *issuer*, *subject*, and optionally *properties* XML elements. The meaning of the *mode* XML element will be explained later in this paper. The *issuer* element consists of a single *entityID* element which contains a public identifier of the credential issuer. Similarly, the *subject* element contains the *entityID* element containing

```
1  <?xml version="1.0" encoding="UTF−8"?>
   <credential xmlns="urn:ewi:namespaces:tulip"
3  notBefore="2007−02−12T20:00:00" notAfter="2008−02−12T20:00:00">
       <permission>
5          <rolename>student</rolename>
           <mode>oi</mode>
7          <issuer><entityID>ut−pub−key</entityID></issuer>
           <subject><entityID>alice−pub−key</entityID></subject>
9          <properties>
               <studentid>0176453</studentid>
11             <department>ewi</department>
               <study>cs</study>
13         </properties>
       </permission>
15     <Signature xmlns="http://www.w3.org/2000/09/xmldsig#">
           <SignedInfo>
17             . . .
               <Reference URI="">
19                 . . .
                   <DigestValue>5WlwStu5ouu94nb5rwQ6BhFOPWc=</DigestValue>
21             </Reference>
           <SignedInfo>
23             <SignatureValue>signature−value</SignatureValue>
           </Signature>
25 </credential>
```

Fig. 1: A basic Standard TuLiP XML credential.

the public identifier of the subject. The optional *properties* XML element can include arbitrary XML content describing additional properties of the issuer and/or the subject. Every credential includes the time period in which it is considered valid - this is done by using the *notBefore* and *notAfter* attributes of the "credential" XML element. Each Standard TuLiP credential is signed by the issuer's private key. Standard TuLiP uses public (RSA) keys as public identifiers. By doing this, every credential can be immediately validated without the need for an external PKI infrastructure. The signature is contained in the *Signature* XML element. We use the enveloped XML signature format [20] (more precisely, a digest value is computed over the top-level element, which is then included in the DigestValue element of the SignedInfo element of the signature, and then the signature is made of the Signed-Info element and included in the SignatureValue element). Notice also the use of the *urn:ewi:namespaces:tulip* namespace in the top level credential XML element. This is required for every valid Standard TuLiP credential. By using namespaces, Standard TuLiP credentials can be easily distinguished from other credential formats and this even allows for different credential formats to be mixed in a single XML document.

Conditional credentials. Sometimes we need more sophisticated types of statement: consider an online store which gives a discount to students of the University of Twente. Instead of giving each student a basic credential granting the discount, it is much more efficient to associate the discount role to everyone who has a student role at the University of Twente, using a variable as subject.

Conditional Standard TuLiP credentials contain an additional *provided* XML element. This element includes one or more *condition* elements which specify additional conditions that must be satisfied before the specified role name can be associated with the credential subject. A *condition* XML element is similar to the *permission* XML element in that it also contains the role name, mode, issuer, subject and optional properties XML elements. In the condition XML element, the issuer, subject, and properties XML elements can contain variables referring to the elements from the preceding conditions and/or to the subject and properties elements from the permission XML element. Notice that the credential issuer cannot contain a variable as the issuer of the credential must always be known (otherwise one would not be able to verify the credential signature). The *provided* part of the credential can also contain a constraint which in turn can refer to built-in functions (to manipulate values taken by the variables). The presence of variables allows us to interface easily with external functions (e.g. arithmetic solvers, constraint solvers, programs written in other languages). The only requirement is that these calls should respect the input-output flow dictated by the mode of the credential; modes are discussed later and it is beyond the scope of this paper to explain in detail how the interfacing with external functions takes place.

A Standard TuLiP security *policy* is defined by a set of credentials.

Queries. When *eStore* wants to check if *alice* is a student of the University of Twente it sends a *query* to the University of Twente. In Standard TuLiP, queries are also encoded as XML documents. The structure of an XML representation of a query is very similar to that of the provided part of a Standard TuLiP XML credential. The top-level element is the *query* XML element. It consists of a one or more condition XML elements each of which contains the role name, mode, issuer, subject, and optionally the properties XML elements. If a query contains only one condition element we call it a *basic query*. Besides the query conditions, every query reports the public identifier of the entity making the query. Each Standard TuLiP query also contains a unique *ID* and *IssueInstant* attributes inside the top-level query XML element. The ID attribute allows the system to check whether the received response corresponds to the earlier issued query. The IssueInstant attribute carries the time and date of the request which allows the responding entity to filter out erroneous requests (like the ones with the time in the future), or to check whether the time matches the validity of the credentials used in answering the query.

A query is always about a specific set of permissions. However, they can be of different types. For instance "Is *alice* a student of the University of Twente?" and "Give me all the students of the University of Twente" are queries of different type. In Standard TuLiP the policy writer can restrict the type of queries one can ask by using modes. We discuss this in Sect. 3.

Semantics. In order to give Standard TuLiP credentials formal meaning they are translated to the equivalent logic programming form. In this representation every credential is represented by a definite clause containing one or more the so called *credential atoms* and/or *built-in constraints*.

Definition 1 (credential atoms,credentials,queries). A *credential atom* is a predicate of the form:

$$rolename(issuer, subject, properties).$$

A *credential* is a definite clause of the form $P \leftarrow C_1, \ldots, C_n$, where P is a credential atom, and $C_1, \ldots, C_n$ are credential atoms or built-in constraints. The credential atom P in the head of the clause corresponds to the permission XML element and every credential atom or built-in constraint C_i in the body of the clause corresponds to a condition in the provided part of the corresponding XML credential encoding. A query is represented by a sequence of credential atoms and/or built-in constraints $C_1, \ldots, C_n$, where each C_i corresponds to a query condition.

The var XML elements are straightforwardly mapped to logical variables. For space reasons, we do not show the actual mapping from the content of the properties XML element to the corresponding logic programming term.

A *policy* is a logic program containing one or more credentials.

Example 1. The policy modelling the scenario presented above is represented by the following logic program:

$$student(ut\text{-}pub\text{-}key, alice\text{-}pub\text{-}key, properties). \tag{1}$$
$$discount(eStore\text{-}pub\text{-}key, X, Y) \leftarrow student(ut\text{-}pub\text{-}key, X, Y). \tag{2}$$

Here credential (1) is a direct translation of credential shown in Fig. 1 and *properties* is the Prolog term representing the content of the corresponding "properties" XML element.

Given a role name p, the set of all credentials having p as a role name of the credential atom occurring in the head is called the *definition* of p. Every credential from the definition of p is called a defining credential of p. For any given credential atom A, we denote the issuer of A by $issuer(A)$ and the subject of A by $subject(A)$.

We will often refer to the logic programming representation of the credentials as it makes the notation easier. For sake of clarity, we will sometimes write the credential atoms without the last argument.

Expressiveness. Standard TuLiP is expressive enough to model complex policies like thresholds and separation of duty. Below we show examples of a threshold and separation of duty policy. In order to emphasise relative simplicity of Standard TuLiP, below we first show the policy encoded in RT^T (in fact we use a dialect of RT called RT_1^T as we also use arguments) and then its equivalent in Standard TuLiP.

Example 2. Threshold Policy: A says that an entity is a member of role $A.r$ and has the properties A_1 and A_2 if one member of $B.s$ and one member of $C.t$ say the same (in RT "?" denotes a variable).

$$RT_1^T : \quad A.r(?A_1,?A_2) \leftarrow A.r_1.r(?A_1,?A_2)$$
$$A.r_1 \leftarrow B.s \odot C.t$$

Standard TuLiP : $r(a,X,\text{prop}:[p_1:A_1,p_2:A_2]) :- s(b,Y),t(c,Z),$
$$r(Y,X,\text{prop}:[p_1:A_1,p_2:A_2]),r(Z,X,\text{prop}:[p_1:A_1,p_2:A_2]).$$

Example 3. Separation of Duty Policy: A says that an entity is a member of role $A.r$ and has the properties A_1 and A_2 if two different entities - one being a member of $B.s$ and the second being a member of $C.t$ - say the same.

$$RT_1^T : \quad A.r(?A_1,?A_2) \leftarrow A.r_1.r(?A_1,?A_2)$$
$$A.r_1 \leftarrow B.s \otimes C.t$$

Standard TuLiP : $r(a,X,\text{prop}:[p_1:A_1,p_2:A_2]) :- s(b,Y),t(c,Z),Y \neq Z.$
$$r(Y,X,\text{prop}:[p_1:A_1,p_2:A_2]),r(Z,X,\text{prop}:[p_1:A_1,p_2:A_2]).$$

RT^T is a member of the RT Trust Management Framework [12]. In order to handle policies like those presented in Example 2 and Example 3, RT^T introduces the so called *manifold roles*, which allow not only entities but also sets of entities to be members of a role. With Standard TuLiP, we have the same syntax and the same semantics for all sorts of supported policies. Notice also, that Standard TuLiP can be easily extended to a general purpose logic programming language by relaxing the restriction on the number of arguments in the credential atoms and their corresponding modes values (though at the cost of limited flexibility of the distributed storage in some cases).

3 Storage and Modes

The content of this section is not new in the sense that the results we report here are a natural extension of the material we present in [6] for Core TuLiP. Nevertheless, we include them for sake of completeness. Standard TuLiP is a distributed system in which credentials are stored by various peers (not necessarily by those issuing the credential). The following standard example shows that the location where the credentials are stored can affect the efficiency and the correctness of the whole TM system.

Example 4. We extend the example presented in Sect. 2. Now, *eStore* gives a discount to any student from any university accredited by *accBoard*. This is modelled as follows (logic notation):

$$discount(eStore\text{-}pub\text{-}key,X) \leftarrow accredited(accBoard\text{-}pub\text{-}key,Y),student(Y,X). \quad (1)$$
$$accredited(accBoard\text{-}pub\text{-}key,ut\text{-}pub\text{-}key). \quad (2)$$
$$student(ut\text{-}pub\text{-}key,alice\text{-}pub\text{-}key). \quad (3)$$

Now, suppose that credential (1) is stored by *eStore*, credential (2) by the *accBoard*, and credential (3) by *alice*: if one wants to know whether *alice* can have a discount at *eStore*, then one needs to evaluate the following query: $\leftarrow accredited(accBoard$

-pub-key,Y), *student*(*Y*, *alice*). The most efficient way of answering this query is first to fetch credential (3) from *alice*. From credential (3), we immediately know that *alice* is a student of *ut*. Now, it is sufficient to check if *ut* is an accredited university. This can be done by either fetching credential (2) from *accBoard*, or from *ut*. Notice however, that if we store both credential (2) and (3) at the *ut* then we would not be able to find them. In this case contacting *alice* would not help as *alice* does not store any related credentials. Similarly, querying *accBoard* will not bring us any closer, as *accBoard* lets universities store the accreditation credentials.

Standard TuLiP uses the notion of *mode* to handle distributed storage. In logic programming, the mode of a predicate indicates which predicate arguments are *input* and which are *output* arguments. An input argument must be ground (completely instantiated) when atom is evaluated. In Standard TuLiP modes are assigned directly to role names and there are only three possible mode values: *ii*, *io*, or *oi*, where *i* stands for "input" and *o* for "output". Here, the first character points to the issuer and the second to the subject. For instance, if role name *r* has mode *oi*, it means that - in order to be able to find a credential of the form *r*(*issuer*, *subject*, *properties*) - "subject" must be known. The most common mode is *io*, but *oi* is also useful to be able to store a credential in a place different from the issuer. The mode value *oo* is not allowed because this would allow queries in which both the issuer and subject are unknown, and we would not know where to start looking.

To be precise, in Standard TuLiP modes determine three things: (1) the storage location of the credentials defining a given role name, (2) the types of queries in which the role name can be used, and (3) they guarantee the soundness and completeness of the method of credential discovery. We now illustrate these three aspects.

Storage. The mode of a role name *p* indicates where the credentials defining the corresponding credential atom should be stored. Standard TuLiP introduces the notion of a *depositary* to be the entity which should store the given credential.

Definition 2 (depositary). Let *p* be a role name and let $c = P \leftarrow C_1, \ldots, C_n$ be a credential defining *p*. Then:

- if $mode(p) \in \{ii, io\}$ then the depositary of *c* is the credential issuer ($= issuer(P)$).
- if $mode(p) = oi$ then the depositary of *c* is the credential subject ($= subject(P)$).

There are exceptions: with mode *oi* it is also possible to store the credential at an entity other than the credential issuer or the subject. For details we refer the reader to [6].

Example 5. Referring to Example 4, assume that we have the following mode assignments: $mode(discount) = ii$, $mode(accredited) = io$, and $mode(student) = oi$. According to Definition 3, credential (1) should be stored by *eStore*, credential (2) by *accBoard*, and credential (3) by *alice*.

Queries. Recall that a Standard TuLiP query is a sequence of one or more credential atoms, each of which can be seen as a basic query itself. In Standard TuLiP we identify three types of (basic) queries:

Type 1: "Given two entities a and b, check if b has role name p as said by a." This query can be answered for any valid mode assignment for p.

Type 2: "Given entity a and role name p, find all entities b such that b has role name p as defined by a." This query can be answered only if $mode(p) = io$.

Type 3: "Given entity b and role name p find all entities a such that a says that b has role name p." This query can be answered if $mode(p) = oi$.

One can also consider a more general form of the query of Type 3: "Given entity b find all role names b has." This query is not supported in Standard TuLiP. The reason for this is purely of syntactic nature as we explain in [6].

The classification above is of purely syntactical nature, and one still has to guarantee that given a supported query, it can be answered. Basically, a query can be answered - either positively or negatively - if all the related credentials can be found. We guarantee this by the soundness and completeness of the credential discovery method.

Soundness and Completeness. Storing the credentials in the right place does not yet guarantee their discoverability. To ensure this we require the credentials to be *traceable*:

Definition 3 (traceable). We say that a credential is *traceable* if it is *well-moded* and the depository of the credential is as given by Definition 2.

We use the standard definition of well-modedness as given in [1]. Standard TuLiP comes with a terminating *sound* and *complete* Lookup and Inference AlgoRithm (LIAR). Assuming that all credentials are traceable and given a well-moded query, the soundness result guarantees that LIAR produces only true answers. The completeness results on the other hand guarantees that if there exists an answer to the query then LIAR will be able to construct the proof of it. In this paper we do not give the detailed description of LIAR. For a formal description, we refer the reader to [6].

4 System Architecture

In this section we describe the architecture of Standard TuLiP. First, we present the system components and their role in the system. Then we show how the system components interoperate and we give a concrete example demonstrating this. Finally, we present the requirements Standard TuLiP has on the underlying infrastructure. In particular, we discuss how public identifiers can be mapped to physical infrastructure nodes.

System Components. In Standard TuLiP we identify the following components: (a) the LIAR engine, (b) the credential server (c) the User Client application, and (d) the mode register (see Fig. 2).

By default, every system user should run an instance of the LIAR engine, but other approaches are also possible. For instance, there can be a preselected set of

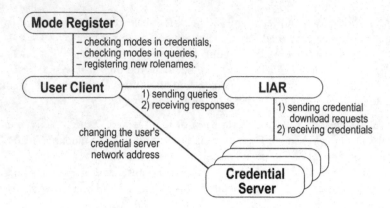

Fig. 2: Components of Standard TuLiP.

nodes having LIAR functionality, or there can even be only one instance of LIAR serving the whole community. The LIAR algorithm is implemented using YAP Prolog [14] with the external interface written in Python. This makes deployment of LIAR easier but allows us to preserve the original logic programming formalism in the "reasoning" part of the system. LIAR operates as an HTTP server when answering the queries and as a client when fetching credentials from *credential servers*. We give a more detailed functional description of LIAR later in this section.

Every user who wants to store her own credentials must run an instance of the credential server. The credential server responds to requests coming from LIAR engines and returns credentials satisfying the request. The credential server is implemented as a simple HTTP server (written in Python) and is internally connected to a *credential store*, which stores all user's credentials.

The *User Client* is a GUI application (written in Flash and Python) and provides user-friendly interface to other Standard TuLiP system components. In particular, the User Client is used for: generating the user private-public key pair, setting up and maintaining the location of the user's credential server, importing user credentials, and querying the Standard TuLiP system. Optionally, additional applications in the form of plugins can be provided. For instance one could provide a plugin having a graphical credential editor functionality. Notice that the User Client application itself does not allow the user to perform any action on a remote resource. Its main purpose is to let the user query the system.

Another important component of Standard TuLiP is the *mode register*, which is a centralised service where all the allowed role names in use and their corresponding modes are stored. The mode register is implemented as an HTTP server with a user-friendly web-interface. The role names and the associated modes are provided as Security Assertion Markup Language (SAML) *assertions* [16]. The mode register responds to SAML *attribute queries*. The answer is returned in the form of an SAML *response* [16] containing one or more assertions, each of which corresponds to the credential atom and its associated mode(s). The mode register uses version 2.0 of the SAML standard [18].

LIAR. The basic functionality of LIAR is to wait for queries and respond to them. Recall that Standard TuLiP queries are themselves XML documents.

When LIAR receives a query from the User Client it first checks the signature on it and then is starts the evaluation process. Every time additional credentials are needed, LIAR fetches them from the location indicated by the mode information obtained by combining the information on the query and the mode register. Actually, by embedding the mode information in the credentials and the queries, the mode register does not have to be contacted in order to determine the storage location for the credentials defining a given role name. The credentials are fetched from the corresponding credential server by sending a so called *credential request*. Credential requests are XML documents specifying which credentials should be fetched. LIAR validates the received credentials by checking the signatures and validity intervals.

After evaluating the query, LIAR sends to the User Client the so called Standard TuLiP *response* (XML) document containing all answers, i.e. all instances of the query conditions satisfying the query. The top-level element of the Standard TuLiP response is the *response* XML element. Besides the unique ID and IssueInstant XML attributes it also contains *InResponseTo* XML attribute containing the value of the ID XML attribute from the corresponding query.

The following example demonstrates the system behaviour in the response to a concrete query.

Example 6. Assume we have the following set of credentials (logic notation):

$$discount(ii, eStore\text{-}pub\text{-}key, X) \leftarrow accredited(io, accBoard\text{-}pub\text{-}key, Y), student(oi, Y, X). \quad (1)$$

$$accredited(io, accBoard\text{-}pub\text{-}key, ut\text{-}pub\text{-}key). \quad (2)$$

$$student(oi, ut\text{-}pub\text{-}key, alice\text{-}pub\text{-}key). \quad (3)$$

This is the same set of credentials as in Example 4 but now including the mode argument indicating the mode of the corresponding role name. Figure 3 presents the steps performed by LIAR during evaluation of the query $\leftarrow discount(ii, eStore\text{-}pub\text{-}key, alice\text{-}pub\text{-}key))$. In Fig. 3 the rounded rectangles represent the (credential servers of) entities, the arrows represent the messages being sent, and numbers above the arrows represent their order. Below, the flow of the algorithm is presented for the given query.

We assume that the instance of the LIAR algorithm is run by a user Jeroen with the public identifier *jeroen-pub-key*. In message $\boxed{1}$ LIAR receives the query in which the query issuer (Jeroen) asks whether the user with public id *alice-pub-key* has a discount at the internet store identified by *eStore-pub-key*. The query is signed by the query issuer. Before evaluating the query, LIAR checks the signature on the query, then it checks the mode of the atom *discount(ii, eStore-pub-key, alice-pub-key)*. As the mode associated with role name *discount* is *ii*, LIAR knows that it should try to fetch credentials matching this query from *eStore*. This is done in messages $\boxed{2}$ and $\boxed{3}$. After receiving the matching credentials, LIAR validates each of them, which means that it checks the signatures and the validity intervals, and then every successfully validated credential rule is instantiated by unifying its head with the query atom. In our case only one credential is fetched (credential (1)) and the resulting instance is:

$$discount(ii, eStore\text{-}pub\text{-}key, alice\text{-}pub\text{-}key) \leftarrow$$
$$accredited(io, accBoard\text{-}pub\text{-}key, Y), student(oi, Y, alice\text{-}pub\text{-}key).$$

We see that in order to prove the initial query, now LIAR has to evaluate the following one:

$$\leftarrow accredited(io, accBoard\text{-}pub\text{-}key, Y), student(oi, Y, alice\text{-}pub\text{-}key).$$

In evaluating this (sub) query, LIAR checks the mode associated with role name *accredited* and notices that the associated mode value is *io*, meaning that the related credentials (if any) should be stored by *accBoard*. The *accBoard* is queried in message ⨄4⨄, resulting in the fact that credential (2) is fetched with message ⨄5⨄, it is validated, and then its instance - *accredited(io, accBoard-pub-key, ut-pub-key)* - is used. As the body of credential (2) is empty, the query reduces to $\leftarrow student(oi, ut\text{-}pub\text{-}key,$ *alice-pub-key*). The mode of role name *student* is *oi* which means that the defining credentials should be stored by their subject: *alice* in this case. Alice is contacted by LIAR with message ⨄6⨄, and asked for all *oi* credentials she stores. In the response, in message ⨄7⨄, credential (3) is returned and then validated. This credential unifies with *student(oi, ut-pub-key, alice-pub-key)* and at this point the original query has been evaluated successfully. The information about successful evaluation, containing only one condition corresponding to the *discount(ii, eStore-pub-key, alice-pub-key)* credential atom, is sent to the User Client in message ⨄8⨄.

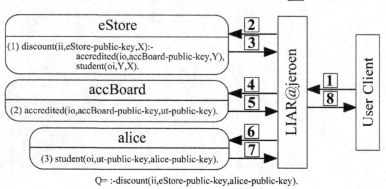

Q= :-discount(ii,eStore-public-key,alice-public-key).

A= discount(ii,eStore-public-key,alice-public-key).

Fig. 3: Credential Discovery with LIAR

Public Identifiers. Recall that Standard TuLiP uses public keys as (public) identifiers of the users. In Example 6 we have silently assumed that there exists a mapping between public identifiers and concrete network addresses. Indeed, Standard TuLiP requires an underlying service to map public identifiers to concrete network addresses.

Distributed Hash Tables (DHT) [19] represent a class of overlay P2P systems with key-based routing functionality. They provide a look up service similar to a hash table. In DHT systems, a network location of a resource is determined by a global unique name of that resource.

Standard TuLiP can be built on top of a DHT system or an another overlay P2P network providing lookup service based on global unique identifiers. We assume that every underlying infrastructure node stores one or more user records containing at the least the current network address of the user, and the network address of the user's credential server. The user should be able to securely change the network address of her credential server. The user's current network address should be synchronised with the actual network address of the User Client application acting in the name of the user.

5 Using Standard TuLiP

In using the Standard TuLiP Trust Management system we can distinguish the following actions that may be performed by the user: (1) issuing credentials, (2) sending the queries and receiving the responses, and (3) revoking credentials and user public identifiers. Below we briefly summarise issues raised by these actions.

Writing Credentials. When issuing credentials one must be sure that any new credential is traceable. The User Client application helps in writing credentials by checking that the credentials are traceable. Before accepting the credential, it checks if *for every* mode value of the credential head there exists a permutation of the credential atoms occurring in the credential body and the corresponding mode values such that the credential is traceable. If this is not the case, the credential is refused. If for a mode value of the head there exists more than one valid mode assignment for the credential atoms in the body, the user will be allowed to choose a preferred one.

The User Client application determines the modes of the credential atoms by querying the mode register. The selected modes are then embedded into the actual credentials so that the mode register does not have to be referred to during query evaluation later. Recall that the assigned modes determine the actual credential storage location. The User Client application automatically uploads the new credentials to the suitable credential server (as given by the user record associated with the given public id).

When a user introduces a credential with a new role name, it has to be registered with the mode register. The mode register can be accessed through the TuLiP homepage, or by using a dedicated application. Each user can request the registration of additional role names and the corresponding modes by requesting it through the TuLiP web-site.

Writing Queries. Every Standard TuLiP query must be well-moded. Therefore, before sending a query, the User Client application checks for well-modedness. If some credential atoms in the query have more than one mode value, it is possible that there will be more than one variant of mode assignment that makes the query well-moded. In such a case, the User Client lets the user to select the preferred mode assignment (e.g. the one that is likely to yield the correct answer most efficiently). The User Client application sends the query to the LIAR engine associated with the user issuing the query and presents the received response.

Revoking Credentials and Public Identifiers. Recall that in Standard TuLiP, the user's public identifier is the user's public key. The use of public keys as user identifiers is convenient as everyone can create her public identifier by simply generating a new key pair. Additionally one can sign the credentials and queries using the corresponding private key. This makes the validation possible *without* the need for any external public key infrastructure. When using public keys as user identifiers, however, one has to deal with the problems of key revocation. Notice that when the user's private key becomes compromised, it is not sufficient to revoke all the credentials issued by this user, but the user's public identifier should not be used anymore. Currently, Standard TuLiP does not support any revocation mechanisms other than the validity period specified in each credential. In the future, we plan to extend LIAR, so that it checks if the selected credential is not revoked. Instead of revoking all the user's credentials, it is also possible to revoke the user id. This can be done by issuing an *id revocation certificate* which would state that the given public identifier cannot be trusted any longer to sign the credentials. A comprehensive revocation framework for Standard TuLiP is our future work.

6 Related Work

The first trust management systems, PolicyMaker [4], KeyNote [3], and SDSI/SPKI [5], as well as e.g. [11, 9] focus on the language design without fully supporting credential distribution. In most systems, public keys are used as the identifiers of the users. This is in contrast to the traditional authorisation mechanisms based on identity-based public-key systems like X.509. The RT family of Trust Management Languages [13, 12] is the first in which the problem of credential discovery is given an extensive treatment. In particular, in [13], a type system is introduced in order to restrict the number of possible credential storage options. In [23] Winsborough and Li identify the features a "good" language for credentials should have, one of those being the support for distributed storage. As we show in [6], our system is at least as flexible as RT and all storage possibilities given by RT can be replicated here.

PeerTrust [15] is a Trust Negotiation language where the problem of the distributed storage is also taken into account. PeerTrust is based on first order Horn clauses of the form $lit_0 \leftarrow lit_1, \ldots, lit_n$, where each lit_i is a positive literal. PeerTrust supports distributed storage by allowing each literal in a rule to have an additional *Issuer* argument: lit_i @ *Issuer*. *Issuer* is the peer responsible for evaluating lit_i. The *Issuer* arguments do not, however, say where a particular credential should be stored but only who is responsible for evaluating it. It means that PeerTrust makes a silent assumption that the credentials are stored in such a way that *Issuer* can find the proof, but it gives no clue of how this should be done. PeerTrust considers only the first two requirements mentioned in the introduction.

From the more practical approaches (but with very strong theoretical foundation as well), Bertino et al. developed Trust-$\mathscr{X}$ - a trust negotiation system [2]. Trust-$\mathscr{X}$ uses the $\mathscr{X}$-TNL trust negotiation language for expressing credentials and disclosure policies. Trust-$\mathscr{X}$ certificates are either credentials or declarations. Credentials state personal characteristics of the owner and are certified by a Credential Authority (CA). Declarations also carry personal information about its owner but are not certified. Trust-$\mathscr{X}$ does not deal with the problem of distributed credential storage and discovery. It means that the second and third requirement is not supported.

The *eXtensible Access Control Markup Language* (XACML) [17] supports distributed policies and also provides a profile for the role based access control (RBAC). However, in XACML, it is the responsibility of the *Policy Decision Point* (PDP) – an entity handling access requests – to know where to look for the missing attribute values in the request. The way missing information is retrieved is application dependent and is not directly visible in the supporting language. Thus, XACML does not support the second and the third requirement presented in Section 1.

7 Conclusions and Future Work

In this paper we presented the architecture of Standard TuLiP - a logic based Trust Management system. Standard TuLiP follows the Trust Management approach in which security decisions are based on security credentials which are issued by different entities and stored at different places. Standard TuLiP basic constituents are the Standard TuLiP Trust Management language, the mode system for the credential storage, and a terminating sound and complete Lookup and Inference AlgoRithm (LIAR) which guarantees that all required credentials can be found when needed.

Standard TuLiP is decentralised. Every user can formulate his/her own security policy and store credentials in the most convenient and efficient way for himself. Standard TuLiP does not require a centralised repository for credential storage, nor does it rely on any external PKI infrastructure. Standard TuLiP credentials are signed directly by their issuers so that no preselected Certification Authority (CA) is needed.

With this we show that it is possible to design and implement a Trust Management system that is theoretically sound yet easy and efficient to deploy and use.

Future Work. Standard TuLiP can be extended in several directions. Firstly, we plan to extend expressiveness of the Standard TuLiP Trust Management language, so that it can be used to express non-monotonic policies. Although Standard TuLiP can already be used as a Trust Negotiation language, we also plan to add a direct support to Trust Negotiation at the language level.

References

1. K. R. Apt and I. Luitjes. Verification of logic programs with delay declarations. In *AMAST*, volume 936 of *LNCS*, pages 66–90. Springer, 1995.
2. E. Bertino, E. Ferrari, and A. C. Squicciarini. Trust-$\mathcal{X}$: A Peer-to-Peer Framework for Trust Establishment. *IEEE Trans. Knowl. Data Eng.*, 16(7):827–842, 2004.
3. M. Blaze, J. Feigenbaum, J. Ioannidis, and A. Keromytis. The KeyNote Trust-Management System, Version 2. IETF RFC 2704, September 1999.
4. M. Blaze, J. Feigenbaum, and J. Lacy. Decentralized Trust Management. In *Proc. 17th IEEE Symposium on Security and Privacy*, pages 164–173. IEEE Computer Society Press, May 1996.
5. D. Clarke, J.E. Elien, C. Ellison, M. Fredette, A. Morcos, and R. L. Rivest. Certificate Chain Discovery in SPKI/SDSI. *Journal of Computer Security*, 9(4):285–322, 2001.
6. M. R. Czenko and S. Etalle. Core TuLiP - Logic Programming for Trust Management. In *Proc. 23rd International Conference on Logic Programming, ICLP 2007, Porto, Portugal*, volume 4670 of *LNCS*, pages 380–394, Berlin, 2007. Springer Verlag.
7. Freeband Communication. *I-Share: Sharing resources in virtual communities for storage, communications, and processing of multimedia data.* URL: *http://www.freeband.nl/project.cfm?language=en&id=520*.
8. S. L. Jarvenpaa, N. Tractinsky, and M. Vitale. Consumer Trust in an Internet Store. *Inf. Tech. and Management*, 1(1-2):45–71, 2000.
9. T. Jim. SD3: A Trust Management System with Certified Evaluation. In *Proc. IEEE Symposium on Security and Privacy*, pages 106–115. IEEE Computer Society Press, 2001.
10. F. Lee, D. Vogel, and M. Limayem. Adoption of informatics to support virtual communities. In *HICSS '02: Proc. 35th Annual Hawaii International Conference on System Sciences (HICSS'02)-Volume 8*, page 214.2. IEEE Computer Society Press, 2002.
11. N. Li, B. Grosof, and J. Feigenbaum. Delegation Logic: A Logic-based Approach to Distributed Authorization. *ACM Transactions on Information and System Security (TISSEC)*, 6(1):128–171, 2003.
12. N. Li, J. Mitchell, and W. Winsborough. Design of a Role-based Trust-management Framework. In *Proc. IEEE Symposium on Security and Privacy*, pages 114–130. IEEE Computer Society Press, 2002.
13. N. Li, W. Winsborough, and J. Mitchell. Distributed Credential Chain Discovery in Trust Management. *Journal of Computer Security*, 11(1):35–86, 2003.
14. LIACC/Universidade do Porto and COPPE Sistemas/UFRJ. *YAP Prolog*, April 2006.
15. W. Nejdl, D. Olmedilla, and M. Winslett. PeerTrust: Automated Trust Negotiation for Peers on the Semantic Web. In *Secure Data Management*, pages 118–132, 2004.
16. OASIS. *Assertions and Protocols for the OASIS: Security Assertion Markup Language (SAML) V2.0*, March 2005.
17. OASIS. *eXtensible Access Control Markup Language (XACML) Version 2.0* URL: *http://www.oasis.org*, Feb 2005.
18. OASIS. *SAML V2.0 Executive Overview*, April 2005.
19. S. Ratnasamy, P. Francis, M. Handley, R. M. Karp, and S. Shenker. A scalable content-addressable network. In *SIGCOMM*, pages 161–172, 2001.
20. W3C. *XML-Signature Syntax and Processing*, Feb 2002.
21. W3C. *Extensible Markup Language (XML) 1.1 (Second Edition)*, Sep 2006.
22. W3C. *Namespaces in XML 1.0 (Second Edition)*, Aug 2006.
23. W. H. Winsborough and N. Li. Towards Practical Automated Trust Negotiation. In *POLICY*, pages 92–103. IEEE Computer Society Press, 2002.

A Trust Evaluation Method Based on Logic and Probability Theory

Reto Kohlas, Jacek Jonczy, and Rolf Haenni

Abstract We introduce a trust evaluation method applicable in a decentralized setting, in which no universally trusted authority exists. The method makes simultaneous use of logic and probability theory. The result of the qualitative part of the method are logical arguments for and against the reliability of an entity. The quantitative part returns the probability that the reliability of an entity can be deduced under the given assumptions and pieces of evidence, as well a corresponding probability for the counter-hypothesis. Our method is a true generalization of existing methods, in particular the Credential Networks. It relies on digital signatures for authenticating messages and accounts for many-to-many relationships between entities and public keys. Moreover, it includes eight different types of trust relations, namely the assumption or the statement that an entity is honest, competent, reliable, or malicious, and their corresponding negations.

1 Introduction

Members of global social networks and e-commerce systems regularly face the question whether they can trust other, a priori unknown entities. A rating system or a *trust evaluation* method can provide decision support in such a situation. It indicates arguments for the reliability of an entity (or a numerical value representing an entity's reliability, respectively) by taking available trust assumptions, recommendations and discredits into account.

The credibility of a statement, for example a recommendation, generally depends on the reliability of its author (i.e., the honesty and the competence of its author). In

Reto Kohlas and Jacek Jonczy
Institute of Computer Science and Applied Mathematics, University of Berne, 3012 Berne, Switzerland, e-mail: kohlas,jonczy@iam.unibe.ch

Rolf Haenni
Bern University of Applied Sciences, 2501 Biel/Bienne, Switzerland, e-mail: rolf.haenni@bfh.ch

Please use the following format when citing this chapter:

Kohlas, R., Jonczy, J. and Haenni, R., 2008, in IFIP International Federation for Information Processing, Volume 263; *Trust Management II*, Yücel Karabulut, John Mitchell, Peter Herrmann, Christian Damsgaard Jensen; (Boston: Springer), pp. 17–32.

a digital setting, messages should be authenticated, since the identity of the alleged sender of a message can typically be forged without effort. The method presented in this paper makes use of *public-key cryptography* and digital signature schemes for message authentication.

The use of public-key cryptography requires the *authentication of public keys*, i.e., the establishment to which physical entity a public key belongs. *Public-key certificates* are digitally signed statements which approve the authenticity of a public-key entity for a physical entity.[1] They contribute thus to public-key authentication and are useful for those physical entities who cannot exchange their public keys personally.

The main purpose of this paper is to introduce a novel trust evaluation method that relies on logic and probability theory. It uses digital signatures for message authentication and extends previously proposed approaches.

1.1 Existing Trust Evaluation Methods

Some authors have noted that early methods for evaluating trust or for authenticating public keys tend to return counter-intuitive results. Deficiencies in PGP's Web of Trust for instance have been identified in [21, 18, 13], principles that such methods should ideally fulfill have been stated in [23, 18]. In search of improved techniques, a vast number of methods has been proposed in the last decade.

Some methods combine the confidence values *specifically*, in the sense that their way of combining the confidence values has been exclusively conceived for trust evaluation. Examples of such specific methods are [2, 22, 23, 26, 1, 19, 20]. Other methods treat trust evaluation as a special case of accepting or rejecting a *hypothesis* (that a public key is authentic or that an entity is reliable) under *uncertain assumptions* and *pieces of evidence* (public-key certificates, recommendations, discredits). Such methods use *formal techniques for reasoning under uncertainty*, and are often based on a *probabilistic* interpretation of the confidence values. Examples are Maurer's Probabilistic Model [21] (based on Probabilistic Logic), Jøsang's Certification Algebra [14] (based on Subjective Logic), Haenni's Key Validation Method [6] and the Credential Networks [12] (both based on the Theory of Probabilistic Argumentation).

We here briefly describe Maurer's probabilistic method (MPM), since it allows us to exemplify in Subsection 1.2 in which sense we intend to extend existing probabilistic methods. The basic idea behind MPM is the combination of *logic* and *probability theory*. MPM's *deterministic* model consists of two so-called *inference rules*. The first inference rule asserts that if a reasoner A knows the authentic public key of X ($\mathrm{Aut}_{A,X}$), if X is trusted by A for issuing public-key certificates ($\mathrm{Trust}_{A,X,1}$)[2], and

---

[1] For reasons explained in Subsection 2.1, these entities are called *public-key* and *physical entities*.

[2] The third index is an integer and corresponds to the *trust level* (its exact meaning is irrelevant for the discussion in this paper).

if X issues a public-key certificate for Y ($\text{Cert}_{X,Y}$)[3], then A can conclude to possess the authentic public key of Y ($\text{Aut}_{A,Y}$). Formally, this rule translates into

$$\forall X \; \forall Y : \; \text{Aut}_{A,X} \wedge \text{Trust}_{A,X,1} \wedge \text{Cert}_{X,Y} \vdash \text{Aut}_{A,Y}.$$

The second inference rule (which we do not print here) describes the role of recommendations for evaluating the reliability of a physical entity. Note that MPM considers positive recommendations only (i.e., there are no statements asserting that some entity is unreliable).

The *probabilistic* model of MPM lets A assign a probability to every assumption. Each probability, also called confidence value, is intended to stand for A's degree of belief with respect to the truth of the judged assumption. MPM then defines confidence value for the hypothesis $\text{Aut}_{A,B}$ as function of the initially attributed probabilities. This confidence value corresponds to the probability that $\text{Aut}_{A,B}$ can be deduced from A's initial view by applying consecutively the two inference rules of the deterministic model.

1.2 Motivation

In accordance with other contributions, we propose to use a probabilistic framework as the basis of our method. However, we suggest to revisit existing probabilistic methods with respect to the type of assumptions and certificates (credentials) they take into account. The following list discusses some important and often neglected modeling aspects:

- *Physical entities may use multiple public-key entities.* Most methods assume that each physical entity uses *at most* one public-key entity. In MPM, for example, the supposed public key of X is precisely for this reason not included in the statement $\text{Aut}_{A,X}$. As a consequence, statements signed by different public-key entities are usually considered independent. However, it is often impossible in a decentralized system to limit the number of keys used, since each entity can generate as many public-key entities and distribute as many public keys as desired. If some physical entity controls two public-key entities, then statements signed by these two public-key entities are by no means independent.
- *Two physical entities can share the use of a public-key entity.* It is usually impossible to assure that one public-key entity is controlled by only *one* physical entity. A key holder can for instance disclose the passphrase for accessing the private key to another physical entity, and thereby share control of the public-key entity. Such sharing of public-key entities can be problematic. If both physical entities control the public-key entity, it is not possible to uniquely assign state-

---

[3] Note that X uses her public-key entity to issue a certificate for Y's public key. But neither X nor Y's public key are parameters in the statement $\text{Cert}_{X,Y}$, because all physical entities are assumed to control *exactly one* public-key entity.

ments signed by the public-key entity to either of the physical entities. As a consequence, if the two physical entities are not equally trusted, it is impossible to determine the credibility of the signed statement in a unique way.

- *The opposite of trust is twofold.* Trust is often modeled as positive assumption only allowing to conclude what trusted introducers say. If an introducer is *not* trusted (e.g., in MPM the statement $Trust_{A,X,1}$ would not be valid), no conclusions are drawn within these methods. But it is possible that malicious entities lie. In the context of public-key authentication, persuading someone to use the "wrong" public key allows to decrypt messages and make statements in someone else's name; providing "false" statements about reliability could convince somebody to enter a deal to the cheating entity's advantage. In Subsection 2.3 we shall therefore differentiate between two opposites of trust: first, as an entity's belief that a given introducer is *incompetent*, and second as the stronger assumption that the introducer is *malicious*, in which case the contrary of what the introducer says can be deduced.

- *Negative statements.* Many existing methods are monotonic. In MPM for instance, if A adds a public certificate to her view, the confidence value $conf(\mathrm{Aut}_{A,B})$ remains the same or increases (but it does not decrease). There is never evidence for the hypothesis that a public key is *not* authentic. The reason for the monotonicity of the methods lies in the fact that only positive statements are taken into account. However, negative and positive statements are equally important. If a honest introducer observes that someone else is spreading false information, or that a public key is not authentic, this honest introducer should have a means at hand to warn other participants. We intend therefore to include different types of negative statements in our model.

1.3 Goal and Outline

The goal of this paper is to propose a trust evaluation method that considers the modeling aspects mentioned in the previous subsection. We base our method on the Theory of Probabilistic Argumentation [16, 9, 7] (TPA), which allows us to cope with conflicting assumptions and evidence. Moreover, hypotheses can be evaluated qualitatively and quantitatively. The qualitative part of the method provides logical arguments for and against a hypothesis. The results of the quantitative evaluation are two corresponding probabilities of derivability.

The emphasis of this paper lies primarily in the preciseness and not in the practicability of the proposed method. By suggesting a more accurate model we hope to understand the mechanisms behind trust evaluation better. Aspects of efficiency and usability will be part of future work.[4]

This paper is organized as follows. In Section 2 we introduce our model. Section 3 describes the logical and probabilistic evaluation of hypotheses concerning

---

[4] We are confident that practicable implementations are possible, as recent experiences in the context of the Credential Networks have shown [11].

reliability and public-key authenticity. We conclude with Section 4 by discussing the contributions of our paper and directions for future research.

2 A Model for Reliability and Public-Key Authenticity

We start by recapitulating an existing entity-relationship model [17], which has been conceived for the public-key authentication problem (Subsection 2.1). The relationships defined within this model are used as predicates in the evidential language $\mathscr{L}$ (described in Subsection 2.2), which allows to formalize the terms of public-key authenticity and trust in Subsection 2.3. Finally, we introduce the concept of a trust and authenticity network in Subsection 2.4.

2.1 Entities and Relationships

The model we consider consists of two types of *entities*. A *physical world entity* (*physical entity* for short) is someone that exists in the reality of the "physical" world. Examples are natural persons (human beings) or legal persons (companies, governmental agencies, sports clubs, etc.). A *public-key entity* consists of a public key and a private key, as well as a signature generation and a signature verification algorithm. Access to the private key is needed for generating signatures in the public-key entity's name.

Finding unique and adequate names for physical entities can be difficult, especially for natural persons. Here we put the naming problem aside and assume that each entity is known under exactly one, unique identifier. We use $p_1, \ldots p_m$ to denote the physical entities of our model, and $k_1, \ldots, k_n$ the n public-key entities. The symbol b represents the entity whose reliability is evaluated. Corresponding capital letters refer to variables, i.e., the indexed variable P_i to a physical entity and K_i to a public-key entity. We use $\mathscr{P}$ to denote the set of physical entities, and $\mathscr{K}$ stands for the set of public-key entities. Entities of our model can stand in the following *relationships*:

- A physical entity `controls` a public-key entity whenever she has access to its private key. Access occurs through knowledge of a password or passphrase, through possession of a physical device such as a smartcard, or through a biometric attribute. The same public-key entity can be controlled by more than one physical entity. A physical entity can control more than one public-key entity.
- The relationship `signs` involves a public-key entity and a statement. It holds if there exists a digital signature under the statement, which has been generated by using the private key of the public-key entity. Note that `signs` does not indicate which physical entity is using or controlling a public-key entity.
- The relationship `authors` stands for the fact that it was in a physical entity's *intention* to be the author of a statement. Authoring a statement can mean to say

it, to write it on a piece of paper, to type it into a computer, or to create any other representation of the statement. The digital signature provides evidence that a physical entity has authored the signed statement.

2.2 An Evidential Language

We use a formal language $\mathscr{L}$ to model assumptions, pieces of evidence, and their logical relationship in the context of trust evaluation. Due to limited space, we cannot provide the exact formal definitions of $\mathscr{L}$ here, but we give at least the basic idea behind $\mathscr{L}$.

The relationships introduced in the previous subsection are used as predicates in $\mathscr{L}$, the elements of $\mathscr{L}$ are called $\mathscr{L}$-formulas. $\mathscr{L}$ is a *many-sorted logic* without function symbols.[5] "Many-sorted" means that all variables and the arguments of the predicates are of a specified sort. We consider three sorts, namely the physical entities, the public-key entities, and the statements. The atoms of $\mathscr{L}$ are the relationships introduced in the previous subsection; a distinguished predicate symbol is the equality sign. An atomic $\mathscr{L}$-formula is a predicate symbol together with arguments of appropriate sort. An argument of predicate is either a constant symbol or a variable. Examples of atomic $\mathscr{L}$-formulas are $\mathtt{controls(p_1,k_3)}$, $\mathtt{controls(P_1,k_3)}$, or $P_1 = p_2$ (note that in the two latter formulas P_1 stands for a *variable* of sort physical entity, and not for a constant). $\mathscr{L}$ contains the usual logical connectives: $\wedge$ (logical and), $\vee$ (logical or), $\neg$ (not), $\rightarrow$ (material implication), $\leftrightarrow$ (bidirectional material implication), and $\forall$ (universal quantifier). In the sequel, let L and the indexed variable L_i stand each for an $\mathscr{L}$-formula.

2.3 Formalizing Reliability and Public-Key Authenticity

2.3.1 Reliability and Maliciousness

We differentiate among three types of introducers in our model. A physical entity is *reliable* if she is competent and honest; statements authored by a reliable principal are believable. The second type of introducers are those who are *incompetent*. If a statement L is authored by an incompetent introducer, it is impossible to decide whether L is true or false; L can be true by chance, independently of the introducer's honesty. Therefore statements made by incompetent entities should be simply ignored. The third type of physical entities are the *malicious* introducers. A malicious entity is competent but dishonest, and tries to deceive other physical entities by spreading credentials that contain a false statement. Under the assumption that someone is malicious one can conclude the contrary of what the suspected in-

---

[5] Except for constant symbols such as p_1, which can be seen as 0-ary function symbols.

troducer says. We therefore define the reliability (rel) and maliciousness (mal) of a physical entity depending on her competence (comp) and honesty (hon) as follows:[6]

Rule 1: *Reliable physical entity.*

$$\forall.P : \big(\text{rel}(P) \leftrightarrow (\text{comp}(P) \wedge \text{hon}(P))\big) \tag{1}$$

Rule 2: *Malicious physical entity.*

$$\forall.P : \big(\text{mal}(P) \leftrightarrow (\text{comp}(P) \wedge \neg\text{hon}(P))\big) \tag{2}$$

The logical relationship between a physical entity P's honesty and her competence, as well as the truth of a statement L authored by P are captured by the following two rules. On the one hand, if P is believed to be reliable, the statement L authored by P can be believed. On the other hand, if P is assumed to be malicious, we invert the truth of the uttered statement L:

Rule 3: *Statement authored by a reliable physical entity.*

$$\forall.P \, \forall.L: \ \big((\text{authors}(P,L) \wedge \text{rel}(P)) \rightarrow L\big) \tag{3}$$

Rule 4: *Statement authored by a malicious physical entity.*

$$\forall.P \, \forall.L: \ \big((\text{authors}(P,L) \wedge \text{mal}(P)) \rightarrow \neg L\big) \tag{4}$$

2.3.2 Public-Key Authenticity

Public-key authenticity of K_1 for P_1 means that P_1, but no other entity P_2, controls K. This formally translates into Rule (5).

Rule 5: *Definition of public-key authenticity.*

$$\forall.P_1 \, \forall.P_2 \, \forall.K : \\ \text{aut}(P_1,K) \leftrightarrow \big(\text{controls}(P_1,K) \wedge ((P_1 \neq P_2) \rightarrow \neg\text{controls}(P_2,K))\big) \tag{5}$$

Because the variables P_1, P_2, and K are universally quantified, Rule (5) is valid for all physical entities P_1 and P_2, as well as all public-key entities K.

Rule (6) formalizes a simplified view of the security of a digital signature scheme: If only P has access to K (i.e., $\text{aut}(P,K)$ holds), and if there is a digital signature under the statement L by K, then P authored the statement L:

Rule 6: *Ascribing digital signatures to physical entities.*

$$\forall.P \, \forall.K \, \forall.L : \ \big((\text{aut}(P,K) \wedge \text{signs}(K,L)) \rightarrow \text{authors}(P,L)\big) \tag{6}$$

---

[6] We do not have to define incompetent introducers at this point, since the assumptions that someone is incompetent allows no conclusion.

2.4 Trust and Authenticity Networks

For evaluating a hypothesis concerning the reliability of a physical entity or the authenticity of a public key, a reasoner A takes certain *assumptions* and collects a set of *credentials*. Assumptions and credentials are either with respect to the authenticity of public keys or the reliability of entities. Assumptions are *subjective*; A decides which assumptions are acceptable for her. A credential is a statement which is either digitally signed by a public-key entity or authored by a physical entity.

A's assumptions and credentials form what we call her *Trust and Authenticity Network (TAN)*. A TAN can be depicted by a *multigraph*. We use drawn-through arrows for authenticity assumptions and credentials, similarly to [21, 6, 12]. The graph in Fig. 1 (a) shows A's assumption that k_1 is authentic for p_1, the graph in Fig. 1 (b) represents the statement that k_2 is authentic for p_2, and is digitally signed by k_1. An example of a *negative* authenticity credential (i.e., a statement that a public key is not authentic) is depicted in Figure 1 (c); negative statements are indicated by the negation sign $\neg$. For the moment, we consider only assumptions and credentials about the aut predicate, but it is conceivable to incorporate controls statements in a future method. Dashed arrows represent trust assumptions and credentials. Whereas

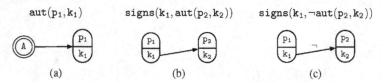

(a)   (b)   (c)

Fig. 1 An authenticity assumption and two authenticity credentials.

A's assumption that p_1 is reliable constitutes a positive trust assumption, her belief that p_1 is incompetent or cheating is negative. We use the following abbreviations: R for a rel assumption and credential, I for incomp, and M for mal. Figure 2 shows

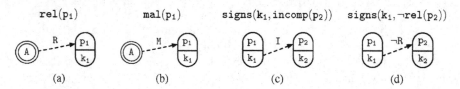

(a)   (b)   (c)   (d)

Fig. 2 Two trust assumptions (of entity A) and two trust credentials (digitally signed by the public-key entity k_1).

examples of trust assumptions and credentials. In the graph of Fig. 2 (a), A believes that p_1 is reliable, in Fig. 2 (b) A assumes that p_1 is malicious. The graph in Fig. 2 (c) shows a statement, digitally signed by k_1, which asserts that p_2 is incompetent. Finally, the graph in Figure 2 (d) provides an example of a negated trust statement: the key owner of k_1 claims that p_2 is not reliable (which is not equal to the statement that p_2 is malicious). TAN-assumptions and credentials can be connected, which results in a multigraph as depicted in Fig. 3.

3 Reasoning about Reliability and Public-Key Authenticity

Our reasoner A is possibly *uncertain* about several of her assumptions; A might doubt the reliability of an introducer; authenticity assumptions can be uncertain if the identification process of an alleged public-key entity owner is error-prone. In analogous manner, credentials can also be uncertain; an introducer can express her uncertainty about an assertion contained within a credential by assigning a *weight* to it. The logical and probabilistic reasoning allows A to evaluate her hypotheses under uncertain assumptions and credentials.

3.1 Logical Reasoning

In this subsection we explain the basic ideas behind *scenarios*, *assumptions* and *arguments*, which are TPA's building blocks for reasoning logically about hypotheses. The definitions coincide to some extent with those provided in [7].

3.1.1 Assumptions

An *assumption* (in the sense of TPA) is a basic unit of concern which is uncertain from the point of view of an entity A. With respect to a TAN, all edges in the multigraph are assumptions, as discussed in the introduction of this section. From a syntactic point of view, an assumption is an $\mathscr{L}$-formula which consists of a predicate symbol and constant symbols of appropriate sort. In the example of Fig. 3 (a), $\mathtt{aut}(p_1,k_1)$, $\mathtt{aut}(p_2,k_2)$, $\mathtt{rel}(p_1)$ $\mathtt{rel}(p_2)$, $\mathtt{signs}(k_1,\mathtt{aut}(b,k_3))$, and $\mathtt{signs}(k_2,\mathtt{aut}(p_3,k_3))$ are assumptions.

3.1.2 Scenarios

A *scenario* is specified by a truth value assigned to each of the assumptions. Given n assumptions, 2^n scenarios exist. A scenario is denoted by the symbol S. If an assumption A is true (false) in S, we write $S(A) = 1$ ($S(A) = 0$). It is assumed that there is exactly one scenario which represents the real state of the world. Unfortunately, A does not know which scenario meets this condition.

With respect to a knowledge base (and hence with respect to a given TAN), the set of scenarios can be divided into *conflicting* and *consistent* scenarios. A conflicting scenario stands in contradiction with the knowledge base, a consistent scenario on the other hand is non-conflicting. In Fig. 3 (a), the scenario in which all assumptions hold is conflicting. An informal explanation is the following: from the two signs and aut assumptions we can conclude - by applying Rule (6) - that p_1 authored $aut(b, k_3)$ and p_2 authored $aut(p_3, k_3)$. Since p_1 and p_2 are trusted, by using Rule (2) $aut(b, k_3)$ and $aut(p_3, k_3)$ can be derived. But Rule (5) asserts that $aut(b, k_3)$ and $aut(p_3, k_3)$ cannot hold both at same time. Hence the scenario is conflicting. All other scenarios are consistent with respect to the TAN of Fig. 3.

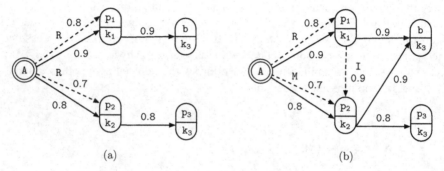

(a)   (b)

Fig. 3 Two simple TANs.

With respect to a hypothesis h, the set of consistent scenarios can be divided into *supporting, refuting*, and *neutral* scenarios [7]. A supporting scenario is a consistent scenario that allows the deduction of h. A refuting scenario is a scenario supporting the counter-hypothesis $\neg h$. A neutral scenario with respect to h is a consistent scenario which is neither supporting nor refuting h. An example of a supporting scenario for $aut(b, k_3)$ is

$$S(aut(p_1, k_1)) = 1, \quad S(rel(p_1)) = 1, \quad S(signs(k_1, aut(b, k_3))) = 1,$$
$$S(aut(p_2, k_2)) = 1, \quad S(rel(p_2)) = 0, \quad S(signs(k_2, aut(p_3, k_3))) = 1.$$

The assumptions $aut(p_1, k_1)$, $signs(k_1, aut(b, k_3))$, and $rel(p_1)$ allow to conclude $aut(b, k_3)$ (by Rule (5) and Rule (2)). The scenario is not conflicting, since by the assumed falsity of $rel(p_2)$ the lower "certification path" in Fig. 3 (a) is broken; hence A cannot conclude $aut(p_3, k_3)$ (otherwise this would lead to a contradiction). An example of a refuting scenario for $aut(b, k_3)$ is

$$S(aut(p_1, k_1)) = 1, \quad S(rel(p_1)) = 0, \quad S(signs(k_1, aut(b, k_3))) = 1,$$
$$S(aut(p_2, k_2)) = 1, \quad S(rel(p_2)) = 1, \quad S(signs(k_2, aut(p_3, k_3))) = 1.$$

The scenario is supporting $aut(p_3, k_3)$, and since we do not accept a public key as authentic for two physical entities, $\neg aut(b, k_3)$ follows.

$qs(\bot)$

(1) $aut(p_1,k_1) \wedge aut(p_2,k_2) \wedge rel(p_1) \wedge rel(p_2) \wedge \; _{\supset}$
$signs(k_1, aut(b,k_3)) \wedge signs(k_2, aut(p_3,k_3))$

$sp(aut(b,k_3))$

(1) $aut(p_1,k_1) \wedge rel(p_1) \wedge signs(k_1, aut(b,k_3)) \wedge \neg aut(p_2,k_2)$
(2) $aut(p_1,k_1) \wedge rel(p_1) \wedge signs(k_1, aut(b,k_3)) \wedge \neg rel(p_2)$
(3) $aut(p_1,k_1) \wedge rel(p_1) \wedge signs(k_1, aut(b,k_3)) \wedge \neg signs(k_2, aut(p_3,k_3))$

$sp(\neg aut(b,k_3))$

(1) $aut(p_2,k_2) \wedge rel(p_2) \wedge signs(k_2, aut(p_3,k_3)) \wedge \neg aut(p_1,k_1)$
(2) $aut(p_2,k_2) \wedge rel(p_2) \wedge signs(k_2, aut(p_3,k_3)) \wedge \neg rel(p_1)$
(3) $aut(p_2,k_2) \wedge rel(p_2) \wedge signs(k_2, aut(p_3,k_3)) \wedge \neg signs(k_1, aut(b,k_3))$

Table 1 $qs(\bot)$, $sp(aut(b,k_3))$, and $sp(\neg aut(b,k_3))$ for the TAN of Fig. 3 (a).

3.1.3 Arguments

A compact logical representation of scenarios is achieved by means of *arguments*. Technically, an *argument* is a conjunction of assumption literals. There are conflicting, supporting anf refuting arguments,, analogously to the different types of scenarios. The expression $qs(\bot)$ represents the set of minimal conflicting assumptions; $sp(h)$ and $sp(\neg h)$ stand for the sets of minimal arguments supporting and refuting h, respectively.

The arguments of the TANs discussed in this paper have been determined by translating first the TAN into a *Propositional Argumentation System* (i.e., a knowledge base in which all variables have been instantiated and the universal quantifiers have been removed). The so-obtained propositional knowledge base was implemented in ABEL [10], a framework for evaluating propositional knowledge bases qualitatively and quantitatively.

3.1.4 Examples

Table 1 shows the minimal argument sets for the example depicted Fig. 3 (a). As mentioned, there is only one conflicting scenario. Hence we have only one conflicting argument containing all assumptions. The common part of the supporting arguments for $aut(b, k_3)$ are the three assumptions of the upper certification path of our example. The assumptions $\neg aut(p_2, k_2)$, $\neg rel(p_2)$, and $\neg signs(k_2, aut(p_3, k_3))$ all guarantee that the argument is not conflicting. Each argument stands for four scenarios (because there are two missing assumptions in each argument supporting $aut(b,k_3)$). The supporting arguments for $\neg aut(b,k_3)$ are in a certain sense symmetric to the arguments for $aut(b,k_3)$. They actually correspond to the supporting arguments for $aut(p,k_3)$. Note that Table 1 lists only the *minimal* arguments. For example, the argument

$$aut(p_1,k_1) \wedge rel(p_1) \wedge signs(k_1,aut(b,k_3)) \wedge \neg aut(p_2,k_2) \wedge rel(p_2)$$

supports also $aut(b,k_3)$, but is contained in argument (1) of $sp(aut(b,k_3))$ of Table 1.

$qs(\bot)$

(1) $aut(p_1,k_1) \wedge rel(p_1) \wedge signs(k_1,incomp(p_2)) \wedge mal(p_2)$

(2) $aut(p_1,k_1) \wedge aut(p_2,k_2) \wedge rel(p_1) \wedge signs(k_1,aut(b,k_3)) \wedge$
$mal(p_2) \wedge signs(k_2,aut(b,k_3))$

$sp(aut(b,k_3))$

(1) $aut(p_1,k_1) \wedge rel(p_1) \wedge signs(k_1,aut(b,k_3)) \wedge \neg mal(p_2)$

(2) $aut(p_1,k_1) \wedge rel(p_1) \wedge signs(k_1,aut(b,k_3)) \wedge$
$\neg signs(k_1,incomp(p_2)) \wedge \neg signs(k_2,aut(b,k_3))$

(3) $aut(p_1,k_1) \wedge rel(p_1) \wedge signs(k_1,aut(b,k_3)) \wedge$
$\neg signs(k_1,incomp(p_2)) \wedge \neg aut(p_2,k_2)$

$sp(\neg aut(b,k_3))$

(1) $aut(p_2,k_2) \wedge mal(p_2) \wedge signs(k_2,aut(b,k_2)) \wedge \neg aut(p_1,k_1)$

(2) $aut(p_2,k_2) \wedge mal(p_2) \wedge signs(k_2,aut(b,k_2)) \wedge \neg rel(p_1)$

(3) $aut(p_2,k_2) \wedge mal(p_2) \wedge signs(k_2,aut(b,k_2)) \wedge$
$\neg signs(k_1,aut(b,k_3)) \wedge \neg signs(k_1,incomp(p_2))$

Table 2 $qs(\bot)$, $sp(aut(b,k_3))$, and $sp(\neg aut(b,k_3))$ for the TAN of Fig. 3 (b).

Figure 3 (b) shows an example which is more complicated. In contrast to the previous example, A believes that p_2 is malicious. There is an additional digitally signed trust credential which claims incompetence for p_2. The owner of k_2 provides conflicting information, as she claims simultaneously public-key authenticity of k_3 for b and p_3.

The qualitative evaluation provides some interesting insights: The second conflicting argument in Table 2 is equal to the only conflicting argument of our first example. Argument (1) of $qs(\bot)$ conflicts with the given TAN because $aut(p_1,k_1)$, $rel(p_1)$, and $signs(k_1,incomp(p_2))$ allow to conclude that p_2 is incompetent. This, however, conflicts with the assumption $mal(p_2)$, which stands for the assumption that p_2 is competent (and dishonest).

All supporting arguments for $aut(b,k_3)$ in the second TAN contain the three assumptions of the upper certification path. Again, some negated assumptions have to be added to guarantee the consistency of the supporting arguments. For example, the first supporting argument contains the literal $\neg mal(p_2)$. By adding this assumption, a contradiction can be prevented. Note that - in contrast to the previous example - there are no supporting arguments for aut(p₃, k₃). If p₂ is indeed *not* malicious, she is incompetent *or* honest. From this clause aut(p₃, k₃) can *not* be deduced.

3.2 Probabilistic Reasoning

The idea of the probabilistic part of TPA (and hence of our method) is that from A's point of view each scenario corresponds with a certain probability to the real state of the world. A has to choose the probabilities such that the sum of the probabilities assigned to the scenarios equals one. Given the exponential number of scenarios, it is infeasible for A to estimate the probability of each single scenario. It is often justifiable to consider the statements of a TAN as being stochastically independent. In this case, A assigns a probability to all of her authenticity and trust assumptions. The weights assigned to each credential are represented by a probability, too. Under

	$dqs(\bot)$	$dsp(h_1)$	$dsp(\neg h_1)$	$dsp(h_2)$	$dsp(\neg h_2)$
TAN of Fig. 3(a)	0.290	0.504	0.222	0.222	0.504
TAN of Fig. 3(b)	0.486	0.403	0.282	0.000	0.654

Table 3 Qualitative evaluation of TANs: $h_1 = $ aut(b, k₃), $h_2 - $ aut(p₃, k₃).

the independence assumption, the probability of a scenario can be computed as the product of the marginal probabilities of the assumptions.

Formally, let A_i stand for the ith assumption, and let p_i be the probability attached to A_i. Given a scenario S, let S^+ denote the assumptions which are positive in S, and S^- the assumptions that occur negatively:

$$S^+ = \{A \in S \mid S(A) = 1\}, \quad S^- = \{A \in S \mid S(A) = 0\}.$$

The probability $P(S)$ of scenario S is then defined as

$$P(S) = \prod_{A_i \in S^+} p_i \cdot \prod_{A_i \in S^-} (1 - p_i).$$

The *degree of conflict*, denoted by $dqs(\bot)$, is obtained by summing up the *probabilities of the conflicting scenarios*. It is a measure of how conflicting the assumptions are with respect to the knowledge base (i.e., the TAN). Let $dqs(h)$ stand for the sum of $dqs(\bot)$ and the probabilities of all the scenarios supporting h (i.e., the sum of the probabilities of all scenarios allowing the deduction of h, including the conflicting ones). The *degree of support* for the hypothesis h, denoted by $dsp(h)$, is the probability that h can be derived, provided that the real scenario is not conflicting.

Formally, the degree of support corresponds to

$$dsp(h) = \frac{dqs(h)}{1 - dqs(\bot)}.$$

Table 3 shows the degrees of support for our two examples of Fig. 3. In example of Fig. 3 (a), $\mathtt{aut}(b, k_3)$ and $\neg\mathtt{aut}(p_3, k_3)$ are quite probable. In the TAN of Fig. 3 (b), $\mathtt{aut}(b, k_3)$ is less probable, but we have no evidence for $\mathtt{aut}(p_3, k_3)$. In both cases, A either accepts $\mathtt{aut}(b, k_3)$ or collects additional evidence to gain more certainty for or against the validity of $\mathtt{aut}(b, k_3)$. A discussion of how to validate a hypothesis based on $dsp(h)$ and $dsp(\neg h)$ can be found in [8].

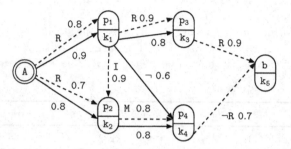

Fig. 4 A more complex TAN.

We end the presentation of our probabilistic method by analyzing the more complicated TAN depicted in Figure 4. The TAN involves most trust and authenticity statements introduced in this paper. It contains a negative authenticity statement $(\mathtt{signs}(k_1, \neg\mathtt{aut}(p_4, k_4)))$, and a negative trust statement $(\mathtt{signs}(k_3, \neg\mathtt{rel}(b)))$. We are interested in the evaluation of the reliability of b, i.e., the hypothesis of interest is $h = \mathtt{rel}(b)$. Although the TAN is not that large, it has already a considerable complexity: there are twelve edges in the TAN, and hence $2^{12} = 4096$ possible scenarios. The qualitative evaluation yields two conflicting and seven supporting arguments (which we do not write down here). One of the two conflicting arguments corresponds to

$$\mathtt{aut}(p_1, k_1) \wedge \mathtt{aut}(p_2, k_2) \wedge \mathtt{rel}(p_1) \wedge \mathtt{rel}(p_2) \wedge$$
$$\mathtt{signs}(k_1, \neg\mathtt{aut}(p_4, k_4)) \wedge \mathtt{signs}(k_2, \mathtt{aut}(p_4, k_4)).$$

The above argument is conflicting, since it allows the deduction of $\mathtt{aut}(p_4, k_4)$ *and* $\neg\mathtt{aut}(p_4, k_4)$. The degree of conflict $dqs(\bot)$ is quite high and is approximately 0.473; the degree of support $dsp(\mathtt{rel}(b))$ is roughly 0.442. Interestingly, there is no argument for the hypothesis that b is not reliable $(dsp(\mathtt{rel}(b)) = 0)$.

4 Conclusion

We have introduced a trust evaluation method, which can also be used for authenticating public keys. The used, extended model considers the possibility that a public-key entity is shared by different physical entities, and that a physical entity controls several public-key entities at the same time. Negative statements are an integral part of the method. Reliability is decomposed into honesty and competence, which allows to differentiate between incompetent and malicious physical entities. The assumptions and the available evidence from the perspective of a physical entity A can be represented by an evidential language and by a multigraph. We make use of the Theory of Probabilistic Argumentation, which allows to cope with conflicting assumptions. TPA provides logical arguments *and* probabilities of derivability for and against the hypotheses in question.

Future work consists in investigating the applicability of our method in concrete systems, and in devising specific algorithms for the evaluation of trust and authenticity networks. Possible extensions of the model are the inclusion of trust scopes and time aspects, as well as modeling the revocation of statements and public keys.

Acknowledgements This research was supported by the Swiss National Science Foundation, Project No. PP002-102652/1.

References

1. The official ebay website. *http://www.ebay.com*, April 2006.
2. T. Beth, M. Borcherding, and B. Klein. Valuation of trust in open networks. In *ES-ORICS'94, 3rd European Symposium on Research in Computer Security*, LNCS 875, pages 3–18. Springer, 1994.
3. M. Burrows, M. Abadi, and R. Needham. A logic of authentication. *ACM Transactions on Computer Systems*, 8(1):18–36, February 1990.
4. W. Diffie and M. E. Hellman. New directions in cryptography. *IEEE Transactions on Information Theory*, IT-22(6):644–654, 1976.
5. L. Gong, R. Needham, and R. Yahalom. Reasoning About Belief in Cryptographic Protocols. In Deborah Cooper and Teresa Lunt, editors, *Proceedings 1990 IEEE Symposium on Research in Security and Privacy*, pages 234–248. IEEE Computer Society, 1990.
6. R. Haenni. Using probabilistic argumentation for key validation in public-key cryptography. *International Journal of Approximate Reasoning*, 38(3):355–376, 2005.
7. R. Haenni. Probabilistic argumentation (submitted). *Elsevier*, 2007.
8. R. Haenni, J. Jonczy, and R. Kohlas. Two-layer models for managing authenticity and trust. In R. Song, L. Korba, and G. Yee, editors, *Trust in E-Services: Technologies, Practices and Challenges*. 2006.
9. R. Haenni, J. Kohlas, and N. Lehmann. Probabilistic argumentation systems. In D. M. Gabbay and P. Smets, editors, *Handbook of Defeasible Reasoning and Uncertainty Management Systems*, volume 5: Algorithms for Uncertainty and Defeasible Reasoning, pages 221–288. Kluwer Academic Publishers, Dordrecht, Netherlands, 2000.
10. R. Haenni and N. Lehmann. ABEL: an interactive tool for probabilistic argumentative reasoning. In *ECSQARU'03, 7th European Conference on Symbolic and Quantitative Approaches to Reasoning under Uncertainty*, pages 588–593, Aalborg, Denmark, 2003.

11. J. Jonczy. Evaluating trust and authenticity with CAUTION. In *iTrust'06, 4rd International Conference on Trust Management*, pages 449–453, Pisa, Italy, 2006.
12. J. Jonczy and R. Haenni. Credential networks: a general model for distributed trust and authenticity management. In A. Ghorbani and S. Marsh, editors, *PST'05: 3rd Annual Conference on Privacy, Security and Trust*, pages 101–112, St. Andrews, Canada, 2005.
13. J. Jonczy, M. Wüthrich, and R. Haenni. A probabilistic trust model for GnuPG. In *23C3, 23rd Chaos Communication Congress*, pages 61–66, Berlin, Germany, 2006.
14. A. Jøsang. An algebra for assessing trust in certification chains. In *NDSS'99: 6th Annual Symposium on Network and Distributed System Security*, San Diego, USA, 1999.
15. A. Jøsang. A logic for uncertain probabilities. *International Journal of Uncertainty, Fuzziness and Knowledge-Based Systems*, 9(3):279–311, 2001.
16. J. Kohlas and P. A. Monney. *A Mathematical Theory of Hints. An Approach to the Dempster-Shafer Theory of Evidence*, volume 425 of *Lecture Notes in Economics and Mathematical Systems*. Springer, 1995.
17. R. Kohlas, R. Haenni, and J. Jonczy. A new model for public-key authentication. In T. Braun, G. Carle, and B. Stiller, editors, *KiVS'07, Kommunikation in Verteilten Systemen*, pages 213–224, Berne, Switzerland, 2007.
18. R. Kohlas and U. Maurer. Confidence valuation in a public-key infrastructure based on uncertain evidence. In H. Imai and Y. Zheng, editors, *PKC'2000, Third International Workshop on Practice and Theory in Public Key Cryptography*, LNCS 1751, pages 93–112, Melbourne, Australia, 2000. Springer.
19. R. Levien and A. Aiken. Attack-resistant trust metrics for public key certification. In *7th on USENIX Security Symposium*, pages 229–242, 1998.
20. G. Mahoney, W. Myrvold, and G. C. Shoja. Generic reliability trust model. In A. Ghorbani and S. Marsh, editors, *PST'05: 3rd Annual Conference on Privacy, Security and Trust*, pages 113–120, St. Andrews, Canada, 2005.
21. U. Maurer. Modelling a public-key infrastructure. In E. Bertino, H. Kurth, G. Martella, and E. Montolivo, editors, *ESORICS, European Symposium on Research in Computer Security*, LNCS 1146, pages 324–350. Springer, 1996.
22. M. K. Reiter and S. G. Stubblebine. Path independence for authentication in large-scale systems. In *CCS'97, 4th ACM Conference on Computer and Communications Security*, pages 57–66, Zürich, Switzerland, 1997. Academic Press.
23. M. K. Reiter and S. G. Stubblebine. Toward acceptable metrics of authentication. In *SP'97: 18th IEEE Symposium on Security and Privacy*, pages 10–20, Oakland, USA, 1997.
24. R. L. Rivest, A. Shamir, and L. M. Adelman. A method for obtaining digital signatures and public-key cryptosystems. Technical Report TM-82, MIT, Cambridge, USA, 1977.
25. C. G. Zarba. Many-sorted logic. http://theory.stanford.edu/~zarba/snow/ch01.pdf.
26. P. R. Zimmermann. *PGP User's Guide Volume I: Essential Topics*, 1994.

A UML-based Method for the Development of Policies to Support Trust Management

Atle Refsdal, Bjørnar Solhaug, and Ketil Stølen

Abstract Most of the existing approaches to trust management focus on the issues of assessing the trustworthiness of other entities and of establishing trust between entities. This is particularly relevant for dynamic, open and distributed systems, where the identity and intentions of other entities may be uncertain. These approaches offer methods to manage trust, and thereby to manage risk and security. The methods are, however, mostly concerned with trust management from the viewpoint of the trustor, and the issue of mitigating risks to which the trustor is exposed. This paper addresses the important, yet quite neglected, challenge of understanding the risks to which a whole system is exposed, in cases where some of the actors within the system make trust-based decisions. The paper contributes by proposing a method for the modeling and analysis of trust, as well as the identification and evaluation of the associated risks and opportunities. The analysis facilitates the capture of trust policies, the enforcement of which optimizes the trust-based decisions within the system. The method is supported by formal, UML-based languages for the modeling of trust scenarios and for trust policy specification.

1 Introduction

When the term trust management was introduced in 1996 [3] it basically referred to the management of authorizations and access rights in distributed systems. Since then, trust management has been subject to increased attention and has more re-

Atle Refsdal
SINTEF ICT, e-mail: Atle.Refsdal@sintef.no

Bjørnar Solhaug
Dep. of Information Science and Media Studies, University of Bergen and SINTEF ICT, e-mail: Bjornar.Solhaug@sintef.no

Ketil Stølen
SINTEF ICT and Dep. of Informatics, University of Oslo, e-mail: Ketil.Stolen@sintef.no

Please use the following format when citing this chapter:

Refsdal, A., Solhaug, B. and Stølen, K., 2008, in IFIP International Federation for Information Processing, Volume 263; *Trust Management II*; Yücel Karabulut, John Mitchell, Peter Herrmann, Christian Damsgaard Jensen; (Boston: Springer), pp. 33–49.

cently been described as an activity "in the intersection between sociology, commerce, law and computer science" [8].

Whatever the approach to or domain of trust management, a fundamental issue is to assess the trustworthiness of other entities and to make decisions based on these assessments. Trust is a relationship between two entities, a trustor and a trustee, and is associated with a particular transaction between these entities. The trustor is the stakeholder in the relationship, and the participation in the transaction is motivated by the opportunities involved in the transaction. Trust is, however, inherently related to risk since there always is a chance of deception or betrayal [16].

In this paper we propose a UML-based method for the development of policies to support trust management. The method goes through three main stages: (1) System modeling, (2) trust analysis, and (3) trust policy specification. The trust analysis should result in an overview of the available choices and the associated risks and opportunities. On the basis of this overview, a trust policy is formalized, the enforcement of which ensures that the most beneficial choices are made.

The next section describes the challenges addressed by this paper. By defining the basic concepts of our approach to trust management and explaining the relations between these concepts, we motivate the various steps and the ultimate goal of the proposed method. A motivating example used to illustrate the method throughout the paper is introduced. We also define a set of success criteria that should be fulfilled by the proposed method. An overview of the method is given in Section 3, followed by an example-driven description of the three main steps of the method in the subsequent sections. Firstly, Section 4 shows the use of Subjective STAIRS [12] to model the target of analysis. Secondly, Section 5 employs the models in Subjective STAIRS to analyze and evaluate the relevant trust relationships. Thirdly, Section 6 shows the use of Deontic STAIRS to specify the trust policy resulting from the analysis. Deontic STAIRS, as well as Subjective STAIRS, are based on UML 2.1 [10] sequence diagrams and STAIRS [6]. Subjecitive STAIRS is furthermore also based on Probabilistic STAIRS [11]. The approach is discussed and evaluated against the success criteria in Section 7, before we conclude in Section 8.

2 The Challenge

The overall challenge addressed by this paper is to establish a method to correctly assess trust and analyze trust-based transactions in order to identify, analyze and evaluate the involved risks and opportunities. The evaluation should result in a trust policy the enforcement of which ensures that risks are minimized and opportunities maximized.

A typical target of evaluation is an enterprise, system or organization in which there are actors whose choices of action may be based on trust. As an example, we consider a local bank and the risks and opportunities involved in loan approval to customers. The evaluation is from the perspective of the bank as a stakeholder, where the main asset of the bank is its revenue. In order to properly identify and assess the involved risks and opportunities, the basis upon which the bank employees grant or reject loan applications must be well understood. To keep the example simple while still illustrating the essential aspects of the approach, we make the following four assumptions: (1) An application for a loan includes the amount a that the customer wants to borrow. Other information, such as the value of the applicant's properties, or other loans the applicant may have, are not considered; (2) The customer either pays back the full loan (including interest), or nothing at all; (3) There is no mortgage securing the loan; (4) If the customer pays back the loan, then the bank's revenue v will increase by a gain g, otherwise it will decrease by a.

In many cases it is obvious whether or not applications should be accepted, typically when the income of the applying customer is very low or very high compared to the loan amount. In this paper we focus on the cases where there might be some doubt or uncertainty with respect to the ability of the customer to repay the loan, and where the decision as to accept an application is made by the individual bank employee. In these cases the level of trust of the employee in the customer may be decisive. Clearly, if the bank employee makes a wrong decision, then money may be lost; either because a loan is granted to a customer who does not pay back, or because a loan is not granted to a customer who would have paid back. The management wishes to develop a policy to ensure that the best possible decisions are made.

Consider first the potential risk involved in loan approval. A risk is defined as the probability of the occurrence of a harmful event [7], i.e. an event with a negative impact on an asset. The harmful event in the bank scenario is that a customer fails to repay the loan, and the impact of this event on the bank's asset is the loss of the loan sum a. The level of risk is given as a function from the consequence (loss) of the harmful event and the probability of its occurrence [1]. If the probability of this event is $p \in [0,1]$, the risk level is $R(p,a)$ for a given risk function R. For sake of simplicity, the risk function is in this paper defined to be multiplication, so $R(p,a) = p \cdot a$.

The dual to a risk is an opportunity, which is defined as the probability of the occurrence of a beneficial event, i.e. an event with a positive impact on an asset. In the bank scenario, the customer having paid all installments represents an opportunity. The positive impact is the gain for the bank, which depends on the loan amount and the interest rate. The opportunity level is given as a function O from the gain, say g, and the probability p for repayment. We use multiplication as the opportunity function also, so $O(p,g) = p \cdot g$.

In cases of doubt, the bank employee must consider the information available on the loan applicant. This may concern job affiliation, age, marital status, previous late settlements of debts, etc. This information may be incomplete or even false, but still a decision has to be made. In such a situation of uncertainty, other factors may also be considered, e.g. the personality of the customer, the impression the customer makes, and even acquaintance if it is a small, local bank. In such cases the trust of the bank employee in the customer may be decisive.

Our notion of trust is based on the definition proposed by Gambetta [5] and defined as the subjective probability by which an actor (the trustor) expects that another entity (the trustee) performs a given action on which the welfare of the trustor depends.

So trust is a probability estimate that ranges from 0 (complete distrust) to 1 (complete trust). It is subjective, which means that it is a belief that may be wrong. The welfare of a trust relation refers to an associated asset of the trustor. If the trustee performs as expected, it will have a positive outcome for the trustee. There is, however, always the possibility of deception, and in that case there will be a negative impact on the welfare. Hence, trust is related to both opportunity and risk.

For the bank being the stakeholder in our example case, it is important to evaluate the effects of the trust-based decisions of the employees in terms of risks and opportunities for the bank. If, for example, an employee has trust $p \in [0, 1]$ in that a given customer will repay a loan of the amount a with a potential gain g, the opportunity is given by $p \cdot g$ as believed by the bank employee. The employee furthermore believes that the risk is $(1 - p) \cdot a$. Decisions are then made by comparing the risk and opportunity. If there is a difference between the trust value and the actual trustworthiness of the customer, the wrong decision may be made.

By trustworthiness we mean the objective probability by which the trustee performs a given action on which the welfare of the trustor depends. Well-founded trust is the case in which trust equals the trustworthiness, and it is only in this case that the involved risks and opportunities are correctly estimated.

If trust is ill-founded, the subjective estimate is either too high or too low. In the former case we have misplaced trust, which is unfortunate as it means that the believed risk level is lower than the actual risk level. In the latter case we have misplaced distrust, which is also unfortunate since then the believed risk level is higher than the actual one, which may lead to valuable transactions being missed.

In existing literature on the subject, trust management is mostly concerned with approaches and methods aimed to support the trustor in making assessments about trustworthiness of other parties. The challenge addressed by this paper is the analysis of the risks and opportunities to which a system is exposed as a result of choices of behavior of entities within the system, where these choices may be based on trust. Some of the entities within the system are subjective entities, and the challenge is to reach an objective understanding of the system as a whole. Moreover, based on this objective understanding, the challenge is also to gain a correct estimation of the risks and opportunities imposed by subjective decisions. Hence, we aim for a method to identify and analyze trust, and thereby capture a policy to avoid risks and seek opportunities, as further explained by the six success criteria described in the following.

The aim of any analysis is to reach an objective understanding of the target of analysis. In this case the target contains actors of a subjective nature, but the challenge is still to reach an objective understanding of the target as a whole: Does the target of analysis function as it should? What is the impact of subjective decisions on the overall behavior? Therefore: *(C1) The method should facilitate the objective modeling of systems whose overall behavior depends on subjective, trust-based behavior of actors within the system.*

Trust is a subjective probability, and in order to properly specify trust relations, the modeling of trust levels of the relevant trust relations must be supported. Therefore: *(C2) The method should facilitate the specification of the level of trust an actor has in another entity with respect to a given transaction.*

The ultimate goal of trust management is to minimize risks and maximize opportunities related to trust. This gives: *(C3) The method should facilitate the identification, estimation and evaluation of system risks and opportunities imposed by the relevant trust relations.*

Through trust modeling and the analysis of risks and opportunities, trust-based choices of behavior that should be avoided are identified, as well as trust-based choices that should be sought. A policy is a set of rules that govern choices in system behavior, and the method should identify the rules that ensure the most advantageous system behavior. In short: *(C4) The method should support the capturing of an adequate trust policy.*

Policy enforcement is facilitated by precise descriptions of the policy rules. Both obligation and prohibition rules should be supported so as to define absolute choices of behavior. In case of choices between potential alternatives that are considered equivalent with respect to a given purpose, permission rules must be expressible. The rules of a trust policy should be specified with triggers that define the circumstance, as well as the levels of trust, under which the rule applies. Hence: *(C5) The method should have sufficient expressiveness to capture obligations, prohibitions and permissions, as well as triggers where required.*

In order to develop a good policy, it is essential that decision makers, developers, analysts, etc. have a clear and shared understanding of the system, the relevant scenarios, and the alternative policy rules. Moreover, the policy rules must be easily understandable for those who are supposed to adhere to them. *(C6) The method should offer description techniques that are understandable to all relevant stakeholders, including end-users, decision makers and engineers.*

3 Overview of Method

In this section we give an overview of the three main steps of the method and motivate its overall structure. The sections thereafter demonstrate the method on the bank example.

Step 1. Modeling of Target. In order to analyze something, we need an understanding of this "something" at a level of abstraction that is suitable for the analysis. Abstraction is necessary since most systems are extremely complex when all details are taken into consideration. For example, our bank example involves human beings, and nobody would even consider to describe a human being in full detail. In order to document the sought understanding and validate it on others, it seems reasonable to make use of a modeling language.

This description of the target should not only show how the actors and components behave, but also what decisions and choices are made by actors in the system, and *why* those decisions and choices are made. More specifically, as our purpose here is to develop a trust policy, we are interested in understanding what decisions are taken on the basis of trust, and what considerations lie behind such decisions.

Subjective STAIRS, which is a language based on UML 2.1 sequence diagrams, has been selected for this purpose. It allows us to specify subjective beliefs about scenarios, as well as actual (objective) scenarios, and also to show how the subjective beliefs influence the choices made by actors. Subjective STAIRS distinguishes between subjective and objective diagrams, and probability may be expressed in both kinds. Trust with respect to a transaction is represented by a probability in a subjective diagram.

We use objective diagrams to capture the actual behavior of the target, while subjective diagrams are employed to express the belief of an actor with respect to a scenario. In Section 4 we demonstrate the use of Subjective STAIRS to describe the banking system as the target of analysis.

There are two main reasons for basing the modeling language on UML sequence diagrams. Firstly, sequence diagrams are well suited to express interactions between entities. As trust is relevant in the context of an interaction between the trustor and the trustee, this makes sequence diagrams a suitable choice. Secondly, sequence diagrams allow systems to be described at a high level of abstraction, in a simple and intuitive manner that can be understood by stakeholders with different background and level of training. These qualities are important in the context of the risk and opportunity analysis that we must conduct in order to develop trust policies.

Step 2. Analysis of Target. After obtaining a suitable description of the target, the next task is to perform an analysis. The analysis proceeds in four sub-steps as described in the following and demonstrated in Section 5 with the banking system as target.

Step 2.1. Identify critical decision points. First, the critical decision points that need to be looked into are identified. Typically, this will be points where decisions are made based on trust. But it may also be points where one could potentially benefit from introducing new trust-based decisions, if the resulting opportunities outweigh the risks.

Step 2.2. Evaluate well-foundedness of trust. Second, we need to evaluate the well-foundedness of the trust on which decisions and choices are based. As trust is a subjective probability estimate, this amounts to finding out to what degree the subjectively estimated probabilities correspond to the actual (objective) probabilities.

Step 2.3. Estimate impact of alternative behavior. Of course, it may well be that the current way of making choices is not optimal. Therefore, the third sub-step is to estimate what would be the impact of other, alternative choices of behavior.

Step 2.4. Evaluate and compare alternative behavior. The final sub-step consists of an evaluation and comparison of alternative behaviors, with the aim to identify the behaviors that should be sought or avoided.

Step 3. Capturing a Policy to Optimize Target. Having identified the desirable behavior, we are finally ready to specify a policy the enforcement of which ensures the optimal choices of behavior.

A policy is a set of rules that determines choices in the behavior of a system [14], and is used in policy based management. Typical domains are security management and the management of networks and services. The method proposed by this paper is an approach to policy based trust management. Each rule determines a system choice of behavior, where a given trust level is a decisive factor for each choice. Enforcement of the given rules ensures the optimal level of the risks and opportunities that are imposed by trust based decisions within the system. As for the target model, it is essential that the policy is unambiguous and understandable for all involved stakeholders. To formalize the policy we use Deontic STAIRS, which is a language for expressing policies, and based on UML sequence diagrams. Employing sequence diagrams as the basis for all modeling, analysis and specification in the method is desirable, both because it facilitates use and understandability, and because specifications can be reused.

Deontic STAIRS has the expressiveness to specify constraints in the form of obligations, prohibitions, and permissions, corresponding to the expressiveness of standard deontic logic [9]. Such constraints are normative rules that describe the desired system behavior. This reflects a key feature of policies, namely that they "define choices in behavior in terms of the conditions under which predefined operations or actions can be invoked rather than changing the functionality of the actual operations themselves" [15]. Furthermore, Deontic STAIRS supports the specification of triggers that define the circumstances under which the various rules apply. In particular, the policy triggers can specify the required trust levels for a particular choice of behavior to be constrained.

4 Modeling the Bank System

We now show how the system to be analyzed is modeled in Subjective STAIRS, focusing only on the case where the bank employee makes a decision based on trust. Subjective STAIRS builds on Probabilistic STAIRS, which has a formal semantics. However, for our purposes here, an intuitive explanation of the diagrams suffices.

Briefly stated, the scenario is as follows: First the customer applies for a loan. The bank employee then grants the loan if she or he believes that the probability of the loan being paid back is sufficiently high. Otherwise, the application is rejected. In the cases where the loan is granted, one of two things may happen: either the customer pays back the loan (with interest), so that the bank's asset value increases, or the bank has to write off the loan, in which case the asset value decreases. The model is given in Fig. 1. The main diagram is loan1, which is an objective diagram showing the actual behavior of the system. Each of the entities taking part in the interaction is represented by a dashed, vertical line called a lifeline, where the box at the top of the line contains the name of the entity, in this case the bank employee

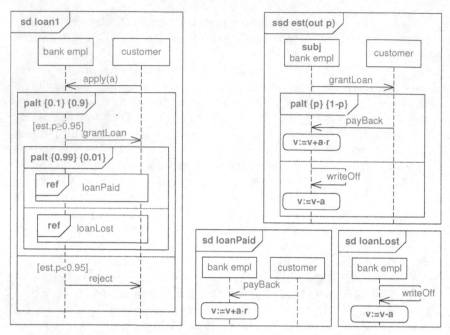

Fig. 1 System model

(bank empl) and the customer (customer). The interaction between the entities are represented by messages, which are shown as horizontal arrows from one lifeline to another (or to itself). Each message defines two events: the transmission of the message, represented by the arrow tail, and the reception of the message, represented by the arrow head. Transmission naturally occurs before reception, and events are ordered from the top on each lifeline, so the first thing that happens is that the customer sends the apply(a) message to the bank employee. This message represents the application, where a is the amount applied for.

At this point, the scenario may continue in one of two alternative ways, as the application may be either granted or rejected. These alternatives are represented by the outermost palt operator. The palt operator expresses alternatives with probabilities. The operator is shown as a frame with the operator name (palt) in the upper left corner. Its operands are separated by a horizontal dashed line. Each operand represents an alternative. The numbers occurring after palt in the upper corner of the operator frame show the probabilities of the operands; the probability for the first (upper) alternative to occur is 0.1, while the probability for the second (lower) is 0.9. As this is an objective diagram, we may imagine that the probabilities have been obtained for example by observing the system for a while and registering frequencies for the alternative behaviors.

At the beginning of each operand, we find a Boolean expression enclosed in square brackets. These constructs, which are called guards, constrain the conditions under which the alternatives may occur; an alternative occurs only if its guard evaluates to true. The expression est.p in the guards of both operands of the outermost paltrepresents the probability subjectively estimated by the bank employee that the customer will pay back the loan if the loan is granted, as will be further explained below. This means that the first alternative, where the loan is granted, occurs only if the bank employee believes that the probability that the loan will be paid back is at least 0.95. The fact that the first alternative has probability 0.1 means that the bank employee holds this belief in 10% of the cases where a loan is applied for.

Assuming the bank employee estimates that the probability of the loan being paid back is at least 0.95, she or he grants the loan, as represented by the grantLoan message. Then we have again two possible alternatives[1]. The first alternative, which has probability 0.99, is that the customer pays back the loan, represented by the payBack message. Notice that there is no assumption about the time interval between events on a lifeline, so the interval between granting the loan and being paid back may be much longer than the time between receiving the application and granting the loan. After the loan is paid back, the bank's asset value v increases by the amount a multiplied by the interest rate r. This is represented in the diagram by the assignment statement v:=v+a·r.

The second alternative, which has probability 0.01, is that the bank employee decides that the money will have to be written off, as the customer will not pay back the loan. This decision is represented by the writeOff from the bank employee to her/himself. In this case the bank's asset value decreases by the amount a, as represented by the assignment statement v:=v-a.

As noted above, the expression est.p represents the probability subjectively estimated by the bank employee that the customer will pay back the loan if the loan is granted. This can be seen from the diagram est in the upper right-hand corner of Fig. 1, which is a subjective diagram representing the belief of the bank employee. Subjective diagrams have the keyword ssd (for subjective sequence diagram) instead of sd in front of the diagram name. In addition, exactly one lifeline is decorated with the keyword subj, indicating that this is the actor (subject) whose belief is represented by the subjective diagram in question. For the est diagram, the bank employee is the subject. The probabilities in the est diagram are given in terms of the symbolic value p rather than a number, as the probability estimate will vary depending on the customer. The statement out p after the diagram name means that the symbolic value p can be referred to from an objective diagram by the expression est.p, as is done in the guards of loan1.

---

[1] For these alternatives we have made use of the UML ref construct. This construct is a reference to the diagram whose name occurs in the frame. Its meaning is the same as if the content of the referenced diagram was inserted in place of the ref construct. The ref construct allows a modular presentation of diagrams, as well as reuse of diagrams.

5 Analyzing the Bank System

In this section we demonstrate the analysis method presented in Section 3 on the bank example by going through the four (sub-)steps of the analysis step.

Step 2.1. Identify critical decision points. For this example, we assume that the only critical decision point we want to consider is the choice between granting or rejecting the application. Other decision points could also have been considered. For example, the bank employee could decide whether further investigations into the customer's previous history are needed before deciding whether to grant the loan, or whether another attempt at demanding payment should be made before writing off the money.

Step 2.2. Evaluate well-foundedness of trust. For the second analysis step, we need to find out whether the trust is well-founded, i.e. to what degree the subjectively estimated probabilities correspond to the objective probabilities. In order to do this, we need a model that describes what happens if the bank employee grants *all* applications. This is necessary in order to evaluate the correctness of the probability estimates also for the cases where the application would normally be rejected. The diagram loan2 in Fig. 2 provides such a model[2]. How the model is obtained is up to the analysis team. It could for example be based on some expert's opinion, historical data, simulation, or be the result of an experiment where all applications are granted for a certain period of time (although the latter is perhaps not likely for this particular example).

In addition to assuming that all applications are granted, we have chosen to distinguish between four different intervals of subjectively estimated probability, as can be seen from the guards in loan2. The number of intervals can be chosen freely by the analysis team, depending on the desired granularity of the analysis. For each interval we have a separate palt operand. This allows us to compare the actual (objective) probability with the interval in which the subjective estimate lies. The first palt operand in loan2 represents the cases where the estimate lies within the interval [0.95, 1], which according to the probability of the first operand happens in 10% of the cases (as the probability for this operand is 0.1). From granted1 referred to in the first operand, we see that the probability of being paid back in this case is 0.99. The second palt operand in loan2 represents the cases where the estimate lies within the interval [0.9, 0.95⟩, which happens in 20% of the cases. The probability of being paid back in these cases is 0.96, as seen from granted2. The third palt operand in loan2 represents the cases where the estimate lies within the interval [0.8, 0.9⟩. For these cases, the probability of being paid back is in fact 0.92, which is slightly outside the estimated interval. Finally, the fourth palt operand in loan2 represents the cases where the estimate is lower than 0.8, and the probability of being paid back in these cases is 0.6 according to granted4.

Step 2.3. Estimate impact of alternative behavior. In addition to showing the correspondence between subjective estimates and objective probabilities, loan2 also describes the overall system behavior resulting from using alternative thresholds

---

[2] The references loanPaid and loanLost are to the diagrams in Fig. 1.

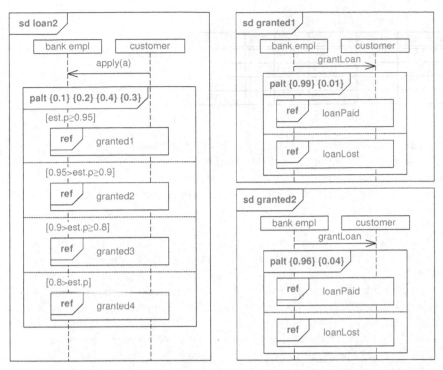

Fig. 2 System model obtained in the analysis in order to evaluate alternatives. The diagrams granted3 and granted4 are omitted. They are identical to the granted1 and granted2 diagrams, except from the probabilities in the palt operand. For granted3, the probabilities are 0.92 for the first operand, and 0.08 for the second operand. For granted4, the probabilities are 0.6 for the first operand, and 0.4 for the second operand.

(against which the estimated probability is compared) when deciding whether to grant loans. Therefore, loan2 already represents an estimate of the impact of some alternative behavior, i.e. what is the impact of using different thresholds. The impact of other alternative behavior could also be considered in this step of the analysis. For example, what would be the impact of always performing investigations into the customer's previous history before deciding whether to grant the loan? However, due to lack of space, we consider only the alternative behavior already described in Fig. 2.

Step 2.4. Evaluate and compare alternative behavior. Table 1 presents the risks and opportunities on the basis of loan2. The numbers are calculated from an interest rate of 8.7%, i.e. $r = 0.087$. The "Threshold" column shows the decision threshold that is analyzed in the corresponding row. For example, the second row in the table shows the results of only granting a loan in cases where the estimated probability of being paid back is at least 0.9.

The "Granted" column shows the percentage of the received applications that will be granted when the relevant decision threshold is used. For example, if a loan

Table 1 The result of using alternative decision thresholds

Threshold	Granted	Paid back	Opp.	Risk	Opp.−Risk
≥ 0.95	10%	99%	0.0086	0.001	0.0076
≥ 0.9	30%	97%	0.025	0.009	0.016
≥ 0.8	70%	94%	0.057	0.041	0.016
≥ 0	100%	84%	0.073	0.16	−0.087

is granted if the estimated probability of being paid back is at least 0.9, then 30% of all applications will be granted. This number is obtained by adding the probabilities of all operands whose guard ensures that the estimated probability is not lower than the decision threshold. For the case where the threshold is 0.9, we add up the probabilities of the two first operands of the palt in the loan2 specification. Thus we obtain 0.3, which corresponds to 30%.

The "Paid back" column shows the percentage of the granted loans that will be paid back. This number is obtained by, for each operand where a loan will be granted, taking the product of the probability of the operand and the probability of being paid back according to this operand. The sum of these products is divided by the percentage of applications being granted. For example, for the second row we get $(0.1 \cdot 0.99 + 0.2 \cdot 0.96)/0.3$, which gives 0.97, i.e. 97%.

The "Opp." column shows the opportunity value we get by choosing the relevant threshold value. The opportunity value is obtained from the formula $0.087 \cdot \sum(p_1 \cdot p_2)$, where $\sum(p_1 \cdot p_2)$ is the sum of the product of the probability p_1 of the operand and the probability p_2 of being paid back for all operands where a loan will be granted when the threshold in the left-hand column is used. For example, for the second row in the table, we get $0.087 \cdot (0.1 \cdot 0.99 + 0.2 \cdot 0.96) = 0.025$. The loan amount a has been factored out, as this would occur only as a common factor in all rows, and we are only interested in the relative values.

The "Risk" column shows the accumulated risk value we get by choosing the relevant threshold value. It is obtained in a similar way as the accumulated opportunity value, except that we use the probability of *not* being paid back for each operand, and that the interest rate is not taken into account. For the second row in the table, we get $(0.1 \cdot 0.01 + 0.2 \cdot 0.04) = 0.009$.

Finally, the "Opp.−Risk" column shows the difference between the two previous columns. From Table 1 we are now able to compare the alternative thresholds in order to decide which of them should be used in order to achieve the most desirable system behavior. The goal of the bank here is to maximize the difference between opportunity and risk, i.e. to achieve the highest possible value for "Contr.-Risk". This goal may or may not coincide with the goals of the bank employee, which has different assets from the bank. However, as the analysis is performed on behalf of the bank, we do not consider the goals of the bank employee.

From the two first rows in the "Opp.-Risk" column we see that the value increases if the threshold is lowered from ≥ 0.95 to ≥ 0.9, i.e. if a loan is granted also in cases where the estimated probability of being paid back is between 0.9 and 0.95, instead of only when the estimated probability is at least 0.95. Even if slightly more of the customers that are granted a loan will not be able to pay back, this is more than made up for by the increased number of customers that will pay back their loan with interest. In other words, the bank loses money by not granting loans in cases where the subjective estimate lies between 0.9 and 0.95. Therefore, the bank should enforce the following trust policy rule: *(R1) It is obligated to grant a loan for the cases in which the trust level is at least 0.9.*

The second and third rows show that the net effect of lowering the threshold one step further, to ≥ 0.8, is zero, as the "Opp.-Risk" value is the same for the thresholds ≥ 0.9 and ≥ 0.8. This means that the bank will neither lose nor gain from granting loans also in the cases where the estimated probability of being paid back is between 0.8 and 0.9. Therefore, the bank may decide to leave the choice up to the individual bank employee. This gives the following two policy rules: *(R2) It is permitted to grant a loan for the cases in which the trust level is lower than 0.9 but at least 0.8; (R3) It is permitted to reject a loan for the cases in which the trust level is lower than 0.9 but at least 0.8.*

The fourth row in the "Opp.−Risk" column, however, shows that granting loans to all applicants will give a risk that is higher than the opportunity. Therefore, the following rule should be enforced: *(R4) It is prohibited to grant a loan for the cases in which the trust level is lower than 0.8.*

6 Policy to Optimize the Bank System

We now show how we may use Deontic STAIRS to formalize the optimized strategies we arrived at in Section 5 as a policy. Deontic STAIRS is an extension of UML 2.1 sequence diagrams and is underpinned by a formal semantics based on the denotational semantics of STAIRS. For the purpose of this paper it suffices to explain the semantics informally.

The analysis of the bank system in the previous section revealed that loan application should be granted in the cases where the trust of the bank employee in that the customer will repay the loan is 0.9 or higher, as captured by rule *(R1)* above. This is expressed by the obligation rule r1 specified to the left in Fig. 3.

The keyword rule in the upper left corner indicates that the diagram specifies a policy rule. The diagram consists of two parts, a trigger and an interaction that is the operand of a deontic modality. The trigger specifies the circumstances under which the rule applies and consists of an event and a condition. The former refers to an event such that when it occurs, the rule applies. In this case the event is the reception by the employee of a loan application. The condition of the trigger limits the applicability of the rule to a set of system states. In this case it refers to the states in which the relevant trust level is 0.9 or higher.

The keyword obligation shows the modality of the rule. It is an operator the operand of which specifies the behavior that is constrained by the rule. In this case, the relevant behavior is the granting of a loan. For simplicity, we model this by a single message only, but in the general case the behavior can be described in any detail with all the expressiveness of UML 2.1 sequence diagrams.

A further result of the analysis in Section 5 is rule *(R4)*, namely that loan should not be granted to customers whose trust value is lower than 0.8, since in that case the risk is higher than the opportunity for the bank. This is captured by diagram r4 to the right in Fig. 3, where the keyword prohibition indicates the modality of the rule.

Obligations and prohibitions specify behavior that must and must not occur, respectively. Permissions, on the other hand, define choices of behavior that should be offered potentially, without disallowing alternative choices to be made instead. That is to say, permissions specify behavior that may occur. The above analysis of the bank system showed that for trust levels in the interval from 0.8 to 0.9, the involved risk and opportunity even out. This means that from the point of view of the bank, both loan approval and rejection are acceptable choices of behavior, i.e. both choices may be permitted.

As indicated by the modality, the rule r2 to the left in Fig. 4 is a permission. It specifies *(R2)* as captured in the analysis, and states that for the mentioned interval of trust levels, the bank employee is permitted to grant the applied loan to the customer. This means that the bank system must always allow the employee to make this choice in case the trigger holds. The employee is, however, free to make any other choice that does not conflict with other policy rules. In order to ensure that a set of potential alternatives should be available, other permissions with the same trigger can be specified. This is exemplified with the permission to the right in Fig. 4, expressing the rule *(R3)* captured in the analysis.

7 Discussion

Ever since trust management became a topic of research, the focus has mostly been on assessing trustworthiness of other entities and establishing trust between entities, as witnessed by a recent survey of state-of-the-art approaches to trust management

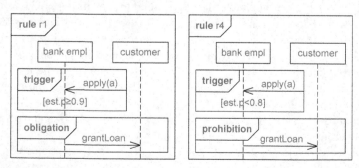

Fig. 3 Obligation and prohibition

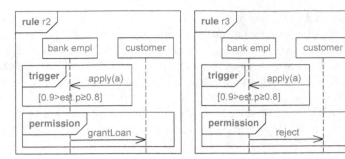

Fig. 4 Permissions

[13]. This is also put forward in [8], where trust management is discussed as an independent research topic and existing methods are reviewed.

Trust management is particularly relevant for distributed systems where the identity and/or intentions of other entities may be uncertain, and it is crucial to develop methods for managing trust, and hence managing risk and security. Importantly, most of the existing approaches focus on trust management from the point of view of the trustor, and the issue of mitigating risks to which the trustor is exposed. In this paper we have focused on the important challenge of understanding the risks to which a system is exposed, where some of the entities within the system are actors that make risk critical decisions based on subjective trust estimates. Moreover, whereas trust management traditionally focuses mostly on risk in relation to trust, we address also the challenge of identifying and evaluating the dual concept, namely opportunity. In the same way as risk is inevitably related to trust, so is opportunity, and in order to derive the most optimal trust policy for a given system, both risks and opportunities must be estimated.

Game theory [4] addresses strategies for describing rational choices in situations in which the outcome of a choice of one actor depends on the subsequent choice of another actor. A payoff structure describes the loss and gain to which the various players are exposed in each of the potential outcomes, and each player seeks the outcome with the most beneficial payoff for itself. Game theory can also be applied to analyze trust, as explained by e.g. Bacharach and Gambetta [2]. They show that the trustor's choice to trust or not, and the trustees subsequent choice to deceit or not, can be modeled in terms of this rational choice theory. The method presented in this paper captures aspects of game theory by the identification and modeling of choices of (trust-based) decisions, as well as the modeling of the associated payoff structure in terms of risks and prospects.

Subjective STAIRS has the expressiveness to model the alternative behaviors of a system, as well as the probabilities of these alternatives. Moreover, the notation supports the objective specification of the subjective probability estimates made by entities within the system, and thereby the trust on which these entities base their decisions. The trust management method proposed in this paper hence fulfills success criteria *C1* and *C2* as formulated in Section 2.

As demonstrated in Section 5, system modeling with Subjective STAIRS facilitates the identification, estimation and evaluation of both the risks and opportunities to which a system is exposed. Criterion *C3* is then also fulfilled by the method, thus allowing the relevant system analysis to be conducted. Through the analysis, the preferable choices of behavior are identified, which in turn facilitates the capture of an adequate trust policy. Hence, also criterion *C4* is fulfilled by the method.

Deontic STAIRS is a customized notation for policy specification, and as shown in Section 6, this notation supports the specification of trust policies. Behavior that should be sought and behavior that should be avoided may be expressed by obligations and prohibitions, respectively, whereas alternative choices of behavior that should be offered by the system may be formalized as permissions. Additionally, the circumstances under which a given rule applies can be expressed by the specification of a trigger consisting of an event and the level of trust of relevance for the policy rule in question. As demonstrated in Section 6, the proposed trust management method then fulfills success criterion *C5*.

The UML has the last decade or so emerged as the *de facto* standard for the specification of information systems. Both Subjective STAIRS and Deontic STAIRS are conservative extensions of the UML 2.1 sequence diagram notation, so people that are already skilled in the UML should be able to understand and use the languages employed by our method. Moreover, contrary to textual, more mathematical notations, the UML should be understandable also for people of non-technical background, at least with some guidance. Arguably, success criterion *C6* is then at least partly fulfilled by the proposed method.

8 Conclusion

This paper contributes by addressing the quite neglected challenge of understanding the risks and opportunities to which a system is exposed in cases where actors within the system make choices based on their trust in other entities. The proposed method offers languages and techniques for the modeling and analysis of the subjective notion of trust in an objective manner, facilitating the identification of risk and opportunity critical decision points. By identifying the set of behavioral alternatives of the target system and precisely estimating the involved risks and prospects, a policy that optimizes system behavior may be captured. The method furthermore contributes by facilitating the formalization of trust policies through an appropriate policy specification language.

Although refinement has not been an issue in this paper, it is certainly of relevance in relation to trust modeling and policy development, as it allows a system to be described, and hence analyzed, at different levels of abstraction. In the future we will address refinement in relation to the trust management method proposed in this paper by utilizing refinement techniques that have already been developed for Subjective STAIRS and Deontic STAIRS.

Acknowledgements The research on which this paper reports has partly been funded by the Research Council of Norway through the ENFORCE project (164382/V30) and partly by the European Commission through the S3MS project (Contract no. 27004) under the IST Sixth Framework Programme.

References

1. AS/NZS. *Australian/New Zealand Standard, AS/NZS 4360:2004, Risk Management*, 2004.
2. M. Bacharach and D. Gambetta. Trust in Signs. In K. S. Cook, editor, *Trust in Society*, volume II of *The Russel Sage Foundation Series on Trust*, pages 148–184. Russel Sage Foundation, 2001.
3. M. Blaze, J. Feigenbaum, and J. Lacy. Decentralized Trust Management. In *Proceedings of the IEEE Symposium on Security and Privacy*, pages 164–173, Oakland, CA, 1996.
4. D. Fudenberg and J. Tirole. *Game Theory*. MIT Press, 1991.
5. D. Gambetta. Can We Trust Trust? In *Trust: Making and Breaking Cooperative Relations*, chapter 13, pages 213–237. Department of Sociology, University of Oxford, 2000. Electronic edition.
6. Ø. Haugen, K. E. Husa, R. K. Runde, and K. Stølen. STAIRS towards formal design with sequence diagrams. *Journal of Software and Systems Modeling*, 4:355–367, 2005.
7. ISO/IEC. *ISO/IEC 13335, Information technology – Guidelines for management of IT security*, 1996–2000.
8. A. Jøsang, C. Keser, and T. Dimitrakos. Can We Manage Trust? In *In Proceedings of the 3rd International Conference on Trust Management (iTrust)*, volume 3477 of *LNCS*, pages 93–107. Springer, 2005.
9. P. McNamara. Deontic Logic. In D. M. Gabbay and J. Woods, editors, *Logic and the Modalities in the Twentieth Century*, volume 7 of *Handbook of the History of Logic*, pages 197–288. Elsevier, 2006.
10. Object Management Group. *Unified Modeling Language: Superstructure, version 2.1.1*, 2007.
11. A. Refsdal, R. K. Runde, and K. Stølen. Underspecification, inherent nondeterminism and probability in sequence diagrams. In *Proceedings of the 8th IFIP International Conference on Formal Methods for Open Object-Based Distributed Systems (FMOODS)*, volume 4037 of *LNCS*, pages 138–155. Springer, 2006.
12. A. Refsdal and K. Stølen. Extending UML sequence diagrams to model trust-dependent behavior with the aim to support risk analysis. In *Proceedings of the 3rd International Workshop on Security and Trust Management (STM)*. ENTCS, to appear.
13. S. Ruohomaa and L. Kutvonen. Trust Management Survey. In *In Proceedings of the 3rd International Conference on Trust Management (iTrust)*, volume 3477 of *LNCS*, pages 77–92. Springer, 2005.
14. M. Sloman. Policy Driven Management for Distributed Systems. *Journal of Network and Systems Management*, 2:333–360, 1994.
15. M. Sloman and E. Lupu. Security and Management Policy Specification. *Network, IEEE*, 16(2):10–19, 2002.
16. B. Solhaug, D. Elgesem, and K. Stølen. Why Trust is not proportional to Risk. In *Proceedings of The 2nd International Conference on Availability, Reliability and Security (ARES)*, pages 11–18. IEEE Computer Society, 2007.

Analyzing the Robustness of CertainTrust

Sebastian Ries, Andreas Heinemann

Abstract Trust in ubiquitous computing is about finding trustworthy partners for risky interactions in presence of uncertainty about identity, motivation, and goals of the potential interactions partners. In this paper, we present new approaches for estimating the trustworthiness of entities and for filtering and weighting recommendations, which we integrate in our trust model, called CertainTrust. We evaluate the robustness of our trust model using an canonical set of population mixes based on a classification of typical entity behaviors. The simulation is based on user traces collected in the Reality Mining project. The evaluation shows the applicability of our trust model to collaboration in opportunistic networks and its advantages in comparison to a distributed variant of the Beta Reputation System.

1 Introduction

The main driving force behind the idea of ubiquitous computing (UC) is to support humans in their everyday life. UC environments are expected to be made up by a huge number of heterogeneous, loosely coupled devices. Thus, collaboration between devices, e.g., sharing information or resources, is an indispensable enabler for the evolution of UC.

Sebastian Ries
Technische Universität Darmstadt, Hochschulstrasse 10, 64289 Darmstadt, Germany,
e-mail: ries@tk.informatik.tu-darmstadt.de
The author's work was supported by the German National Science Foundation (DFG)
as part of the PhD program "Enabling Technologies for Electronic Commerce"

Andreas Heinemann
Technische Universität Darmstadt, Hochschulstrasse 10, 64289 Darmstadt, Germany,
e-mail: aheine@tk.informatik.tu-darmstadt.de

Please use the following format when citing this chapter:

Ries, S. and Heinemann, A., 2008, in IFIP International Federation for Information Processing, Volume 263; *Trust Management II*; Yücel
Karabulut, John Mitchell, Peter Herrmann, Christian Damsgaard Jensen; (Boston: Springer), pp. 51–67.

Frequent collaboration requires frequent decisions about who to interact with, demanding for a non-intrusive way of decision making. This can be done based on certificates or by hard-coded policies, which, e.g., only allow for the interaction with a set of pre-defined partners. However, in an unmanaged domain we can neither expect pre-defined or certified partners to be available all the time, nor that all suitable interaction partners are certified. The shortcomings of both approaches become obvious, when considering opportunistic [7] or pocket switched networking [8] in which information is disseminated in absence of an end-to-end connectivity, but rather in an one hop manner from one mobile node (user) to the next one.

Thus, we favor the approach of selecting interaction partners based on trust, which is built on experiences from past interactions. Although, one may be uncertain about the identity, motivation or goals of potential interaction partners, direct experiences from past interactions are a good indicator whether to interact another time. As direct experiences may be rare, indirect experiences (recommendations) need to be considered as additional information. As recommendations may be more or less accurate, techniques for filtering and weighting recommendations are important.

In this paper, we show how our trust model improves the selection of interaction partners, and thus improves the quality of interactions, i.e., positive outcome and feedback. For that purpose, we evaluate the trust model against a canonical set of populations with respect to its users' behaviors and by varying stability of the users' behaviors, i.e., varying the adherence of the users to a behavior. To cope with bad interaction partners and lying recommenders we introduce new approaches for calculating the trustworthiness of entities, and provide a new way to handle recommendations.

The remainder of the paper is structured as follows: First, we present related work in Sec. 2. Then, we briefly describe the scenario for our analysis, i.e., content distribution in an opportunistic network (see Sec. 3). In Sec. 4, we explain the parts of our trust model, called CertainTrust, that are relevant for the evaluation. In Sec. 5 we introduce our classification of entity behaviors and derive the possible population mixes. In Sec. 6, we present our simulation setup and the gained results. We discuss the results and summarize this work in a conclusion.

2 Related Work

Our scenario is motivated by an application, called *musicClouds* [7], which allows for autonomous sharing of music files in opportunistic networks. It focuses on defining filters for specifying the meta information of files of interest, but not on the selection of the interaction partner. In [8], Hui et al. argue for the relevance of pocket switched networking since there are numerous scenarios in which local connectivity might be preferred over an internet-based connection, due to bandwidth, latency or costs. Although, the authors focus on analyzing mobility patterns and consequences for data forwarding, they state that, among other aspects, establishing and maintaining trust relationships, as well as the provision of incentives for participating in the network are important.

Besides the seminal work on trust in [11], which focuses on modeling trust for only two agents, and centralized approaches [6], there is a growing number of trust models which allow for a decentralized computation of trust, being more suitable for UC (see below).

Distributed trust models usually compute trust based on direct experiences from past interactions in a certain context and indirect ones (via recommendations) [1, 9, 10, 12]. A few approaches integrate additional knowledge from similar contexts [2] or related aspects [14], which requires an additional modeling of ontologies expressing the relations between those contexts or aspects. In this paper, we focus on modeling trust in a single context, as this is the most appropriate for our scenario.

The trust model in [1] focuses on virtual organizations, and provides a label-based approach for representing trust, but includes only a rudimental approach for treating uncertainty. In [12], Quercia et al. provide a trust model that allows for a discrete, non-binary representation of trust. The model is capable of expressing the confidence of a trust value, mainly based on the variance derived from the data about experiences in past interactions, and the number of past experiences. A general approach to model trust, called "Subjective Logic", proposed by Jøsang [9], integrates the Bayesian update mechanism together with a representation reflecting a human notion of belief, capable of expressing uncertainty. This model also provides a method for integrating continuous feedback [10]. Both approaches do not allow to explicitly define how many experiences are necessary to reach the maximal level of certainty. Thus, they treat (un-)certainty equally for all contexts, and in a rather static manner. Furthermore, their filtering and weighting techniques focus on scenarios with a majority of positive recommendations. The trust model provided by Buchegger in [3] proposes a filtering of recommendations based on the similarity of the recommendations to the direct experiences, which may be circumvented if direct experience is missing, or by a repeated stepwise providing of misleading recommendations. The approach introduced in [15] is close to our approach, as it uses the past accuracy of past recommendations per entity for weighting its recommendations. But it takes a long time until it totally excludes misleading recommendations from a recommender. Furthermore, it introduces the assumption that it is necessary to learn the trust in recommenders depending on the actual values of the recommendations.

3 Scenario

For the evaluation of the impact of our trust model, we choose a scenario in which humans with mobile devices share music in an opportunistic network. In the following we refer to users with their mobile devices as entities. As these entities move, they will meet other entities, and interact with each other, e.g., they exchange music (mp3 files) or recommendations, in a spontaneous manner. Due to different goals or motivation, the users will show different behaviors when providing files to others. The goal of a typical user is to interact only with trustworthy interactors, i.e., interactors from which he expects to receive a good file (correct file, no viruses, complete song, and expected quality).

We assume that a user appreciates the support of a software component including a trust model, which supports him with information about the trustworthiness of the available candidates for an interaction, or is even capable of making decisions and interacting on its own. This will be especially true, if it allows for increasing the quality of a user's interactions, i.e., the number of received good files.

After an interaction, the *quality of the interaction* is determined by feedback. The generation of the feedback does not necessarily require user interaction. In some cases this can also be done automatically, e.g., by scanning the mp3 file for viruses, checking the size, the bitrate, and noise. This allows the software component to create histories about interactors and recommenders.

4 Trust Model

In this section, we introduce our system model. For self-containment of this paper, we briefly describe the representational trust model (for details see [13]), which defines how trust is modeled. Then, we present our approach of deriving an expectation value from the collected evidences. Furthermore, we present a new approach for filtering and weighting recommendations. At last we introduce the update mechanism based on feedback on past interactions. For an overview of the different steps in establishing trust between entities and selecting entities based on trust see Fig. 1.

4.1 System Model

The participants in the system are called `entities`. Entities can be either `active` or `passive`. Active entities can be humans with mobile devices, or autonomous software components, e.g., web services. Active entities have a behavior which can be more or less trustworthy. A passive entity is any kind

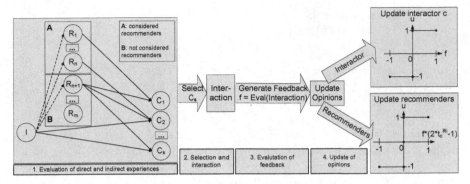

Fig. 1 Main steps in establishing trust between entities and selecting entities

of object, which can be rated, but does not have any behavior, e.g., a music file. For the evaluation in this paper, we only consider active entities.

Furthermore, we define the following roles for an entity (see Fig. 1): **initiator (I)**, **candidate (C)**, **recommender (R)**. The initiator is an entity which wants to initiate an interaction. The candidates – sometimes referred to as *interactors* – are the potential partners for this interaction. The entities which pass recommendations about the candidates to the initiator have the role of the recommenders. The initiators as well as the recommenders will always be active entities. The candidates may be active or passive.

4.2 Representational Trust Model

The representational trust model of CertainTrust has already been published in [13]. In general, this trust model can be used for different contexts. However, for simplifying the notation, we assume there is only one.

Let entities be denoted by capital letters $A, B, \ldots$. The opinion of entity A about the trustworthiness of entity B as *candidate* is denoted as o_B^A. The opinion of an entity A about the trustworthiness of B as *recommender* will be denoted as o_B^A. Furthermore, a parameter, called the *maximal number of expected evidences*, expresses how many evidences an entity expects to reach the maximal certainty of an opinion (see below) and is denoted as e.

Evidence Model: The evidence based representation allows to derive beta probability density functions from the collected evidence. The beta distribution, denoted as $Beta(\alpha, \beta)$, can be used to model the posteriori probabilities of binary events; typically using $\alpha = r + 1$ and $\beta = s + 1$, where $r \geq 0$ and $s \geq 0$ represent the number of collected positive and negative evidence, respectively. The *number of collected evidence* is represented by $r + s$. If an opinion is represented by the parameters r and s, we use the notation

$o = (r,s)^{rs}$. This representation allows for easily integrating feedback in the trust model (see Sec. 4.6).

Human Trust Interface: In the HTI an opinion o is a 2-dimensional expression, represented by a 2-tuple $o = (t,c)^{HTI} \in [0,1] \times [0,1]$, where the superscript refers to the representational model. The opinion $o_b^A = (t_b^A, c_b^A)^{HTI}$ expresses the opinion of A about the trustworthiness of entity B as *interactor*. The value of t_b^A represents the past experience of A with B as interactor, calculated as relative frequency of good interactions. This value is referred to as the *trust value*. The value c_b^A is referred to as *certainty value*. This value expresses, which certainty the provider of an opinion assigns to the trust value, e.g., a low certainty value expresses that the trust value can easily change, whereas a high certainty parameter indicates that the trust value is rather fixed, and thus will be a good estimate for the future behavior. The certainty increases with the ratio between the number of collected evidences and the number of expected evidences. For opinions with certainty $c_b^A = 0$ the trust value is initialized with $t_b^A = 0.5$. For details of the calculation see [13].

4.3 Expectation Value

The opinion about the trustworthiness of an entity is based on information collected from past interactions. As the trust model is to support users in future interactions, we extend our model with new approaches to derive an expectation from the opinions. The certainty of an opinion is to indicate whether the trust value is expected to be a good prediction or not; thus, both values need to be included in the expectation value.

In case that certainty $c = 1$, the trust value should be used as expectation value; if the certainty $c = 0$, i.e., complete uncertainty, the expectation value should be an appropriate initial value; in-between it seems natural, that the expectation value moves from this initial value towards the trust value with increasing certainty. For an opinion $o = (t,c)^{HTI}$, this can be expressed as:

$$E(o) = c \cdot t + (1-c) \cdot f \text{ ,where } 1-c \text{ is the uncertainty}$$

The parameter f can be used to determine the initial expectation value in case of complete uncertainty and influences the expectation value until complete certainty $c = 1$ is reached. Thus f can be used to express a user's general attitude (dispositional trust) or depend on additional knowledge about the distribution of trustworthy and untrustworthy entities. In the following, we briefly introduce several strategies to initialize f.

Pessimistic $(f = 0)$: The pessimistic strategy for calculating an expectation value uses only the evidences on which the opinion was based. According to this strategy, the expectation value is 0.0, if there has not been collected any evidence at all (complete uncertainty). This reflects a user's attitude like

"I believe entities are untrustworthy, unless I know the opposite with high certainty".

$$E_{pessimistic}(o) = t \cdot c$$

Moderate ($f = 0.5$): The moderate approach is especially suitable for binary decisions, in the case that positive and negative results happen with the same probability. According to this strategy the expectation value is 0.5, if there has not been collected any evidence at all (complete uncertainty). This reflects a user's attitude like "I believe there are as many trustworthy as untrustworthy entities."

$$E_{moderate}(o) = t \cdot c + (1 - c) \cdot 0.5$$

Optimistic ($f = 1$): The optimistic behavior reflects a user's attitude like "I believe entities are trustworthy, unless I know the opposite with high certainty".

$$E_{optimistic}(o) = t \cdot c + (1 - c)$$

Dynamic Recalculation of f: As an entity's experiences within a community grows it might be reasonable that it dynamically updates the parameter f that expresses its initial believes. To evaluate whether a dynamic expectation value may have positive effects on the trust model, we designed an ad-hoc heuristic. We define a new variable *community factor* cf, that each entities calculates based on its own experiences and is used as the initial parameter f.

The basic idea is to derive the community factor from the opinions about the known entities. For the community factor used for the expectation value about recommenders we provide the update mechanism in pseudo code:

```
r = 0;  s = 0;  for  (Entity E:  known  Recommenders){
    u = trustValue(o_E^A);
    r = r + u;  s = s + (1 - u);  }
o_cf = (r, s)^{r,s};  cf = E_moderate(o_cf);
```

For the interactors the calculation is similar. But due to the fact, that all entities prefer to interact with good interactors, we adjust the value u in the pseudo code according to $u = trustValue(o_e^A) * (1 - certaintyValue(o_e^A)/2)$.

Comparison with the Mean Value of the Beta Distribution: For the Beta distribution $Beta(r + 1, s + 1)$ the expectation value (mean) E_{mean} is defined as $(r + 1)/(r + s + 2)$. This mean value only depends on the number of collected evidences. It gets closer to the mode of the distribution as the number of collected evidences grows, but this relation is static. This means, it does not depend on the number of maximal expected evidences, and thus, it does not properly integrate the certainty of an opinion in our model.

Our moderate approach for calculating the expectation value produces the most similar results to E_{mean}. We are currently working on a mapping of our strategies for determining the expectation value to adequate counterparts derived from the Beta distribution. This can be done using $\alpha = r + r_0$ and $\beta = s + s_0$, adjusting r_0, s_0 depending on the value of f, the number of collected evidences, and the number of expected evidences.

4.4 Computational Trust Model

The task of the computational trust model is trust propagation, i.e., to aggregate the direct and indirect evidences. As proposed in [13] we propagate trust based on the two operators *consensus* – summing up several opinions to a single one – and *discounting* – weighting recommendations based on the opinion about the recommender.

Consensus: For the consensus of the opinions $o_c^{B_1}$, ..., $o_c^{B_n}$ we use: $consensus(o_c^{B_1}, ..., o_c^{B_n}) := \sum_{i=1}^{n} o_c^{B_i} := o_c^{B_1} \oplus ... \oplus o_c^{B_n} := (\sum_{i=1}^{n} r_c^{B_i}, \sum_{i=1}^{n} s_c^{B_i})^{rs}$.

Discounting: Let the opinion of entity A about the trustworthiness of B_i as recommender be $o_{B_i}^A$, and $o_c^{B_i}$ is B's recommendation about entity C as candidate. For the discounting we propose: $discounting(o_{B_i}^A, o_c^{B_i}) := o_{B_i}^A \otimes o_c^{B_i} := (E(o_{B_i}^A) * r_c^{B_i}, E(o_{B_i}^A) * s_c^{B_i})^{rs}$. Thus, using the pessimistic strategy for the expectation value, is equal to the discounting operator defined in [13].

Simple Trust Propagation: Let the direct experience of entity A with candidate C be o_c^A; furthermore A has collected indirect experiences from the recommenders $B_1, ..., B_n$. The aggregated opinion of A about C is denoted as $\tilde{o}_c^A$, and can be calculated as:

$$\tilde{o}_c^A = o_c^A \oplus \sum_{i=1}^{n} o_{B_i}^A \otimes o_c^{B_i} \tag{1}$$

This variant of trust propagation has some shortcomings:
1. The opinions of recommenders which are known to provide bad recommendations are still considered.
2. All available recommendations are used. Thus, it would be possible, just by creating a huge number of "fake" entities to dominate the resulting opinion, even if the weight of a single recommendation is very low.

More Robust Trust Propagation: For the more robust variant of the trust propagation we propose a few enhancements to overcome the shortcomings pointed out above. To deal with the first issue, it seems reasonable that the initiator I only considers recommendations from recommenders which provided mostly accurate recommendations in the past, i.e., the trust value of o_R^I is greater than or equal to 0.5. Furthermore, we also consider recommendations of unknown recommenders.

To overcome the second issue, we use another feature of our trust model to limit the considered recommendations. We sort the recommendations descending by the expectation value of calculated by the initiator for the recommenders. Then, we consider only recommendations as long as the certainty of the aggregated opinion is less or equal to 1. Thus, we only use the best recommendations, until the sum of direct evidences and weighted indirect evidences is equal to the number of maximal expected evidences.

These arrangements together are supposed to improve the robustness of our model to false recommendations (either false praise or false accusation), since we use only the recommenders which have been known to be the best recommenders from their past recommendations. Furthermore, in the case that we have enough direct evidences and good recommendations, this makes our model also quite robust to sybil attacks [4], since it is no longer possible to overtake an opinion based on sufficient direct experiences and good recommendations only by providing an arbitrary huge number of recommendations using specially created recommenders.

Although, it is possible to further increase the robustness to false recommendations and sybil attacks by introducing further criteria for considering recommendations, e.g., excluding unknown recommenders, we are not going to extensively evaluate this aspects, since it would be beyond the scope of this paper.

4.5 Selection of a Candidate

The selection of the most trustworthy candidate for an interaction of a set of candidates C_1, ...,C_n is done based on the expectation value. Let $\bar{o}^A_{C_i}$, ..., $\bar{o}^A_{C_n}$ be the aggregated opinions of A about the candidates. The most trustworthy candidate is selected as an entity with maximal expectation value. Depending on the initiator the expectation value is calculated by one of the strategies proposed above.

4.6 Update Mechanism

After each interaction, the entity that initiated the interaction updates the opinions about its interaction partner (selected candidate) and the recommenders (see Fig. 1). In the case of a dynamical recalculation of the expectation value, the community factor also is updated after an interaction. The quality of an interaction, which for now is equal to the generate feedback fb, can be in $[-1; 1]$. Here, -1 is the worst possible feedback, 1 is the best one. The feedback for an interaction, can be either user generated or by an external software component.

Update the Opinion for the Selected Candidate: Let the opinion (direct experiences) of A about the selected candidate C be $o^A_C = (r^A_{C_{old}}, s^A_{C_{old}})^{rs}$;

for the feedback f, the direct experiences are updated to $(r^A_{C_{new}}, s^A_{C_{new}})^{rs}$ using (with $u := fb$):

$$(r^A_{C_{new}}, s^A_{C_{new}})^{rs} = (r^A_{C_{old}} + (u+1)/2), s^A_{C_{old}} + (1-u)/2)^{rs} \qquad (2)$$

Update the Opinions for the Recommenders: The update of the opinions about the recommenders is performed according to the accuracy of their recommendations. For this reason, the trust value of the recommendation of B about the candidate C is compared with the feedback with which A rated the interaction. If both have the "same tendency", then the recommendation is supposed to be positive and the opinion of A about B as recommender is updated positively, else there is a negative update.

More formally: If the opinion of A about entity B as recommender was $o^A_B = (r^A_{B_{old}}, s_{B_{old}})^{rs}$ and the recommendation by B about the candidate C was $o^B_C = (t^B_c, c^B_c)^{HTI}$ with $(c^B_c > 0)$, and $A's$ feedback for the interaction with C is fb, we calculate u as:

$$u := \begin{cases} 1 & \text{, if } (2*t^B_c - 1)*fb > 0 \\ -1 & \text{, if } (2*t^B_c - 1)*fb < 0 \\ 0 & \text{, else .} \end{cases} \qquad (3)$$

The update of o^A_B is done using u in Eq. 2. For example, if the trust value of the recommendation was in $]0,1]$ and the interaction was positive $(f > 0)$, then the recommendation is considered to be good ($u = 1$), and the positive evidences of the opinion about the recommender are increased by 1; the negative evidences are kept unchanged.

In the case the interaction behavior of C depends on the initiator of the interaction, and C shows different interaction behavior towards R and I, the recommendations of R will be misleading, and I will negatively update the recommender trust for R. This is due to the fact that I is not capable of distinguishing between R is lying and C interaction behavior is interactor dependent.

Furthermore, we point out that the *normalization* as described in [13] introduces an implicit aging of the evidences, if the collected evidences exceed the maximal number of expected evidences.

5 Basic Types of Behavior and Population Mixes

Entities may be recommenders or interactors. In both roles, an entity can be good (+) or bad (-). This means a good interactor provides good interactions, leading to positive feedback ($fb = 1$), a bad interactor provides interactions leading to negative feedback ($fb = -1$). A good recommender provides recommendations which reflect its real experiences. The model for bad (lying) recommenders is derived from [15]. Bad recommenders try to provide recommendations with a maximal misleading expectation value, i.e., if $E_{mean}(o_x^B)$ is the expectation value calculated by recommender B for interactor x, the recommendation of B would be an opinion with the expectation value $1 - E_{mean}(o_x^B)$. This can be achieved by switching the positive and negative evidences. Thus, we identified 4 basic types of behaviors, see Fig. 2.

Combining these basic types of behaviors, we can derive 15 canonical population mixes: h, m, s, w, hm, hs, hw, ms, mw, sw, hms, hsw, hmw, msw, $hmsw$. The numbers of entities with a specific behavior within a population are set to be equal, e.g., the population mix h contains only entities with honest behavior, the population mix hm contains 50% entities with honest behavior and 50% malicious, and so on.

Basic entity behaviors		Recommendation behavior	
		+	-
Interaction behavior	+	honest (h)	selfish (s)
	-	malicious (m)	worst (w)

Fig. 2 Basic entity behaviors

Furthermore, we believe that the interaction behavior of an entity may be unstable, i.e., good interactors may sometimes provide bad interactions and vice versa. Therefore, we introduce an additional parameter called stability y. In the case of stability $y = 1$ an entity totally adheres to its assigned interaction behavior. In the case the stability of entity is set to 0.9 it adheres only in 90% of its interactions to the behavior it has been assigned, in the other 10% it will do the opposite. Knowing the stability of an entity and its behavior, it is easy to derive the probability for positive interactions with this entity. For simplicity, we assume stability only influences the interaction behavior, the recommendations behavior is assumed to be stable.

We use two different settings for the stability factor per population mix. In the first setting we set the stability factor to 1 for all entities, in the second one the stability factor is randomly (and uniformly distributed) chosen from the interval $[0.5; 1]$. In case of the population hm, a stability of 1 leads to a population in which 50% of all entities provide only good interactions and 50% provide only bad interactions. Using the same population but choosing the stability factor from the interval $[0.5; 1]$ per entity, the probabilities for good interactions over all entities are uniformly distributed in $[0; 1]$.

6 Simulation

The simulation is based on the scenario described in Sec. 3. For having realistic user traces as mobility model, we use the user traces collected in the Reality Mining project [5]. The data provides information about 97 users of mobile phones and their location as the ID of the cell tower the mobile phones were connected to.

For our evaluation we choose a single week of this data set, in which a big number of users were connected to a small number of cell towers; thus, we expected to have a big number of possible interactions. Based on [7], we assume that a group of users is in proximity to each other if the users are connected to the same cell tower within a 15 minute time interval. For the evaluation, we consider a so-called *meeting* to happen in intervals in which six or more users are connected to the same cell tower. The reason is, that we want to evaluate the trust model's capabilities in selecting the most trustworthy candidate from a set of candidates. The set of candidates is determined randomly as half of the available entities, i.c., an initiator has at least 3 candidates for an interaction. In the restricted data set, there are 68 distinct users (entities), which met each other in 556 meetings. In average an entity took part in 59.94 meetings, and met 46.76 distinct entities. The average number of entities per meeting is 7.33. By repeating the selected week three times in our simulation, we are able to evaluate the value of direct experiences as well as indirect ones. Although these assumptions might look a little simplistic, we believe that using real world user traces allows for a more realistic evaluation than using artificially created user profiles as a basis for the simulation.

We do the simulation for all 15 populations, each with stability $y = 1$ and $y \in [0.5; 1]$. Each simulation was repeated 20 times per trust model and population mix using the same seeds for the comparison of the different models and baselines.

6.1 Meeting Procedure

Each meeting proceeds as follows. In each meeting each entity has to interact with one candidate, i.e., each entity is the initiator of one interaction. The candidates for an interaction are randomly chosen as the half of the entities which are part of the meeting, i.e., we expect that half of the entities in the meeting can provide a specific mp3-file. If the trust model includes recommendations, the initiator asks all entities that are part of the meeting for providing recommendations about the candidates. Then, the initiator evaluates the trustworthiness of the candidates, and selects the most trustworthy one, i.e., the one with the greatest expectation value. We chose this setting in contrast to a setting in which each entity has the choice whether to interact or not, since we want to evaluate the trust model and not the decision making component. After each interaction, the initiator updates the opinions about its interaction partner (selected candidate) and the recommenders based on the outcome of the interaction as described in Sec. 4.6.

6.2 Baselines and Models

The first baseline is the random strategy (referred to as *const_0.5* in Fig. 4). This strategy selects the partner for the interaction randomly – expecting positive interactions from any candidate with probability 0.5. Furthermore, we use the *perfect strategy* that always selects the best candidate based on the behavior it has been assigned by the simulation environment. In a way, this is similar to a "best possible" selection process in a hypothetic world, in which all entities have labels on their forehead stating the behavior (and the probability for a positive interaction). We compare the following trust models in our evaluation:

1. CT_M: CertainTrust using the mean as expectation value and $e = 20$.
2. CT_C: CertainTrust using the expectation value based on a dynamically calculated expectation value and $e = 20$.
3. BetaRepSys: The beta reputation system was proposed in [10]. Since the goal of our research is to provide a trust model for UC, we use a distributed variant of this reputation system in which each entity is its own reputation centre. The reputation centre stores only direct experiences. The expectation value (reputation) for an interaction partner is calculated using the consensus operator for combining the direct experiences with the available recommendations.

6.3 Evaluation Metrics

The evaluation is based on three metrics.

1. Each entity B is assigned a characteristic probability for providing good interactions (denoted as p_B) at the beginning of the simulation (as described in Sec. 5). For the first metric, we calculate the mean absolute error $err(A)$ an entity makes when estimating this probability for all entities in the population P. For entity A this error is calculated as: $err(A) = (\sum_{B \in P} | E(o_b^A) - p_B |)/ | P |$. For the calculation of $E(o_b^A)$ entity A may ask all entities in P for recommendations. The *average error in estimating the trustworthiness* err is defined as: $err = (\sum_{A \in P} err(A))/ | P |$. The average error should be close to 0.

2. We define the reputation $R(A)$ of an entity A as the average of the expectation values calculated by each entity B in the population P for entity A: $R(A) = (\sum_{B \in P} E(o_a^B))/ | P |$. Again, entity A may ask all entities in P for recommendations. As the average reputation over all entities in the population depends on the population mix, we calculate the average only over the entities belonging to the same behavior.

$$average\_R(behavior_i) = \frac{\sum_{A \text{ is assigned } behavior_i} R(A)}{| A \text{ is assigned } behavior_i |} \qquad (4)$$

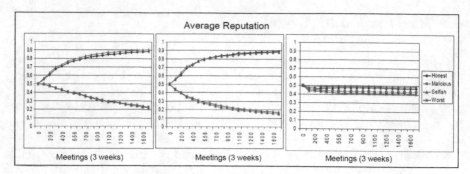

Fig. 3 Reputation evaluation over time in population *hmsw* with stability 1 (order: CT_C, CT_M, BetaRepSys)

3. For each interaction, the feedback can be either 1 or −1. The accumulated sum of feedback (*acc_sum*) is calculated for each entity as sum of the feedback over its past interactions. This value strongly depends on the population mix. In a population with stability $y = 1$ and only honest entities are only positive interactions; in a population with only malicious entities are only negative ones. Therefore, we define the *average percentage of accumulated sum of feedback* as the portion of the accumulated sum of feedback achieved using the considered trust model relative to the accumulated sum achieved using the *perfect strategy*:

$$percentage\_acc\_sum(model\_X) = \frac{\sum_{A \in P} acc\_sum(entity\_A, model\_X)}{\sum_{A \in P} acc\_sum(entity\_A, perfect\ strategy)}$$
(5)

The *average percentage of accumulated sum of feedback* is the third metric for comparing the different trust model. The closer the average percentage of accumulated sum of feedback is to 1.0, the more positive interactions had an entity, and the closer is trust model to the perfect selection strategy.

6.4 Results

Reputation Evaluation Over Time: The three diagrams in Fig. 3 show the evaluation of the reputation over time for the models CT_M, CT_C, and the BetaRepSys. As space is limited we provide these diagrams only for the population *hmsw*. As we can see from these diagrams both CertainTrust variants are capable of detecting the different behaviors of the entities. The true reputation of honest and selfish entities would be 1 and for malicious and worst entities it would be 0. The BetaRepSys is hardly capable of detecting differences as 50% of the recommendations are misleading.

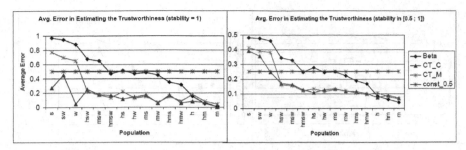

Fig. 4 Average percentage of accumulated sum per population (at the end of the simulation) - Populations sorted according to the percentage of good recommenders (the lines are only for ease of reading)

Average Error in Estimating the Trustworthiness: Fig. 4 shows the results of the error in estimating the trustworthiness at the end of each simulation (averaged over all runs) per population and stability of behaviors.

From the results we can see that whenever there are 33% or more misleading recommendations, our CertainTrust variants have a considerable better performance than the BetaRepSys. Only in case of populations with only good recommenders the BetaRepSys has slight advantages. The CT_C model produces the best results in populations with only bad recommenders.

For stability in $[0.5; 1]$ the absolute numbers for the error are less than for stability $y = 1$. This can be explained as in the first case the average probability of good interactions per entity is in the interval $[0.25; 0.75]$ and in the latter case in the interval $[0; 1]$.

Average Percentage of the Accumulated Sum: Fig. 5 shows the results of the average percentage of the accumulated sum at the end of each simulation (averaged over all runs) per population and stability of behaviors. In the populations m, w, and mw the accumulated sum for the perfect strategy as well as the accumulated sum for all other models is negative. Therefore, we omitted the results here.

In the case of stability $y = 1$ the BetaRepSys only produces similar results as the CT variants in the populations h, s, hs (this is trivial as there are 100% good interactors), and in the population hm. In the other populations the CT variants outperform with similar results.

In the case of stability in $[0.5; 1]$ the BetaRepSys can only compete in the populations hm and h. Both CT variants show similar performance.

7 Discussion

In contrast to the simulations in $[12, 15]$, our simulation presents results over a huge set of populations and uses a mobility model as basis for the interactions and recommendations. The population mixes are derived from our

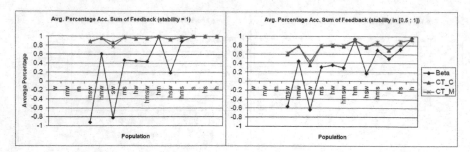

Fig. 5 Average percentage of accumulated sum per population (at the end of the simulation) - Populations sorted according to the percentage of good interactors (the lines are only for ease of reading)

classification of the basic types of behaviors. As we consider all kinds of combinations the results present an good overview of the performance of the considered models. The possibilities for interactions and recommendations between entities are based on real world user trace. This is especially important as we develop a trust model for opportunistic collaboration and UC applications.

The results for the average accumulated sum of feedback (see Fig. 5) show that our trust model achieves good results in all considered populations. Compared to the perfect selection strategy CT_C is capable of achieving more than 75% of maximally reachable results in 21 of 24 populations. Compared to the BetaRepSys we see that CertainTrust variants outperform in most population mixes. This is especially important as a user will evaluate not the trust models itself, but the improvement of the quality of his interactions. The reason for the improved overall quality of interactions can be the smaller error in the estimated trustworthiness (see Fig. 4) for most of the populations. Furthermore, we have shown that our CertainTrust model CT_C using the dynamically updated community factor may have advantages in estimating the trustworthiness of interactors.

We learn that the main drawback of the distributed variant of the BetaRep-Sys is that it does not weight recommendations. The discounting, as proposed in [10], is based on the assumption that the behavior of an entity as recommender is equal to the behavior of this entity as interactor and may still be misleading. Furthermore, the discounting would discard the recommendations by unknown interactors. Thus, it heavily depends on direct experiences. The filtering techniques for the BetaRepSys as proposed in [16] will only work if the majority of recommenders provides good recommendations. This is also true for the filtering techniques proposed in [12]. As the representational model of the BetaRepSys as well as our model are based on collected evidences, it should be possible to define a mapping between both representations. Thus, the filtering mechanisms presented in this paper can easily be transferred to the BetaRepSys and other models based on collected evidences.

8 Conclusion

We presented and evaluated new approaches for discounting opinions and estimating the trustworthiness of entities. We showed that our trust model allows to significantly improve the quality of interactions especially in presence of lying recommenders. Furthermore, we showed our trust model's robustness over different populations and varying stability of the users' behaviors. The dynamical calculation positively influences the trust models' performance. We will investigate on this in future work.

References

1. Abdul-Rahman, A., Hailes, S.: Supporting trust in virtual communities. In: Proceedings of Hawaii International Conference on System Sciences (2000).
2. Billhardt, H. et al.: Trust-based service provider selection in open environments. In: ACM SAC '07, pp. 1375–1380. ACM Press, New York, NY, USA (2007).
3. Buchegger, S., Le Boudec, J.Y.,: A Robust Reputation System for Peer-to-Peer and Mobile Ad-hoc Networks. In: P2PEcon 2004 (2004)
4. Douceur, J.R.: The sybil attack. In: IPTPS '01: Revised Papers from the 1st Int. Workshop on Peer-to-Peer Systems, pp. 251–260 (2002)
5. Eagle, N., Pentland, A.S.: Reality mining: sensing complex social systems. Personal Ubiquitous Comput. 10(4), 255–268 (2006).
6. Golbeck, J.: Computing and applying trust in web-based social networks. Ph.D. thesis, University of Maryland, College Park (2005)
7. Heinemann, A.: Collaboration in Opportunistic Networks. Ph.D. thesis, Technische Universität Darmstadt (2007).
8. Hui, P. et al.: Pocket switched networks and human mobility in conference environments. In: WDTN '05: Proceeding of the 2005 ACM SIGCOMM workshop on Delay-tolerant networking, pp. 244–251 (2005).
9. Jøsang, A.: A logic for uncertain probabilities. International Journal of Uncertainty, Fuzziness and Knowledge-Based Systems 9(3), 279–212 (2001)
10. Jøsang, A., Ismail, R.: The beta reputation system. In: Proceedings of the 15th Bled Conference on Electronic Commerce (2002)
11. Marsh, S.: Formalising trust as a computational concept. Ph.D. thesis, University of Stirling (1994).
12. Quercia, D., Hailes, S., Capra, L.: B-Trust: Bayesian trust framework for pervasive computing. In: 4th Int. Conf. on Trust Management, pp. 298–312 (2006)
13. Ries, S.: CertainTrust: A trust model for users and agents. In: ACM SAC '07, pp. 1599 – 1604 (2007)
14. Sabater, J., Sierra, C.: Reputation and social network analysis in multi-agent systems. In: Proceedings of the AAMAS, pp. 475–482 (2002).
15. Teacy, W.T. et al.: TRAVOS: Trust and reputation in the context of inaccurate information sources. In: Proceedings of the AAMAS 12(2), 183–198 (2006).
16. Whitby, A., Jøsang, A., Indulska., J.: Filtering out unfair ratings in bayesian reputation systems. Icfain Journal of Management Research 4(2), 48 – 64 (2005)

An Intensional Functional Model of Trust*

Kaiyu Wan and Vasu Alagar

Abstract Computers have been in use for many years to build high confidence systems in safety-critical domains such as aircraft control, space transportation and exploration, and nuclear power plant management. However, due to the recent rush in developing ubiquitous and pervasive computing applications and a demand from across the world to access information from shared sources, the mosaic of computing ecosystem has undergone a radical change. It is in this context that computing has to be made *trustworthy*. To build and manage a trustworthy system it is necessary to blend and harmonize socially acceptable and technically feasible norms of trust. This in turn requires a generic formal model in which trust categories can be specified, trusted communication can be enabled, and trustworthy transactions can be specified and reasoned about. In this paper we introduce a formal *intensional* model of trust and suggest how it can be integrated into a trust management system.

1 Introduction

Trust is a broad social concept, which defies a precise definition. We generally understand what trust is not when the outcome of an event or a transaction or an action is not something that we expected. In almost all societies trust is related to honesty, truthfulness, reliability, and competence. But none of these attributes can be precisely stated for use in automatic computing systems. The Oxford Reference

Kaiyu Wan
Department of Computer Science, East China Normal University, e-mail: kywan@cs.ecnu.edu.cn

V. Alagar
Department of Computer Science and Software Engineering, Concordia University, e-mail: alagar@cs.concordia.ca

* The research is supported by a grant from Natural Sciences and Engineering Research Council, Canada.

Please use the following format when citing this chapter:

Wan, K. and Alagar, V., 2008, in IFIP International Federation for Information Processing, Volume 263; *Trust Management II*; Yücel Karabulut, John Mitchell, Peter Herrmann, Christian Damsgaard Jensen; (Boston: Springer), pp. 69–85.

Dictionary (ORD) states that trust is "the firm *belief* in the *reliability* or *truth* or *strength* of an *entity*." The European Commission Joint Research Center (ECJRC) [11] defines trust as the "*property* of a business *relationship*, such that *reliance* can be placed on the business *partners* and the business *transactions* developed with them." Putting together both definitions and abstracting it we see that trust notion is a fundamental requirement for reliance. The definitions also suggest that trust is a *relation* between (groups of) entities, and the attributes that associates a *value* to it are reliability, truth, integrity (strength), (reliance) security. In this paper we refine this definition and provide a formal of it in order that trustworthy computing systems can be rigorously developed and trust management systems (TMS) can administer trust policies uniformly across different applications.

Grandison and Sloman [9] have provided a survey of trust in internet applications. Trust is thereby classified according to the different *contexts* in which services are demanded. Without defining what a context is, they have considered *access to a trustor's resources, certification of trustees, delegation*, and *infrastructure trust* as four possible contexts. As a consequence the classification may be regarded only as ad hoc. In this paper we use context in its full formality, as was first introduced by Alagar [3], and subsequently refined by Wan [16]. In the formal trust model that we define context is a parameter to a higher order function that defines trust. We call the function *intensional* for reasons explained below. The term "intension" has a different meaning from the term "intention" (an aim or plan), as explained below.

Intensional logic is a branch of mathematical logic used to precisely describe context-dependent entities. According to Carnap, the real meaning of a natural language expression whose truth-value depends on the context in which it is uttered is its *intension*. The *extension* of that expression is its actual truth-value in the different possible contexts of utterance. For an instance, the statement "*The capital of China is Beijing*" is intensional because its valuation depends on the context (here is the time) in which it is uttered. If this statement is uttered before 1949, the extensions of this statement are *False* (before 1949 the capital was Nanjing). However, if it is uttered after 1949, the extensions of this statement are *True*. Thus the real meaning of an expression is a function from contexts to values, and the value of the intension at any particular context is obtained by applying context operators to the intension. Basically, intensional paradigm provides intension on the representation level, and extensions on the evaluation level. Hence, intensional paradigm allows for a more declarative way of specifying trust and programming it without loss of accuracy.

McKnight and Chervany [13] have given a typology for classifying trusting behavior in domains such as sociology, psychology, political sciences, and management. A trusting behavior, when expressed in natural language and semantically interpreted through Carnap's intensional logic, becomes an intensional statement. The six-fold classification of trusting behavior of an entity *a*, called *trustor*, on another entity *b*, called *trustee*, given by McKnight and Chervany [13] are (1) *disposition* (an entity *a* is naturally <u>inclined</u> to trust, (2) *situation* (an entity *a* trusts *b* in a <u>particular scenario</u>, (3) *structure* (entity *a* trusts the structure (<u>institution</u>) of which the entity *b* is a member), (4) *belief* (entity *a* <u>believes</u> that *b* is trustworthy), (5) *behavior* (entity *a* <u>voluntarily depends</u> on entity *b*), and (6) *intention* (entity *a* is willing to depend on entity b). McKnight and Chervany [13] have also classified the behavior of trustees in categories. The most relevant reasons for trusting b are *competence, benevolence, integrity*, or *predictability*. The natural language statements corresponding to these trusting behaviors have a natural intensional logic interpretation.

In our formalism, context is multi-dimensional and is much more general and expressive than the *situational* notion. The intensional functional definition of trust has context as a parameter, and has the expressive power to express the six-fold trusting behavior categories. Hence, trust contexts and trust categories that we define in this paper are not to be confused with the trusting behavior categories. However, our trust model can be integrated into the application environments of the domains considered by McKnight and Chervany [13].

With respect to our formalism itself, the two most relevant related works are the seminal work of Weeks [19] and Carbone [5]. Weeks first recognized *least fixed point* as a way to compute global trust, assuming a complete partial order of the trust domain. Carbone strengthened the work of Weeks by adding *information ordering* to *trust value ordering*. According to Carbone, trust value ordering is to measure the degree of trustworthiness, while information ordering is to measure the degree of uncertainty present in the information content on which trust is based. Information ordering enables the refinement of trust values. In [8] the notion of context is recognized as important for trust management, however no formal treatment of it has been attempted. Context formalization has found applications in different application domains, such as language design, multi-agent systems, and system security [3, 18, 17]. The distinct properties of our formalism are the following: (1)Trust definition is intensional. The benefits of an intensional model are explained earlier; (2) Trust values are restricted to a domain which is a complete partial order (cpo) and a lattice and a metric space. This allows formalizing the degree of trust and trust measure; (3) Trust calculation formulas are automatically developed based on formal context calculus. Thus subjectivity in calculation is eliminated; (4) Global trust computation is both context dependent and dynamic. Thus, during *delegation* the principals should adhere to the specific context in which the cooperation is sought and the global trusting rules that are relevant to that context; and (5) Homomorphism between trust domains (chosen by participants) must exist, otherwise global trust can not be defined. This property is particularly important for distributed systems.

2 Formal Trust Model

We start with a set of requirements for trust. Trust is relation between a trustor, the subject that trusts a target entity, and a trustee, the entity that is trusted. It is possible to measure the level of trust, called trust value, of a trustor on a trustee in any given context. Trust values must be comparable. It must be possible to manipulate trust values across different contexts, and aggregation of contexts. It should be possible to refine trust values, going from a general (specific) to a specific (general) context. It must be possible to express indirect trust relations and compute indirect trust values between a trustor and a trustee. It must be possible to ground the theoretical results in practice. A formal model that fulfills the above requirements must be comprehensive enough to cover most of the trust categories [13]. This is an important requirement because in a practical application more than one trust category will arise.

A number of choices exist in choosing a relation model of trust. The model depends on the inclusion/exclusion of the properties *reflexive*, *symmetric*, and *transitive*. In addition, it is also possible to allow or disallow one of the properties *one-to-many*, *many-to-one* and *many-to-many*. The choice is essentially dictated by the application domain. We get around this web of choices by choosing an intensional function definition for assigning trust value. We require the domain of trust values, hereafter called trust domain, to be a lattice with a minimum element. We turn the trust domain into a metric space. This will enable us to compare trust values and compute trust values from trust expressions. We define trust categories, motivate how contexts may be constructed within a trust category and arrive at extensions to the intensional trust definition within each category.

2.1 Intensional Function Definition

Trust involves *entities* ($\mathscr{E}$), their *interactions* ($\mathscr{I}$) and *policies* ($\mathscr{P}$). An *active* entity, called a *principal* (or an *agent*), can initiate a transaction, negotiate a deal, and communicate its intentions. A *passive* entity is a resource which can only be acted upon by an active entity. Data stores, files, printers, and programs are passive entities. An interaction is always initiated by an active entity. A human being accessing the internet, a program that reads data from a data base, and a component requesting a service from another component are examples of typical interactions. When an entity a requests service from another entity b, there is an implicit trust involved in that a trusts in the ability of b to provide the requested service. The credentials of the service provider, in this case b, and the *contract* announced by b that binds the service are convincing enough for a to trust b. Credentials and contracts, similar to utterances as explained earlier, are declarative statements. Trust is usually not absolute, it is always relative and contextual. Consequently declarative trust statements are regarded as intensions. That is, a trust statement (policy) must be evaluated at different contexts to extract their extensions. Hence, the hypothesis that a policy, although will be stated declaratively, will always be applicable to one or more specific contexts, is both fair and sound. This is the rationale for formally introducing *context* ($\mathscr{C}$) as another modeling element. Context and contextual information provide the qualitative aspect of trust, and trust domain ($\mathscr{D}$) provides the quantitative aspect to the model. That is, the information in the context justifies the trust value assigned. A formal treatment of context appears in [17], and a logic of reasoning with context for multi-agent systems appears in [16]. We briefly summarize the most relevant results in section 3.

2.1.1 Properties of Trust Domain

We require that the elements of a trust domain, also called trust values, are chosen as the most appropriate ordinal type to indicate the level (degree) of trust of a on b in a context c. Trust values can be either simple values, such as numbers or symbols, or vectors. The numeric values themselves may be either discrete, such as natural numbers or rational, or continuous such as real values. If symbols are used then we regard it as an *enumerated* type, the order being implicit in the enumeration. As an example, in the enumeration $\{hold, sell\}$, the degree of trust in *sell* recommendation is higher than the degree of trust in *hold* recommendation. Real numbers, natural numbers, and rational numbers are totally ordered sets, and hence degree of trusts are comparable. In the case of vector values, it is necessary to define an ordering. In general, it is sufficient to require that the trust values are partially ordered, which is the weakest relation necessary to compare an element with at least one other element in the set.

2.1.2 Partial Order

Assume that $\simeq$ is a reflexive partial order defined on $\mathscr{D}$. Consequently trust relationship is transitive, which goes against the opinion expressed in [15]. Since context was not a factor in previously published trust definitions the transitivity property promoted a wide open trust delegation policy, which was not always desirable. Because of the introduction of context, transitivity is constrained to contexts that are *compatible* and delegation can be enabled only in such contexts. As an example, if Alice delegates her trust decisions to Bob in the context of *installing a virus protection software in her computer,* and Bob trusts Cathy in the context of *Linux installation,* then the installation of virus protection cannot be delegated to Cathy. We also remark that computing transitivity is part of global trust computation and it should not change the local trust policies of any entity. With these safeguards, the partially ordered domain $(\mathscr{D}, \simeq)$ is quite safe. We also require $(\mathscr{D}, \simeq)$ to have a least element $\bot$, in the sense that $\forall d \in \mathscr{D},\ \bot \simeq d$. An ω-chain on $(\mathscr{D}, \simeq)$ is a monotone function $\iota : \omega \to \mathscr{D}$, where ω is the set of natural numbers. That is in the sequence $\iota = (\iota_n)_{n \in \omega}$, $\iota_1 \simeq \iota_2 \simeq \ldots \iota_n$. An element $\iota_u \in \mathscr{D}$ such that $\iota_k \simeq \iota_u$, $k = 1, \ldots, n$ is called a *least upper bound (lub)* of ω. In order that $(\mathscr{D}, \simeq)$ be a cpo every ω-chain in it must have a least upper bound. Interpreting $\bot$ to mean "undefined trust value" the function defined below becomes a total function.

Definition 1 *The function,* $\tau : \mathscr{E} \times \mathscr{E} \times \mathscr{C} \to \mathscr{D}$ *associates for* $a, b \in \mathscr{E}$, *and* $c \in \mathscr{C}$ *a unique element* $d \in \mathscr{D}$, *called the trust that a has on b in context c. That is,* $\tau(a, b, c) = d$. *The function* τ *is context-dependent and expresses the trust intension in different contexts. So we call* τ *an intensional function.* □

2.2 Further Properties of Trust Domain

By imposing a metric, in addition to a partial order, we can measure the disparity between two trust levels. Finally, we also define a homomorphism between trust domains in order that trust value from one domain may be carried into the other trust domain. In a distributed system, where each site may have a different trust domain, without a homomorphic mapping it is not possible to calculate and compare trust globally.

2.2.1 Metric Space

Let $(\mathcal{D}, \simeq)$ be a cpo. We define a total monotone function $\rho :: \mathcal{D} \to \omega$ which assigns a non-negative integer value to each trust value such that for $d_1, d_2 \in \mathcal{D}$

- if $d_1 \simeq d_2$ then $\rho(d_1) \le \rho(d_2)$, and
- for every ω-chain $\iota : \omega \to \mathcal{D}$, $\rho(\iota_1) \le \rho(\iota_2) \le \ldots \rho(\iota_n)$.

The function $\delta : \mathcal{D} \times \mathcal{D} \to \omega$ defined by $\delta(d_1, d_2) = \mid \rho(d_1) - \rho(d_2) \mid$ satisfies the properties

- $\delta(d_1, d_2) \ge 0$
- $\delta(d_1, d_2) = \delta(d_2, d_1)$, and
- for $d_1, d_2, d_3 \in \mathcal{D}$, $\delta(d_1, d_3) \le \delta(d_1, d_2) + \delta(d_2, d_3)$

Hence $(\mathcal{D}, \rho, \delta)$ is a metric space. The usefulness of this exercise is clear when we want to quantify the disparity between $d_1 = \tau(a, b, c)$ and $d_2 = \tau(a, b, c')$, which is precisely $\delta(d_1, d_2)$. If $d_1 < d_2$, then by going from context c to context c', a's trust in b has increased by the amount $\delta(d_1, d_2)$. That is, metrication helps to reason about trust refinement and trust evolution.

2.2.2 Homomorphism

The trust domain may be chosen differently by different developers for the same application domain. In a distributed network, each local site may have a different trust domain. In order that trust values across sites can be compared and global trust computed it is necessary that the homomorphism f, defined below, is a continuous function on the ω chains.
$$f : (\mathcal{D}, \simeq, \rho) \to (\mathcal{D}', \simeq', \rho')$$

- for $d_1, d_2 \in \mathcal{D}, f(d_1 \simeq d_2) = f(d_1) \simeq' f(d_2)$
- $f(\bot) = \bot'$,
- $f(\rho(d_1, d_2)) = \rho'(f(d_1), f(d_2))$

Theorem 1 *For every ω-chain ι in $(\mathcal{D}, \simeq)$, $\iota' = f(\iota)$ is a ω-chain of $(\mathcal{D}', \simeq')$, and $f(\iota_u) = \iota'_u$,*

Proof: Since $\iota : \omega \to \mathscr{D}$ *is monotonic and f is continuous the composition* $f \circ \iota$ *is monotonic. But,* $\iota' : \omega \to \mathscr{D}'$ *satisfies the equation* $\iota' = f \circ \iota$. *Hence* ι' *is monotonic.*

Theorem 2 *Let* $\tau : \mathscr{E} \times \mathscr{E} \times \mathscr{C} \to \mathscr{D}$ *and* $\tau' : \mathscr{E} \times \mathscr{E} \times \mathscr{C} \to \mathscr{D}'$ *be two intensional functions that give the trust values on the trust domains* $\mathscr{D}$ *and* $\mathscr{D}'$. *Then* $f \circ \tau = \tau'$
Proof: The proof follows from the two facts $f \circ \rho = \rho'$ *and* $f \circ \iota = \iota'$.

2.3 Trust Expressions

By requiring that every subset $\mathscr{S} \subset \mathscr{D}$ has a least upper bound (lub) and a greatest lower bound (glb) in $\mathscr{D}$ we turn the trust structure to a complete lattice. For $d_1, d_2 \in \mathscr{D}$, we write $lub(d_1, d_2) = d_1 \vee d_2$ and $glb(d_1, d_2) = d_1 \wedge d_2$. In general $lub(\mathscr{S}) = \bigvee_{d \in \mathscr{S}} d$ and is written $\bigvee \mathscr{S}$. Similarly, $glb(\mathscr{S}) = \bigwedge_{d \in \mathscr{S}} d$, and is written $\bigwedge \mathscr{S}$. We also define $\rho(d_1 \wedge d_2) = min\{\rho(d_1), \rho(d_2)\}$, and $\rho(d_1 \vee d_2) = max\{\rho(d_1), \rho(d_2)\}$. In general, $\rho(glb(\mathscr{S})) = min_{d \in \mathscr{S}}\{\rho(d)\}$ and $\rho(lub(\mathscr{S})) = max_{d \in \mathscr{S}}\{\rho(d)\}$. A trust expression over $(\mathscr{D}, \simeq, \rho)$ is defined by the syntax $\tau_e = d \mid \tau_e \vee \tau_e \mid \tau_e \wedge \tau_e$. An expression τ_e is evaluated from left to right. In an evaluation we let $d \vee \perp = d$, and $d \wedge \perp = \perp$. Thus every expression uniquely evaluates to a trust value $d \in \mathscr{D}$, and hence a unique $\rho(d)$, although not every expression can be assigned a meaning. As an example, the expression $\tau(a_1, b, c) \wedge \tau(a_2, b, c)$ represents the trust level that both a_1 and a_2 can agree upon the entity b in context c. However, the expression $\tau(a_1, b_1, c_1) \vee \tau(a_2, b_2, c_2)$, where $a_1 \neq a_2$, $b_1 \neq b_2$, and $c_1 \neq c_2$ has a unique value in $\mathscr{D}$, but the value is hard to interpret in a meaningful way. With this extension we can write many other trust expressions of the form $\tau_e \vee (\bigwedge \mathscr{S})$, $\tau_e \wedge (\bigvee \mathscr{S})$.

3 Trust Contexts - a formalization

In this section we discuss the notion of *trust contexts* (TC), motivate the need to formalize this notion in a discussion of trust modeling, and their importance in trust management. We follow the formal definition of context, the syntax for context representation, and review the basics of context calculus given by Wan in [17].

In [9] trust is defined as "the firm belief in the competence of an entity to act independently, securely, and reliably within a *specified context*". It is observed in [8, 9] that "the notion of *context* is important in the SECURE trust model". In the former, context is not defined. In the later, trust is regarded as a *multi-dimensional* quantity and the different dimensions are called trust contexts. However, no formal treatment of context is attempted. The definition of context in [17] includes dimensions, and *tags* (indexes) along the dimensions. The term "dimension" used by Dimmock ectal; [8] essentially refers to a knowledge domain, as suggested by the statement "...by analogy, a person who is trusted to *drive a car* may not be trusted to *fly a plane*." In the above statement "driving a car" and "flying a plane" are defined as dimensions by Dimmock [8]. However in the work of Wan [17] "driving a car" and "flying a plane" are regarded as "different worlds of knowledge (information)" and the term "dimension" is used to systematically break down the structural information content in each world. For instance, in the world "driving a car" knowledge on the drivers, cars, and their associations are available. That is, information on the name (N) of driver, address (A) of the driver, date of issue (DI) of the driving permit, termination date (DT) of the driving permit, driving status (DS), car type (CT) and restrictions on the driver (RD) are available. In Wan's formalization these information categories are regarded as dimensions. The tag sets and their types for these dimensions are shown in Table 3.

Dimension Name	Tag Set	Type
N	a set of driver names	*alpha* (string)
A	a set of addresses	record type (string, string, string)
DI, DT	a set of dates	record type (int,int,int)
DS	a set of discrete values	enumerated type Example:(`learner`, `good`, `dangerous`)
CT	a set of car models	enumerated type Example:(`mini`, `compact`, `sport`)
RD	a set of restrictions	enumerated type Example: (day-time only, must wear glasses)

Table 1 Dimensions and Tag Sets for "Driving a Car"

We assume that a TMS exists whose major goal is *compliance checking*. It provides a systematic, and application-independent framework to managing security policies, credentials, and trust relationships. When a principal submits a request to perform an action, the access control manager (ACM) in TMS should dynamically determine dimensions, construct contexts and provide context-sensitive services that are correct with respect to the trust policy in that context. A policy usually specifies *who is trusted to do what*. In our model we attach a context condition along with a rule, as explained later.

3.1 Review of Context Formalization

We have motivated in [16] that five dimensions are essential for dynamically constructing contexts. These are [1.] *perception- who* (which entity) provides the service or requires the service?, [2.] *interaction - what* type of service (resource allocation, algorithms for problem solving) is required?, [3.] *locality - where* to provide the service?, [4.] *timeliness- when* to provide the service (what time bounds, or delay, or duration should be satisfied)?, and [5.] *reasoning - why* a certain action is required in providing the service (due to obligation, adaption, or context-aware requirements)? Example 1 illustrates the construction of contexts and compliance checking by a TMS.

Example 1 *Consider the policy* Policy1: *Either the surgeon a on-duty in a hospital or any surgeon b whom a trusts can be trusted to perform surgery of patients either admitted by a or treated by a. This policy is in the "health care" trust category. The policy refers to physician name, her current status (on-duty or off-duty), patients admitted by her, and patients under her care. The context for enforcing the policy is suggested by the above information. The dimensions and their tag sets are are PN (a finite set of physician names), PS (a finite set of statuses of physicians), WS (a finite collection of work schedules), PA (a finite set of patients admitted) and PC (a finite set of patients cared). An example of a context c with these dimensions is represented in the syntax $[PN : Bob, PS : on - duty, WS : 1, PA : Alice, PC : Tom]$. This context describes the setting in which "physician Bob is on duty on the first day of the week, admitted Alice and cared for Tom". To check the compliance of "Policy1", the TMS constructs the current context c_1, and retrieves from its database the context c_2 in which the patient was admitted. The physician a_1 in context c_1 and the physician a_2 in context c_2 are both trusted to perform the surgery. Assume that the degree of trust demanded by a_1 on another surgeon is at least ε_1, and the degree of trust demanded by a_2 on another surgeon is at least ε_2. The TMS allows the b_1 or b_2 as stand-by surgeon for performing the surgery if $\rho(\tau(a_1, b_1, c_1)) \geq \varepsilon_1$ and $\rho(\tau(a_2, b_2, c_2)) \geq \varepsilon_2$.*

What is important is to make clear that "Alice" and "Tom" are patients and not hospital personnel. That is, context definition requires a unique dimension name for each entity type, because a hospital patient may also be an employee in the hospital. The set of dimensions and the tag sets for dimensions are usually suggested by the world knowledge associated with the trust category. In many applications, such as pervasive computing, contexts must be constructed dynamically in real-time. As an example, once again consider a hospital environment. Assume every nurse possesses a hand-held device equipped with sensory and communication capabilities. As the nurse goes around hospital wards the sensory information gathered by the device at any instant is transformed into a context. The dimensions for such contexts may be chosen as $CLOC$ (the ward where the nurse is), $NLOC$ (the next ward to be visited), $TIME$ (current local time), and DUR (time taken to walk the distance between the wards). In general, once the dimensions and tags are determined context is formalized as a *typed relation*.

Definition 2 *Let DIM denote the set of all possible dimensions and TAG denote a set of totally ordered sets. Let $\bigcup TAG$ be the set of tags for all dimensions in DIM. The set of all un-typed contexts is*

$$CO = \mathbb{P}(DIM \times \bigcup TAG)$$

By letting each set in TAG to assume all possible tag values for some dimension in DIM we get typed contexts. Let CO^* denote the set of non-empty un-typed contexts, and $CT = DIM \rightarrow TAG$ be the type of all total surjective functions with DIM as domain and TAG as range. Let $\kappa \in CT$. The set

$$G(\kappa) = \{c \mid c \in CO^* \wedge dom\ c \subseteq dom\ \kappa \wedge \forall (X, x) \in c \bullet X \in DIM, x \in \kappa(X)\}$$

denotes the set of typed contexts for the given type τ. □

If $DIM = \{X_1, \ldots, X_n\}$ and $\kappa(X_i), i = 1, \ldots, n$ are respectively the tag sets for X_i, $i = 1, \ldots, n$, the syntax for a context is $[X_1 : x_1, \ldots, X_n : x_n]$, where $x_i \in X_i$. In the rest of the paper by context we mean a finite non-empty context, and omit explicit reference to κ unless our discussion demands it. A context in which the dimensions are distinct is called *simple context*. It is shown in [17] that a non-simple context is equivalent to a set of simple contexts. In this paper we encounter only simple contexts.

operator name	symbol	meaning	precedence
Union	$\sqcup$	Set Union	3
Intersection	$\sqcap$	Set Intersection	3
Difference	$\ominus$	Set Difference	4
Subcontext	$\subseteq$	Subset	6
Supcontext	$\supseteq$	Superset	6
Override	$\oplus$	Function overwrite	4
Projection	$\downarrow$	Domain Restriction	1
Hiding	$\uparrow$	Range Restriction	1
Undirected Range	$\rightleftharpoons$	Range of simple contexts with same domain	5
Directed Range	$\rightharpoonup$	Range of simple contexts with same domain	5

Table 2 Context Operators and Precedence

3.1.1 Context Calculus

A set of context operators are formally defined by Wan [17]. We review them here, give examples, and illustrate the evaluation of context expressions. For the sake of simplicity we assume that tag sets are the set of natural numbers.

Table 2 shows the context operators, their functionalities, and precedences. Example 2 illustrates the application of a few context operators.

Example 2 :
Let $c_1 = [d:1, e:4, f:3], D = \{d, e\}$
$c_1 \downarrow D = [d:1, e:4]; c_1 \uparrow D = [f:3]$
Let $c_2 = [e:3, d:1, f:4], c_3 = [e:1, d:3]$
   $c_2 \oplus c_1 = [e:4, d:1, f:3]; c_1 \oplus c_2 = [e:3, d:1, f:4]$
   $c_1 \ominus c_2 = [e:4, f:3]; c_1 \sqcap c_2 = [d:1]$
   $c_3 = c_1 \sqcup c_2 = [d:1, e:3, e:4, f:3, f:4]$.
Using the result in [17] c_3 *can be written as a set of simple contexts:*
   $c_3 = \{[d:1, e:3, f:3], [d:1, e:3, f:4], [d:1, e:4, f:3], [d:1, e:4, f:4]\}$
   $c_2 \rightleftharpoons c_3 = \{[e:1,d:1,f:4],[e:1,d:2,f:4],[e:1,d:3,f:4],[e:2,d:1,f:4],$
               $[e:2,d:2,f:4],[e:2,d:3,f:4],[e:3,d:1,f:4],[e:3,d:2,f:4],$
               $[e:3,d:3,f:4]\}$
   $c_2 \rightharpoonup c_3 = \{[d:1,f:4],[d:2,f:4],[d:3,f:4]\}$

3.1.2 Context Expression

A context expression is a well-formed expression in which only contexts, context variables, and context operators occur. A well-formed context expression will evaluate to a context. As an example, $c_3 \uparrow D \oplus c_1 \mid c_2$, where $c_1 = [x : 3, y : 4, z : 5]$, $c_2 = [y : 5]$, and $c_3 = [x : 5, y : 6, w : 5]$, $D = \{w\}$ is a well-formed expression. The steps for evaluating the expression according to the precedence rules shown in Table 2 are shown below:

[Step1]. $c_3 \uparrow D = [x : 5, y : 6]$ [$\uparrow$ Definition]

[Step2]. $c_1 \mid c_2 = c_1 \ or \ c_2$ [$\mid$ Definition]

[Step3]. *Suppose in Step2, c_1 is chosen,*

$\qquad c_3 \uparrow D \oplus c_1 = [x : 3, y : 4, z : 5]$ [$\oplus$ Definition]

else if c_2 is chosen,

$\qquad c_3 \uparrow D \oplus c_2 = [x : 5, y : 5]$ [$\oplus$ Definition]

3.1.3 Trust Context Categories

A *trust context category* is a set of trust contexts relevant to capture the knowledge in that category. As an example, the set of contexts $\{[N : n, DT : t, DS : s] \mid ct \leq t + 6 \wedge s = \text{learner}\}$ belongs to the category "driving a car". These contexts are relevant to the action "determine the drivers who were granted `learner's permit` within the last six months (here ct stands for current time)". A trust category has its own trust domain which has the structural properties discussed in Section 2.

Every principal will choose its trust categories and submit it to the TMS, who in conjunction with ACS, has the knowledge and resources to determine the contexts for each trust category. For instance, if principal a submits the categories $\pi_a = \{\pi_{a_1}, \ldots, \pi_{a_{k_a}}\}$ to the TMS then for each category $\pi_{a_i} \in \pi_a$ the TMS will determine a set $DIM_{a_i} = \{X_{a_i}^1, \ldots, X_{a_i}^{k_i}\}$ of dimensions, and a tag set $\kappa(X_{a_i}^j)$ for each dimension $X_{a_i}^j \in DIM_{a_i}$. Whenever principal a submits a request for action belonging to that category, with the help of the context tool kit, the TMS will construct contexts that are relevant for the action. In this scheme, the trust categories and contexts in those categories of a principal a are known only TMS, ACS, and itself. The context toolkit is an implementation package of the context calculus. As an example, using the toolkit the TMS can calculate the set s of simple contexts corresponding to a non-simple context c. It uses the rule

$\{s \mid \forall c' \in s \bullet dim(c') = dim(c) \wedge (X, x) \in c' \rightarrow (X, x) \in c\}$

As another example, the TMS can determine the set of contexts such that a given logical expression is true at every context in that set. To check the compliance with respect to the policy "A `learner` should pass road test examination within `six months` of the *date of expiry* of the learner's permit" the TMS should determine the contexts where the logical expression $(ct \leq t + 6 \wedge s = \text{learner})$ is true. An application of this policy is warranted when the action " determine the set L of drivers with

a-Dimensions	b-Dimensions	c-Dimensions
LOC	WHERE	PLACE
	WHEN	DATE
WHO	NAME	USER
WHAT		ACTION
WHY	PURPOSE	

Table 3 Mapping Between Dimensions

learner permit issued within the last six months" is initiated. We call ($ct \leq t+6 \wedge s =$ learner) a context condition. It is clear that a context condition, in general, may satisfy a set of contexts. We write $\mathbf{ist}(\alpha, c)$ to denote that expression α is true (valid) in context c. The context condition α for a context c is an assertion on the *evidence* relevant to the context c. Example 3 illustrates the usefulness of context conditions.

Example 3 *Let Bob trust a driver a if a can be certified to comply with the learner policy stated above. The degree to which Bob trusts the driving of Alice is at least as much as his trust on any learner who has complied with learner policy. We can formally express this trust policy of Bob as*

$$\rho(\tau(Bob, Alice, c)) \geq minimum\{\rho(\tau(Bob, a, c))\},$$
where $a \in L \wedge \mathbf{ist}(\alpha, c)$, and $\alpha = ct \leq t+6 \wedge a = learner$

After constructing the trust contexts for all categories of a principal the TMS must resolve *conflict* among dimension names and *construct ontology* for "equivalent" dimensions.

- *resolve conflicts:* A conflict arises when a dimension name is common for two different categories of a principal and the tag sets of the dimensions are of different types. If these two types are sub types of a super type then the conflict is resolved by replacing the tag types with the super type. If a super type does not exist then the conflict is resolved by renaming the dimension in one trust category.
- *ontology:* It is possible that some principals have a common trust category, but the dimension names (with their tag names) chosen by the principals may be different. The TMS maintains an ontology table in which *equivalent* dimension names are listed. An example of the mapping between dimensions chosen by three principals is shown in Table 3. Informally, dimensions X and Y are equivalent if either they have the same tag set or the types of tag sets can be lifted to a unique super type. As an example, the dimensions *LOC*, *WHERE*, and *PLACE* are equivalent under the assumption that they have the "set of city names" as their tag.

4 Trust Calculation

Without loss of generality assume that all trust categories in π_a have a common trust domain, say $\mathscr{D}_a$. For a given evidence α_i in the context category π_{a_i}, the trust of a on b over all contexts in the context category π_{a_i} that satisfy the evidence α_i can be calculated in more than one way. Let $\mathscr{C}_{a_i}$ be the set of contexts in the trust category π_{a_i}.

- *minimum trust:* $\tau_i^l(a,b \mid \alpha_i) = \bigwedge_{\mathbf{ist}(\alpha_i,c) \,\wedge\, c \,\in\, \mathscr{C}_{a_i}} \tau(a,b,c)$
- *maximum trust:* $\tau_i^h(a,b \mid \alpha_i) = \bigvee_{\mathbf{ist}(\alpha_i,c) \,\wedge\, c \,\in\, \mathscr{C}_{a_i}} \tau(a,b,c)$
- *uncertainty:* Since trust is not absolute in any context there is an element of uncertainty associated with the assignment of trust values. The two potential approaches to deal with uncertainty in trust calculation are based on *trust intervals* and *trust probabilities*.

  - *trust interval* A domain of *trust intervals* $\mathscr{I}(\mathscr{D}_a)$ is constructed from $\mathscr{D}_a$ which is a cpo and a function μ
    $$\mu : \mathscr{E} \times \mathscr{E} \times \mathscr{C}_{a_i} \to \mathscr{I}(\mathscr{D}_a)$$
    that assigns trust values to intervals is defined. This method is followed in [5]. We refine this approach, emphasizing that the interval $\mathscr{I}(\mathscr{D})$ must be a *sub interval* of the interval $[\tau_i^l(a,b \mid \alpha_i), \tau_i^h(a,b \mid \alpha_i)]$
  - *Probabilistic Model*: Trust values are considered as random variables over the domain $\mathscr{D}_a$. With respect to a probabilistic distribution in the trust domain $\mathscr{D}_a$ a probability $P(\tau(a,b,c) = d)$ is computed. That is, with probability $P(\tau(a,b,c) = d)$ the degree of trust of a on b is d in context $c \in \mathscr{C}_{a_i}$. The principal a may choose $d_{max} \in \mathscr{D}_a$ such that $d_{max} = max_{d \in \mathscr{D}_a}\{P(\tau(a,b,c) = d)\}$ is a maximum, and assign it as the trust of a on b in context c. Further, a can choose a threshold β_a, and may decide not to trust b in context c if the maximum probability is less than β_a.

Choosing any one of the above methods to calculate trust, the principal a will have a trust vector
$$\tau'(a,b \mid \alpha_a) = \langle \tau_1'(a,b \mid \alpha_{a_1}), \ldots, \tau_k'(a,b \mid \alpha_{a_k}) \rangle,$$
where $\alpha_a = \alpha_{a_1} \wedge \alpha_{a_2} \wedge \ldots \alpha_{a_k}$, α_{a_i} is the evidence for context category π_{a_i}. The set $\{\tau'(a,b \mid \alpha_a) \mid a \in \mathscr{E}_b\}$ is the set of trust vectors of principals in $\mathscr{E}$ who have calculated their trust for the participant b. At any instant the collection of all such vectors is part of the global trust in the system.

4.1 Trust Delegation and Refinement

Assume that $\alpha' \to \alpha$, where α and α' are context conditions. If $\mathbf{ist}(\alpha',c')$, and $\mathbf{ist}(\alpha,c)$, then a trust policy enforced in a context c is quite relevant in context c' defined by α' and should be enforced there. Hence for a principal a and entity b the trust degree $\tau_i(a,b \mid \alpha')$ is known then we conclude that $\tau_i(a,b \mid \alpha) = \tau_i(a,b \mid \alpha')$

for trust category π_i. In other words, logical implication propagates trust values from one context to another.

Trust Delegation: We can justify now that trust delegation is a form of trust propagation. Suppose principal a_1 has a trust policy "my trust on the entity a_3 is the same as the trust of a_2 on a_3. Assume that the policy is to be applied by a_1 in context c_1, and ist(α_1, c_1). In context c_1, which is local to a_1, let $\tau(a_2, a_3, c_2) = d$, and α_2 be the justification for computing this trust value. If $\alpha_2 \to \alpha_1$ the trust propagation happens, and $\tau(a_1, a_3, c_1) = d$. If $\alpha_2 \nrightarrow \alpha_1$ the trust delegation cannot happen.

Refinement: Refinement refers to calculating a more precise trust value than the one already available. Informally, the trust of a on b in context c is *refined* when either some additional constraints are imposed on the information $W(c)$ or some additional information becomes available, thus creating a new context c'. Thus the trust value evolves as well as refined. Refinement need not be *monotonic*, meaning the addition of new information or the imposition of additional constraints on existing information may decrease the trust value.

Consider information content refinement by imposing constraints on existing information. For context $c \in \mathscr{C}$, let $W(c)$ denote the world of information referenced by c. Suppose for contexts $c_1, c_2 \in \mathscr{C}$, the world $W(c_2)$ referenced by c_2 is a restricted subset of the information in the world $W(c_1)$ referenced by c_1. The restriction is often imposed by constraints on the entity described in the world $W(c_1)$. Then the information in the world $W(c_2)$ is more precise or special than the information $W(c_1)$. This kind of sub-setting can be realized either semantically or syntactically. In the former case, a logical expression may be used. An example is $W(c_1)$ is the set of physicians and $W(c_2)$ is the set of surgeons. In the case of syntactic sub-setting, more dimensions are added to the set $dim(c_1)$ such that the world referenced by new contexts obtained by the addition of dimensions do not go outside $W(c_1)$. Formally a context c_2 is constructed such that $dim(c_2) = dim(c_1) \cup D$, where $D \subset DIM$, $D \cap dim(c_1) = \varnothing$, such that $W(c_2) \subset W(c_1)$. Thus, the additional dimensions in the set $dim(c_2) \setminus dim(c_1)$ have no extraneous influence on the information along the dimensions in the set $dim(c_1)$, instead it can only constrain it. An example is the context $c_2 \subset c_1$, where $c_2 = [GPS : Newyork, TIME : 10, NS : 12, EW : 3]$, and $c_1 = [GPS : Newyork, TIME : 10]$, with the interpretation that every event happening in context c_2 can be seen from context c_1. Hence, if α is a valid formula in $W(c_2)$ then it is possible to prove in context c_1 that α is true in context c_2. We define such a relationship between contexts as *visible*.

Definition 3 *A context $c_2 \in S$ is said to be* visible *from context $c_1 \in S$, written $c_1 \succeq c_2$, if $c_1 \subset c_2$ and $W(c_2) \subset W(c_1)$.* □

From Definition 3 it follows that ist$(c_2, \alpha) \Rightarrow$ ist$(c_1, \text{ist}(c_2, \alpha))$. Consequently, the current context c_1 in which the value $\tau(a, b, c_2)$ is computed must satisfy the relation $c_1 \succeq c_2$. When information is added on to existing information context condition will change, and consequently contexts will change. For this case we offer a few axioms for simple situations. We write $d' \gtrsim d$ to mean that d' is the refinement of d.

- *arbitrary subset:* $c_1 \subset c_2 \Rightarrow \tau(a, b, c_2) \gtrsim \tau(a, b, c_1)$

- *intersection:* $\tau(a,b,c_1) \gtrsim \tau(a,b,c_1 \sqcap c_2)$
  $\tau(a,b,c_2) \gtrsim \tau(a,b,c_1 \sqcap c_2)$
  $\tau(a,b,c_1) \wedge \tau(a,b,c_2) \gtrsim \tau(a,b,c_1 \sqcap c_2)$
- *disjoint union:* $\tau(a,b,c_1 \sqcup c_2) \gtrsim \tau(a,b,c_1)$
  $\tau(a,b,c_1 \sqcup c_2) \gtrsim \tau(a,b,c_2)$
  $\tau(a,b,c_1 \sqcup c_2) \gtrsim \tau(a,b,c_1) \vee \tau(ab,c_2)$

5 Trust Policy Framework

A trust model must include a formal framework for policy representation and policy application. A trust policy mentions entities (principals and objects), and suggests either directly or indirectly a sequence of actions to be done when the rule is followed. A Policy may mention a *role*, in which case it is applied to every entity playing that role. A policy in every trust category is a rule, an intensional statement. An example trust policy in health care category is *a physician can be trusted to access medical information on the patients under her care*. A policy, being a declarative statement, does not dictate how it should be represented in organizational databases and how it should be implemented. However we recommend that the policy representation include information on where it is applicable.

5.1 Policy Representation

A policy can be represented by a rule $H \Leftarrow B$, where H is called the *head (consequent)* of the rule and B is called the *body (antecedent)* of the rule. In general, the body of a rule is a conjunction of one or more conditions; no disjunction is allowed in the body. The head of a rule, expressed declaratively, is an action specification. We associate a context condition U with each rule to suggest that the rule is applicable in any context that satisfies this condition. By separating the context condition from the rule we achieve rule generality, and flexibility in the application of the rule.

Example 4 *Consider the rule* $U : \iota(x,y,z) == \iota(x',y,z) \Leftarrow \rho(\iota(w,x',z)) \geq \rho(\iota(w,y,z))$, *where the context condition is* $U \equiv physician(x) \wedge nurse(y) \wedge head\_nurse(w) \wedge physician(x') \wedge c \in \mathscr{C}$. *The rule states that in context c that satisfies the context condition U, physician x trusts nurse y to the same degree that physician x' trusts y provided nurse w trusts physician x' more than the trust she has for nurse y".*

The TMS maintains the policy bases, one for each principal in the system. Let $\{PB_a \mid a \in \mathscr{E}\}$ denote the set of policy bases. The policy bases are secured in the sense that PB_a can be accessed only by the principal a and the ACS within the TMS. For an efficient processing of transactions, we propose two methods to organize the rules in each policy base.

- *partitioning:* The set PB_a of rules is partitioned so that each subset has policies associated with a specific trust category. As an example, corresponding to the trust categories π_a of the principal a, the policy base PB_a is partitioned into $\{PB_{a_1}, \ldots, PB_{a_k}\}$.
- *Linking Partitions:* A rule $r :: U : H \Leftarrow B$ is relevant to the rule $r' :: U' : H' \Leftarrow B'$ if $U' \rightarrow U$. For a rule $r \in PB_{a_i}$ the rules in PB_{a_i} that are relevant to r are linked.

Following the links and applying the trust propagation rule the global trust can be computed at any instant. The global state of the TMS at any instant is given by the elements of the trust model, the organization of the policy base and the global trust computed from them.

6 Conclusion

The formal trust model proposed in this paper is both new and novel, yet it shares many properties of other trust models [5]. The basic function that computes trust is context-specific. This function is made use of in defining trust in trust categories. The explicit introduction of context in the computation of trust, annotating trust policies with context conditions, and defining delegation through related contexts are some of our new results given in this paper. The important benefits in the intensional definition of trust are (1) Context is independent of what it references. As a consequence, context-based trust definition captures different kinds information conveyed by events that happen in a context; (2)Context calculus enables the construction of new contexts from existing contexts, and the logic of contexts [16] enables one to reason about the information in the newly constructed context with respect to the information contents in the contexts from which the new one is constructed. As a consequence context-based trust definition is well-suited to handle trust in dynamic networks, in which contexts and their respective information contents may dynamically change independent of each other; (3) The model becomes more general and expressive because we incorporate what Grandison and Sloman [9] and [8] have strongly proposed, but failed to formalize.

The contribution made by us in this paper is a quick summary of what we have been doing during the last few months. With the full support of context theory and its logic of reasoning [16] we plan to add more formal arsenal to our trust model. These include devising rules for reasoning, and transporting our formalism to a practical stage in which trustworthy systems can be developed. We expect this work to follow very closely the ongoing work [1, 2].

References

1. Vasu Alagar and Mubarak Mohammad. *A Component Model for Trustworthy Real-Time Reactive Systems Development.* In *Proceedings of the 4th International Workshop on Formal*

Aspects of Component Systems (FACS'07), September 19 - 21, 2007. Sophia-Atipolis, France.

2. Vasu Alagar and Mubarak Mohammad. *Specification and Verification of Trustworthy Component-Based Real-Time Reactive Systems.* In *Proceedings of the Specification and Verification of Component-Based Systems Workshop (SAVCBS'07)*, September 03 - 04, 2007, Dubrovnik, Croatia. (ACM Portal   http://portal.acm.org/citation.cfm?id=1292316.1292327 & coll=GUIDE & dl=)

3. V.S. Alagar, J. Paquet, K. Wan. *Intensional Programming for Agent Communication.* Proceedings of the 2nd International Workshop on Declarative Agent Languages and Technologies (DALT) 2004, New York, U.S.A., June 2004, LNAI Springer-Verlag, Vol. 3476, Page 239-255. ISBN: 3-540-26172-9.

4. R. Carnap. *Meaning and Necessity.* Chicago University Press, 1947. Enlarged Edition 1956.

5. Marco Carbone, Mogens Nielsen, and Vladimiro Sassone. *A formal model for trust in dynamic networks.* Research Series RS-03-04, BRICS, Department of Computer Science, University of Aarhus, January 2003, EU Project SECURE IST-2001-32486 Deliverable 1.1.

6. N. Damianou, N. Dulay, E. Lupu, and M. Solomon. *The Ponder Policy Specification Language.* Proceedings Policy 2001: Workshop on Policies for Distributed Systems and Networks, Bristol, UK, 29–31, Jan. 2001.

7. J. DeTreville. *Binder, a logic-based security language.* Proceedings of the 2002 IEEE Symposium on Security and Privacy, IEEE Computer Society Press, May 2002, 105-113.

8. Nathan Dimmock, András Belokosztolszki, and David Eyers. *Using Trust and Risk in Role-Based Access Control Policies.*, In *Ninth ACM Symposium on Access Control Models and Technologies (SACMAT)*, Yorktown Heights, New York, June 2004.

9. Tyrone Grandison and Morris Sloman. *A Survey of Trust in Internet Applications.* IEEE Communications Surveys, Fourth Quarter 2000, 1-16.

10. Audun Jøsang, Elizabeth Gray, and Michael Kinateder. *Analyzing topologies of transitive trust.* In *Proceedings of the Workshop of Formal Aspects of Security and Trust (FAST)*, September 2003.

11. S. Jones. *TRUST-EC: Requirements for Trust and Confidence in E-Commerce.* European Commission, Joint Research Center, 1999.

12. G. Klyne. www.ninebynine.org/iTrust/Intro.html, 2008.

13. D. Harrison McKnight and Norman L. Chervany. *Trust and Distrust Definitions: One Bite at a Time.* In *Trust in Cyber Societies - LNAI*, 2246:27-54, 2001.

14. Craig Mundie, Peter de Vries, Peter Haynes, and Matt Corwine. *Trustworthy Computing - Microsoft White Paper,* Microsoft Corporation, October 2002.

15. D. Povey. *Trust Management,* 1999, http://security.dstc.edu.au/presentations/trust.

16. KaiYu Wan, Vasu Alagar. *A Context Theory for Multi-agent Systems.* Revised Draft, January 2008.

17. Kaiyu Wan, *Lucx: Lucid Enriched with Context,* Ph.d Thesis, Department of Computer Science and Software Engineering, Concordia University, Montreal, Canada, January 2006.

18. K. Wan, V.S. Alagar. *An Intensional Programming Approach to Multi-agent Coordination in a Distributed Network of Agents.* Proceedings of the 3rd International Workshop on Declarative Agent Languages and Technologies (DALT) 2005, Utrecht, The Netherlands, July 25, 2005. Page 148-164, LNCS Springer-Verlag, Vol. 3904, pp. 205-222.

19. Stephen Weeks. *Understanding trust management systems.* In *Proceedings of IEEE Symposium on Security and Privacy.*, Oakland, 2001.

A Translation Mechanism for Recommendations

Pierpaolo Dondio, Luca Longo and Stephen Barrett

Abstract An important class of distributed Trust-based solutions is based on the information sharing. A basic requirement of such systems is the ability of participating agents to effectively communicate, receiving and sending messages that can be interpreted correctly. Unfortunately, in open systems it is not possible to postulate a common agreement about the representation of a rating, its semantic meaning and cognitive and computational mechanisms behind a trust-rating formation. Social scientists agree to consider unqualified trust values not transferable, but a more pragmatic approach would conclude that qualified trust judgments are worth being transferred as far as decisions taken considering others' opinion are better than the ones taken in isolation. In this paper we investigate the problem of trust transferability in open distributed environments, proposing a translation mechanism able to make information exchanged from one agent to another more accurate and useful. Our strategy implies that the parties involved disclose some elements of their trust models in order to understand how compatible the two systems are. This degree of compatibility is used to weight exchanged trust judgements. If agents are not compatible enough, transmitted values can be discarded. We define a complete simulation environment where agents are modelled with characteristics that may differ. We show how agents' differences deteriorate the value of recommendations so that agents obtain better predictions on their own. We then show how different translation mechanisms based on the degree of compatibility improve drastically the quality of recommendations.

Distributed System Group
Department of Computer Science and Statistics
Trinity College Dublin, Dublin 2,
e-mail: dondiop@cs.tcd.ie e-mail: longol@cs.tcd.ie e-mail: stephen.barrett@cs.tcd.ie

Please use the following format when citing this chapter:

Dondio, P., Longo, L. and Barrett, S., 2008, in IFIP International Federation for Information Processing, Volume 263; *Trust Management II*; Yücel Karabulut, John Mitchell, Peter Herrmann, Christian Damsgaard Jensen; (Boston: Springer), pp. 87–102.

1 Introduction

An important class of distributed Trust-based solutions is based on information sharing. This class encompasses Recommendation, Reputation systems and Social Networks. A basic requirement of such systems is the ability of participating agents
to effectively communicate with others, receiving and sending messages that can
be correctly interpreted. Unfortunately, in open systems, it is not possible to postulate a common agreement about the representation of a rating, its semantic meaning, the cognitive and computational mechanisms behind a trust-rating formation.
The mentioned problem is logically precedent to any other: if agents cannot understand each other, the feasibility of these trust solutions is fatally undermined, even
when all agents are acting honestly. Social scientists agree to consider unqualified
trust values not transferable and computational trust researchers are aware of the not
completely transitivity of trust, proposing conditions and uncertain models like the
one by Josang [1]. A more pragmatic approach would conclude that qualified trust
judgements are worth being transferred as far as decisions taken considering others'
opinions are better than the ones taken in isolation.

Our research seeks to define a distributed translation mechanism able to make
information, exchanged from one agent to another, more accurate and useful. We
define the problem by analysing the potential differences that two trust systems may
encounter. A generic trust systems may be depicted as a multi-layer architecture encompassing: a trust value representation, a trust metric used to compute such values,
a trust ontology that defines concepts quantified by the trust metric and a function of
satisfaction that represents how an agent consider the interaction performed. Moreover, each agent is interacting in a specific domain and therefore it is equipped with
a domain representation (for instance an ontology) and a collection of past experiences. Each of these level may be affected by differences, as we describe in section
3. Referring to an eBay-like scenario, an agent may rate very high a seller for its low
packaging time, while another may consider this information marginal as far as the
item sold is of good quality. In section 4 we review the state-of-the-art solutions that
focus mainly on the definition of a common ontology for reasoning about trust. Our
complementary strategy implies that the parties involved disclose some elements of
their trust model in order to understand how compatible the two systems are. This
degree of compatibility is used to weight exchanged trust judgements. If agents are
not compatible enough, transmitted values are discarded, while values received from
highly compatible agents are strengthened. The strategy has an unsupervised nature
that, under some conditions, skips or limits the ontology processing. We define a
complete simulation environment where agents are modelled with characteristics
that may differ. For instance, our simulator allows agents to have different trust metrics, thresholds and functions of satisfaction. Its distributed nature allows agents to
have a personal database for pieces of evidences. In our evaluation we start considering some aspects of the problem, restricting the case where the agents share the
same domain representation and they have trust metric exclusively dependant on a
combination of direct past experience and recommendations. Further experiments

are left for future works. This paper is structured as follows: in section 2 we review how the trust transferability problem is discussed among social scientists, in section 3 we define the problem by analysing which differences may affect a generic model of a trust system, then in section 4 we review present and potential solutions. In section 5 we describe the simulator environment while in section 6 we describe our evaluation, defining goals and metrics used. Conclusions and future works end our contribution.

2 Trust Transferability in Computational Trust

Before asking how we can effectively transfer trust, a first question is whether trust has a degree of objectivity. Studies in social science seem to agree about the subjective nature of trust. In the classical definition by Gambetta [5], this is represented by the subjective probability that the trustor assigns to the trustee, that vary according to the trustee, the situation and the level of perceived risk. Any attempt at objective measurement can dangerously mislead agents into thinking that the value is transferable and be used by another trustor, which is not true for trust. In other words, trust is not transitive, which has also been formally shown in [7]. As Luhmann wrote [8]: *Trust is not transferable to other objects or to other people who trust.* To say that one trusts another without further qualification of that statement is meaningless. But, on the contrary, the success and the diffusion of systems like Social Networks or Ratings Systems make the problem worth to be investigated. Therefore, the problem is to qualify correctly trust judgements, and build a mechanism to translate values produced by two different systems to allow meaningful communications. Josang and Pope [1], investigated the transferability of trust by analysing under which formal condition trust may be considered transitive. Their conditional transitivity construct adds conditions for considering trust values, propagated by transitivity, more plausible. The concept is present also in Abdul-Rahman and Hailes distributed trust model [2]. The conditional transitivity requires that:

- A has direct knowledge of B
- B has direct knowledge of C
- A has knowledge of B as a recommender
- A can use B's trust value in C

Using Joasng words: "a transitive trust path therefore stops ... when there are no more outgoing referral trust", where referral trust is the trust in an agent as a recommender. These works clearly shows how trust transferability is not a valid concept, but a plausible one that deserves to be investigated. By respecting additional conditions and by adding explanation about the semantic meaning of its rating, an agent should consider transferred trust value still useful in its decision making process.

3 Defining the problem

In order to focus the problem, in figure 1 we depicted a high-view of the components of a trust-based system. At each level, differences among the systems may cause lack of trust transferability. In order to keep our discussion more realistic, we often refer to a scenario where agents have to select trustworthy open software. Each system is depicted as a multi-layer pile with the components described in the follow:

- *Domain Perception*. It includes all the information that an agent has available about the domain where it is interacting. It is generally composed by a domain ontology and a facts database (or evidence DB).

  - *Domain Ontology*: agent's representation and understanding of the domain it is interacting in. We model it as an ontology that describes terminology and relationships related to the domain under analysis.
  - *Evidence DB:* the facts the agent collected from its experience that are used to ground trust-based decisions. A possible evidence could be: "The component1 by developer XYZ crashed twice in the last two weeks".

- *Trust System*. It contains the agent notion of Trust, its computational model represented by a trust metric, a trust value representation, a decision making process and a function of satisfaction.

  - *Trust Value*: the quantification of the trust judgement.
  - *Trust Ontology (model of trust)*: agent's definition of trust in the context. It implies to define which are the elements composing its notion of trust. We can generalize a trust model as an ontology. An example of trust model, for open software, could be: trust is a combination of stability of the software, programming techniques used and experience of the authors or in absence of past evidences a recommendation from other users.
  - *Trust metric*: the actual computation performed over the available inputs to generate a trust value. The trust metric specifies how trust model's elements are converted into numerical values and how each of them concurs to the final aggregated trust value. Different metric has been defined, even starting from the same inputs.
  - *Function of Satisfaction*: each agent has a mechanism to evaluate the quality of an interaction just completed with the trustee agent. We model this mechanism as a function defined as follows: $S : O \to [0,1]$ that goes from the set O of possible outcomes to a value that represents agent's level of satisfaction associated with a specific outcome. The function models an essential concept in trust computation: the trustor should have a mechanism to understand if the trustee fulfilled its expectations, quantified by the function S. Using function S trustee's trust value can be automatically updated according to trustor level of satisfaction. For example, an agent may be satisfied if the software has clear comments and it does not crash in the first two months and therefore he can decide to give to that software a high rating.

– *Decision making process*: this component, also referred as trust management, describes how the agent exploits the computed trust values to support its decision making process. Generally, a threshold T defines the minimum trust value required to start an interaction. The decision making process could be more articulated and it is usually represented by a set of policies (see for instance the SECURE policy language [11]) or a set of (fuzzy) rules like in the REGRET trust model by Sabater [3].

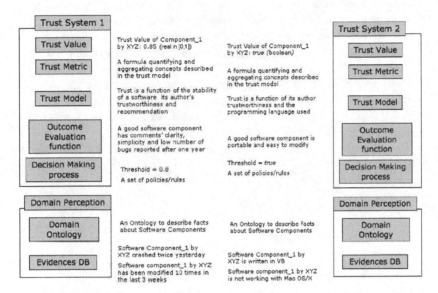

Fig. 1 Trust Transferability scenario

In any of the above levels, differences may reduce the transferability of trust.

- *Trust Value differences.* The two systems may have a different values representation. For example, a system may have trust value represented with a real number in the range [0, 1] while the other may represent values with five discrete levels from 0 to 4. A second problem is the identification of the agent whose trust values belong to: the two systems may have different names for the same agent or the same label could not be bounded to the same agent.
- *Trust metric differences.* Even when the two agents are using the same trust representation, i.e., they have the same trust ontology, they may compute trust in different ways. An entity may compute 90% of its trust value on the number of bugs reported, while another may assign to it a marginal role.
- *Trust models (ontology) differences.* Systems may have different representation and understanding of what trust is. An agent may define trust as a prediction of software quality based on its author, while another agent may include many other factors, like the author popularity, the stability and persistence of the software or the programming technique used.

- *Different Threshold.* An agent can be more optimistic about and have a lower threshold than another one, that may have more strict requirements in order to start cooperating. This implies that an exchanged trust value could be sufficient for A to start an interaction even if for B was not enough, leading to substantial differences in agents' behaviour.
- *Different function of Satisfactions.* Two agents may judge differently the same interaction because, for example, of different expectations. A user may not care about the clarity of the code or comments in a software component, as far as the component does not crash, while another entity may consider confusing code as an important negative factor, maybe because he wants to modify it.
- *Domain Representation differences.* Agents may have different knowledge of the domain structure in which they are interacting. An agent may have a limited knowledge, ignoring elements that are known to other agents. Two entities may have different names and representations for the same concept, define diverse relationships among domain elements and use concepts that are aggregation of elements, so that the same evidence using agent A's domain ontology can only partially described by agent B.
- *Evidence Database differences.* Two agents may have a dissimilar database of evidences. In a distributed scenario this is a common situation: each entity has a limited set of experience and its partial vision of the world.

4 State-of-the-art solutions

A general solution implies that the parties involved disclose some elements of their trust model in order to understand how similar the two systems can be considered. Referring again to figure 1, a matching between two systems can be performed at various levels: trust values, trust model, evidences.

Trust value matching. At the level of trust value representation, a conversion may be performed in order to reduce trust values to a common representation. Since during the conversion some information is lost, an estimation of this loss has to be part of the process. Pinyol et al. [3] performed an analytical study of trust value conversion. The authors consider four common trust value representations: boolean, bounded real, discrete sets and probabilistic distribution representation. The authors proposed a conversion between these four representations and they define a factor taking into account the uncertainty involved in the conversion. They propose to compute this factor considering the entropy of the trust value seen as a random variable. As it is easy to understand, high level of uncertainty are associated when a conversion is from a simpler to a richer representation, while no uncertainty is associated with the opposite conversion.

Trust model matching. ElMessery [4] proposes to enhance trust values by declaring the expectations that the trustee has. In this way, it is possible to understand which elements may affect positively a trust value or not from the point of view of that particular trustee. If two agents share the same expectations, it is likely that they will judge situations in similar ways and consequently trust values could be transferred. The proposed solution has, as a condition, the fact that the two systems are able to understand the terminology (and the semantic) of each trust model. Methodology that are based on ontology matching have a great potential, but the problem that so far has not been investigated in trust studies and that represents a challenging task where some results has been achieved in a specific domain with semi-automatic tools. Another possible solution is the definition of a generic and basic ontology for trust representation that may act as a starting point where personalised ontology may be matched in order to be compared. This ontology does not want to force agents to a common trust model, but offer a generic and flexible mean of communications of trust information among agents. In Computational Trust this problem has been studied using high-level concept present in any trust-based decisions. The European project eRep [9] defines a set of terms about reputation concepts has been defined. The aim of this effort is to define an ontology that all partners participating in the project could use as a consensual starting point. This ontology is based on the cognitive theory of reputation defined by Conte and Paolucci [10]. Punyol at al. [3] propose a generic ontology as a possible common base for mapping different trust models. The authors describe a generic belief about an entity as a combination of SimpleBelief, a belief that the holding agent acknowledges as true, and MetaBelief, a belief about others' belief.

Evidence matching and unsupervised learning of similarity: extending collaborative filtering. If agents are acting in the same or similar domain, it may be likely that they encountered similar situations. A degree of similarity can be deduced by simply matching evidences and corresponding trust values. This could be performed in several ways as we describe in the next section, but the common idea is to compute a degree of compatibility based on common data or behaviours in recognized situations. Leaving details in the next section, a basic difference between these classes of solutions and the previous ones, is that it does not take in consideration the elements of a trust model, but it focuses on the comparison of common data in order to understand the similarity between the two systems. It is therefore an implicit and unsupervised solution that limits the need of a common ontology, but that still requires that, at least, the two agents speak a language partially understandable.

Privacy issues. The disclosure of extra information rather than a trust value implies, at least, an issue of privacy. One or both the parties may not want to share information about their trust judgements or their reasoning model. The problem was described by Seigneur [6] as the trade-off between trust and security: in order to trust an agent we need information that may reduce its privacy.

5 Our strategy

Our solution requires that two parties disclose some information in order to understand the degree of compatibility of their trust systems. Common to all the following solutions is the hypothesis that agents have been designed to interact with each other in a domain. We therefore assume that their domain representations partially overlap. Differences can arise in their preferences, trust models or their past experiences, but we postulate that they are partially able to communicate facts happening in the domain: this means that the domain ontology partially matches. Each strategy should be evaluated at least with the following criteria: impact on the quality of recommended trust values, privacy issues, risk and communication overload. The choice of adopting a specific strategy will be a trade-off dependant on situational factors like bandwidth, need for recommendations, privacy constraints. In this first paper we analyze three strategies: the sharing of trust values database or past interactions database, the direct comparisons of the function of satisfaction S or the trust metric T in presence of an accepted common domain ontology and the approximation of the function S or T using stereotypes situations without common ontology. In all the strategies the agents' goal is to get an idea of other agent's trust metric T or function of satisfaction S. Note how these goals are only partially linked: in the first case the agent is interested in understanding how the other agent assigns trust value, while in the second it is interested in other agent's preferences. Knowing T may not guarantee the expected S, exactly like knowing that a person is considered very trustworthy for another person does not guarantee that it will satisfy my expectations. Knowing the preferences of another agent (function S) does not guarantee on its ability to predict others trustworthiness. We are now ready to describe these three preliminary solutions, remembering that this paper, as the first on the topic, does not claim to be comprehensive.

- 1a. *Sharing of Trust Value DB*. In this strategy agents share a DB containing at least the couple $< agent\ name, trust\ value >$. The idea is that two agents check if they have some acquaintances in common, and they use common connections' trust value to compute a compatibility degree. A hypothesis is that agents are using the same ID for the same agent, hypothesis not always valid. Some statistical indicators like correlation, can be used, and supplemental information like number of accepted/rejected interactions with an agent can make the computation more plausible. If agents have different trust value representations, a conversion may be performed as described in Punyol at al. [3]. This strategy predicts the agents trust metric T, it does not require any knowledge of the Trust model and according to the number of agents in common could became an accurate indicator. On the contrary, privacy is very poor; communication overload can be heavy like the risk involved. Several systems have been implemented to add an extra-layer of security to guarantee the confidentiality of the information shared that relies on trusting computing and encryption keys policies.
- 1b. *Sharing of Evidences*. This solution is similar to the first one, but the data shared are single interactions and how each agent evaluated each interaction.

In this way agents predict the function S rather than T. Communication overload is even bigger, but privacy concerns are less relevant since evidences are anonymous in the sense that they describe situations rather than agents' personal information.

- 2. *Direct Comparison of function S.* When there is a common ontology describing facts that is accepted by all agents, each of them can easily map its function S over this common ontology and directly compare it with the others'. The simplest case, that we evaluate in section 6, is when function S has the same basic form (for example a linear combination of factors). An example of such an ontology is the recent evolution of the eBay feedback system, where four fixed criteria have been introduced to assess the validity of an item sold, representing a first common base for comparing feedbacks. By directly comparing the two functions, agents compute an accurate degree of compatibility, without disclosing sensitive information about other agents or personal experience, and with a few communication overload (unlike the previous two solutions). On the contrary, the hypothesis on which this solution relies can be hard to satisfy.

- 3. *Predicting S and T using stereotypes situations.* Solution 1 scales poor and suffers from privacy constraints. Solution 2 is better in any respects, but it requires the strong hypothesis of a common ontology for outcome evaluations. When there is no common ontology, but agents, at least, partially can understand each other, a solution can be build by using stereotypes situations. Here we describe the prediction of the function *S*, but the method can be applied to the prediction of the trust metric *T* using trust values instead of values of satisfaction and stereotypes agents instead of stereotype situation. Agents' goal is to accurately predict other agent's function *S* using the minimum number of messages. In the generic situation, each function S is any function defined from some domain concepts or elements to a value

$$S_1 : f(X_1, X_2, ..., X_n) \quad S_2 : f(Y_1, Y_2, ..., Y_m) \tag{1}$$

We assume that, if the agents have different value representation, they translate it using the technique described in [3]. Each agent sends stereotypes situation that it considers meaningful to the other agent and wait for its evaluation of the situation. For instance, an agent considering the low shipping time, essential for being a good eBay seller, may propose two situations where this factor varies drastically. Agents can propose situations where only one key-factor changes, in order to understand the importance of that specific factors, with the drawback of not understanding the mutual dependence of the factors in the formula. In general, agents need a strategy to generate the appropriate next situation after having received the other agent's feedback. The strategy should indicate when the process should stop, i.e., enough information has been collected to understand other's agent model. In general, agents may employ an unsupervised learning system or adopt statistical tools like regression and correlation to understand other's agent reasoning model, performing an on-the-fly negotiation of their preferences. The solution appears a good trade-off between the previous ones: using stereotypes situations sensitive data are not disclosed, communication overload is relatively small, varying from the perfect situation of solution 2 to the case where many messages have to be exchanged in order to understand other agents. Number of messages will in general depend on how close the two agents representations are, how many of the situations proposed are relevant and fully understood. It may happen that an agent may reply not with a value but with an "Unknown situation" message if it was not able to understand the specific situation proposed. The analysis of this issue requires further investigation beyond the scope of this paper.

6 Our simulator

In order to test the validity of our strategy, we designed a complete simulator where agents' community is divided in Buyers and Sellers. A Seller is modelled as a function that defines the quality of the items he can sell. Each item is described as a n-tuple $(f_1, f_2, .., f_n)$ of factors indicating item quality. In our evaluation, we propose an eBay-like scenario where each item is described by the five eBay factors: (1) *Item as described* (2) *Communication* (3) *Shipping Time* (4) *Shipping Cost* (5) *Pricing*. Each value is in the interval $[-1, 1]$. Therefore the seller function S is defined as follows:

$$Q_R : \Re^n \to [-1, 1] \tag{2}$$

When a buyer decides to buy from a seller, a seller will produce a n-tuple describing the quality of the item purchased. The buyer will then assess its satisfaction. A seller produces its n-tuple as follows. Each quality factors f_i is a uniformly distributed random variable in $[base\ value \pm service\ variance]$. Base value is a uniformed random variable in $[-0.9, 0.9]$. It is decided at the start of the simulation and it does not change, meaning that a seller does not change its average quality of service during the simulation. The service variance is a uniformed variable in $[0, 0.3]$ decided at start-up, that models how variable the service provided by a seller is, introducing a more realistic change variation. Values lower than -1 and value greater than 1 are rounded to -1 and 1. A seller is therefore modelled by an n-tuple $< base\ value, service\ variance >$, therefore 2^n value. A buyer is modelled with the following functions: a trust metric producing a trust value for a seller and a function of satisfaction that evaluates the degree of satisfaction of the buyer after purchasing an item. The buyer decides to buy only according to the seller trust value computed. Each buyer has a threshold T, the minimum seller's trust value needed to buy from it. After deciding to buy or not, the 5 quality factors of the item sold are disclosed to understand if the buyer's decision was correct. Each buyer has a local database of trust values shown in table 1. It also keeps a history DB of its transactions described in table 2 and a third database containing all the buyers known with a degree of similarity between it and other buyers, as depicted in table 3.

Seller ID	ID of the seller
Trust Value Local	a trust value for the seller
Num_Transaction	number of transactions engaged with that seller
Num_Transaction_OK	number of item purchased from that seller

Table 1 Local buyer's database

Seller ID	ID of the seller
Time	time of the transaction
n-tuple	description of the item engaged with that seller
Purchased	boolean value, true means item purchased from that seller
Level of satisfaction	a value in [0, 1], described as follows, representing the level of satisfaction of the buyer about the item

Table 2 Local buyer's history database

Seller ID	ID of the seller
Compatibility_Value	a value in [-1, 1] that represents how the two buyers are comparable (1: very similar, 0: non comparable, -1: opposite).

Table 3 Local buyer's similarity database

6.1 Computations

Computation of Trust Value. In this first evaluation, the trust metric will be dependant only on direct and indirect experience, i.e., recommendations. In details, the trust value is computed as follows:

$$T_{value} : i \cdot T_{value}^{local} + (1 - i) \cdot T_{value}^{recommended} \tag{3}$$

where T_{value}^{local} is the value stored in the trust-value database of the buyer; $T_{value}^{recommended}$ is the value that the buyer collects from other buyers and i is a uniform random variable in $[0.1, 0.9]$, assigned at the start of the simulation to the buyer, that represents in which proportion recommended value and local trust value influence the final trust value. The local trust value is totally dependent on direct past experiences between the buyer and a specific seller. In absence of interactions, the buyer uses a dispositional trust value that is a property of each buyer. The dispositional trust value is again a uniformed random variable in $[0.1, 1]$, representing buyer with a strong disposition to trust (value close to one) or diffident buyers (close to 0.1). After an interaction, the local trust value is updated like this:

$$T_{value}^{local} : m \cdot T_{value} + (m - i) \cdot V_{satisfaction} \tag{4}$$

where m is uniformly distributed in $[0.1, 0.9]$ representing the effect of memory, i.e. how much the last interaction count on the new local trust value. The value of satisfaction is a value in $[0, 1]$ computed as described in the next section. The recommended trust value is computed as follows: the buyer asks to all the buyers in the community if they know the seller. All the buyers that know the seller will reply submitting their local trust value and the number of transactions used to compute that trust value. The recommended value is a weighted average of all of these trust values using the number of interactions completed.

Value of satisfaction computation. For each transaction a value of satisfaction of the buyer is computed in any case (item sold or not). Each buyer has a vector of preferences defined as a n-tuple of value between $[-1, 1]$, uniformly distributed random variable decided at the simulation start-up for each buyer. This vector is in correspondence with the seller's n-tuple of item quality factors. Each value of the buyer's n-tuple represents how important it considers each factor. A value of 1 means that the factor is essential for its satisfaction, a value of 0 means that the factor does not influence the buyer' s satisfaction and a value of -1 means that the buyer satisfaction increases when the correspondent factor is low (remind that quality factors are between 0 and 1). The negative values are inserted to model the situation where two buyers may have opposite view about a quality factors. For instance, the fact that in a movie there is a specific actor may be a strong negative factor for a person and a negative for another one. We can visualize the computation of the value of satisfaction using a vector representation. The n-tuple of vector preferences of the buyer and the n-tuple of the quality factors generated by the seller for an item are two vectors in an R^n space, P and Q_s. It seems appropriate to model the computation of the value of satisfaction as the scalar product between the two vectors. As displayed in figure 2, the scalar product is maximum when the two vectors have the same direction and versus, equal to zero when they are orthogonal and minimum when they are opposite. These three circumstances correspond to a situation where the quality of factors and the preferences are very similar (fig. 2 dx), not comparable (centre) and opposite (sx). By normalizing the vectors with then R^n norm, the value of satisfaction Vs is generally a value in $[-1, 1]$. In our case, it is a value in $[0, 1]$ because we discarded negative numbers for the preferences. The level of satisfaction is used, in case the buyer decided to buy from that seller, to update the local trust value of the buyer associated to that seller. Finally, we summarise, in table 4, the random variable that defines a buyer: these variables are all local to each buyer.

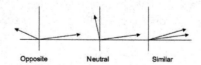

Opposite   Neutral   Similar

Fig. 2 Buyer dissimilarities in the preferences space

Similarity Value Computation. This value is computed using the strategy 2, by directly comparing the functions S of the two buyers, represented by a linear combination of the 5 quality factors. Thus the computation is a scalar product among two 5-dimension normalized vectors and values are properly uniformly re-distributed in $[-1, 1]$.

Tr	Agent's threshold [0,0.8]
I	proportion direct/indirect experience in [-0.7, 0.7]
Dispositional Tvalue	Dispositional trust value
M	buyer memory [0.1, 0.9]
n-tuple preferences	preferences coefficients in [-1, 1]

Table 4 Random variable for a buyer

6.2 How the simulation works

1. A couple buyer, seller $< B_{uyer}, S_{eller} >$ is selected
2. B_{uyer} computes the trust value of S_{eller}

   - a) B_{uyer} retrieves the local trust value
   - b) B_{uyer} collects the recommended trust values
   - c) B_{uyer} computes the degree of compatibility for each recommending Buyer
   - e) B_{uyer} computes the trust value

3. IF $T_{value} >$ threshold $\geq B_{uyer}$ THEN buys from S_{eller}

   - a) S_{eller} generates item quality factors n-tuple
   - b) B_{uyer} computes its level of satisfaction
   - c) B_{uyer} updates its local trust value for S_{eller}
   - d) B_{uyer} updates its interaction DB

   ELSE: e. b. d. (trust value not updated)

When the simulation is running without the degree of compatibility, step 2c is skipped. If agents don't use recommended values, step 2b and 2d are also skipped.

7 Evaluation

In this section we evaluate the benefit of recommendations enhanced by a degree of compatibility. We used our simulator with 20 sellers, 50 buyers and we simulated 1 000, 2 000, 10 000 and 20 000 transactions in the following cases:

- A) buyers don't use recommendations at all;
- B) buyers use recommendations without degree of compatibility ;
- C) buyers filter recommendations using a degree of compatibility: this degree is generated by directly comparing the two functions S as described in the previous section, strategy 2. The threshold of compatibility is set to 0.5, meaning that an agent discards all the values transmitted from an agent with degree of compatibility lower than 0.5.

Our first evaluation covers only the basic strategy 2 described in section 5, where all the agents have a function of satisfaction represented by a linear combination of fixed quality factors. The definition and evaluation of other's strategies are an interesting future development of this work. We assume that agents are not malicious: they always transmit their real values. The study of the robustness of our solutions is regarded as an interesting future works. Here our goal is to show that:

- When agents are different, the quality of recommendation is deteriorated, and the case A and B results became very close. It may happen that the case A performs better than B (i.e., an agent decides better on its own)
- By using the compatibility value, the quality of recommendations is better than case B and "even if not always predictable" results are better than case B.

The metrics used are:

- P_{ok}. (True Positive): the number of transactions completed by the buyer whose level of satisfaction was more than the buyer's threshold, i.e., the number of time it was a good idea to trust the seller;
- P_{no} (True Negative): the number of transactions correctly rejected by the buyer, i.e., the transactions whose level of satisfaction would have been smaller than buyer's expectations;
- N_{ok} (False Positive): the number of transactions accepted by the buyer whose level of satisfaction was smaller than buyer's threshold, i.e., it would have been better to decline the transaction;
- N_{no} (False Negative): the number of transactions erroneously rejected by the buyer, i.e., the transactions whose level of satisfaction would have been greater than buyer's expectations.

The metrics are computed locally and globally and their metrics represent the ability of the buyer of making good predictions in good and bad cases. The Case A is better than the case A if P_{ok} and N_{ok} are greater than P_{no} and N_{no}. We decided to assign (for good or bad) more importance to P_{ok} and N_{ok} than P_{no} and N_{no} , since the first two metrics represent a real benefit or damage, while the second ones are a potential benefit or damage. Therefore we defined a summarizing metric as in the following:

$$F = \frac{P_{ok}}{N_{ok}} \sqrt{\frac{P_{no}}{N_{no}}} \tag{5}$$

In the discussion we will also compare the value of P and N metrics in each case. Before describing the results obtained, we perform an analytical evaluation of the expected results. The case A, where agents do not use recommendations, is expected to perform very good when the number of transactions is very high, since each agent has sufficient number of past interactions to predict correctly sellers' behaviour. For small number of transactions, agents have not enough information on sellers and they follow they dispositional trust that, in our settings, encourages interactions. Therefore, we expect deteriorated values since the first interactions have a strong blind component. Recommendations should work better than the case A even for a small number of transactions, since agents share their information. In the long term, recommendations will perform like the case A. The above prediction is valid only if recommendations are meaningful for the agent. In case of recommendations from agents with strong differences, their effect will be reduced both in the short and in the long term. Therefore, we expect that the case C results, obtained with our compatibility degree, will perform better than the case B independently from the number of transactions. In the short term, the case C should perform better than the case A, for the effect of meaningful recommendations, while in the long term the case C should tend to the case A's results, since agents receive recommendations only from other agents very compatible with them. The case B, even in the long run should be the worst case, since the effect of recommendations from different agents causes deterioration in the value of recommended values. Results are summarized in figure 3 and table 5 confirming many of our predictions. In particular:

1. 1 000 transactions. The case A performs poorly as expected, but the other two cases are worst. This means that in the case B and C recommendations are not yet effective. In the case C the degree of compatibility is not fully applicable yet, since it is hard to find compatible agents that interacted with the same seller.
2. 5 000 transactions. The case B and C close the gap with the case A. The case C is the best case showing the effect of recommendation based on the degree of similarity. The case B is still the worst case, but the gap with the other cases is the lowest.
3. 10 000 transactions. The case A is now the more effective, meaning that agents have gained enough direct past experience to predict sellers' trustworthiness correctly. The case C performs well, with metrics similar to the case A. The case B shows a growing inefficiency: recommendations without a compatibility degree are deteriorating the predictions
4. 20 000 or more transactions. After 20 000 transactions, the three cases reach an almost steady state (similar results were obtained with 100 000 transactions). The case A is the best case as predicted, the case C performs well, slightly less than A and the case B is very far from the other two. Looking at Table 5's results for 20 000 transactions, the case C, based on the degree of compatibility, appears the most precise in selecting a trustworthy patner, since the value of P_{ok} is even greater than the case A. Note that the case B has a high number of P_{ok}, but this is due to the fact that the system allows more transactions than in the other cases. It has the highest number of P_{ok} (7054 against 6638), but it has also a four time greater number of mistakes N_{ok} (2397 against 890 of the case A).

Transactions	1 000				5 000			
	P_{ok}	N_{ok}	P_{no}	N_{no}	P_{ok}	N_{ok}	P_{no}	N_{no}
Case A	364	223	400	13	1600	713	2559	128
Case B	297	208	424	71	1542	689	2583	186
Case C	348	281	351	20	1532	451	2821	196
Transactions	10 000				20 000			
	P_{ok}	N_{ok}	P_{no}	N_{no}	P_{ok}	N_{ok}	P_{no}	N_{no}
Case A	3565	700	5501	234	6563	890	11797	850
Case B	3678	1444	4757	121	7054	2397	10190	359
Case C	3524	667	5534	275	6638	1094	11518	750

Table 5 Metrics' Value in the four cases analyzed

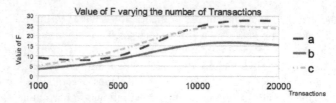

Fig. 3 Evaluation results

8 Open issues and future works

In this paper we analyze the problem of trust transferability. We defined the problem and we analysed the state-of-the-art of solutions. We showed how a degree of compatibility based on sharing common situations keeps the quality of recommendations even in presence of strong difference among agents. Future works are in the investigation of different solutions and their evaluation in the presence of malicious agents. In particular, our simulations show how, when the number of recommnedations are high, our strategy shows results comparable with a strategy purely based on past direct experience, while for an interval of interactions, our method works better than the others tested. We think that a study of trust ontology-matching will represent an important contribution and a complementary solution to our work. We think that an efficeint ontology matching could largely benefit from the support of unsupervised techniques to assist the matching process an viceversa, an macthing at the level of ontology can support a better computation of similarity.

References

1. A. Josang, S. Pope. *Semantic Constraints for Trust Transitivity.* Proceedings of the Second Asia-Pacific Conference on Conceptual Modelling, Newcastle, Australia, 2005
2. Abdul-Rahman 1997. *A distributed trust model.* In New Security Paradigms Workshop, UK.
3. I. Pinyol, M. Paolucci, J. Sabater-Mir *How to Talk About Reputation Using a Common Ontology: From Definition to Implementation.* 9th Workshop on Trust in Agent Societies, Hawaii.
4. A. Elmessery. *Expectations enhanced Trust value.* AAMAS 2006, Hawaii, USA.
5. D Gambetta. *Can we trust trust?* In Diego Gambetta, editor, Trust. Basil Blackwell, 1988.
6. Jm Seigneur, C. Jensen. *Trading Trust for Privacy,* Proceedings of iTrust'04 the International Conference on Trust Management, LNCS 2995, Springer-Verlag, 2004.
7. B. Christianson, William S. Harbison. *Why isn't trust transitive?* In Proceedings of the Security Protocols International Workshop, University of Cambridge, 1996.
8. N. Luhmann. *Familiarity, confidence, trust: Problems and alternatives.* Blackwell, 1988.
9. eRep. *eRep:Social Knowledge for e-Governance.* http://megatron.iiia.csic.es/eRep, 2006.
10. R. Conte, M. Paolucci. *Reputation in artificial societies: Social beliefs for social order.* Kluwer Academic Publishers, 2002.
11. Cahill, V. et al., 2003. *Using Trust for Secure Collaboration in Uncertain Environments.* IEEE Pervasive Computing Magazine, July-September 2003.
12. J. Sabater, C. Sierra. *Reputation and social network analysis in multi-agent systems.* In Proceedings of the 1st AAMAS conference, pages 475-482, New York, NY, USA, 2002. ACM.

Modeling Trust for Recommender Systems using Similarity Metrics

Georgios Pitsilis and Lindsay F. Marshall

Abstract. In this paper we present novel techniques for modeling trust relationships that can be used in recommender systems. Such environments exist with the voluntary collaboration of the community members who have as a common purpose the provision of accurate recommendations to each other. The performance of such systems can be enhanced if the potential trust between the members is properly exploited. This requires that trust relationships are appropriately established between them. Our model provides a link between the existing knowledge, expressed in similarity metrics, and beliefs which are required for establishing a trust community. Although we explore this challenge using an empirical approach, we attempt a comparison between the alternative candidate formulas with the aim of finding the optimal one. A statistical analysis of the evaluation results shows which one is the best. We also compare our new model with existing techniques that can be used for the same purpose.

1 Introduction

Recommender systems have become popular nowadays as they are widely used in e-commerce. Examples of services which use recommender systems for helping users to choose products they might like are epinions [1], eBay [2] and Amazon [3]. The contribution of recommender systems comes in two forms, either as predicted ratings of services that a user wants to know about, or as lists of services that users might find of interest. The effectiveness of a *Recommender system* can be measured by the accuracy of the predictions that it makes. *Collaborative filtering* (CF) [4] is

Georgios Pitsilis and Lindsay F. Marshall
School of Computing Science, University of Newcastle Upon-Tyne, Newcastle Upon Tyne, NE1 7RU, U.K., e-mail: Georgios.Pitsilis@ncl.ac.uk

Please use the following format when citing this chapter:

Pitsilis, G. and Marshall, L. F., 2008, in IFIP International Federation for Information Processing, Volume 263; *Trust Management II*; Yücel Karabulut, John Mitchell, Peter Herrmann, Christian Damsgaard Jensen, (Boston: Springer), pp. 103–118.

the most widely known technique used in Recommender systems and is based on the idea of making predictions using similarity metrics to correlate users.

However, *Recommender Systems* and particularly *Collaborative Filtering* are not perfect and as it is well known that they appear to have weaknesses such as a low quality of predictions (known as the *false negatives* and *false positives* problems [5]), caused by sparsity in the dataset. Also, the architectural characteristics of CF are known to be vulnerable to attacks from malicious and libelous users. CF systems employ statistical techniques to develop virtual relationships between users, and in this way, neighborhoods of users can be formed consisting of those who have a history of agreeing and who are thus assumed to be similar. The virtual relationships are built upon a metric that is used for correlating the users based on their experiences and is called *Similarity*. In order to know how similar two users are with each other, a number of common experiences must exist.

Trust has been investigated by many researchers of recommender systems in the past [23] and proposed also as a potential solution to alleviate the previously mentioned problems of recommender systems [6,7]. Trust can also express integrity in relationships between entities and so can be used to express the quality of service providers. So, service consumers should be able to assess reliably the quality of services before they decide to depend on a particular instance. In order to know the trustworthiness of a service provider evidence needs to be provided to potential consumers from which they can derive their own trust for the provider.

Under appropriate circumstances (with regard to a common purpose), trust relationships can also support transitivity [8] whereas similarity generally does not. In order to benefit from the special characteristics of trust such as the ability to propagate along chains of trusted users, a formula for deriving it from similarity and vice versa is needed. In this way user entities that cannot be correlated due to lack of common experiences can benefit from each other and thus extend the quantity and/or the quality of predictions they can make about their future choices. Our contribution to this research problem is the provision of appropriate formulas that can be used for converting trust to similarity.

The rest of the paper is organized as follows. In the next section, there is a more detailed description of the problem. Section 3 includes related work in the field and in section 4 we analyze our approach to the problem, showing the formulas we have introduced. Next in section 5 we present the evaluation we performed and some comparative results which show the best candidate. Finally, in section 6 we discuss some future issues concerning the applicability of the proposed method.

2   Motivation

The main idea of collaborative filtering is to make predictions of scores based on the heuristic that two people who agreed (or disagreed) in the past will probably agree (disagree) again. A typical collaborative filtering system runs as a centralized service and the information it holds can be represented by a matrix of users and items. Each value of the matrix represents the score that a particular user has given to some item. The number of empty cells is known as sparsity and as we mentioned in the previous section, it is the main reason that recommender systems behave poorly, because not much evidence can be gathered to support a recommendation. This is usually because users themselves are unwilling to invest much time or effort in rating items. In existing CF systems users can only be correlated through their common experiences, so in the presence of limited data they turn out to be unable to make accurate predictions. The idea to enhance the neighboring base of users, by using the potentially developed trust relationships between them, could make it possible to reach other members of the community through them.

Assuming that the potential trust between the users could help in reducing the number of empty cells in the matrix by allowing missing values to be predicted from existing ones, finding a way of computing that trust from the existing data (user experiences) might help to alleviate the problem.

For such an idea to be applicable, it is necessary that, somehow, users must be able to place trust on their neighbors. In some centralized consumer opinion sites [1] it is a requirement that this trust measure should be provided by the users themselves. However, this requires that users should have developed some instinct in judging things accurately, and this cannot be assured. Poor judging abilities introduce the danger of establishing relationships with wrong counterparts. Our approach to this issue is to introduce a technique for mapping between similarity measures and trust, and which will be done automatically on behalf of the users.

In our model we use ordinary measures of similarity taken from CF to form the potential trust between the correlated entities which would be propagated in a similar way to the word-of-mouth scheme. In that scheme the trust that the first entity should place on the distant one is derived through a trust graph. Finally, by transforming the value back into similarity measure terms it could be made appropriate for use in CF algorithms. However, to our knowledge, today there is no standard approach for modeling trust from such type of existing evidence. In this work as well as in a previous one [9] we express trust in the form of opinions as they are modeled in *Subjective Logic* [10]. In this theory *trust* is considered as a subjective measure and introduces the important idea that there is always imperfect knowledge when judging things. The latter is expressed with a notion called *uncertainty* and is present when trust is based on user observations. Another interesting point of subjective logic is that it provides an algebra for combining *direct* and *indirect* trust along chains of users. *Direct* trust is considered the trust that is built upon first hand evidence or else derived from experience with the trustee. *Indirect* trust is built upon recommendations from others when first hand evidence is not present.

The use of trust in transitive chains requires the existence of a common purpose [8] which needs recommender trust to be derived or given from a specific transitive chain. This has either to be modeled from relevant evidence or, somehow, trustors must be enabled to derive it from past experiences.

Our work in this paper is concerned with the construction of trust relationships using first hand evidence, which in our case is the users' ratings. More specifically we try various similarity-to-trust transformation formulas with the purpose of finding the most suitable one. In the future we aim to evaluate the accuracy of a whole recommender system that employs the proposed transformation formula.

3   Background Research

Trust has long been a concern for scientists and much work has been done to formalize it in computing environments [11,12]. As well as being context specific, it has important characteristics such as asymmetry, subjectivity, and under specific circumstances, transitivity. It is also related to tasks in the sense that entities are trusted to perform a particular task. A simplistic approach would be to determine the levels of trust and distrust that should be placed on some entity from its probabilistic behavior as seen from trustor's point of view. In this sense, trust can be thought of as the level of belief established between two entities in relation to a certain context. In uncertain probabilities theory [13] the metric which expresses the belief is called *opinion*. Because there is always imperfect knowledge as opinions are based on observations, lack of knowledge should be considered when assessing them. *Subjective Logic* framework deals with the absence of both trust and distrust by introducing the *uncertainty* property in opinions. This framework uses a simple intuitive representation of uncertain probabilities by using a three dimensional metric that comprises belief (b), disbelief (d) and uncertainty (u). Between *b,d* and *u* the following equation holds b+d+u=1 which is known as the *Belief Function Additivity Theorem*. Building up opinions requires the existence of evidence, but even though opinions in the form (b,d,u) are better manageable due to the quite flexible calculus that opinion space provides, evidence is usually available only in other forms, that are essentially more understandable to humans.

Having this in mind, we could use the ratings given by the users as evidence, also called behavioral data, for forming trust relationships between them in a CF system. The *Beta Distribution Probability Function* can offer an alternative representation of uncertain probabilities [14], making it possible to approximate opinions from behavioral data. However, data in that evidence space are considered as sets of observations and therefore must be provided strictly in binary form representing the possible two outcomes of a process, x or $\bar{x}$. So, a behavior is described by the number of x and $\bar{x}$ that derives from the set of observations. In [10] there is a mapping between Evidence Spaces and Opinion Spaces where the uncertainty property (u) is solely dependent on the quantity of observations. In contrast, other similarity based approaches such as that in [15] are based on the idea of linking users indirectly using predictability measures, but, to our knowledge, these have not been tested in real environments.

As we mentioned above, the requirement for trust to become transitive in long chains is that a common purpose exists along the chain. According to this, only the last relationship should be concerned with trust for a certain purpose and all the other trust relationships in the chain should be with respect to the ability to recommend for the given purpose. The former is called *functional* trust and the latter *recommender* trust. It is worth mentioning the existence of other approaches to making recommender systems trust-enabled such as [16] where there is no distinction between functional and recommender trust. Also in some other solutions [17] that are used for predicting scores in recommender systems using webs of trust, the notion of trust is confused with similarity even though they are essentially different. Subjective logic provides a useful algebra for calculating trust in long chains of neighbors but it requires that opinions be expressed in (b,d,u) format which existing modeling techniques are not suitable to handle. This is because existing solutions for encoding trust either deal with data in an unsuitable form (see [14] beta pdf) or do not provide links to similarity. In our opinion it is not appropriate for users to be asked to provide trust measures for others, mainly because this requires skills and adequate experience that not all users have.

4   Our Approaches

In general, trust models are used to enable the parties involved in a trust relationship to know how much reliance to place on each other. Our model aims to provide a method for estimating how much trust two entities can place in each other, given the similarities between them.

The problem that emerges when Trust is to be used in a recommender system is the fact that the entities involved usually provide their views in the form of ratings about items and not as their trust estimates about other entities. That means, to benefit from such model it is required that all user ratings be transformed into trust values. We are contributing to solving this issue by proposing and comparing various formulas for encoding direct trust. The first formula we propose in paragraph 4.1 has already been used in an experimental P2P recommender system which has been studied in [18]. The other new modeling approaches we propose are extensions of the same idea. The significant difference, though, between the existing and the new approaches is found in the way we model the uncertainty property. In all the new approaches we keep the main method of modeling uncertainty the same but we change the way that the remaining properties (belief and disbelief) are shaped.

4.1   The existing approach

Unlike the other modeling concepts we discussed above, such as beta pdf modeling, in our first approach we use both quantitative and qualitative criteria on the evidence to derive uncertainty. In order to achieve this, we consider the ratings that users have given to items as the behavioral data required for the composition of opinions. In order to capture this requirement in our model we assume that the level of trust that develops between every pair of entities is based on how similar they perceive each other's choices to be. We used the *Pearson* coefficient, as this is the best known and most suitable coefficient for this type of application. It can take values between -1 and 1 where two entities are considered as having higher similarity when their Pearson values are close to 1 and as completely dissimilar when the Pearson Coefficient is -1. A value of 0 would mean that there is no relationship between the two entities at all. Bearing in mind the idea that those entities whose ratings can be accurately predicted should be considered as trustworthy sources of information, the uncertainty in such relationships should be lower.

Thus, in this approach we have re-defined the perception of *Uncertainty* as the inability of some entity to make accurate predictions about the choices of the other counterpart in the relationship. A low ability value should result from the existence of conflicting data and this should make the observer unable to fill in the uncertainty gap. When there are not enough observations to distinguish rating trends data might appear to be highly conflicting.

We propose the following formula to model uncertainty from prediction error:

$$u = \frac{1}{k} \sum_{x=1}^{k} \frac{|p_x - r_x|}{m} \qquad (4.1)$$

where k is the number of common experiences (ratings) of the two entities that form a relationship, p_x is the predicted rating of item x calculated using some prediction calculation formula and r_x is the real rate that the entity has given to item x. m represents the maximum value that a rating can take and it is used here as a measure of rating. As can be seen, uncertainty is inversely proportional to the number of experiences. This agrees with the definition of uncertainty we presented in the previous section.

The logical reasoning for deriving formula (4.1) for Uncertainty is the following: Uncertainty is proportional to the prediction error for every user's single experience; therefore the numerator represents the absolute error between the predicted value (using a rating prediction formula) and the real (rated) value. The denominator m has been used for normalizing the error to the range 0-1. The summing symbol has been used to include all the experiences (k in number) of a particular user. Finally, the division by the total number of experiences (k) is done to get the average normalized error. In the sum we take every pair of common ratings and try to predict what the rate p would be. Therefore it is assumed that on every prediction calculation all but the real rating of the value that is to be predicted exist.

Unlike Beta mapping [14] where u tends to 0 as the number of experiences grows, in our model the trend remains quite uncertain because u is also dependent on the average prediction error. In the extreme case where there is high controversy in the data, u will reach a value close to 1, leaving a small space for belief and disbelief. Another interesting characteristic of our model is the asymmetry in the trust relationships produced, which adheres to the natural form of relationships since the levels of trust that two entities place on each other may not be necessarily the same.

As regards the other two properties b (belief) and d (disbelief), we set them up in such a way that they are dependent on the value of the Correlation Coefficient CC. We made the following two assumptions:
• The belief (disbelief) property reaches its maximum value (1-u) when CC=1 (or CC=-1 respectively)
• The belief (disbelief) property reaches its minimum value (1-u) when CC= -1 (or CC=1 respectively)
which are expressed by the two formulae:

$$b = \frac{(1-u)}{2}(1 + CC) \qquad (4.2)$$

$$d = \frac{(1-u)}{2}(1 - CC) \qquad (4.3)$$

As can be seen, the ratio of belief and disbelief is shaped by the CC value. In this way, a positive Correlation Coefficient would be expected to strengthen the belief property at the expense of disbelief. In the same way, disbelief appears to be stronger than belief between entities that are negatively correlated (CC<0).

These two formulae can be used in the opposite way too: for estimating how similar the two entities should consider each other, given their trust properties. The asymmetry in the trust relationships is mainly responsible for having unequal similarities between the original one and the one derived from the backward application of the formula. The different points of view are responsible for this difference as well as the formula used to work out the predictions p_x in (4.1). The formulas proposed in [15] as well as Resnick's [19] empirical one built for the Grouplens CF system can be used for the calculation of p_x.

As we can see in this proposed model, belief/disbelief increases/decreases linearly with the Correlation Coefficient and in terms of computational complexity, the uncertainty formula is $O(n^2)$. This seems to be a significant drawback to this method because the calculation of uncertainty requires the prediction formula to run for n times which in turn requires the calculation of similarity value k times. This has to be repeated whenever a new score is entered by any of the two parties.

4.2 The new proposed model

Since the above formula is found to be computationally intensive we came up with other less complex alternative formulas for modeling the same notions.

The first thing that we changed was the calculation of uncertainty. In contrast to the old approach, in the new design it is calculated exclusively from the quantity of experiences similarly as is done in the beta pdf mapping in Josang's approach [14]. However, in our new model we propose that every pair of common scores is counted as a different experience and for the uncertainty calculation we use the formula: $u = (n+1)^{-1}$, where n is the number of common scores.

As to *belief* and *disbelief* we tried various associations with CC such as linear, non-linear and circular. Amongst the pros of the alternative formulas is the significantly lower complexity $O(n)$ which means lower calculation time since it is now dependent only on the number of common ratings.

For a linear approach to shaping belief and disbelief the formulae used should be the same as before in the original model expressed in (4.2) and (4.3). For non-linear approaches we tried equations which are shown as figures of various skewnesses. The belief property alternatives are expressed in table 1. To save space, the formulas from which disbelief (d) is derived are not presented but for all cases d is considered as the remainder since d = 1 − b − u and it is symmetric to belief.

In addition to the two assumptions we made for the linear mapping shown in the previous paragraph, we included a third which is:

• A zero correlation coefficient (CC=0) should mean that belief equals disbelief.

Next, in Table 1 we present all formulas we came up with for shaping the b property and conform with the 3 assumptions we made.

1.
$$b = \frac{1}{2}\left(\sin(CC \cdot \frac{\pi}{2}) + 1 \right) \cdot (1 - u) \qquad (4.4)$$

2.
$$b = \frac{1}{2} + \left(\frac{\arcsin(CC)}{\pi} \right) \cdot (1 - u) \qquad (4.5)$$

3.
$$b = \frac{1}{2}(1 - u)\left(1 + CC^{\frac{1}{K}} \right) \qquad (4.6)$$

4.
$$b = \frac{1}{2}(1 - u)\left(1 + CC^{K} \right) \qquad (4.7)$$

Table 1..The proposed formulas for belief property.

Fig. 1 shows the form of all formulas used for shaping the belief property presented in Table 1, type 1 and 2 as well as for types 3 and 4 for various skewness k. The linear approach that we described in paragraph 4.1 is also shown in Fig.1

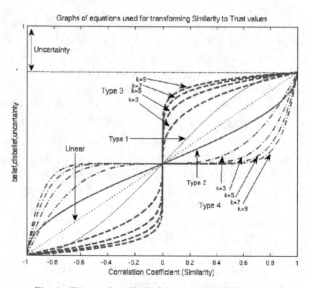

Fig. 1. The graphs of belief property for all formulas

5   Evaluation

When carrying out this experiment we faced the challenge of how to evaluate every alternative formula and what measures to use for comparing the accuracy of our modeling approach. Therefore, we developed and applied the following plan.

5.1   The plan

Since the goal was to test the accuracy of each candidate formula we considered as the best scenario comparing a known and accepted value of similarity against one that is derived by applying our trust derivation mechanism. More specifically, for each pair of users, lets call them A and B, we first calculated how similar they are, applying Pearson's CC formula over the common experiences of A and B, and then we calculated the indirect trust between them. Next, this trust value was converted to a similarity metric using our formula and, finally, the derived value was compared against the original similarity we calculated first. The latter similarity is derived from the resulting indirect trust between A and B when subjective logic rules are applied to the graph built by the trust relationships that exist between A and B. (see figure 2.) In order to accomplish this, the primary trust between every pair of users has to be built pro-actively when making up the trust graph.

Figure 2 is a pictorial representation of the entities involved in the evaluation scheme. We call $S_{A,B}$ the similarity that is derived from the common experiences between A and B, and $S'_{A,B}$ the similarity that is derived from the indirect trust of A for B. In the evaluation we compare these two values and we calculate the mean error.

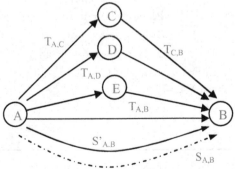

Fig. 2. .The evaluation diagram.

$T_{A,C}$ and $T_{A,D}$ are two of the direct trust values that are used for calculating the indirect (or secondary) trust of A for B.

Due to the fact that Pearson's coefficient has unstable behavior when there is a low number of common experiences between two parties, we considered as similar neighbors those who have at least 10 common experiences and we choose to perform the evaluation test on these pairs of entities as Pearson's similarity is calculable.

To measure the accuracy we calculated the Mean Absolute Error between the directly calculated similarity S and the one derived from the transitive trust S'. We use the following formula in which C_{max} and C_{min} are the maximum/minimum values of the Correlation Coefficient (1 and -1 respectively):

$$MAE = \frac{|S - S'|}{C_{max} - C_{min}} \tag{5.1}$$

The evaluation algorithm can be described in pseudo-code as in fig. 3. Let us call $dt_{i,j}$ the direct trust between entities i and j and $it_{i,j}$ the indirect one. Assuming that j is within 2 hops of i in the constructed trust graph, the indirect trust of i for j can be calculated using subjective logic in two steps: First, the derived trust of every alternative path that begins from i and ends to j is calculated separately as a transitive relationship using the suggestion operator $\otimes$. Then all the values of the alternative paths along with $dT_{i,j}$ are combined together using the consensus operator $\oplus$ which gives the value of $iT_{i,j}$. In general the consensus is expressed in the following formula where A and B are two different agents which hold about the statement p respectively the opinions ω_p^A and ω_p^B.

```
Let K be the set of all users
Let R be the set of all ratings over items
Let Rᵤ ⊂ R be the set of the ratings of some user u
Let Ki ⊂ K : |Rᵤ| ≥ 10        *   Cardinality of set of ratings of user i *
For i in Ki
    Let Eᵢ ⊂ R                 *   The set of ratings of user i  *
    Let M ⊂ Ki : ∀ p ∈ M , Eₚ ⊂ R and |Eᵢ ∩ Eₚ| ≥ 10
    For j in M do              *   p has 10 common ratings with i
        S ← CC(i, j)           *   Pearson's similarity *
        T ← iTrust(i, j)       *   Derived Indirect trust *
        S' ← f(T)              *   Derived Similarity from our formula f *
        MAE ← |S - S'|/(Cmax - Cmin)   * Absolute Mean Error value *
    End For j
End For i
Average(MAE)
```

Fig. 3. The evaluation algorithm

The consensus opinion held by an imaginary agent A,B is:

$$\omega_p^{A,B} = \omega_p^A \oplus \omega_p^B = \{b_p^{A,B}, d_p^{A,B}, u_p^{A,B}\} \tag{5.2}$$

More about this can be found in [20]. In our particular case the statement p is the trustworthiness of the target j. A, B represent the alternative paths from i to j.

The algorithm for calculating the indirect trust between the origin i and the target j is shown in figure 4.

$it_{i,j} \leftarrow dt_{i,l}$	* direct trust is considered *
Let $E_i \subset R$	* the set of ratings of i *
Let $P \subset K_i : \forall f \in P, E_f \subset R$ and $\|E_i \cap E_f\| \geq 10$	
For j in P do	* i has 10 common ratings with f *
$\quad t_{l,j} \leftarrow dt_{l,j}$	
$\quad t_{i,l,j} \leftarrow t_{i,l} \otimes t_{l,j}$	* Serial graph composition *
$\quad it_{i,j} \leftarrow it_{i,j} \oplus t_{i,l,j}$	* Parallel graph composition *
End For j	
Return $it_{i,j}$ as $iTrust$	* return the indirect trust *

Fig. 4. The indirect trust calculation.

The choice for exploring the trust graphs up to maximum distance of 2 hops was made mostly for reasons of simplicity since with a third hop the number of required calculations increases significantly without a corresponding substantial gain in accuracy.

Assuming that the trust transitivity mechanism of Subjective logic is accurate enough then any error measured via our experiment should be considered as error derived from our Similarity-to-Trust transformation formula. In order to evaluate our modeling approach we needed a suitable dataset of user's scores. We chose a publicly available dataset taken from a real CF system known as *MovieLens* [21]. MovieLens is a movie recommendation system based on collaborative filtering established at the University of Minnesota. The available dataset contains 1.000.209 anonymous ratings of approximately 3.900 movies made by 6.040 users who joined the service over the year 2000. For our experiment we used a subset of MovieLens that comprised 130000 ratings which were given by 1000 randomly selected users.

5.2   Comparative Results and Discussion

In our tests, we applied each candidate formula to 10 different data sets and the results were averaged. Each 100 user dataset built trust graphs of approximately 5000 relationships.

First, for each pair of users for which indirect trust is calculable the real and the trust-derived similarity are compared. The results are shown in figure 5. Also interesting to see is the measured correlation between the number of common experiences of i and j and the calculated error. Figure 6.a shows the above result pictorially including each pair of trusted entities.

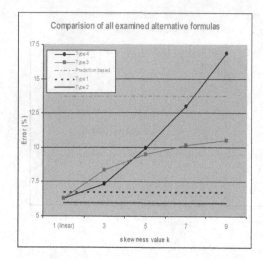

Existing approach		13.71
Type 4	k=1, linear	6.27
Type 4	k=3	7.33
Type 4	k=5	9.96
Type 4	k=7	12.96
Type 4	k=9	16.88
Type 3	k=3	8.34
Type 3	k=5	9.48
Type 3	k=7	10.11
Type 3	k=9	10.49
Type 1	-	6.74
Type 2	-	5.96

Fig. 5. Comparison of the alternative formulas.

Due to space limitations we present only the last candidate formula we tested (Type 2 of table 1) and which appears to give the best results (lowest error) compared to all other candidates. As can be seen from figure 6.a there is a stochastic relationship between the error of the transformation formula applied on pairs of users and the number of common scores of those users. It can also be seen that the maximum error observed is just above 35% as opposed to our first (*Existing*) approach which produced max error 70%. In terms of average error the new formula is better than twice as good. Another interesting, and obvious, observation from the figure is that as the number of common scores increases the error follows the opposite trend. Also, the deviation of the error decreases as the common scores increase. The importance of this observation is that it may have a practical value since it makes it possible to predict how accurately the derived trust will be calculated. Thus, when a recommendation is to be created a decision can be formed about whether or not a particular relationship should be considered in the process of secondary trust calculation. Hence, according to some quality criteria that can be applied, such primary trust relationships that have been built upon 'poor' data can be disclosed as they do not provide adequate contribution in the secondary trust calculation.

In figure 6.b we also show the variance of the similarity prediction error which has the practical meaning of how accurately the trust could be approximated using our model. That could have a practical use: for example it might be used as a criterion for choosing the right threshold value for the minimum number of common scores. In this way, the expected error can be determined according to some quality of service criteria that need to be met when building a web of trust.

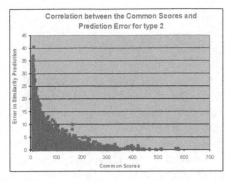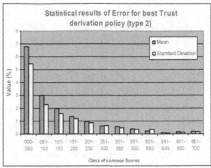

Fig. 6a (left) and **6.b.** (right). Graphical presentation of results.

We also looked to see if there is any correlation between the error of our trust derivation method and the number of common experiences between the two parties and the results show that there is slight correlation when considering linear approximation between error and common experiences. More specifically the correlation value declines as the k factor which expresses the skewness (see fig.1) increases. A more detailed study revealed that the error adapts best to a non-linear approximation. The regression analysis on the results presented in fig.6.a. and are referred to the type 2 equation showed that the best value of Coefficient of Determination (R^2) for the above data had a relatively low value of -0.4135.

The increased divergence that is observed for the error as the number of common scores declines can be justified as the result of the noisy behavior of the Correlation Coefficient; therefore the quality of predictions is quite uncertain. Finally, it worth noticing that we observed higher prediction error when the correlation coefficient was between 0 and -1. This can be interpreted as: prediction is easier when users tastes agree and vice versa, or else the proposed formula is not as useful for disagreeing tastes as it is when users agree. This means that using a unique mapping formula for the whole range of correlation coefficient values is not an ideal solution. Otherwise, the first assumption we have made in which, a similarity value of zero would mean that the trustworthiness with the other party should be the half of which corresponds to similarity value 1, is not absolutely right.

6   Future Work

As shown from a more careful examination of the results, there is high variation in the error in a way that follows different trends as k changes. For example the error that is measured between a certain pair of nodes i and j does not follow the same trend as that of the average. As also shown in figure 6.b and as discussed in the previous paragraph, the varied deviations in the error need a more detailed analysis of the results to see if it will be possible to justify this observation.

For these two reasons it is worth investigating if and how the topological properties of the derived network might be responsible for the variation and if it might be possible to decrease the error even more.

The assumption we have made in our modeling that the value of trustworthiness should correspond to a similarity value of zero seems to be not an optimum choice, therefore more investigation is needed towards finding the optimum fitting. As mentioned in paragraph 4.1 and 4.2 about the complexity of the formulas used, there is a potential problem since these computations need to be repeated for every user in the system. So, whenever a new user joins the system the trust and similarity computations will have to be redone against all existing users. As the system grows the computation time will increase significantly raising a scalability issue. A possible solution to this problem is to restrict the correlation process to a subset of participants rather the whole world. A focus of a future research is to investigate if clustering [22], a technique that is used for tackling a similar problem in recommender systems, can be quite effective here.

We intend to apply our technique to a real recommender system, with the expectation that it will improve the quality of the derived recommendations. Another idea is to make use of the web-of-trust that could evolve from the establishment of direct trust relationships between users. Our aim is to improve recommendations by exploiting the experiences of any entities not neighboring the querying one but which can be reached via the web-of-trust. The question that arises from this is how accurate these predictions can be. Short tests we performed, showed a significant increase in the coverage, which translates into reduced sparsity, without significant impact on the error in predictions. Our short-term plans include a thorough study and analysis of the various parameters that may have some impact on the results as well as a performance analysis of the resulting system. The long-term plans include the deployment of a totally distributed recommender system.

Recommender trust can be derived in a similar way to that described for *functional* trust in this paper. The basic idea is that someone's (lets call it the trustee) recommender trust can be estimated by some other entity (lets call it the trustor) by comparing any recommendations that trustee has provided in the past about statements for which the trustor also maintains its own evidence. Then the trustor, by comparing its relevant personal experiences with the trustee's recommendations, will be able to estimate how good in doing recommendations the trustee has been. Similarly to *direct* trust, *recommender* trust is a subjective measure, which means, every trustor has to maintain its own picture of the community.

No matter the quality of the recommendations such architecture can provide, there are weaknesses concerning security for the recommender systems that must also be covered. In particular, any deployed solution must be resistant to attacks from users that try maliciously to influence the system.

7   Conclusion

We presented an empirical technique for modeling the trustworthiness of entities using evidence that describe their rating behavior. The novelty comes from way that trustworthiness is derived from Similarity using a non-linear mapping.

We coded our derived trust opinions into metrics taken from Shaferian belief theory and we attempted an evaluation of our model by comparing the resulting similarity to that derived from secondary trust.

We also compared the proposed approach against another that has been used in the past and in which the shaping of the derived uncertainty is dependent on a predictability measure and thus on the quality of the evidence. The comparison showed that using qualitative measures for deriving trust not only incur a computation penalty but also provide lower accuracy when compared with less complex approaches for describing the user's behavior.

In conclusion, the strong points of the proposed technique can be summarized as its ability to incorporate similarity measures in its properties, the low computation complexity and its flexibility in accepting datasets in which user ratings are expressed in continuous values. In terms of accuracy in deriving trust opinions, a comparison against the older alternative shows that the new one is more than twice as accurate. We would suggest that the method is very suitable for use in CF recommender systems.

References

1. http://www.epinions.com
2. http://www.ebay.com
3. http://www.amazon.com
4. D.Goldberg, D.Nichols, B.M.Oki, D.Terry, "Using Collaborative filtering to weave an information tapestry", Communication of ACM, 35(12):61-70, 1992
5. B.Sarwar, G.Karypis, J.Konstan, J.Reidl, "Analysis of Recommendation Algorithms for ECommerce", In Proceedings of the Second ACM Conference on Electronic Commerce pg 158-168,ACM Press 2000.
6. M.P. O'Mahony , N.J. Hurley , G.C.M. Silvestre, "Detecting noise in recommender system databases", Proceedings of the 11th international conference on Intelligent user interfaces, January 29-February 01, 2006, Sydney, Australia
7. B. M.Sarwar , J.T.Riedl, "Sparsity, scalability, and distribution in recommender systems," 2001, ISBN:0-493-04207-5, University of Minnesota.
8. A. Jøsang, E. Gray and M. Kinateder. "Analysing Topologies of Transitive Trust", In the proceedings of the Workshop of Formal Aspects of Security and Trust (FAST) 2003, Pisa, September 2003.
9. G.Pitsilis., L.F.Marshall, "A model for trust derivation from evidence for use in recommender systems", Newcastle University, Technical report CS-TR-874, 2004.
10. A.Josang, "A Logic for Uncertain probabilities", International Journal of Uncertainty, fuzziness and Knowledge based systems, Vol.9,No.3, June 2001.
11. S.Marsh, "Formalizing Trust as Computational concept", PhD Thesis, University of Stirling, Scotland 1994.
12. A.Rahman, S.Heiles,"Supporting trust in Virtual Communities", In proceedings of International conference On System Sciences, Jan 4-7-2000, Hawaii.
13. G.Shafer, "A Mathematical Theory of Evidence", Princeton University Press. 1976
14. A. Jøsang, R. Ismail. "The Beta Reputation System". In the proceedings of the 15th Bled Conference on Electronic Commerce, Bled, Slovenia, 17-19 June 2002.
15. C.C.Aggarwal, J.L.Wolf, K.Wu, P.S.Yu,,"Horting Hatches an Egg: A New Graph-theoretic Approach to Collaborative Filtering", In Proceedings of the ACM KDD'99 Conference. San Diego, CA, pp.201-212.
16. P.Massa – P.Avesani, "Trust-aware Collaborative Filtering for recommender Systems", CoopIS/DOA/ODBASE (1) 2004: 492-508

17. M.Papagelis, D.Plexousakis, T.Kutsuras, "Alleviating the Sparsity Problem of Collaborative Filtering using Trust Inferences", In Proceedings of iTrust, pp.224-239, 2005.
18. G.Pitsilis, L.F.Marshal, "Trust as a Key to Improving Recommendation Systems". In Proceedings of iTrust, Paris - France : pp.210-223, 2005
19. P.Resnick, N.Iacovou, M.Suchak, P.Bergstrom, J.Riedl, "Grouplens. An OpenArchitecture for Collaborative filtering of Netnews" In Proceedings of ACM 1994, Conf. On Computer Supported Cooperative.
20. A. Jøsang, "An Algebra for Assessing Trust in Certification Chains", In Proceedings of the Network and Distributed Systems Security (NDSS'99) Symposium, Internet Society, 1999
21. B.N.Miller,I.Albert, S.K.Lam, J.A. Konstan, J.Riedl, "MovieLens Unplugged: Experiences with an Occasionally Connected Recommender System",.In Proceedings of ACM 2003 International Conference on Intelligent User Interfaces (IUI'03) (Poster), January 2003.
22. B.M.Sarwar, G.Karypis, J.Konstan, J.Riedl, "Recommender Systems for Large-Scale E-Commerce: Scalable Neighborhood Formation Using Clustering",In Proceedings of the Fifth International Conference on Computer and Information Technology, December 2002, East West University, Bangladesh.
23. J. O'Donovan , B. Smyth,"Trust in recommender systems", Proceedings of the 10th international conference on Intelligent user interfaces, January 10-13, 2005, San Diego, USA

Trust-Based Collaborative Filtering

Neal Lathia, Stephen Hailes, Licia Capra

Abstract k-nearest neighbour (kNN) collaborative filtering (CF), the widely successful algorithm supporting recommender systems, attempts to relieve the problem of information overload by generating predicted ratings for items users have not expressed their opinions about; to do so, each predicted rating is computed based on ratings given by like-minded individuals. Like-mindedness, or similarity-based recommendation, is the cause of a variety of problems that plague recommender systems. An alternative view of the problem, based on trust, offers the potential to address many of the previous limiations in CF. In this work we present a varation of kNN, the trusted k-nearest recommenders (or kNR) algorithm, which allows users to learn who and how much to trust one another by evaluating the utility of the rating information they receive. This method redefines the way CF is performed, and while avoiding some of the pitfalls that similarity-based CF is prone to, outperforms the basic similarity-based methods in terms of prediction accuracy.

1 Introduction

Over the last decade, recommender systems have had a rising presence on the web, transitioning from novelty components of e-commerce portals to become focal points of many web services. Implemented throughout e-commerce, movie and music profiling web sites, the goal of recommender systems is the flipside of classical information retrieval; these systems aim to present users with interesting content based on their historical behaviour, rather than answering a specific query. Collaborative Filtering [1], or CF, has emerged as the dominant algorithm behind recommender systems, and, as the name describes, it uses the collaborative effort of an entire community of users to help each individual sift through the endless amounts

Neal Lathia, Stephen Hailes, Licia Capra
Department of Computer Science, University College London, London WC1E 6BT, UK
e-mail: n.lathia, s.hailes, l.capra @cs.ucl.ac.uk

Please use the following format when citing this chapter:

Lathia, N., Hailes, S. and Capra, L., 2008, in IFIP International Federation for Information Processing, Volume 263; *Trust Management II*; Yücel Karabulut, John Mitchell, Peter Herrmann, Christian Damsgaard Jensen; (Boston: Springer), pp. 119–134.

of online content. The current assumptions of CF are that historically like-minded individuals will also share similar tastes in the future. Measuring similarity plays a central role; only the top-k most similar users are allowed to contribute their ratings, and each contribution is weighted according to the specific degree of similarity the neighbour shares with the current user.

Grounding the prediction engine of CF algorithms in similarity measures hides a number of pitfalls, which stem from the fact that user profiles are incredibly sparse and limited in breadth. When users have no profile, there is no way to measure their similarity to anyone else's; the *cold-start* problem arises and no predictions can be made for the user. When users do have a profile, the neighbours they are assigned often cannot provide information about new items of interest; prediction *coverage* problems appear. Lastly, users look to recommender systems to provide both useful and *serendipitous* (or "surprising") results, and although this is a very difficult quality to measure in an algorithm, the lack of this property finds its provenance in locking measurably similar users together. These three problems originate from the fact that user profiles are incredibly sparse. The set of items that a user has rated, and hence expressed an opinion about varies in size from one user to the next. Based on the ratings each user has provided and the varying degrees of overlap between user profiles, we are currently unable to know exactly which other users would be perfect recommenders. Since CF systems hold a highly incomplete picture of the participating users they need to deal with an immense amount of uncertainty, and the current similarity-based methods often fall short of the desired performance.

An alternative view of CF systems, based on trust, has the potential to address many of the problems outline above. As detailed in [2], trust has been applied to a wide range of scenarios, including (but not limited to) *access* problems, or deciding who should be trusted to access content or services [3], problems involving *sanctioning*, or punishing network nodes that misbehave in a given context [4], and *signaling*: or helping users decide whether to access a resource or not. The last problem is surprisingly similar to problem the CF aims to solve. Descriptions of information overload [5] tell us that there is simply too much content for users to find all the items that they will like, and recommender systems alleviate this problem by helping each user decide which content to access. However, trust broadens the limited view of similarity to encompass a wider range of characteristics; we define recommenders to be *trustworthy* if they are consistent sources of valuable information, which can be appropriately interpreted when predicting how much a user will rate an item. We therefore propose to tackle the problem of information overload as a trust-management problem, and introduce and evaluate the following:

- **Selecting Neighbours Based on Trust**: neighbour selection based on profile similarity is replaced by a utilitarian evaluation of the *value* that each user provides to others, and trust is awarded accordingly, as described in Section 2.1. In particular,
- **Lack of Information is Informative**: our method awards varying degrees of trust to all those who were potential recommenders for each item a user rates, and downgrades trust scores for users who could not provide any information. In

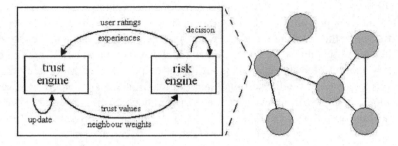

Fig. 1 A Trust Principal in a Web of Trust

other words, the presence (or lack) of information is used when computing trust values.

- **Retrieve Ratings from Recommenders, Not Neighbourhoods**: Limiting users to a top-k neighbourhood damages the prediction coverage that is possible. We propose to operate according to a top-k recommenders, or users who have the required information to make a prediction, in Section 2.2.
- **Divergent Ratings can be Useful**. The fact that two users completely disagree in their ratings does not imply that this information cannot be successfully used: an appropriate *interpretation* is required, as we discuss in Section 2.3.

2 Filtering as a Trust Problem

Can we use the properties of trust systems to address the difficulties faced by recommender systems? To answer this question, we need to understand how a trust system works, and then explore whether the methods it describes are applicable to CF or not. A trust system is a network of interacting peers, or trust *principals* [2]. Formal models of trust often divide the process of building a trust relationship with another entity into an interaction between two internal components, as we have depicted in Figure 1. The first is the *risk engine*, a component that decides whether to enter into a transaction with the entity or not. Assuming that it does enter into this transaction, then the risk engine will observe the results, and report these observations to the *trust engine*. The trust engine evaluates the interaction, and updates its trust in that entity according to rules defined in a trust policy. Each principal has a subjective view of the environment around it, and the entire community of principals forms a web of trust.

In CF, each user can be described as a trust principal, which needs to decide what content to access. To do so, the risk engine needs to decide whether to recommend an item to the end user, by generating predicted ratings. Each predicted rating is computed by collecting rating information from a subset of the other principals in the system. Which principals should be selected? Here the risk engine queries the trust engine, which maintains and updates a table of trusted peers. Traditional CF dictates that only provably similar neighbours should be considered, and the rest disregarded. Once the actual rating is received from the end user, the actual experience with the content is known, and the trust principal can look back on the prediction it made to not only see if it was correct, but if it also appropriately weighted the contributions it received from the surrounding principals, and can update its trust values accordingly. A CF environment, where a decision mechanism is needed in order to *select* an appropriate subset of users to act as recommenders, therefore, can be described as an instance of a trust based system. If CF is considered as an instance of a trust-management problem, the reverse approach can be adopted; we begin from the perspective of a trust-management system and construct a CF algorithm, by describing the operation of each component of the trust principal.

2.1 The Trust Engine

The first decision that must be made in a CF system is who to interact with; each user needs a defined neighbourhood of recommenders. This step is supported by the assumption that collecting information from everybody (and basing predictions on item *reputations*) will not be as useful as only aggregating the information from the "appropriate" sources; and thus involves deciding who these appropriate users will be. Traditionally, a user's neighbourhood has been populated with the top-k most similar users in the system. To do so, the common ratings in two user's profiles, r_a and r_b, are compared to each other, using measures such as the Pearson Correlation Coeffiecient [6]:

$$w_{a,b} = \frac{\Sigma_{i=1}^{N}(r_{a,i} - \bar{r}_a)(r_{b,i} - \bar{r}_b)}{\sqrt{\Sigma_{i=1}^{N}(r_{a,i} - \bar{r}_a)^2 \Sigma_{i=1}^{N}(r_{b,i} - \bar{r}_b)^2}} \quad (1)$$

The similarity $w_{a,b}$ between users a and b is computed as the degree of linearity between the ratings. Many other similarity measures have been proposed [1, 7], yet they all share the same characteristic; they rely on a non-empty intersection between two user's profiles in order to find a measure of similarity, and only measure similarity using co-rated items. This assumption is the primary cause for the cold-start problem (since users may have no historical profile), and can lead to poor prediction coverage (as the only rating information for certain items may belong to recommenders with zero-similarity). It also has been shown that the various similarity measures tend to disagree with one another; there is no way of finding the optimal method [8]. What we propose is a new method based on trust.

Transferring the current idea of CF into a trust based context means "I trust the best k users who can show that they have similar opinions to my own, and I do not trust anyone else." However, the broader approach put forward by trust management research, is also worthy of exploration. The equivalent quote would be "I trust the users who I have had a positive experience with, and *do not know* how much to trust the rest." This quote introduces two new important concepts, which may offer an escape route from the pitfalls of CF algorithms:

- **Uncertainty**: Users should not necessarily be excluded from contributing to one another's predicted ratings if they have no measurable value of similarity. They can still be sources of serendipitous and valuable information, if there is a means of dealing with the uncertainty.
- **Value**: Being the optimal recommender is not simply a matter of high similarity, but can be described according to two further qualities. The best neighbours will have the information necessary to participate in the user's predicted ratings and positively influence the predicted rating towards the opinion that the user will provide. In other words, the neighbour's opinion should be heavily weighted in the user's predictions, and thus similarity will be an emergent property of the trust relationship, rather than being the cause of it.

When the user a enters a rating $r_{a,i}$ for an item i, the system examines all the rating information available for item i, and asks; how much *should* the user have trusted each of these recommenders? If we were considering this problem from the perspective of a user-item rating matrix, this process would iterate over item i's column, and for each row (i.e. recommender) b make a utilitarian evaluation of the entry compared to the user's rating r:

$$value(a,b,i) = \frac{-1}{5}|r_{a,i} - r_{b,i}| + 1 \qquad (2)$$

If the recommender b has not rated item i, a trust score of 0 is returned. The equation, which assumes a five-star rating scale, awards the highest trust to users who rated the item exactly as the user did. As the distance between the user's rating and the recommender's rating increases, trust decreases linearly. However, if a recommender b has rated the item, the trust score will be positive, even if the recommender's rating was the complete opposite of the user's. This captures the fact that even if $r_{a,i}$ was $1*$, and $r_{b,i}$ was $5*$ (so the absolute difference between the ratings is 4), the recommender b was able to provide a with information regarding i, even if the opinion was very distant to a's. A measure of value, therefore, departs significantly from similarity measures by awarding discordant ratings. The computed value is used to update the trust for recommender b, which is an average of the value contributed over all the n historical ratings:

$$trust(a,b,n) = \frac{\sum_{i=0}^{n} value(a,b,i)}{n} \qquad (3)$$

The idea is to reward recommenders who can provide information, varying the reward according to the perceived quality of the information, and to downgrade recommenders who do not have any information available. The trust values that are assigned to other users in this system will range from 0 to $+1$. Similarity measures, on the other hand, range from -1 to $+1$; we therefore disregard the concept of dissimilarity or distrust [9], in favour of rewarding sources of information. The reward scheme we implemented is a linear function based on the absolute distance between the user's and recommender's ratings. We could have also implemented value functions with higher degrees, such that the amount of trust rewarded falls at a sharper rate as the distance increases. In this work, for the sake of simplicity and the encouraging results we obtain, we focus only on the linear case. Structuring the selection of neighbours based on learned trust has the added benefit that it need not be fully recomputed every time that a system update is performed; much like other learning algorithms [10], trust is learned incrementally as the user inputs more ratings.

Users are no longer weighted according to how like-minded they are, but will be weighted according to the quality of the information that they exchange with each other. Since the amount of information that a user provides to others may vary from how much information that user receives, weightings between user pairs are no longer guaranteed to be symmetrical. Furthermore, based on each users' initial disposition to trust the other nodes around it, users will no longer ignore the potentially useful information they receive from neighbors they have never interacted with, or a neighbor that they bear zero similarity to. Rating information will be weighted according to trust, a value that will reflect a history of interactions rather than a history of similar ratings.

2.2 Finding Opinions: k-Nearest Recommenders

Once the ranking of neighbours is complete, and trust values have been assigned to all users, a second decision must be made: CF needs to determine what neighbours will be acceptable sources of information. There are a variety of methods that can be implemented, which we define here:

- **Threshold-based**: All neighbours with weights above a pre-determind threshold are potential recommenders. Selecting such a threshold is a difficult decision, since it is dependent on the distribution of weights over the community [8], and hence is also dependent on the method that is used to rank neighbours.
- **k-Nearest Neighbours**: Traditional CF operates by limiting interactions to the top-k neighbours. The limitations are two-fold: on the one hand the user can have no more than k neighbours; on the other the algorithm only works if the user shares a measurable degree of similarity with these neighbours. If this is not the case, neighbours are assigned a zero-weighting, and any contribution from them is disregarded. Each user's neighbourhood can therefore be considered a *static* group of users, which may only change when the system is updated.
- **k-Nearest Recommenders**: A further change we introduce is a slight modification to kNN, by allowing users to search for the top-k neighbours who can actually provide information about the item that requires a predicted rating. Ranking the users is a job for the trust engine, but in order to maximise coverage we look to those who can provide information when making a prediction; a method we define as the k-nearest recommender, or kNR, strategy. Unlike kNN, each user's neighbourhood will be dynamic, and the selection of neighbours will be guided by the item that a prediction is being made for.

2.3 The Risk Engine

Now that we have outlined how the trust engine works, we have a means of selecting and updating each user's neighbourhood. This neighbourhood defines the breadth and quality of information that is available to generate predicted ratings for each user, and will hopefully be populated with neighbours who are good sources of valuable information, as we have constructed above. We now require a means of combining, or aggregating, the information that a user receives from his neighbours in order to generate a predicted rating. The predicted rating will determine whether the item should be recommended to the end user or not, and thus the aim is to minimise the *risk* of accessing (or even being recommended) uninteresting items. Traditional CF defines this task as a job for the prediction engine [6], we however chose to align our terminology with trust management research [2] and call it a risk engine. The role of this component will be to select the top-k neighbours $N(a,i)$ of user a who have rated the item i we want to make a prediction about, and can combine the ratings with trust values in one of two ways:

$$p_{a,i} = \frac{\Sigma_{b \in N(a,i)} r_{b,i} \times w_{a,b}}{\Sigma_{b \in N(a,i)} w_{a,b}} \qquad (4)$$

This equation simply takes a weighted average of each neighbours rating, and has been used widely [11]. The second method converts each neighbours rating into an *opinion*, by seeing how much it deviates from that neighbour's mean rating, and can thus derive a predicted rating for a user that is centred around that user's mean, by taking a weighted average of neighbour opinions [6]:

$$p_{a,i} = \bar{r}_a + \frac{\Sigma_{b \in N(a,i)} (r_{b,i} - \bar{r}_b) \times w_{a,b}}{\Sigma_{b \in N(a,i)} w_{a,b}} \qquad (5)$$

Both of these equations share a common assumption: they assume that the people who are rating items share a common interpretation of the rating scale, and thus two users who have input different valued ratings disagree with each other. Rating items, however, is a human activity, and is only guided by descriptive adjectives of what each value should represent (1 = poor, 5 = excellent). Each user of a recommender system can and will interpret these adjectives differently, and form their own mental model of the rating scale, to then use it subjectively, even if in general their opinions may tend to agree. We therefore introduce an additional characteristic of a trust-relationship: learning to interpret the opinion that we receive from a recommender. This idea has previously only been applied to trust management systems, by finding the *semantic distance* between a recommendation and one's own opinion [12]. The interpretation will serve to boost the prediction accuracy of Equations 4 and 5, and is best demonstrated by introducing an example. Our example uses actual rating information of two individuals in the MovieLens[1] movie rating dataset, collected by the GroupLens team at the University of Minnesota. The dataset consists of 100,000

---

[1] http://www.grouplens.org/

	1*	2*	3*	4*	5*
1*	0	0	0	0	0
2*	0	0	0	2	0
3*	0	0	0	3	3
4*	0	0	0	3	1
5*	0	0	1	6	3

	Lower	Same	Higher	Transpose
1*	0	0	0	1.00
2*	0	0	0	2.00
3*	0	0	1	4.00
4*	5	3	6	4.07
5*	4	3	0	4.43

Table 1 Two-Way Contingency Table   **Table 2** Interpreting Bob's Ratings

ratings, from 943 users on 1682 movies. Each user has rated at least 20 movies, using a five-star rating scale. The dataset has been subdivided into five disjoint training/test sets ($u1$, $u2$, ... $u5$), in order to use the training sets to set any necessary values (such as finding similarity measures), measure the predictive power of a CF method on the test set, and perform five-fold cross validation of experimental results.

2.3.1 An Example

Let us consider two users from the MovieLens $u1$ subset, the users with ids 1 and 10, who we respectively rename Alice and Bob. A quick look at their training set profiles shows that Alice has rated 135 items, and Bob has rated 94 items. The overlap, or number of co-rated items, between the two profiles, has size 22. For the sake of simplicity, let us assume that predictions for unrated items will be done with a single recommender (i.e. $k = 1$), and that the underlying neighbourhood selection procedure has determined that Bob is the best recommender for Alice. We can therefore proceed to make predictions of the items in Alice's test set, using the opinions expressed in Bob's profile.

The first point we can observe is that the overlap between Alice's test set and her recommender's training set has size 18. Therefore, we can only make predictions on 18 of her 137 test items, and so the coverage we achieve will be around 13%. Since we are using a single recommender, the amount that we weight Bob's opinions is unimportant; we simply go ahead and make 18 predictions, and only collect error measures from these items. In other words, in this case we are only interested in how well we perform when we can make a prediction, and disregard all uncovered items from the accuracy error measure.

If the predictions are made with Equation 4, the achieved mean absolute error (MAE) between the predictions and actual ratings is 0.888, while if we use the opinion-based Equation 5, we do slightly worse with a MAE of 0.948. However, both methods assume that Alice and Bob are using their rating scales in the same way. In other words, if both Alice and Bob agreed about the quality of a movie, they would both give it the same rating, and therefore the main task of CF algorithms becomes that of finding two users who not only rate the same items, but rate them in the exact same way as well. However, Alice and Bob may be using the rating scale differently from one another. Therefore, Alice's "excellent" rating may be equivalent to Bob's "great," and in the same way Bob's "very poor" (1 star) may be Alice's "poor" (2 stars). In general, they tend to agree about the items they rate, but the error remains high due to the misalignment between their use of the rating scale.

We can visualise the extent to which Alice and Bob's opinions diverge from one another by combining their ratings into a two-way contingency table, as shown in Table 1. Each entry in the table corresponds to the frequency that Alice and Bob gave a particular rating; a 6 in the last cell from the right of the bottom row tells us that on 6 separate occasions Bob's recommendation was 5 stars, and Alice's rating was 4 stars.

This table highlights a number of characteristics, such as the fact that Alice's training ratings are never lower than 3 stars, reflecting the positive skew of rating distributions that is common to CF datasets. This approach has been used to determine the extent to which two movie raters agree in their opinions [13], yet in this work we use it to interpret the information that we receive from a recommender. In fact, Table 2.3 can be reduced to a 5×3 table recording the experiences that Alice has compared to Bob's recommendations, and Alice can learn to transpose the ratings she receives from Bob in order to correctly interpret, or transpose, them based on the experiences she has shared with him.

The transpose of a recommender's rating is found by computing a weighted mean of the experiences shared with the recommender when receiving that rating. For example, when Alice receives a 5 star recommendation from Bob, she knows that of the seven times she received 5 stars from him before, four of those times her opinion was slightly less than 5. She thus interprets 5 stars from Bob as 4.43 stars on her own scale, as shown in Table 2. This is described by the following formula:

$$transpose(r) = \frac{(r - 1 \times lower_r) + (r \times same_r) + (r + 1 \times higher_r)}{lower_r + same_r + higher_r} \qquad (6)$$

For the ratings that have no recorded historical experience the transpose remains the same as the rating. When a rating can be transposed, however, it replaces the actual rating in Equations 4 and 5. In other words, we learn to interpret the opinions we receive from recommenders as we interact with them. If we recompute the predictions on Alice's test set using Equation 4 and Bob's transposed ratings, the error in the predicted ratings falls from 0.888 to 0.710, while if we use Equation 5, the mean absolute error is reduced from 0.948 to 0.791. In other words, in this toy example, we were able to improve the recommendation accuracy of the items we could make predictions on by including the *interpretation* of the neighbour's rating into the trust relationship. Using these ideas, we can now perform a full scale evaluation on the entire MovieLens dataset.

3 Evaluation

To evaluate the performance of our method, we used the MovieLens dataset, the same dataset we used in Section 2.3.1. In this paper, we report the full results from the $u1$ subset and provide summarised results from the rest of the subsets.

	Trust-Learning		Weighted-PCC		Co-rated Proportion	
Neighbours	X-MAE	Covered (%)	X-MAE	Covered (%)	X-MAE	Covered (%)
1	0.8705	99.84	0.8723	45.44	0.9164	38.45
2	0.8226	99.84	0.8513	63.18	0.8946	54.02
5	0.7913	99.84	0.8195	81.32	0.8464	74.28
10	0.7821	99.84	0.7906	90.42	0.8139	85.24
30	0.7791	99.84	0.7565	96.80	0.7781	94.77
50	0.7794	99.84	0.7476	97.94	0.7673	97.02
100	0.7804	99.84	0.7434	99.0	0.7590	98.65

Table 3 MovieLens u1 XMAE and Coverage Results

	Trust-Learning		Weighted-PCC		Co-rated Proportion	
Dataset	X-MAE	Covered (%)	X-MAE	Covered (%)	X-MAE	Covered (%)
u1	0.7916	99.84	0.8195	81.32	0.8464	74.28
u2	0.7793	99.82	0.8159	79.16	0.8380	76.58
u3	0.7729	99.82	0.8158	79.84	0.8488	77.04
u4	0.7717	99.87	0.8247	80.24	0.8399	76.68
u5	0.7752	99.82	0.8263	81.52	0.8461	74.26
Average	0.7781	99.83	0.8204	80.42	0.8438	75.77

Table 4 MovieLens Subset Results, $k = 5$

One of the major problems concerning the evaluation of CF systems is the power of the error measures used; the primary focus of research to date is to achieve the highest possible mean accuracy. The primary error measures have therefore been the MAE, as used in the above example, and the root mean squared error (RMSE). In this work we collect error measures exclusively on the items that we can make predictions for, as we did in Section 2.3.1. We call this error exclusive-MAE, or X-MAE, values. This error measure must go hand in hand with coverage statistics, and thus leaves the trade-off decision between coverage and accuracy to those implementing recommender systems. The results are shown in Tables 3 and 4.

We compare the performance of our method to two similarity measures: the weighted-PCC in the second column, and the proportion of co-rated items in the third, which have both demonstrated to be accurate and successful means of similarity-based CF [8, 6]. When using similarity measures, we report results from using the traditional kNN strategy.

The immediate highlight of the results is the improvement in accuracy and coverage when very small neighbourhoods (k) are used; while co-rated similarity-based prediction achieves a MAE of 0.9164 on 38.45% of the dataset, the trust learning method nearly covers all predictions, 99.84%, and reduces the MAE to 0.8705. The improved coverage comes from the kNR strategy: we look for recommenders who have rated the item in order to generate a predicted rating, and even when doing so manage to maintain an improved level of accuracy. Coverage is not boosted to a maximum value since the dataset contains ratings for which there are no existing ratings.

k = 5		Number of Opinions				
Method	Total	1	2	3	4	5
Co-Rated	14,856	4,268	3,714	3,029	2,345	1,500
Weighted-PCC	16,263	4,119	4,020	3,686	2,863	1,575
Trust-Learning	19,968	38	53	97	65	**19,715**

Table 5 MovieLens $u1$ Neighbour Participation Results, for $k = 5$

k = 100		Number of Opinions				
Method	Total	1	(1-25)	(25-50)	(50-75)	(75-100)
Co-Rated	14,856	4,268	3,714	3,029	2,345	1,500
Weighted-PCC	16,263	4,119	4,020	3,686	2,863	1575
Trust-Learning	19,968	38	1,945	2,538	2,417	**13,030**

Table 6 MovieLens $u1$ Neighbour Participation Results, for $k = 100$

As the neighbourhood size increases, the accuracy results improve across all methods, and the difference between the methods is found in the coverage results. In fact, neither of the similarity measures achieve maximal coverage with fewer than 100 neighbours, which is a very large proportion of the 943-user dataset. These results also appear in the subset summary of Table 4: when k is 5, the trust method will, on average, cover a near-maximal proportion of the dataset with a higher level of accuracy than the similarity measures accomplish on smaller amounts of the same datasets. However, accuracy and coverage results are not the sole descriptors of the performance of CF algorithms, and other methods have been proposed [14]. In particular, little work has been done at understanding why one method may outperform another. For example, why does trust perform better than similarity with small neighbourhoods, but loses its advantage over similarity when neighbourhood sizes are larger?

One aspect that influences the accuracy of generated recommendations is the *participation* of recommenders. In other words, when the neighbourhood k is restricted to a specific value x (such as 5), does that mean that all predictions are made with x opinions? We show the result for $k = 5$ in Table 5. For each method we report the total number of predictions that were possible along with the individual number of predictions that were made using a varying number of opinions. We preferred using the actual values rather than proportions due to the the very low values found in the trust-learning method. As is visible in the table, restricting a user's neighbourhood in kNN methods does not guarantee that each prediction will be made using k opinions; on the contrary, the number of opinions used will vary. Only a very small proportion, about $1,500$ of between 14 and $16,000$ predictions, are made using contributions from the full neighbourhood. The alternative strategy adopted by our trust-learning method, kNR, guarantees that nearly all predictions will be made using the specified number of opinions. This may account for the improved accuracy that we measured.

However, this characteristic may also be the downfall of the trust-based method as neighbourhood sizes increase. In Table 6, we collected the same participation results for $k = 100$. Once again, the trust method includes a significantly larger number

Method	X-MAE	Covered (%)
trust kNN	0.8785	67.54
trust kNR	0.9191	99.84
trust kNR-T	0.8705	99.84
trust kNR-TO	0.8301	65.4
trust kNR-TOP	0.8182	59.24
trust kNR-TOPB (0.5)	0.8177	59.03

Table 7 MovieLens u1 Subset Results, $k = 1$

of opinions within its predicted ratings. To do so, it must include information from neighbours that it has a minimal, near-negligible history of interactions with. Ratings will therefore be difficult to interpret, or transpose correctly, and the rating will diminish the value of the predicted rating.

This sort of analysis begs the question as to whether k recommendations are necessary when making each prediction. It thus questions what the added value of each opinion will be to the specific *prediction* (rather than the considerations of value done in Section 2.1), and whether this added value can be computed when making the prediction. We leave this matter for future work.

4 Trust Results Summary

In this work we have outlined a number of techniques for performing CF from the point of view of a trust-management problem, including the kNR strategy, learning trust by evaluating recommender's *value*, and *transposing* (T) recommender's ratings by learning to interpret their opinions. The results we reported above explore the predictive performance of a trust-based CF algorithm when all of these components have been implemented. In this section we will take a brief look at how each of these components influences the performance. As the results in Table 7 show, the trust-learning method works relatively well with the kNN strategy. Changing to kNR boosts the coverage to a maximum, forsaking some of the accuracy. Adding the interpretation of recommender ratings (T), maintains the coverage while returning the accuracy to the level we found at first. There are a number of further characteristics that can be considered when generating recommendations, which we introduce below. The main conclusion remains that each of these individual components can be implemented separately; the decision should be based on the recommendation context, or domain, and the user search mode [15].

4.1 Positive Opinions, Potential Recommenders, and Initial Trust

In this section we describe three additional characterisics of trust relationships that can be applied to CF; each of them exerts its own influence on the accuracy and coverage performance metrics, and is included in Table 7.

- **O: Positive Opinions**: One choice that can be applied to our k-NR strategy is to limit the predictions that are made to those that include at least one *positive* opinion. The reason for this is that, while the goal of CF is to predict ratings accurately, in order to rank items and then decide whether to recommend the item to the user or not, recommender systems in general are more interested in finding the items that users *like*, or rather, ones that they would also have a positive opinion about. If predictions that do not include at least one positive opinion are disregarded, and marked as *uncovered*, the accuracy increases at the expense of prediction coverage.
- **P: Potential Recommenders**: Computing trust and similarity share a common trait. Both are subject to the size of the profile of the current user; as it increases the possible set of co-rated items with neighbours increases as well, and both trust and similarity measures become more reliable. A further consideration would be to reward trust to *potential* recommenders, by rewarding them with trust for items they have rated that the current user has not. This is an attempt to capture how much "knowledge" the neighbour's profile contains, and pair this with the value judgements that are computed on shared opinions. In Table 7, the reward value was set to 0.1.
- **B: Initial Trust**: The computation of trust we have described thus far requires the user to have rated items in order to find valuable neighbours. If the user has no such ratings, no predictions can be made at all, and the *cold-start* problem appears. This problem can be side stepped if users are allowed to set initial trust values in others [16], or trust values are set to an inital constant. How much should a principal trust another if they have never interacted before, or if the current user has no profile? This is a question of trust *bootstrapping*, a non-trivial problem that has been studied extensively [17] that is beyond the scope of our work here. Limiting ourselves to bootstrapping trust values in all neighbors to an initial value β, which will then be molded by the measures of value found as the user's profile grows requires a small modification of Equation 3:

$$trust(a,b,n) = \frac{\beta + \Sigma_{i=0}^{n} value(a,b,i)}{n+1} \qquad (7)$$

In terms of how this affects recommendations, the initial predictions that a system will be able to make (based on no historical profile) will be the same as items' reputation, since all neighbours will have equal weighting. Recommendations will become more accurate as the number of ratings the user inputs grows, trust values become more reliable, and the risk engine, as will be explored in Section 2.3, can operate more effectively. Table 7 reflects an experiment done with $\beta = 0.5$.

5 Related Work

Computational trust is a topic that is experiencing a rising influence in the field of recommender systems. Not only does it provide an interesting metaphor that can be used to explain the implicit interactions that occur as CF algorithms operate, but also suggests methods that can improve on the work that has been done to date. Trust, however, is applicable to different aspects of recommender systems. In this short review we focus on the influence of trust on the algorithm deriving predicted ratings, and not, for example, on the interactions between users and the interface to the recommender system.

Amongst the first applications of trust to CF is the work done by Massa et al [16]; in order to overcome problems that arise from similarity measures, which require co-rated items in order to function, users can be asked to input trust values in other users. This method is particularly useful if a *trust propagation* algorithm is also implemented, and allows both the breadth and accuracy of predicted ratings to improve. Our work differs from [16] by performing trust evaluations based on *computed* added value, rather than pushing the decision to the end users, a scenario that may be more appropriate when user profiles need to are restricted in the interest of privacy. We also did not include trust propagation as we assume a centralised domain, where the user-rating matrix is available for complete analysis.

The trust-learning method that we propose more closely resembles the work done by O'Donovan and Smyth in [14]; they define a recommender's rating to be correct if the difference between it and the user's rating is less than a threshold value. Correctness is defined as a binary value, and, in doing so, begins to return to the domain of similarity. Our trust-learning method rewards sources of information, regardless of the opinion that was expressed, in order to differentiate between trustworthy recommenders (sources) and opinions (transposed ratings).

Trust has also been explored in decentralised recommender systems [18, 19]. As above, similarity relationsips can be viewed as a limited instance of trust relationships, thus allowing trust to be propagated over networks and then reconverted into similarity in order to reduce data sparsity. [18] extends this work, exploring whether trust models can be feasibly implemented in these systems, observing the effect of the trust model on bandwith usage, response time, and on user's patience.

All these solutions, however, focus on profile similarity. Our approach to the problem moves away from similarity by considering trust as a question of value rather than similarity. All users learn who their trusted recommenders are, and at different points in time they will have both varying levels of information with regards to their community. This idea deviates from the traditional assumption of similarity-based user interaction, towards encompassing further requirements of successful interaction, such as information sharing and honesty, into the recommendation process.

It is important to note that the implementations of trust in CF contexts are parallel to work being done by the clustering community, which include many interesting techniques that aim towards the same goals we stated above: finding a subset of the community of users that are the "appropriate" ones. Work such as [20] describes clustering from the perspective of message-passing, performing clustering by imitating the way people group together around common interests. Although lacking in the language used within trust-management research, these fields of work can offer a wide variety of important techniques that are equally applicable using the trust metaphor of CF.

6 Conclusion

In this work we have addressed the problem of learning how much to trust rating information that is received from other users in a recommender system. We thus transform the formation of predicted ratings from "how did *similar* users to me rate this item?" to "how much do those I *trust* like this item, and how should I *interpret* their opinion?" The results we have achieved not only offer a means for CF to be performed successfully under a new trust-based metaphor and perform within similar ranges of similarity-based methods, but offer novel ways of interpreting profile data when generating predicted ratings. Constructing a CF algorithm based on trust will thus include similarity as an emergent property of trust relationships, but not the cause of it. The performance of CF algorithms are known to be subjective to the dataset that they operate on; the contribution of this work can only be further validated by experimenting with more datasets. In particular, the optimal initial trust may vary between datasets, and designing a means of learning what this value is would be a great advantage.

The trust-based perspective and methodology also reduces the vulnerability that CF has to profile injection attacks; inserting a profile of ratings would not affect a target user's trust values in others unless the inserted ratings cover items that the target user has yet to rate. This is due to the fact that building trust relationships inherently includes a temporal component, and thus only users who have input ratings for an item prior to the active user inputting the rating will be considered for trust updates. Therefore an attacker can only target users who have yet to rate the items that meet the injected profile. It is possible to mimic this scenario in a controlled, experimental set up, but makes attacks much harder to design in the broader settings of online recommender systems. Our evaluation at this point has also implicitly assumed that all the users who are participating in the CF environment will not alter it or try to "game" the system in any way. Our future work will focus on removing these assumptions and observing the effect that these new scenarios will have on the recommendation process. Since we have defined interactions in this work on a user-pair basis, a malicious node can still attack each user in the system before all will have lost their trust in it. This entails defining suitable attack models for these kind of systems, and methods for users to defend themselves from malicious peers, by propagating trust values throughout the community, such as in techniques provided in [17].

References

1. J. Herlocker, J. Konstan, L. Terveen, and J. Riedl. Evaluating collaborative filtering recommender systems. In *ACM Transactions on Information Systems*, volume 22, pages 5–53. ACM Press, 2004.
2. M. Carbone, M. Nielsen, and V. Sassone. A formal model for trust in dynamic networks. In *In Proceedings of Int. Conference on Software Engineering and Formal Methods, (SEFM)*, 2003.
3. Daniele Quercia, Manish Lad, Stephen Hailes, Licia Capra, and Saleem Bhatti. Strudel: Supporting trust in the dynamic establishment of peering coalitions. In *Proceedings of the 21st ACM Symposium on Applied Computing*, pages 1870–1874, Dijon, France, April 2006.
4. L. Yan, S. Hailes, and L. Capra. Analysis of packet relaying models and incentive strategies in wireless ad hoc networks with game theory. In *Proc. IEEE 22nd International Conference on Advanced Information Networking and Applications (AINA08)*, GinoWan, Okinawa, Japan, March 2008. IEE Computer Society.
5. J.B. Schafer, J. Konstan, and J. Riedl. Recommender systems in e-commerce. In *Proceedings of the ACM Conference on Electronic Commerce*, 1999.
6. J. L. Herlocker, J. A. Konstan, A. Borchers, and J. Riedl. An Algorithmic Framework for Performing Collaborative Filtering. In *Proceedings of the 22nd Annual International ACM SIGIR Conference on Research and Development in Information Retrieval*, pages 230–237, 1999.
7. G. Linden, B. Smith, and Y. York. Amazon.com recommendations: Item-to-item collaborative filtering. In *IEEE Internet Computing*, pages 76–80, 2003.
8. N. Lathia, S. Hailes, and L. Capra. The effect of correlation coefficients on communities of recommenders. In *To Appear in ACM SAC TRECK*, 2008.
9. R. Guha, R. Kumar, P. Raghavan, and A. Tomkins. Propagation of trust and distrust. In *Proceedings of the 13th international conference on World Wide Web*, pages 403–412, 2004.
10. K. Crammer and Y. Singer. Pranking with ranking. In *Proceedings of the Conference on Neural Information Processing Systems (NIPS)*, 2001.
11. R. Bell and Y. Koren. Scalable collaborative filtering with jointly derived neighborhood interpolation weights. In *IEEE International Conference on Data Mining (ICDM'07)*. IEEE, 2007.
12. A. Abdul-Rahman and S. Hailes. Supporting trust in virtual communities. In *Proceedings of the 33rd International Conference on System Sciences*, Hawaii, USA, 2000.
13. A. Agresti and L. Winner. Evaluating agreement and disagreement among movie reviewers. In *Chance*, volume 10, 1997.
14. J. O'Donovan and B. Smyth. Trust in recommender systems. In *IUI '05: Proceedings of the 10th international conference on Intelligent user interfaces*, pages 167–174. ACM Press, 2005.
15. I. Im and A. Hars. Does a one-size recommendation system fit all? the effectiveness of collaborative filtering based recommendation systems across different domains and search modes. In *ACM Transactions on Information Systems (TOIS)*, volume 26, November 2007.
16. P. Massa and P. Avesani. Trust-aware recommender systems. In *Proceedings of Recommender Systems (RecSys)*, 2007.
17. D. Quercia, S. Hailes, and L. Capra. Lightweight distributed trust propagation. In *Proceedings of the 7th IEEE International Conference on Data Mining*, Omaha, US, October 2007.
18. G. Pitsilis and L. Marshall. A trust-enabled p2p recommender system. In *Proceedings of the 15th IEEE International Workshops on Enabling Technologies: Infrastructure for Collaborative Enterprises*, pages 59–64. IEEE, 2006.
19. G. Pitsilis and L. Marshall. *Trust as a Key to Improving Recommendation Systems, Trust Management*, pages 210–223. Springer Berlin / Heidelberg, 2005.
20. H. Geng, X. Deng, and H. Ali. A new clustering algorithm using message passing and its applications in analyzing microarray data. In *Proceedings of the Fourth International Conference on Machine Learning and Applications*, 2005.

SOFIA: Social Filtering for Robust Recommendations

Matteo Dell'Amico and Licia Capra

Abstract Digital content production and distribution has radically changed our business models. An unprecedented volume of supply is now on offer, whetted by the demand of millions of users from all over the world. Since users cannot be expected to browse through millions of different items to find what they might like, filtering has become a popular technique to connect supply and demand: *trusted* users are first identified, and their opinions are then used to create recommendations. In this domain, users' trustworthiness has been measured according to one of the following two criteria: *taste similarity* (i.e., "I trust those who agree with me"), or *social ties* (i.e., "I trust my friends, and the people that my friends trust"). The former criterion aims at identifying *competent* users, but is subject to abuse by malicious behaviours. The latter aims at detecting *well-intentioned* users, but fails to capture the natural subjectivity of tastes. We argue that, in order to be trusted, users must be *both* well-intentioned and competent. Based on this observation, we propose a novel approach that we call *social filtering*. We describe SOFIA, an algorithm realising this approach, and validate its performance, in terms of accuracy and robustness, on two real large-scale datasets.

1 Introduction

In his 2006 bestseller "The Long Tail" [1], Chris Anderson emphasizes how digital distribution has dramatically changed retailers' business models. Traditional retailers have a limited space they can use to stock items; market forces drive them to carry only a limited number of items, in particular, those that have the best chance to sell, thus losing less popular ones. With the advent of the Internet, retailers are not bound by the same physical constraints, so that a much wider variety of items can be offered from the 'long tail'. As a result, while a traditional bookshop can

Matteo Dell'Amico, Università di Genova, Italy e-mail: dellamico@disi.unige.it
Licia Capra, University College London, UK e-mail: l.capra@cs.ucl.ac.uk

Please use the following format when citing this chapter:

Dell'Amico, M. and Capra, L., 2008, in IFIP International Federation for Information Processing, Volume 263, *Trust Management II*, Yücel Karabulut, John Mitchell, Peter Herrmann, Christian Damsgaard Jensen; (Boston: Springer), pp. 135–150.

hardly be expected to sell more than 100,000 different titles, an online service such as Amazon.com can offer its costumers millions of different products. However, as Anderson points out, providing people with a massive choice is pointless, if that means they have to browse through thousands, or even millions, of potentially relevant items. Rather, people must be assisted in finding what they want. Filters can be used to *connect supply and demand*, making it easier for users to find the particular content that they would enjoy.

The most popular technique to realise this connection is collaborative filtering (CF) [7]. Most of the work on collaborative filtering has been focusing on identifying users with similar preferences, and then recommending items that people with similar tastes have approved. Traditional collaborative filtering techniques have worked quite well for the mass market and under the assumption of collaborative behaviours. However, these techniques have been subject to abuse by malicious behaviours [11]: for example, malicious users could copy honest users' reviews, to gain high similarity scores with them; they could subsequently inject inflated reviews in the system, to trick those users into buying an item or, viceversa, to disrupt an item's sales.

We argue that *accurate* and *robust* filtering techniques can be devised by exploiting information from a user's social network. We call this approach *social filtering*. The core idea is to give higher weight to recommendations received from *trusted* users. To be trusted, a user must be both *well intentioned* and *competent*. Traditional collaborative filtering techniques focus only on competence (i.e., the ability to give useful - in a subjective way - recommendations), without considering the fact that competent users may indeed be malicious. Rather than relying on all recommendations from similar (i.e., competent) users, our approach specifically looks for well-intentioned users (i.e., users who are willing to provide honest recommendations) among those with whom we have stronger social relationships.

Social ties are a warranty against malicious behaviors: if the trust inference algorithm is robust, it would be very costly for an attacker to build enough friendships with 'honest' users to effectively subvert the system. Indeed, the robustness of CF systems is usually measured in terms of the proportion of malicious nodes in the network, under the assumptions that attackers are not able to create unlimited new identities at will, and they are not aware of the judgements expressed by each peer [18, 2, 16, 15]. In our approach, these assumptions can be dropped, and the impact of an attack becomes limited by the "intent" ranking of the attacker, which is in turn determined only by the connectivity of malicious nodes in the social network.

The remainder of the paper is structured as follows: Section 2 describes the concept motivating social filtering, focusing on the two distinct aspects of intent and competence. In Section 3 we discuss SOFIA (SOcial FIltering Algorithm), that is, a specific realisation of social filtering. In Section 4 we analyse attacks against which filtering must defend itself, and in Section 5 we demonstrate the accuracy and robustness of SOFIA against two large real dataset, namely Citeseer and Last.fm. Finally, Section 6 concludes the paper.

2 Philosophy of the Approach

Social filtering relies on the identification of *trusted* recommenders. In the scope of this work, we call trusted a recommender that is both well-intentioned and competent. The three questions we are thus trying to answer are: (1) how to evaluate intention; (2) how to evaluate competence; and (3) how to combine this information to find trusted recommenders.

Intent - Trust over Users

We define intent as the the *willingness* of a user to provide honest judgements[1], differentiating "spammers" from people who are legitimately using the application. Note that a judgement given with good intent is not necessarily useful, since users may have different tastes and preferences; this section will illustrate how to find competent users among well-intentioned ones.

Users' intent can be represented as a *web of trust*, that is, as a a directed graph where nodes are users and an edge from user A to B indicates that A considers B a well-intentioned one; in other words, A trusts B. Webs of trust are thus instances of social networks where links represent assessments on the behaviour of nodes rather than simple acquaintance.

The web of trust can be built in many different ways. For example, by means of explicit social network creation (e.g., "Add as a friend" in sites like MySpace or FaceBook); using email/phone-book contacts; via automated creation as described in ReferralWeb [9], and so on. We are not concerned with what specific technique is used to create the web of trust; however, we expect it to be difficult, for malicious nodes, to obtain endorsements from honest ones: this condition is key for the robustness of social filtering. For this reason, we discourage the creation of the web of trust via automated matching purely based on users' similarity.

The web of trust can then be traversed in order to obtain *reputation*[2] information about users we do not directly know and trust. We propose to do so by means of the *transitive trust propagation pattern*. A peer A obviously trusts the nodes that can be reached from itself via an edge; since A believes these nodes behave honestly, their recommendations for other nodes are believed by A to some extent, and some trust is propagated to them. The pattern repeats iteratively, propagating trust to all nodes reachable with a directed path starting from A.

The principle of trust transitivity has been criticized since the judgement of who deserves trust is subjective [12, 8] (i.e., we are not guaranteed to like all the friends of our friends). However, we argue that benevolent intent (unlike competence) is a concept where subjectivity does not apply strongly. Moreover, if the web of trust is

---

[1] In the following, we will use the more general term 'judgements', instead of 'recommendations', as our approach is equally applicable to recommendations (i.e., endorsements of products or content) as to 'negative' or purely informative judgements (e.g., "avoid that restaurant" or "this is relaxing music").

[2] We use the word 'reputation' here in its most general sense, that is, 'the estimation in which a person or object is held by the community or public' (source: Oxford Dictionary)

built using evaluations of past behavior, reputation provides incentives to cooperation via reciprocative behavior [17, 4].

Competence - Trust over Judgements

Together with intent, competence is a key component in evaluating the trustworthiness of recommenders. In this work, we define *competent* those users who are able
to make correct judgments; since the definition of "correct" judgments is inherently
subjective, competence is a subjective matter as well.

A sensible way of evaluating competence is via the so called *co-citation pattern*.
A bipartite graph is used to represent a *network of judgments*: users (e.g., $\{A,B\}$)
and judgments (e.g., $\{X,Y\}$) form two disjoint sets of vertices; an edge (A,X) is
present if user A expressed the judgment X. If users A and B agree on judgment X
(i.e., there exist edges $A \rightarrow X$ and $B \rightarrow X$), then A may consider B a competent user.
Using the co-citation pattern, she may then *propagate trust over competence* on the
other judgements that B expressed.

However, users' competence is not sufficient to warrant trust to their judgements.
For instance, let us consider a malicious user Mallory, wishing to trick Alice in
believing a dishonest judgement Z stating that "Mallory's Greasy Restaurant offers
very good food". In order to do so, Mallory could simply copy Alice's judgements;
using the co-citation trust propagation pattern, Alice would deem Mallory a very
competent evaluator, and would consequently believe/trust judgement Z too.

We argue that competence should thus be combined with intent to identify *trustworthy recommenders*, that is, recommenders who are willing to provide us with
honest judgements and that we are likely to find useful.

The Combined Approach

As discussed above, using the *transitivity* trust propagation pattern alone is not
enough, as subjectivity of tastes, which is an intrinsic characteristic of judgements,
is lost. On the other hand, using the *co-citation* trust propagation pattern alone is
subject to abuse by malicious users.

We propose a novel approach that combines the strengths of the two patterns,
while circumventing their individual weaknesses: we exploit the transitivity trust
propagation pattern on the web of trust to determine well intentioned users, and the
co-citation trust propagation pattern on the network of judgements to evaluate their
competence. By so doing, we are capable of inferring trust over judgements, in a
way that is both accurate and robust. The underpinning idea is that, in order to be
trusted, a judgement must have been expressed by a user who is both *willing* (intent)
and *able* (competence) to give useful judgements. We call the new approach *social
filtering*. Based on the interpretation of trust propagation over intent and competence
we gave in the previous two sections, A can infer trust for a judgement Y expressed
by a user D (Fig. 1) if:

1. there exists a directed path from A to D in the web of trust (e.g., $A \rightarrow B \rightarrow C \rightarrow D$);
2. A and D both expressed at least one common judgement (e.g., X).

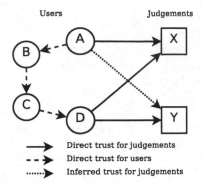

Fig. 1: Combined trust-propagation approach.

This is the first approach that aims at increasing the utility of recommendations, by exploiting information coming from the social network *and* from individual's preferences at the same time. We are aware of only two other works where the transitivity and co-citation trust propagation patterns have been used together, but with rather different goals and following a different philosophy: in [6], trust is propagated using *either* co-citation or transitivity in a social network where links represent similarity in preferences; in [14], the transitive trust propagation pattern is used as an *alternative to* the co-citation pattern, in order to bootstrap trust when traditional user similarity cannot be computed, again because of lack of information. These approaches work well in those scenarios where there is a strong correlation between social ties and individual preferences. On the contrary, our approach is best suited to those scenarios where the social network is not just a surrogate of users' preferences. As we shall demonstrate in Section 5, when separate information is available about the web of trust and judgements, an approach that reasons about intent and competence *at the same time* can yield the biggest increase in the utility of recommendations, even in the absence of malign behavior. Before doing so, we discuss how we have realised social filtering in practice.

3 Realization of the Approach

In the previous section, we have introduced social filtering from a conceptual viewpoint, highlighting the advantages of propagating trust over both intent and competence, in order to give users *trusted judgements*. To be of practical use, an implementation of social filtering would need to attribute a numeric value to the *amount* of trust a judgement deserves. This would ultimately allow users to rank judgements and/or to filter out unreliable ones. In this section, we describe how the transitive and co-citation patterns have been uniquely combined in SOFIA, our own implementation of social filtering. In describing our implementation, we will refer to the general case of weighted social networks, with weights expressing the strength of social ties. The user-judgement edges can be weighted as well, representing the level of confidence of a user towards a given judgement. The unweighted case is just a specific instance of the more general one, with all instances of trust relationships and/or judgements having the same weight.

Evaluating Intent

There exist various algorithms to quantify the amount of trust that is propagated transitively on a weighted social network. Desirable properties that most algorithms guarantee are: *longer paths disperse trust* (i.e., if there is a trust path $A \rightarrow \ldots \rightarrow B \rightarrow C$, then the amount of trust inferred from A to C is not greater than the trust inferred from A to B); *adding paths increases trust* (i.e., if there are two paths from A to B, then the trust that A infers for B is at least as high as if only one path was present).

A popular approach that guarantees these properties is the simulation of a random walk on the web of trust, as done by PageRank [19], the algorithm used by Google for ranking search results. The algorithm considers a random walk over the graph of WWW pages and their links, starting from a random node and stopping with a probability $1 - \alpha$ at each step. Nodes are then ranked according to the probability that this random walk stops at them[3]. Pages that receive many incoming links, and pages that are being linked by another heavily-linked page, are then ranked higher. Intuitively speaking, the same approach could be used to propagate trust over a social network: the higher the number of paths (equivalent to links) leading to a node (equivalent to a WWW page), the more reputable the node is assumed to be (the higher it ranks).

The standard version of PageRank misses on subjectivity, as it ranks pages regardless of the evaluating node. As a consequence, any node in the system would propagate trust to a node X in the same way. To obtain a subjective version of the algorithm, two simple changes are required: first, we force the starting point of the random walk to be the evaluating node itself (thus avoiding walks that originate at malicious nodes); second, rather than having the same probability of jumping to another node (as done in the original version of PageRank), we chose such probability to be proportional to the weight (i.e., the strength) of the edge itself. A walk starting at A will thus result in trust propagation from A's subjective viewpoint only. This modified version of the original algorithm is sometimes referred to as *Personalised PageRank* (PPR).

Note that the original version of PageRank is subject to Sybil attacks[4] [5, 3]: in scenarios where new virtual identities can be cheaply created, a malicious node S_0 could create an unlimited number of siblings $S_1, S_2, \ldots$, add a web of strong (fake) ties between S_0 and its Sybil nodes S_i to the social network, and exploit this setup to gain a disproportionately large trust. To defend against this type of attack, trust propagation algorithms should limit the amount of trust gained by any Sybil node S_i

---

[3] The most common PageRank definition corresponds to the *equilibrium distribution* of a random walk, with a $1 - \alpha$ probability of jumping to a random node. The two definitions are equivalent.

[4] This style of attack is also known as 'shilling' in recommender systems, 'profile injection' in collaborative filtering, and 'web spamming' in webpage ranking.

by a function of the trust that S_0 has 'legitimately' gained. Personalised PageRank does exactly so: an attacker S_0 can only divert, towards the Sybil region, those paths that pass through S_0 itself; if the probability that a random walk reaches S_0 is p, then the cumulative value of all one-step paths from S_0 is αp; for two steps, it is $\alpha^2 p$, and so on. Thus, the maximal total rank for the Sybil region amounts to $\sum_{i=0}^{\infty} \alpha^i p = \frac{p}{1-\alpha}$. The α parameter thus influences the resilience to Sybil attacks: the lower the value of α, the better the robustness. Low values of α also increase subjectivity, as they reward short paths over long ones, while when α approaches 1 the outcome of the algorithm becomes more and more similar, regardless of the initiator node. Finally, the lower the value of α the faster the convergence speed of the algorithm (with $\alpha = 0.5$, more than 99.9% of the overall ranking weight comes from paths of length up to 10). Note, however, that low values of α may cause honest nodes who are 'socially far-away' not to be considered, thus discarding potentially useful information. This may affect the accuracy of our algorithm, with respect to traditional collaborative filtering techniques where the full dataset is considered instead. We will analyse optimal choices of α with respect to accuracy vs. robustness in Section 5.

In our realisation of social filtering, we have chosen to deploy Personalised Page-Rank to quantify the transitive trust propagation over the social network, as it combines our requirements of subjectivity and robustness.

Evaluating Competence

The co-citation trust propagation pattern has been widely studied and applied to the problem of ranking Web pages. One of the most famous algorithms realising this pattern is HITS [10]. HITS conceptually divides pages in two subsets: authorities (i.e., pages whose content satisfy the query), and hubs (i.c., pages that link to relevant documents, that is, to authorities). Using an iterative process, HITS traverses the linkage structure of Web documents, and computes both a hub weight and an authority weight for each visited page at every step, so that:

1. Forward Step (from hubs to authorities): the weight given to an authority is proportional to the sum of the weights of those hubs linking to it;
2. Backward Step (from authorities to hubs): the weight given to a hub is proportional to the sum of the weights of those authorities being linked by it.

If weights expressing confidence are present in the network of judgements, they can be used as a multiplicative factor (i.e., a link with weight 2 acts as two separate links, each with weight 1). The process continues (renormalizing scores at every iteration) until it converges, and the top ranking pages, according to their authority scores, are then returned.

The principle behind HITS is that good hubs link good authorities, and good authorities are linked by good hubs, in a mutually reinforcing way. We argue that the same principle holds in our scenario, where we can expect competent users to give valuable judgements, and valuable judgements to be given by competent users. If we map users to hubs and judgements to authorities, we can run an HITS-like iterative algorithm to rank judgements, which is our ultimate goal. This would not realise our social filtering method though, as the following caveats must be addressed first.

(1) Solving the TKC Problem. It has been demonstrated that the HITS algorithm suffers from the "Tightly Knit Community" (TKC) syndrome [13]: if a community of users all gave the same (or very similar) judgements (thus resulting in a highly connected bipartite graph), the competence weight of the community would disproportionately increase, with the judgements they express being excessively high-ranked, even if they are not authoritative. A set of malicious users could thus artificially create a TKC in order to artificially boost their ranking. To solve this problem, we adopt the solution proposed in SALSA [13]: we divide the weight that each hub transfers at each forward step by its outdegree (the sum of weights on outgoing edges), and we do the same for authorities and their indegree at each backward step. After a forward step, the total weight transferred from a single hub to its linked authorities is thus equal to the weight on that hub; viceversa, after a backward step, the total weight that is redistributed from a single authority to the set of hubs linking to it equals the weight gained by the authority. Thus, the sum of weights remains constant at every step, removing the need for normalization. A very desirable side-effect of this alteration is that users who express "niche" judgements are rewarded more than those expressing only mainstream (redundant) ones.

(2) Subjectivity of Ranking. HITS-like algorithms provide non-subjective results, as they are independent of the user A starting the search. To cater for the subjectivity required by our scenario, we initialize the algorithm so that the only hub (user) with a non-zero weight is the reference node A itself (instead of assigning an equal weight to any hub in the network). In so doing, the first forward step of the algorithm only considers the judgements given by the reference node, thus tailoring the ranking results to his/her tastes. To limit the propagation of trust to judgements that are too dissimilar from the tastes of A, after each backward step, the weights associated to each user are multiplied by a parameter $\beta \in (0, 1)$, and the trust given to A is increased by $1 - \beta$. These two changes are similar, in spirit, to the modifications already suggested for PageRank, where we forced the random walk to start from the very same node; the β parameter plays the same role that α plays in PageRank, ensuring the convergence of the algorithm, with lower values of β impling faster convergence and higher subjectivity.

(3) Catering for Well-Intentioned Users. As discussed in Section 2, trust propagation over competence alone is susceptible to attacks. We propose to add robustness to HITS-like algorithms, by incorporating users' intent assessment as follows. To begin with, Personalised PageRank is run on the social network, thus obtaining a vector with nodes' reputation, as seen by the reference node A. We then run the subjective HITS-like algorithm, so that, at every backward step, trust is redistributed from judgements to users in a way that is *proportional to users' intent*, as measured by PPR. In other words, *reputation becomes a multiplicative factor for backward trust propagation*. As discussed in Section 3, a Sybil coalition can obtain only a limited amount of trust from the social network, so the amount of trust that can be transferred to malicious nodes is limited too.

We call the algorithm that results from modifying the HITS-like approach in the three ways described above SOFIA, that is, SOcial FIltering Algorithm. The resulting pseudocode is shown in Algorithm 1. The result of running SOFIA is a vector

---

Algorithm 1 SOFIA.

Parameters: a judgement bipartite network $G = (V, E)$, where V is the union of the set of users U and the set of judgements J; an evaluating node $A \in U$; weights such that w_{uj} is the weight of edge (u, j); an intent ranking vector r computed using Personalised PageRank over the web of trust, so that r_u is the intent ranking of user u; a $0 < \beta < 1$ parameter.
Returns: a trust vector $\hat{t}$ such that $\hat{t}_j$ is the trust ranking of judgement j.
$n \Leftarrow$ size of U; $m \Leftarrow$ size of J; $t \Leftarrow 0^n$; $t_A \Leftarrow 1$
while algorithm has not converged **do**
    {Forward Step: from users to judgements}
    $\hat{t} \Leftarrow 0^m$
    for all $(u, j) \in E$ **do**
        $\hat{t}_j \Leftarrow \hat{t}_j + \dfrac{w_{uj}}{\sum_{k \in J} w_{uk}} t_u$
    end for
    {Backward Step: from judgements to users}
    $t \Leftarrow 0^n$; $t_A \Leftarrow 1 - \beta$
    for all $(u, j) \in E$ **do**
        $t_u \Leftarrow t_u + \beta \dfrac{w_{uj} r_u}{\sum_{v \in U} w_{vj} r_v} \hat{t}_j$
    end for
end while
return $\hat{t}$

$\hat{t}$ containing a *trust* numeric value for each judgement in J, computed considering both the intent and the competence of the users in U, as seen by the reference node A. The normalization parameters ($\sum_{k \in J} w_{uk}$, $\sum_{v \in U} w_{vj} r_v$) can be calculated outside the loops, so the computational cost of the full algorithm is proportional to the number of edges in E times the number of iterations of the algorithm.

4 Attack Model

In order to validate our social filtering algorithm, we have conducted a variety of experiments on two very large real datasets. While ideal to measure accuracy, real datasets are unsuitable to test the robustness of the algorithm while varying threat intensity. To demonstrate the robustness of SOFIA, we thus have to manually inject attacks on top of real datasets, and run experiments under different configuration settings. In this section, we analyse threat strategies, leaving their enactment and corresponding experimental validation to Section 5.

In the scenario we are considering, the most plausible goal of an attacker would be to alter the rating of a certain judgement X. It may do so either to trick a single user A, or more extensively to deviate the judgements of all users, in favour of (or against) X. Let us analyse how an attacker could achieve such goal. In the first case, since the attacker wants to be rated by A as a very competent user, it could first copy the judgements that A expressed, and then add a new judgement X. In the second case, there is no single set of judgements the attacker can copy, as each user would have expressed different ones: copying popular judgements would yield to very little reward, as a consequence of our strategy to reward users who gave niche judgements more; on the contrary, copying 'niche' judgements would yield to very high appeal, but to rather few users. We will thus model this attack as we modeled the targeted attack, that is, by copying the judgements of a randomly chosen node A and adding the judgement for X; however, rather than studying the impact of the attack on A, we will study the 'collateral damage' that the attack has on other users.

To increase the impact of the attack itself (i.e., to increase the ranking of judgement X), we also consider the case of an attacker who has the ability to create an unlimited number of Sybil identities, all endorsing X. We assume that each Sybil can create any number of outgoing edges in the web of trust, from the Sybil node to any other user. They can also create any number of incoming edges, originating within the Sybil coalition. However, what they cannot do is create incoming edges from honest nodes at will, since obtaining trust from well-intentioned peers is costly. It is thus reasonable to expect a low cut between the "honest" and the "Sybil" region [20]. In our experiments, we will thus create Sybil regions that are highly interconnected internally; we will then set the amount of incoming links from honest nodes as a parameter, and analyse the robustness of SOFIA (i.e., how highly ranked can X become) against it.

5 Experimental Validation

We have evaluated SOFIA along two dimensions: accuracy and robustness against Sybil attacks. Both experiments were conducted using data from two real datasets: the Citeseer online scientific digital library, and the Last.fm music and social networking website. The key characteristics of these datasets are briefly summarised below.

The Datasets
Citeseer (http://citeseer.ist.psu.edu/oai.html) is an online scientific literature digital library, containing over 750,000 documents. From this repository, we have extracted a social network based on the co-authorship relation: if A and B have co-authored n papers together, then an edge between the two will be added to the social network, with weight n. The judgement network is built from the citations instead: if a paper X authored by A cites paper Y, then an (unweighted) edge from A to Y is added to the judgement network; the rationale is that, by citing Y, the authors of X have expressed the judgement "Y is relevant with respect to the topic discussed in X". To obtain a more manageable subset of the whole network, we isolated a highly-clustered subset of 10,000 authors, and took in consideration only the papers that had them as authors. The result is a set of 182,675 different papers; 48,998 of them received at least one citation by one of the others.

Last.fm (http://last.fm/) is a "social music" website that creates profiles of musical tastes, by tracking which songs users listen more often to. Users explicitly create a social network by adding other users to their friend-list. We gathered our social network with a breadth-first crawl of 10,000 users using the Audioscrobbler Web Services available at http://www.audioscrobbler.net/data/webservices/. We then considered the 50 most listened artists of each user, and ended up with a total of 51,654 different artists. The judgement network was finally created by linking users to their most listened artists (thus representing the judgement "user A likes to listen to songs by X"), and by weighting each judgement edge with the number of times the user listened to songs by that artist.

Accuracy

To assess the accuracy of SOFIA in giving recommendations, we performed the following experiment on both datasets: we "hid" one random edge $A \rightarrow X$ from the judgement network, run SOFIA on the modified network, and used its output (i.e., a vector of weights) to rank all judgements from A's viewpoint; this is equivalent to producing recommendations, tailored to A, based on the computed ranking of judgements. Since X is a judgement that A expressed (before we hid it), A obviously approves of it, so a good recommendation engine should return X at a very high ranking. Thus, the highest the position of X in the ranked list of judgements, the better the accuracy of the ranking algorithm. In the Citeseer dataset, the experiment is equivalent to guessing a missing citation from a paper; in Last.fm, it means finding the missing artist in the top-50 chart of a user. In the following, all the results shown (for a given algorithm and set of parameter) were computed from 1,000 individual instances of the experiment.

The first set of experiments aimed at analysing the impact that the two different trust propagation patterns (transitivity and co-citation) individually had on prediction accuracy; at the same time, we wanted to quantify the effect that different choices of parameters had on it (namely α, β and the number of iterations). We thus separated the two "halves" of SOFIA into:

Personalised PageRank (PPR):   each user u is first ranked using PPR; the ranking r_u is then simply divided between all the judgements u has expressed (proportionally to the edge weight). PPR thus enables us to measure the impact of trust transitivity, while disregarding the network of judgements;

Non-SOcial FIltering Algorithm (N-SOFIA):   all nodes in the web of trust are given equal intent ranking, instead of relying on the PPR output. N-SOFIA thus enables us to study the impact of the co-citation pattern while disregarding the social network.

The first parameter we have studied is the *number of iterations* needed to obtain satisfying results. Table 1 shows the percentiles of the ranking of the "hidden" judgements, when running both PPR and N-SOFIA on the Citeseer dataset, with α and β parameters chosen to optimize the results. As the table shows, a rather small number of iterations is enough to obtain very good results: for instance, after 10 iterations, 10% of the hidden judgements can be found in the top 2 returned results (i.e., recommendations) of PPR, and at the very top for N-SOFIA; half of the hidden judgements (50th percentile) were returned within the top 29 recommendations

Algorithm	Iterations	Ranking percentiles						
		5	10	25	50	75	90	95
PPR ($\alpha = 0.3$)	3	**1**	**2**	8	32	161	4,293	–
	5	**1**	**2**	8	30	**115**	**1,709**	**11,609**
	10	**1**	**2**	7	**29**	141	3,341	20,287
N-SOFIA ($\beta = 0.05$)	3	**1**	**1**	3	12	67	**1,060**	–
	5	**1**	**1**	3	12	**63**	1,136	–
	10	**1**	**1**	3	**11**	72	1,020	–

Table 1: Hidden judgement ranking of PPR and N-SOFIA (best results in bold) with different numbers of iterations on the Citeseer dataset.

made by PPR, and in the top 11 by N-SOFIA, and so on[5]. In the following, the number of iterations for both parts of the algorithm has been set to 5.

We then studied the impact that parameters α and β had on the accuracy of PPR and N-SOFIA on the specific datasets at hand[6]. Tables 2a and 2b report the results for different values of α on PPR, and of β on N-SOFIA, respectively. The key observation obtained from these numbers is that, on both datasets, N-SOFIA performs better than PPR, suggesting that the information on tastes is more valuable than the information that can be inferred from the social network. On both datasets, the optimal value for β is much lower than the optimal value for α, suggesting that taste similarity propagates effectively on short paths only. Also, the optimal values for α are remarkably lower in our experiments than the "traditional" recommended $\alpha = 0.85$ for PageRank, reflecting the fact these datasets reward higher subjectivity. We have also compared the accuracy of N-SOFIA with traditional Collaborative Filtering techniques (in particular, using the cosine-based similarity mea-

Dataset	α	Ranking percentiles					
		5	10	25	50	75	90
Citeseer	0.2	**1**	**2**	8	33	132	3,076
	0.3	**1**	**2**	8	**30**	**115**	**1,709**
	0.85	2	4	11	48	242	3,473
Last.fm	0.3	5	14	75	361	**2,107**	**15,064**
	0.5	5	**12**	**66**	**344**	2,188	16,025
	0.85	5	14	71	367	2,289	15,648

(a)

Dataset	β	Ranking percentiles					
		5	10	25	50	75	90
Citeseer	0.02	**1**	**1**	3	14	87	2,820
	0.05	**1**	**1**	3	**12**	**63**	**1,136**
	0.3	**1**	**1**	4	17	93	1,603
Citeseer (CF)	–	1	1	3	15	88	
Last.fm	0.01	2	**6**	**32**	**157**	**822**	**3,954**
	0.1	5	13	58	269	1,305	10,599
	0.3	8	20	89	404	1,742	9,878
Last.fm (CF)	–	3	8	36	204	1,061	7,735

(b)

Table 2: (a) Impact of α on hidden judgement ranking with Personalised PageRank. (b) Impact of β on hidden judgement ranking with N-SOFIA.

---

[5] Note that the judgements returned with ranking higher than of X are not mistakes: they are simply other recommendations that these algorithms compute but, given that such judgements were never made by A (unlike X), we have no way of measuring how accurate those are.

[6] Note that a single optimal choice of these parameters do not exist, as they intrinsically depend on the characteristics of the dataset (in terms of "level of transitivity").

Algorithm	Ranking percentiles						
	5	10	25	50	75	90	95
SOFIA	1	1	1	4	31	855	–
N-SOFIA	1	1	3	12	63	1,136	–
PPR	1	2	8	30	115	1,709	**11,609**

(a)

Algorithm	Ranking percentiles						
	5	10	25	50	75	90	95
SOFIA	2	6	32	174	992	7,429	–
SOFIA (2)	3	8	46	240	1,347	11,919	–
N-SOFIA	2	6	32	157	822	**6,954**	–
PPR	5	12	66	344	2,188	16,025	–

(b)

Table 3: (a) Hidden judgement ranking comparison on the Citeseer dataset. The α and β parameters were tuned for best performance ($\alpha = 0.5$, $\beta = 0.3$ for SOFIA, $\beta = 0.05$ for N-SOFIA, $\alpha = 0.3$ for PPR). (b) Hidden judgement ranking comparison on the Last.fm dataset ($\alpha = 0.9$ and $\beta = 0.05$ for SOFIA, $\alpha = 0.5$ and $\beta = 0.1$ for SOFIA (2), $\beta = 0.01$ for N-SOFIA, $\alpha = 0.5$ for PPR).

sure): given that N-SOFIA produces recommendations based only on the network of judgements, while discarding social relations, we expect N-SOFIA and traditional CF to exhibit similar accuracy. As Table 2b illustrates (rows labeled CF), the accuracy is indeed comparable on both datasets. Note that attacks have not been considered yet: once introduced, results will change dramatically, with approaches based on competence only (i.e., CF-like techniques) suffering the most.

As a final set of experiments, we have compared the accuracy of PPR and N-SOFIA with SOFIA, under the best choice of parameters for both datasets. Results are shown in Tables 3a and 3b, for Citeseer and Last.fm respectively. Using the Citeseer dataset, SOFIA outperforms both algorithms, with 50% of the hidden judgements being ranked in the top 4 positions, against 12 for N-SOFIA and 30 for PPR. The accuracy gain of SOFIA is perhaps more striking when considering up to 75% of the hidden judgements: using SOFIA, a user would find the hidden judgement in the the top-30 list of recommended papers, while using PPR the top-115 would have to be investigated. Of particular relevance is the observation that, even now that malicious attacks are *not* considered, SOFIA outperforms N-SOFIA, despite the fact that SOFIA throws away (potentially useful) information coming from (honest) socially far-away nodes. This means that SOFIA effectively exploits knowledge gathered from the social network to counter-balance this loss of data, and the gain is higher than the cost for datasets that, like Citeseer, exhibit the intrinsic property of having "socially close" nodes more likely to share tastes.

The performance gain of SOFIA on the Last.fm dataset is less striking. As Table 3b demonstrates, SOFIA still outperforms PPR by a factor of 2. However, the performance of SOFIA and N-SOFIA are almost undistinguishable: with this dataset, the loss of data that SOFIA suffers from not considering far away nodes, and the added knowledge it gathers from the social network, balance each other out. However, even in these circumstances, we argue that running the whole SOFIA, instead of N-SOFIA alone, pays off: as we shall demonstrate in the next section, once attacks are in place, SOFIA outperforms N-SOFIA by far, thus yielding the best results overall in terms of accuracy *and* robustness. Note that Table 3b also reports the results of running SOFIA on an additional set of parameters (row labelled SOFIA

(2)), in particular, with a lower value of α; while accuracy becomes worse, we shall demonstrate, in the next section, that robustness to attacks becomes better, as shorter paths are considered, thus reducing the chance of traversing an attack region.

Robustness

As discussed in Section 4, we are interested in evaluating how much an attacker, with the ability of creating an unlimited number of Sybils, can raise the ranking of a given judgement X. We assume that, while it is relatively cheap to create a fully connected Sybil sub-network, it is costly for any Sybil node to enter the social network of an honest node (i.e., to be directly trusted by an honest user). We have thus designed our experiments as follows: we have created a completely connected Sybil sub-network of 100 nodes, and attached it to the honest part of the web of trust with a parametric number k of *attack edges*; each attack edge is given a weight of 1, and the honest node to which it connects is chosen at random. All Sybil nodes copy all the judgements given by a random "victim" V, and then create another edge towards a malicious judgement X (in Last.fm, where judgements are weighted, the weight is set as the maximum between the judgements of the victim). We then study how the ranking of X changes, before and after the attack, both on V and on other random nodes in the network, *for different values of* k. Once again, for each algorithm and set of parameters, the results have been obtained with 1,000 instances of the experiment. Note that the number of Sybil nodes is not relevant for PPR- and SOFIA-like algorithms, where the impact of the attacker is limited by the total ranking of the Sybil region. We have thus fixed the number of Sybils to 100, while varying k (which does influence the ranking of the Sybil region instead).

Table 4 shows how the ranking of malicious judgement X varies, with respect to parameter k, when enacting the attack on the Last.fm dataset (the results of the same experiment on the Citeseer dataset, not shown here for lack of space, are qualitatively equivalent, and all remarks expressed here are valid for both datasets). The α and β parameters were the same as those used for the experiments shown in Table 3b. The first row of the table shows the ranking of X when no attack is in place.

Let us consider N-SOFIA and cosine-based collaborative filtering (CF) first. Since these algorithms do not take into account the social network, the number of attack edges k is irrelevant in these cases. As shown, the malicious judgement X comes always at the very top of the recommendations made for the victim node V, even though, before the attack, such judgement was in position 2.5K or above! The ranking of X becomes very high even for nodes who are not specifically under attack, thus confirming the fact that both N-SOFIA and traditional collaborative filtering techniques based on taste similarity only are highly vulnerable to Sybil attacks. On the contrary, the impact of the attack on PPR is marginal. In this case, being a victim is undistinguishable from being any node in the network, given that individual opinions are not taken into consideration. As the table shows, even when the Sybil region has conquered 100 attack edges, the ranking of the malicious judgement X is at position 2000 or above in 50% of the cases.

Algorithm	k	Role	Percentiles						
			5	10	25	50	75	90	95
Any		no attack	2,583	5,165	12,914	25,827	38,741	46,489	49,071
N-SOFIA		victim	1	1	1	1	1	1	1
		other	34	85	348	1,185	3,132	5,875	7,482
CF		victim	1	1	1	1	1	1	1
		other	25	54	214	1,522	27,367	–	–
PPR	1		2,297	4,459	10,730	20,493	33,322	–	–
	10		1,285	2,353	4,759	8,757	13,371	19,648	26,846
	100		334	559	1,092	2,012	3,101	4,434	5,290
SOFIA	1	victim	679	1,386	3,406	11,182	31,765	–	–
		other	2,264	4,409	9,599	19,186	33,064	–	–
	10	victim	41	132	469	1,311	2,815	7,039	34,725
		other	1,082	2,126	4,612	8,779	14,718	22,254	26,959
	100	victim	1	2	13	74	197	377	564
		other	215	391	1,040	2,649	5,571	8,395	10,179
SOFIA (2)	100	victim	15	46	138	353	697	1,042	1,234
		other	448	705	1,578	3,106	5,128	7,447	9,187

Table 4: Ranking of the "malicious judgement" after a Sybil attack on the Last.fm dataset.

The robustness of SOFIA is comparable to that of PPR when considering non-victim nodes. The victim node clearly suffers instead, but much less than when using N-SOFIA: for example, when the Sybil region has 10 attack edges to the honest part of the network, 50% of the times the malicious judgement X is ranked at around position 1300 or above by the victim node using SOFIA, instead of position 1 using N-SOFIA. The impact of the attack becomes non-negligible for victim nodes running SOFIA once the number of attack edges reaches $k = 100$. Note, however, that this is a rather costly attack: in fact, it requires tricking 1% of the 10,000-node network into trusting dishonest nodes, and all this effort just to change the ranking of judgement X by a single node V, with X only gaining marginally in other nodes' viewpoints. This result supports the claim we made at the end of the previous section, that is, that running SOFIA pays off, as its accuracy is at least as good as that of N-SOFIA, but its robustness to Sybil attacks is way higher. Last but not least, it is worth observing the impact of different choices of parameters on the robustness of SOFIA; the last set of results shown in Table 4 are obtained using the alternative set of parameters for SOFIA that were specified in Table 3b: while the accuracy of the recommendations using this second set of parameters was shown to be worse, the use of a lower α value makes the system more attack-resilient. As expected, there is a tradeoff between accuracy and robustness, and the desired balance between the two features can be obtained by adjusting the parameters to the specific characteristics and requirements of the domain at hand.

6 Conclusions

In this paper, we have proposed *social filtering*, a novel approach to realise accurate and robust recommendation systems, based on a combination of taste similarity and user intent. We have illustrated SOFIA, our realisation of social filtering, and demonstrated its accuracy against two real datasets, as well as its robustness against attacks of different magnitude. As shown, SOFIA achieves the best results in scenarios where judgements are subjective, and where users with similar tastes tend to form social ties.

References

1. C. Anderson. *The Long Tail: Why the Future of Business Is Selling Less of More*. Hyperion, 2006.
2. R. Burke, B. Mobasher, R. Bhaumik, and C. Williams. Segment-based injection attacks against collaborative filtering recommender systems. In *Proc. IEEE ICDM '05*, 2005.
3. J. R. Douceur. The Sybil attack. In *Proc. IPTPS '02*, March 2002.
4. M. Feldman, K. Lai, I. Stoica, and J. Chuang. Robust incentive techniques for peer-to-peer networks. In *Proc. ACM EC '04*, 2004.
5. E. J. Friedman and A. Cheng. Manipulability of pagerank under sybil strategies. In *Proc. NetEcon06*, 2006.
6. R. V. Guha, R. Kumar, P. Raghavan, and A. Tomkins. Propagation of trust and distrust. In *ACM WWW '04*, 2004.
7. J. L. Herlocker, J. A. Konstan, A. Borchers, and J. Riedl. An algorithmic framework for performing collaborative filtering. In *Proc. ACM SIGIR '99*, 1999.
8. A. Josang. The right type of trust for distributed systems. Proc. *Proc. ACM NSPW '96*, 1996.
9. H. Kautz, B. Selman, and M. Shah. Referral web: combining social networks and collaborative filtering. *Commun. ACM*, 40(3):63–65, March 1997.
10. J. M. Kleinberg. Authoritative sources in a hyperlinked environment. *JACM*, 46, 1999.
11. S. Lam, D. Frankowski, and J. Riedl. Do You Trust Your Recommendations? An Exploration of Security and Privacy Issues in Recommender Systems. In *Proc. ETRICS '06*, 2006.
12. M. Langheinrich. When trust does not compute – the role of trust in ubiquitous computing. Workshop on Privacy at Ubicomp 2003, October 2003.
13. R. Lempel and S. Moran. Salsa: the stochastic approach for link-structure analysis. *ACM Trans. Inf. Syst.*, 19(2):131–160, April 2001.
14. P. Massa and P. Avesani. Trust-aware recommender systems. In *Proc. ACM RecSys '07*, 2007.
15. B. Mobasher, R. Burke, R. Bhaumik, and C. Williams. Toward trustworthy recommender systems: An analysis of attack models and algorithm robustness. *ACM TOIT*, 7(4):23, 2007.
16. B. Mobasher, R. Burke, and J. J. Sandvig. Model-based collaborative filtering as a defense against profile injection attacks. In *Proc. AAAI'06*, 2006.
17. M. A. Nowak and K. Sigmund. Evolution of indirect reciprocity by image scoring. *Nature*, 393(6685):573–577, 1998.
18. M. O'Mahony, N. Hurley, and G. Silvestre. Promoting Recommendations: An Attack on Collaborative Filtering. In *Database and Expert Systems Applications*. Springer, 2002.
19. L. Page, S. Brin, R. Motwani and T. Winograd. The PageRank Citation Ranking: Bringing Order to the Web. Digital Libraries Project 1999-66, Stanford University, 1999.
20. H. Yu, M. Kaminsky, P. B. Gibbons, and A. Flaxman. Sybilguard: defending against Sybil attacks via social networks. In *ACM SIGCOMM 2006*, pages 267–278. ACM, 2006.

Continuous Ratings in Discrete Bayesian Reputation Systems

Audun Jøsang, Xixi Luo and Xiaowu Chen

Abstract Reputation systems take as input ratings from members in a community, and can produce measures of reputation, trustworthiness or reliability of entities in the same community. Binomial and multinomial Bayesian reputation systems are discrete in nature meaning that they normally take discrete ratings such as "average" or "good" as input. However, in many situations it is natural to provide input ratings to reputation systems based on continuous measures. This paper describes the principles of discrete Bayesian reputation systems, and how continuous measures can provide input ratings to such systems. The method is based on fuzzy set membership functions.

1 Introduction

Online reputation systems have emerged as important decision support tools that can help reduce the risk of engaging in transactions and interactions on the Internet. Reputation systems stimulate higher quality online services, and are also being investigated as a general method of social control in the online environment.

The same basic principles for creation and propagation of reputation in the physical world used by online reputation systems. The main difference is that online reputation systems are supported by extremely efficient network and computer systems. While reputation formation in the physical world is mostly limited to local communities, online reputation systems have no geographical limits.

Audun Jøsang
University of Oslo, UNIK Graduate Center, Norway e-mail: josang@unik.no

Xixi Luo
Beihang University e-mail: xixiluo@cse.buaa.edu.cn

Xiaowu Chen
Beihang University e-mail: chen@vrlab.buaa.edu.cn

Please use the following format when citing this chapter:

Jøsang, A., Luo, X. and Chen, X., 2008, in IFIP International Federation for Information Processing, Volume 263, *Trust Management II*, Yücel Karabulut, John Mitchell, Peter Herrmann, Christian Damsgaard Jensen; (Boston: Springer), pp. 151–166.

Reputation systems collect information about the performance of a given entity as ratings from other community participants who have had direct experience with that entity. In the typical case of centralised reputation systems, the reputation centre collects all the ratings and derives a reputation score for every party. The reputation scores are published online so that they represent the public reputation of every party in the community. Participants can then use each other's scores, for example, when deciding whether or not to transact with a particular party. The idea is that transactions with reputable parties are likely to result in more favourable outcomes than transactions with disreputable parties.

Fig.1 shows a typical centralised reputation system architecture, where A and B denote parties with a history of transactions in the past, and who consider transacting with each other in the present.

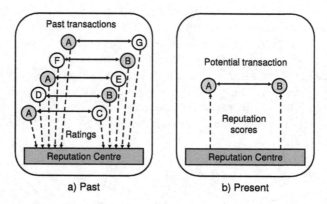

a) Past   b) Present

Fig. 1 General reputation system architecture

Fig.1.a shows that the parties provide ratings about each other's performance after each transaction. The reputation centre collects ratings from all the agents, and continuously updates each agent's reputation score as a function of the received ratings.

Fig.1.b shows that updated reputation scores are provided online for all the parties to see. These are used by party A and B to decide whether or not to transact with each other.

Two fundamental elements of reputation systems are:

1. *Communication protocols* that allow participants to provide ratings about transaction partners to the reputation centre, as well as to obtain reputation scores of potential transaction partners from the reputation centre.
2. *A reputation computation engine* used by the reputation centre to derive reputation scores for each participant, based on received ratings, and possibly also on other information.

This paper focuses on the reputation computation engine. Bayesian reputation systems represent a type of mathematically sound and well studied computation engines. We have previously proposed and studied binomial and multinomial Bayesian reputation systems [3, 4, 5, 8]. Binomial reputation systems allow ratings to be expressed with two values, as either positive (e.g. *good*) or negative (e.g. *bad*). Multinomial reputation systems allow the possibility of providing ratings with graded levels such as e.g. *mediocre - bad - average - good - excellent*. In addition, multinomial models are able to distinguish between the case of polarised ratings (i.e. a combination of strictly good and bad ratings) and the case of only average ratings. The ability to indicate when ratings are polarised can provide valuable clues to the user in many situations. Multinomial reputation systems therefore provide great flexibility when collecting ratings and providing reputation scores.

However, it is common that the subject matter to be rated is measured on a continuous scale, such as time, throughput or relative ranking, to name a few examples. Even when it is natural to provide discrete ratings, it may be difficult to express that something is strictly good or average, so that combinations of discrete ratings, such as *"average-to-good"* would better reflect the rater's opinion. Such ratings can then be considered continuous. To handle this, it is important to have a sound and consistent method for including continuous measures as normal ratings in reputation systems. This paper investigates principles for including ratings based on continuous measures in reputation systems, and combining them with traditional discrete measures. We show that this can be done through membership functions in the same way as fuzzy set membership is computed in traditional fuzzy set theory.

The rest of the paper is structured as follows. Sec.2 briefly reviews the Bayesian multinomial model, and Sec.3 describes how to design reputation systems based on this model. Sec.4 describes how continuous measures can be taken as input ratings in Bayesian reputation systems, and Sec.5 describes an example of using this method. Sec.6 concludes.

2 The Multinomial Bayesian Model

This section briefly reviews the principles of the multinomial Bayesian model which forms the basis for Bayesian reputation systems. For details, see [5, 1].

2.1 The Dirichlet Distribution

Multinomial Bayesian reputation systems allow ratings to be provided over k different levels which can be considered as a set of k disjoint elements. Let this set be denoted as $\Lambda = \{L_1, \ldots L_k\}$, and assume that ratings are provided as votes on the elements of Λ. This leads to a Dirichlet probability density function over the k-component random probability variable $\mathbf{p}(L_i)$, $i = 1 \ldots k$ with sample space $[0, 1]^k$, subject to the simple additivity requirement $\sum_{i=1}^{k} \mathbf{p}(L_i) = 1$.

The Dirichlet distribution with prior captures a sequence of observations of the k possible outcomes with k positive real rating parameters $\mathbf{r}(L_i)$, $i = 1 \ldots k$, each corresponding to one of the possible levels. In order to have a compact notation we define a vector $\mathbf{p} = \{\mathbf{p}(L_i) \mid 1 \le i \le k\}$ to denote the k-component probability variable, and a vector $\mathbf{r} = \{r_i \mid 1 \le i \le k\}$ to denote the k-component rating variable.

In order to distinguish between the *a priori* default base rate, and the *a posteriori* ratings, the Dirichlet distribution must be expressed with prior information represented as a base rate vector $\mathbf{a}$ over the state space. This will be called the Dirichlet Distribution with Prior.

Definition 1 (Dirichlet Distribution with Prior).
Let $\Lambda = \{L_1, \ldots L_k\}$ be a state space consisting of k mutually disjoint elements. Let $\mathbf{r}$ represent the rating vector over the elements of Λ and let $\mathbf{a}$ represent the base rate vector over the same elements. Then the multinomial probability density function over Λ is expressed as:

$$f(\mathbf{p} \mid \mathbf{r}, \mathbf{a}) = \frac{\Gamma\left(\sum_{i=1}^{k}(\mathbf{r}(L_i) + C\mathbf{a}(L_i))\right)}{\prod_{i=1}^{k}\Gamma(\mathbf{r}(L_i) + C\mathbf{a}(L_i))} \prod_{i=1}^{k} \mathbf{p}(L_i)^{(\mathbf{r}(L_i) + C\mathbf{a}(L_i) - 1)} ,$$

$$\text{where} \begin{cases} \sum_{i=1}^{k} \mathbf{p}(L_i) = 1 \\ \\ \mathbf{p}(L_i) \ge 0, \forall i \end{cases} \text{and} \begin{cases} \sum_{i=1}^{k} \mathbf{a}(L_i) = 1 \\ \\ \mathbf{a}(L_i) > 0, \forall i . \end{cases} \tag{1}$$

The vector $\mathbf{p}$ represents probability variables, so that for a given $\mathbf{p}$ the probability density $f(\mathbf{p} \mid \mathbf{r}, \mathbf{a})$ represents their second order probability. The first-order variables of $\mathbf{p}$ represent probabilities of rating levels, whereas the density $f(\mathbf{p} \mid \mathbf{r}, \mathbf{a})$ represents the probability of specific values for the first-order variables. Since the first-order variables $\mathbf{p}$ are continuous, the second-order probability $f(\mathbf{p} \mid \mathbf{r}, \mathbf{a})$ for any given value of $\mathbf{p}(L_i) \in [0, 1]$ is vanishingly small and therefore meaningless as such. It is only meaningful to compute $\int_{p_1}^{p_2} f(\mathbf{p}(L_i) \mid \mathbf{r}, \mathbf{a})$ for a given interval $[p_1, p_2]$ and level L_i, or simply to compute the expectation value of $\mathbf{p}(L_i)$. The most natural is to define the reputation score as a function of the expectation value. This provides a sound mathematical basis for combining ratings and for expressing reputation scores. The probability expectation of any of the k random probability variables can be written as:

$$\mathrm{E}(\mathbf{p}(L_i) \mid \mathbf{r}, \mathbf{a}) = \frac{\mathbf{r}(L_i) + C\mathbf{a}(L_i)}{C + \sum_{i=1}^{k} \mathbf{r}(L_i)} . \tag{2}$$

The *a priori* constant C will normally be set to $C = 2$ when a uniform distribution over binary state spaces is assumed. Selecting a larger value for C will result in new observations having less influence over the Dirichlet distribution, and can in fact represent specific *a priori* information provided by a domain expert or by another reputation system. It can be noted that it would be unnatural to require a uniform distribution over arbitrary large state spaces because it would make the sensitivity to new evidence arbitrarily small.

For example, requiring a uniform *a priori* distribution over a state space of cardinality 100, would force $C = 100$. In case an event of interest has been observed 100 times, and no other event has been observed, the derived probability expectation value of the event of interest will still only be about $\frac{1}{2}$, which would seem totally counterintuitive. In contrast, when a uniform *a priori* distribution is assumed in the binary case, and the same 100 observations are taken as input, the derived probability expectation of the event of interest would be close to 1, as intuition would dictate.

The value of C determines the approximate number of votes needed for a particular level to influence the probability expectation value of that level from 0 to 0.5

2.2 Visualising Dirichlet Distributions

Visualising Dirichlet distributions is challenging because it is a density function over $k-1$ dimensions, where k is the state space cardinality. For this reason, Dirichlet distributions over ternary state spaces are the largest that can be easily visualised.

With $k = 3$, the probability distribution has 2 degrees of freedom, and the equation $\mathbf{p}(L_1) + \mathbf{p}(L_2) + \mathbf{p}(L_3) = 1$ defines a triangular plane as illustrated in Fig.2.

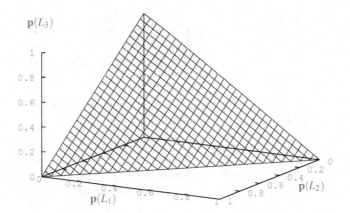

Fig. 2 Triangular plane

In order to visualise probability density over the triangular plane, it is convenient to lay the triangular plane horizontally in the x-y plane, and visualise the density dimension along the z-axis.

Let us consider the example of a reputation system with three discrete rating levels: L_1, L_2 and L_3 (i.e. $k = 3$). Let us first assume that no other information than the cardinality is available, meaning that the default base rate is $\mathbf{a}(L_i) = 1/3$ for all states, and $\mathbf{r}(L_1) = \mathbf{r}(L_2) = \mathbf{r}(L_3) = 0$. Then Eq.(2) dictates that the expected *a priori* probability of picking a ball of any specific colour is the default base rate probability, which is $\frac{1}{3}$. The *a priori* Dirichlet density function is illustrated in Fig.3.

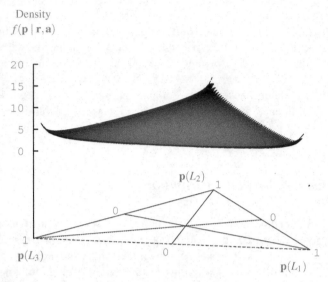

Fig. 3 Prior Dirichlet distribution in case of three rating levels

Let us now assume that ratings have been given as $\mathbf{r}(L_1) = 6$, $\mathbf{r}(L_2) = 1$, and $\mathbf{r}(L_3) = 1$. Then the *a posteriori* expected probability of level L_1 can be computed as $\mathrm{E}(\mathbf{p}(L_1)) = \frac{2}{3}$. The *a posteriori* Dirichlet density function is illustrated in Fig.4.

3 The Dirichlet Reputation System

Multinomial Bayesian systems are based on computing reputation scores by statistical updating of Dirichlet Probability Density Function (PDF). This can be called Dirichlet reputation system [5]. The *a posteriori* (i.e. the updated) reputation score is computed by combining the *a priori* (i.e. previous) reputation score with the new rating. The same principle is also used for binomial Bayesian reputation systems based on the Beta distribution [2, 4, 6, 7].

In Dirichlet reputation systems, an agent is allowed to rate another agent or service, with any level from a set of predefined rating levels, and the reputation scores are not static but will gradually change with time as a function of the received ratings. Initially, each agent's reputation is defined by the base rate reputation which is distributed evenly among all agents. After evidence about a particular agent is gathered, its reputation will change accordingly. Moreover, the reputation score can be represented on different forms.

Density
$f(\mathbf{p} \mid \mathbf{r}, \mathbf{a})$

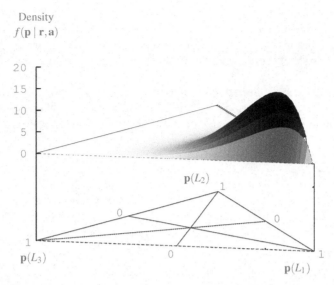

Fig. 4 *A posteriori* Dirichlet distribution after 6 L_1-ratings 1 L_2-rating and 1 L_3-rating

3.1 Collecting Ratings

A general reputation system allows for an agent to rate another agent or service, with any level from a set of predefined rating levels. Some form of control over what and when ratings can be given is normally required, such as e.g. after a transaction has taken place, but this issue will not be discussed here. Let there be k different discrete rating levels. This translates into having a state space of cardinality k for the Dirichlet distribution. Let the rating level be indexed by i. The aggregate ratings for a particular agent y are stored as a cumulative vector, expressed as:

$$\mathbf{R}_y = (\mathbf{R}_y(L_i) \mid i = 1 \ldots k) . \tag{3}$$

The simplest way of updating a rating vector as a result of a new rating is by adding the newly received rating vector $\mathbf{r}$ to the previously stored vector $\mathbf{R}$. The case when old ratings are aged is described in Sec.3.2.

Each new discrete rating of agent y by an agent x takes the form of a trivial vector $\mathbf{r}_y^x$ where only one element has value 1, and all other vector elements have value 0. The index i of the vector element with value 1 refers to the specific rating level.

3.2 Aggregating Ratings with Aging

Ratings may be aggregated by simple addition of the components (vector addition).

Agents (and in particular human agents) may change their behaviour over time, so it is desirable to give relatively greater weight to more recent ratings. This can be achieved by introducing a longevity factor $\lambda \in [0,1]$, which controls the rapidity with which old ratings are aged and discounted as a function of time. With $\lambda = 0$, ratings are completely forgotten after a single time period. With $\lambda = 1$, ratings are never forgotten.

Let new ratings be collected in discrete time periods. Let the sum of the ratings of a particular agent y in period t be denoted by the vector $\mathbf{r}_{y,t}$. More specifically, it is the sum of all ratings $\mathbf{r}_y^x$ of agent y by other agents x during that period, expressed by:

$$\mathbf{r}_{y,t} = \sum_{x \in M_{y,t}} \mathbf{r}_y^x \tag{4}$$

where $M_{y,t}$ is the set of all agents who rated agent y during period t.

Let the total accumulated ratings (with aging) of agent y after the time period t be denoted by $\mathbf{R}_{y,t}$. Then the new accumulated rating after time period $t+1$ can be expressed as:

$$\mathbf{R}_{y,(t+1)} = \lambda \cdot \mathbf{R}_{y,t} + \mathbf{r}_{y,(t+1)}, \text{ where } 0 \leq \lambda \leq 1 . \tag{5}$$

Eq.(5) represents a recursive updating algorithm that can be executed once every period for all agents. Assuming that new ratings are received between time t and time $t+n$, then the new rating can be computed as:

$$\mathbf{R}_{y,(t+n)} = \lambda^n \cdot \mathbf{R}_{y,t} + \mathbf{r}_{y,(t+n)} , \ 0 \leq \lambda \leq 1. \tag{6}$$

3.3 Convergence Values for Reputation Scores

The recursive algorithm of Eq.(5) makes it possible to compute convergence values for the rating vectors, as well as for reputation scores. Assuming that a particular agent receives the same ratings every period, the Eq.(5) defines a geometric series. We use the well known result of geometric series:

$$\sum_{j=0}^{\infty} \lambda^j = \frac{1}{1-\lambda} \text{ for } -1 < \lambda < 1 . \tag{7}$$

Let $\mathbf{r}_y$ represent the rating vector of agent y for each period. The Total accumulated rating vector after an infinite number of periods is then expressed as:

$$\mathbf{R}_{y,\infty} = \frac{\mathbf{r}_y}{1-\lambda}, \text{ where } 0 \leq \lambda < 1 . \tag{8}$$

Eq.(8) shows that the longevity factor determines the convergence values for the accumulated rating vectors.

3.4 Reputation Representation

A reputation score applies to member agents in a community M. Before any evidence is known about a particular agent y, its reputation is defined by the base rate reputation which is the same for all agents. As evidence about a particular agent is gathered, its reputation will change accordingly.

The reputation score of a multinomial system can be represented on different forms, which can be *evidence representation*, *density representation*, *multinomial probability representation*, or *point estimate representation*. Each form will be described in turn below.

3.4.1 Evidence Representation

The most direct form of representation is to simply express the aggregate evidence vector $\mathbf{R}_y$. The amount of ratings of level i for agent y is denoted by $\mathbf{R}_y(L_i)$.

It is not necessary to express individual base rate vectors, as it will be the same for all agents.

3.4.2 Density Representation

The reputation score of an agent can be expressed as a multinomial probability density function (PDF) in the form of Eq.(1). For ternary state spaces, the PDF can be visualised as in Fig.4. Visualisation of PDFs for state spaces larger than ternary is not practical.

3.4.3 Multinomial Probability Representation

The most natural is to define the reputation score as a function of the probability expectation values of each element in the state space. The expectation value for each rating level can be computed with Eq.(2).

Let $\mathbf{R}$ represent a target agent's aggregate ratings. Then the vector $\mathbf{S}$ defined by:

$$\mathbf{S}_y : \left(\mathbf{S}_y(L_i) = \frac{\mathbf{R}_y(L_i) + C\mathbf{a}(L_i)}{C + \sum_{j=1}^{k} \mathbf{R}_y(L_j)}; \mid i = 1\ldots k \right). \tag{9}$$

is the corresponding multinomial probability reputation score. As already stated, $C = 2$ is the value of choice, but larger value for the constant C can be chosen if a reduced influence of new evidence over the base rate is required.

The reputation score $\mathbf{S}$ can be interpreted like a multinomial probability measure as an indication of how a particular agent is expected to behave in future transactions. It can easily be verified that

$$\sum_{i=1}^{k} S(L_i) = 1 . \tag{10}$$

The multinomial reputation score can for example be visualised as columns, which would clearly indicate if ratings are polarised. Assume for example 5 levels:

$$\text{Discrete rating levels:} \begin{cases} L_1 : \text{Mediocre,} \\ L_2 : \text{Bad,} \\ L_3 : \text{Average,} \\ L_4 : \text{Good,} \\ L_5 : \text{Excellent.} \end{cases} \tag{11}$$

We assume a default base rate distribution. Before any ratings have been received, the multinomial probability reputation score will be equal to $1/5$ for all levels. Let us assume that 10 ratings are received. In the first case, 10 *average* ratings are received, which translates into the multinomial probability reputation score of Fig.5.a. In the second case, 5 mediocre and 5 excellent ratings are received, which translates into the multinomial probability reputation score of Fig.5.b.

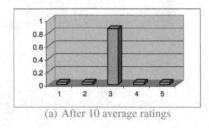
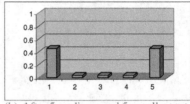

(a) After 10 average ratings

(b) After 5 mediocre and 5 excellent ratings

Fig. 5 Illustrating score difference resulting from average and polarised ratings

With a binomial reputation system, the difference between these two rating scenarios would not have been visible.

In case an agent receives the same ratings every period, the reputation scores will converge to specific values. These values emerge by inserting the convergence values of Eq.(8) into Eq.(9). Let $\mathbf{r}_y$ be the constant ratings that agent y receives every period. The convergence score value for each rating level i can then be expressed as:

$$\mathbf{S}_{y,\infty}(L_i) = \frac{\lambda \cdot \mathbf{r}_y(L_i) + (1-\lambda)C\mathbf{a}(L_i)}{(1-\lambda)C + \lambda \sum_{j=1}^{k} \mathbf{r}_y(L_j)} \tag{12}$$

In particular it can be seen that when no ratings are received (i.e. $\mathbf{r}_y$ is the null vector), then the convergence score value for each level is simply the base rate for that level.

3.4.4 Point Estimate Representation

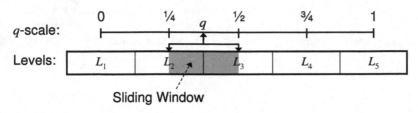

Fig. 6 Sliding windows

While informative, the multinomial probability representation can require considerable space to be displayed on a computer screen. A more compact form can be to express the reputation score as a single value in some predefined interval. This can be done by assigning a point value v to each rating level i, and computing the normalised weighted point estimate score σ.

Assume e.g. k different rating levels with point values evenly distributed in the range [0,1], so that $v(L_i) = \frac{i-1}{k-1}$. The point estimate reputation score is then computed as:

$$\sigma = \sum_{i=1}^{k} v(L_i)S(L_i) .\tag{13}$$

However, this point estimate removes information, so that for example the difference between the average ratings and the polarised ratings of Fig.5.a and Fig.5.b is no longer visible. The point estimates of the reputation scores of Fig.5.a and Fig.5.b are both 0.5, although the ratings in fact are quite different. A point estimate in the range [0,1] can be mapped to any range, such as 1-5 stars, a percentage or a probability.

3.5 Dynamic Community Base Rates

Bootstrapping a reputation system to a stable and conservative state is important. In the framework described above, the base rate distribution **a** will define initial default reputation for all agents. The base rate can for example be evenly distributed, or biased towards either a negative or a positive reputation. This must be defined by those who set up the reputation system in a specific market or community.

Agents will come and go during the lifetime of a market, and it is important to be able to assign new members a reasonable base rate reputation. In the simplest case, this can be the same as the initial default reputation that was given to all agents during bootstrap.

However, it is possible to track the average reputation score of the whole community, and this can be used to set the base rate for new agents, either directly or with a certain additional bias.

Not only new agents, but also existing agents with a standing track record can get the dynamic base rate. After all, a dynamic community base rate reflects the whole community, and should therefore be applied to all the members of that community.

The aggregate reputation vector for the whole community at time t can be computed as:

$$\mathbf{R}_{M,t} = \sum_{y_j \in M} \mathbf{R}_{y,t} \tag{14}$$

This vector then needs to be normalised to a base rate vector as follows:

Definition 2 (Community Base Rate). Let $\mathbf{R}_{M,t}$ be an aggregate reputation vector for a whole community, and let $\mathbf{S}_{M,t}$ be the corresponding multinomial probability reputation vector which can be computed with Eq.(9). The community base rate as a function of existing reputations at time $t+1$ is then simply expressed as the community score at time t:

$$\mathbf{a}_{M,(t+1)} = \mathbf{S}_{M,t}. \tag{15}$$

The base rate vector of Eq.(15) can be given to every new agent that joins the community. In addition, the community base rate vector can be used for every agent every time their reputation score is computed. In this way, the base rate will dynamically reflect the quality of the market at any one time.

If desirable, the base rate for new agents can be biased in either negative or positive direction in order to make it harder or easier to enter the market.

When base rates are a function of the community reputation, the expressions for convergence values with constant ratings can no longer be defined with Eq.(8), and will instead converge towards the average score from all the ratings.

4 Taking Continuous Ratings

This section describes a method for taking continuous ratings as a basis for input to multinomial and binomial Bayesian reputation systems.

4.1 The Multinomial Case

For a multinomial reputation system with k discrete levels, the parameters of the Dirichlet distribution are $\mathbf{r}$. Our method is based on a sliding window for determining the discrete rating as a function of the continuous rating.

In general, when there are k rating levels, the parameters $(\mathbf{r}(L_1), \mathbf{r}(L_2), ..., \mathbf{r}(L_k))$ can be computed as a function of the continuous rating q according to fuzzy triangular membership functions.

Let each rating level L_t be a fuzzy subset, and each rating q is assigned a membership grade $\mathbf{r}(L_i, q)$ taking values in $[0, 1]$, with $\mathbf{r}(L_i, q) = 0$ corresponding to non-membership in L_i, $0 < \mathbf{r}(L_i, q) < 1$ to partial membership in L_i, and $\mathbf{r}(L_i, q) = 1$ to full membership in L_i. According to the above analysis, the fuzzy set triangular membership functions can be expressed in terms of Eq.(16), Eq.(17), and Eq.(18).

Membership function for L_1 :

$$\mathbf{r}(L_1, q) = \begin{cases} 1 - q(k-1) & \text{IF } 0 \leq q \leq \frac{1}{(k-1)} \\ 0 & \text{ELSE} \end{cases} \tag{16}$$

Membership function for L_i where $1 < i < k$:

$$\mathbf{r}(L_i, q) = \begin{cases} i - q(k-1) & \text{IF } \frac{(i-1)}{(k-1)} \leq q \leq \frac{i}{(k-1)} \\ 2 - i + q(k-1) & \text{IF } \frac{(i-2)}{(k-1)} \leq q \leq \frac{(i-1)}{(k-1)} \\ 0 & \text{ELSE} \end{cases} \tag{17}$$

Membership function for L_k :

$$\mathbf{r}(L_k, q) = \begin{cases} 2 - k + q(k-1) & \text{IF } \frac{(k-2)}{(k-1)} \leq q \leq 1 \\ 0 & \text{ELSE} \end{cases} \tag{18}$$

For example with five rating levels the sliding window function can be illustrated as in Fig.6.

The continuous q-value determines the position of the sliding window. The relative overlap between the window and a specific level determines the r-value for that level.

As an example, Fig.6 indicates the continuous value $q = 3/8$, which causes the sliding window to overlap with rating levels L_2 and L_3. It can be seen that $q = 3/8$ results in the level rating vector expressed by:

$$\text{Discrete level ratings resulting from } q = 3/8: \begin{cases} \mathbf{r}(L_1) = 0.0 \\ \mathbf{r}(L_2) = 0.5 \\ \mathbf{r}(L_3) = 0.5 \\ \mathbf{r}(L_4) = 0.0 \\ \mathbf{r}(L_5) = 0.0 \end{cases} \tag{19}$$

These r-ratings can then be fed into the reputation system described in Sec.3.

Visualisation of fuzzy membership functions provide an alternative way of intuitively deriving the discrete level ratings. The fuzzy membership functions in the case of 5 discrete rating levels are illustrated in Fig.7.

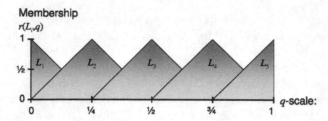

Fig. 7 Fuzzy triangular membership functions

A discrete rating vector derived from a continuous measure will have either one or two vector elements with positive value, where the sum is always one. This property emerges from the formal expressions of Eqs.(16), (17) and (18). The same property becomes immediately obvious through the visualisation of the fuzzy membership functions in Fig.7.

4.2 The Binomial Case

The binomial case is simply a special case of the multinomial case. Let (r_1, r_2) be the parameters of the Beta distribution. Let q be the continuous rating in the range $[0,1]$. Then (r_1, r_2) can be determined by the fuzzy set membership function

$$\begin{cases} r_1(q) = 1 - q \\ r_2(q) = q \end{cases} \tag{20}$$

For every continuous rating, we can compute its membership value to each rating level, and then taking this membership value to be the rating of that level. The Eq.(4)$\cdots$Eq.(13) are the same with continuous ratings, and the parameter r is allowed to be any number between 0 and 1, but not limited to be 0 and 1.

5 Example

In this example, agents can be rated on continuous measures in the range $[0,1]$, and the reputation system has 5 discrete levels, with base rates evenly distributed. Let an agent be rated over 10 time periods as expressed in Table 1. The longevity factor is set to $\lambda = 0.9$.

Computing the rating levels with Eqs.(16), (17), and (18), we can get the level ratings expressed in the middle row of Table 1.

Then applying Eq.(9), we can get the corresponding multinomial reputation scores in the bottom row of Table 1. The same scores are visualized as a function of the time period in Fig.8.

Time Period	0	1	2	3	4	5	6	7	8	9	10
Continuous ratings:	0.05	0.05	0.05	0.00	0.10	0.90	0.80	0.80	0.80	0.90	
Level ratings	↓	↓	↓	↓	↓	↓	↓	↓	↓	↓	↓
L_1		0.8	0.8	0.8	1.0	0.6					
L_2		0.2	0.2	0.2	0	0.4					
L_3											
L_4							0.4	0.8	0.8	0.8	0.4
L_5							0.6	0.2	0.2	0.2	0.6
Level scores	↓	↓	↓	↓	↓	↓	↓	↓	↓	↓	↓
L_1	0.2	0.4	0.4923	0.5452	0.6161	0.5998	0.4982	0.4209	0.3604	0.3121	0.2728
L_2	0.2	0.2	0.2	0.2	0.1632	0.2033	0.1728	0.1496	0.1315	0.1170	0.1052
L_3	0.2	0.1333	0.1026	0.0849	0.0735	0.0656	0.0598	0.0554	0.0520	0.0492	0.0470
L_4	0.2	0.1333	0.1026	0.0849	0.0735	0.0656	0.1197	0.2162	0.2916	0.3519	0.3540
L_5	0.2	0.1333	0.1026	0.0849	0.0735	0.0656	0.1496	0.1580	0.1645	0.1698	0.2210

Table 1 Scalar ratings translated into level ratings that in turn generate level scores

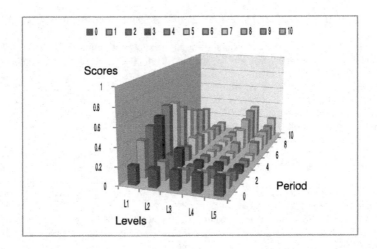

Fig. 8 Evolution of an agent's reputation scores after the rating sequence of Table 1

It can be seen that the first five periods are characterised by very low continuous ratings, resulting in the score for L_1 increasing rapidly. Then in the five last periods, the continuous rating is relatively high, resulting in increasing scores for L_4 and L_5 and decreasing scores for L_1, L_2 and L_3.

6 Conclusion

Bayesian reputation systems normally take discrete ratings as input. This could represent a limitation to the applicability of such reputation systems when the observations to be rated are continuous in nature. This paper focuses on transforming continuous ratings into discrete ratings by using fuzzy set membership function. This work makes the Bayesian reputation systems more practical and generally applicable. The traditional reputation system principles such as aggregating rating with aging, convergence value for reputation scores, methods for reputation representation, and dynamic community base rates are equally applicable both with discrete and continuous ratings.

References

1. A. Gelman et al. *Bayesian Data Analysis, 2nd ed*. Chapman and Hall/CRC, Florida, USA, 2004.
2. A. Jøsang. Trust-Based Decision Making for Electronic Transactions. In L. Yngström and T. Svensson, editors, *Proceedings of the 4th Nordic Workshop on Secure Computer Systems (NORDSEC'99)*. Stockholm University, Sweden, 1999.
3. A. Jøsang, S. Hird, and E. Faccer. Simulating the Effect of Reputation Systems on e-Markets. In P. Nixon and S. Terzis, editors, *Proceedings of the First International Conference on Trust Management (iTrust)*, Crete, May 2003.
4. A. Jøsang and R. Ismail. The Beta Reputation System. In *Proceedings of the 15th Bled Electronic Commerce Conference*, June 2002.
5. A. Jøsang and Haller J. Dirichlet Reputation Systems. In *In the Proceedings of the International Conference on Availability, Reliability and Security (ARES 2007)*, Vienna, Austria, April 2007.
6. L. Mui, M. Mohtashemi, C. Ang, P. Szolovits, and A. Halberstadt. Ratings in Distributed Systems: A Bayesian Approach. In *Proceedings of the Workshop on Information Technologies and Systems (WITS)*, 2001.
7. L. Mui, M. Mohtashemi, and A. Halberstadt. A Computational Model of Trust and Reputation. In *Proceedings of the 35th Hawaii International Conference on System Science (HICSS)*, 2002.
8. A. Withby, A. Jøsang, and J. Indulska. Filtering Out Unfair Ratings in Bayesian Reputation Systems. *The Icfain Journal of Management Research*, 4(2):48–64, 2005.

A Robust and Knot-Aware Trust-Based Reputation Model

Nurit Gal-Oz, Ehud Gudes and Danny Hendler

Abstract Virtual communities become more and more heterogeneous as their scale increases. This implies that, rather than being a single, homogeneous community, they become a collection of *knots* (or sub-communities) of users. For the computation of a member's reputation to be useful, the system must therefore identify the community knot to which this member belongs and to interpret its reputation data correctly. Unfortunately, to the best of our knowledge existing trust-based reputation models treat a community as a single entity and do not explicitly address this issue. In this paper, we introduce the *knot-aware* trust-based reputation model for large-scale virtual communities. We define a *knot* as a group of community members having overall "strong" trust relations between them. Different knots typically represent different view points and preferences. It is therefore plausible that the reputation of the same member in different knots assign may differ significantly. Using our knot-aware approach, we can deal with heterogeneous communities where a member's reputation may be distributed in a multi modal manner. As we show, an interesting and beneficial feature of our knot-aware model is that it naturally prevents malicious attempts to bias community members' reputation.

Nurit Gal-Oz
Deutsche Telekom Laboratories at Ben-Gurion University, Beer-Sheva, 84105, Israel, e-mail: ga-loz@cs.bgu.ac.il

Ehud Gudes
Deutsche Telekom Laboratories at Ben-Gurion University, Beer-Sheva, 84105, Israel, e-mail: ehud@cs.bgu.ac.il

Danny Hendler
Deutsche Telekom Laboratories at Ben-Gurion University, Beer-Sheva, 84105, Israel, e-mail: hendlerd@cs.bgu.ac.il

Please use the following format when citing this chapter:

Gal-Oz, N., Gudes, E. and Hendler, D., 2008, in IFIP International Federation for Information Processing, Volume 263, *Trust Management II*; Yücel Karabulut, John Mitchell, Peter Herrmann, Christian Damsgaard Jensen; (Boston: Springer), pp. 167–182.

1 Introduction

The Internet has enabled the creation of virtual worlds and communities, where user interactions imitate and, to some extent, even replace the more traditional "real-life" equivalents on a larger scale. The existence of easily accessible virtual communities makes it both possible and legitimate to communicate with total strangers. We can now anonymously interact with other virtual community members whom we do not really know in ways that are, in general, not possible in the "real world".

Many of our real-life decisions, such as, e.g., which book to buy or which physician to consult with, are based on information that we collect based on our social interactions. Our decisions are often based on our own direct experience, but when direct experience is lacking, we have to rely on the opinions of people we know. In the latter case, the weight we assign to these opinions is directly correlated to the extent by which we trust these people. This decision-making process is obviously individual and is often based on hunches and intuitions: we are not always fully aware of why we eventually decide as we do. While representing the data used for such decisions electronically is relatively straightforward, it is much harder to imitate human decision making processes once that information is available. This is a key difficulty in devising effective virtual communities. Another difficulty is that virtual communities expose their members to new types of fraud and deception since impersonation is much easier in virtual communities than in the "real-world".

Trust and reputation systems are considered key enablers of virtual communities, especially communities of strangers, where users are not required to reveal their real identities and use nicknames or pseudonyms instead. These systems support the accumulation of member reputation information and leverage this information to increase the likelihood of successful member interactions and to better protect the community from fraudulent members. Unlike cryptographic-based security mechanisms to which a user typically must be explicitly aware, trust and reputation systems are often considered to be a *soft security* mechanism [15]: "Soft security accepts and even expects that there might be unwanted intruders in the system. The idea is to identify them and prevent them from harming the other actors".

As the scale of virtual communities continues to increase, they become more and more heterogeneous. This implies that, rather than being a single, homogenous community, they become a collection of loosely-coupled *knots* (i.e. sub-communities) of users. We define a *knot* as a group of community members having overall "strong" trust relations between themselves (see Section 3.3 for a formal definition). Typically, members belonging to the same knot are more likely to have similar viewpoints and preferences as compared to members that belong to different knots.

In this paper, we present the knot-aware trust-based reputation model. We model virtual communities of strangers, where members seek services or expert advice from other members. Two key examples of such communities are eBay [1] and Experts-Exchange [2]. A major implication of the fact that community members do not necessarily expose their real identity is that trust must rely on reputation accumulated by member ratings and cannot be derived from "real-world" social familiarity. The assumption underlying our knot-aware model is that "less is more":

the use of relatively small, but carefully selected, subsets of the overall community's reputation data yields better results than those represented by the full data set. The application of this principle is done by (1) partitioning the community into knots of members who rated other members in a similar manner, and (2) assigning higher weight to the reputation information of intra-knot members than that of members outside the knot. Since members are primarily influenced by members that shared their preferences in the past, a useful feature of our model is that it naturally prevents malicious attempts to bias community members' decisions. Another advantage is that smaller sub-communities, whose viewpoints differ from the overall community average, can maintain their distinctive preferences without having their opinions "diluted' by those of the majority of users outside their knot.

We have implemented an algorithm that adheres to our knot-aware model and conducted experiments to evaluate it by using the publicly available database of the MovieLens [3] movie recommendations community. Our preliminary evaluation results establish that our knot-aware approach improves system predictions as compared with non-knot aware trust computation.

The rest of the paper is organized as follows. Section 2 provides an overview of the related work. In section 3, we formally define our knots-aware model. Simulation results are presented in Section 4. We conclude by discussing future research directions in Section 5.

2 Related Work

Trust and reputation models for virtual communities are gaining increasing research attention. Several such models have been proposed over the last decade. These models differ mainly in how they define trust and reputation, in their assumptions on how the system obtains data on trust relationships, in how they compute new trust relationships based on existing data, and in the set of trust *attributes* (i.e., different trust dimensions) used by them.

Abdul-Rahman and Hailes [4] proposed a model in which the trust attributed to one member by another falls into one of four levels: *VeryTrustworthy*, *Trustworthy*, *Untrustworthy* and *VeryUntrustworthy*. As they mention, trust in their model is not transitive, hence a member only relies on recommenders with which it has "personal experience". *Ratings* are the smallest building block on which trust and reputation models are built. [4] use the *semantic distance* of ratings to identify recommenders that are *over-raters* or *under-raters* and adjust their recommendation accordingly. The trust in a recommender is calculated after a transaction between two members is completed, by evaluating the distance between the recommendation and the actual experience. In computing a recommended trust value (reputation), the model gives higher (fixed) weight to information coming from members with a more similar point of view.

Yu and Singh [18] use Dempster-Shafer's theory of evidence to represent and propagate the ratings given by agents to others. In their model, a user rates an agent upon each transaction as either trusted or untrusted. These ratings are collected and used as evidence to determine the user's level of trust in that agent. Transitive trust-chains of predefined length are generated, in order to identify the *witnesses* of the target agent, and information from different witnesses is aggregated using Demp-ster's rule of combination.

The Beta reputation system introduced by Josang [8] is based on using beta prob-ability density functions to combine feedback and derive reputation ratings. In their model, the authors use a *forgetting factor* to overcome the growing irrelevance of old feedback due to changing behavior of agents over time. However it only con-siders the order of experiences but does not factor in the elapsed time. That is, the one-before-last feedback is "forgotten" to the same degree regardless of whether it was given yesterday or a year ago. An aging factor is used also in Kinateder [11] to update trust. This factor determines how fast new experiences change the trust compared to previous experiences, regardless of the time distance.

Some of the prior art works do not distinguish between trust in a target agent (service provider) and trust in a recommender [10, 19]. These assume that a good service provider will be a reliable witness as well. While this may be true for some systems (e.g., in file sharing systems), it is not necessarily the case for other com-munities. In other works [4, 11], the requesting user is required to rate the recom-mendation she got after the transaction took place. In their paper [11], the authors argue that in ratings that consist of multiple attributes, the process of collecting user feedback cannot be automated and every single recommendation must be rated. This requirement is highly challenging, since soliciting member feedback on transactions is a major challenge in reputation systems; receiving feedback on each and every recommendation might not be feasible. TrustBAC [5] relies on the agents' ability to provide recommendations but it is not clear how these recommendations are ob-tained. TrustBAC is a trust-based access control model that is somewhat different from other models of trust and reputation, as it actually extends the conventional role-based access control model with the notion of trust levels. The trust an agent puts in another is represented by a vector with three components: (1) the *experience* with the target agent, (2) *knowledge*, specifying whether the experience is direct or indirect, and (3) *recommendation* - the cumulative effect of all recommendations from different sources.

In Jimminy [12], the authors present an honesty assessment algorithm and a re-ward model for encouraging honest ratings. Their computation of honesty is based on the probability distribution of all ratings available for a subject. Their model as-sumes there is a correlation between the extent by which a member's ratings disagree with the ratings of others and the probability that the member is dishonest.

In the group based reputation system proposed in [17], groups are constructed according to users shared interests and trust is calculated based on user ratings be-tween peers, between groups and peers, and between groups. A similarity based clustering is used to identify the set of trustworthy raters within a group and filter unfair ratings, however this approach is aimed at certain types of applications (e.g. file sharing).

A review on trust and reputation systems is provided by Josang et al in [9]. Their review discusses the semantics of the trust and reputation concepts and the relations between them, and suggest a classification of trust and reputation measures according to two dimensions: *specific* vs. *general*, and *subjective* vs. *objective*. The authors also provide an overview of reputation computation models and existing applications of online reputation systems. Sabater et al [16] also presents an overview of several computational trust and reputation models that have been implemented and classify them according to a few criteria, such as the source of the information used, the assumptions made on agents' behavior, the visibility of trust, and whether reputation is considered as a personal/subjective property or as a global property.

3 Trust Based Reputation Model

The knots model is composed of three separate modules: the *member trust inference module*, the *knots construction module*, and the *reputation computation module*. The member trust inference module identifies trust relations among members; the knots construction module utilizes these relations to to generate trust knots; the reputation computation module computes local reputations within knots and global reputations for the community as a whole. We describe the key responsibilities of these modules later in this section.

3.1 Trust and Reputation

As mentioned before, our model is designed for communities in which members typically do not reveal their real identities. We consider communities in which experts in specific fields offer their advice and consulting services to community members seeking such services. A community consists of *members*, all of which may participate in community activities, such as searching for an expert, interacting with an expert, and sharing recommendations about experts with other members. *Experts* are a subclass of *members*. Experts may provide professional services and advice to members. Although experts are also members, in what follows we regard experts and members as two disjoint sets for presentation simplicity.

The literature proposes several definitions of the term *trust*. We adopt Mui's definition [14] because it emphasizes the two major aspects of trust - the subjectivity of trust and the importance of accumulated experience - and extend it to capture a third aspect: the transitivity of trust. When searching for an expert, a member takes into consideration the extent to which the members she trusts trust relevant experts.

Definition 1. *Trust* is a subjective expectation an agent has about another's future behavior based on the history of that agent, and other reliable agents' encounters with that other agent.

As suggested in [5], we use the term trust in two different contexts.

Definition 2. *TrustMember* (TM) is Trust in the context of recommendations. More specifically, it is a trust value that quantifies the extent by which one member relies on another member to rate experts "correctly". *TrustExpert* (TE) is Trust in the context of experts. More specifically, it is a trust value that quantifies the extent by which a member relies on an expert to successfully provide the service it requires.

Reputation systems suggest various metrics for calculating reputations. Most of them compile an aggregated "general opinion" of all recommending members. Some of these systems disregard ratings that are too far from the popular rating score or even consider them as malicious [12]. We maintain that it is possible for the same experience to be perceived differently by different people. For example, the same PC expert may get excellent ratings from inexperienced PC users and very poor ratings from highly experienced PC user. When there is no clear normal distribution of the rating scores given, we cannot ignore the opinion of a minority or even try to aggregate the scores to one measure that will surely result in loss of valuable information.

We define reputation according to [14] and add the word "aggregated" to emphasize the fact that reputation is an aggregated quantity. This definition captures the time-dependency as well as the subjective nature of reputation.

Definition 3. *Reputation* is the aggregated perception that an agent creates through past actions about its intentions and norms.

3.2 Member Similarity and Trust Sets

Member ratings are the foundation of most trust and reputation models. *Rating* is a member's evaluation of the quality of a transaction after its completion. There are various aspects on which one can evaluate a transaction. A dimension based rating is a vector of values in the range [0,1], each representing the degree to which a member is pleased with the transaction from a certain aspect. While some of the dimensions depend on the type of transaction performed, others, such as, e.g., promptness or politeness, are more general and may be considered universal dimensions. Our model views a ratings as vectors of dimension weights with total weights sum of 1.

Definition 4. *Rating Similarity* quantifies the similarity between two comparable ratings (i.e., ratings given on the same expert in the same context within some limited time interval). The rating similarity of two ratings is defined as the Euclidean distance between the two rating vectors.

In trust-based reputation models of communities of strangers, such as [4, 10, 5], the trust a member has in another is based on how the trusting member rates the trusted party upon the completion of a transaction. In contrast, in models of communities in which members *are* familiar with each other, trust is based on personal acquaintance.

No explicit recommendations on experts are given by members in our model. Instead, we use the notion of *Member Similarity* (formally defined shortly) to calculate implicit trust among members. Let us elaborate on this idea. We observe that, in communities were explicit recommendations are provided, a recommendation given by one member to the other may be viewed as a transaction between the two members; rating the recommendation is a statement of how valuable it was. One way a member can evaluate the quality of recommendations provided by another member is to compare that member's recommendations with her own experience. In our model, member Similarity quantifies the extent of similarity between the ratings given by two members to the same experts. If the ratings of two members are very similar, this may be viewed as good ratings of the implicit recommendations given by each of them to the other. Hence, the influence of member A's ratings on the results of an expert-search done by member B increases as much as the member Similarity between A and B is higher.

Technically, member Similarity is a value in $[0,1]$, quantifying the extent to which two members are considered similar based on their common experience. Member Similarity may change over time and should thus be calculated based on all comparable ratings while assigning more weight to more recent ones. Our model takes time into account, by splitting history into a set of *time intervals*, each of which is assigned a different weight. This set may change over time. In any instance of time, the sum of interval weights is 1. Typically, more recent time intervals will be assigned higher weights as in [5]. In any instance of time, we only compare two ratings if they belong to the same time interval. The length of a time interval, the number of relevant time intervals and the weight assigned to each time interval are parameters that can be set according to the nature and maturity of the community. Formally, we define member Similarity as the opposite of member Difference, defined in the following.

Definition 5. Let $R^t(A,x)$ denote a rating vector given by member A at time t with respect to expert x. Let $R^{T_i}(A,x)$ denote the average (vector) of all ratings given by A with respect to x in time interval T_i. If there are no such ratings, then $R^{T_i}(A,x)$ is defined as the zero vector. Let X be a set of experts and let $TI \subseteq \{T_1,..,T_i\}$ be the set of time intervals for which comparable ratings with respect to the set of experts X were found. Let W_{T_i} denote the weight of interval T_i.

Then the *Difference* between two users in time $t \in T_i$ is given by:

$$Difference^t(A,B) = \sum_{T_j \in TI} W_{T_j} \cdot Average_{x \in X}(Distance(R^{T_j}(A,x), R^{T_j}(B,x)))$$

Definition 6. The Similarity of two members A and B at time t is defined by:

$$SIM^t(A,B) = 1 - (Difference^t(A,B))$$

Next, we define the *confidence* of member A in member B, which computes the significance of the transactions between A and B relative to the overall transactions in which A was involved.

Definition 7. Let $n(A,B)$ denote the number of ratings used to compare between A and B, let $N_A = \{n(A,B)|B \text{ has comparable ratings with } A\}$. Then the confidence of A in the similarity with B is defined as:

$$SConf_\beta(A,B) = (\beta + (1-\beta) \cdot CDF(N_A, n_B)).$$

Where CDF is the Cumulative Distribution Function. This function describes the statistical distribution of the number of comparable ratings A has with any other member. $CDF(N_A, n_B)$ returns for n_B in the sample N_A the probability of receiving this outcome or a lower one. β is the maximum Trust we allow A to have in B given perfect similarity $Sim(A,B) = 1$ and minimum experience; $(1 - \beta)$ gives weight to previous experience.

Definition 8. The TrustMember function of A in B, denoted by $TM(A,B)$, quantifies the extent by which member A relies on the ratings of member B. It is defined as follows:

$$TM^t(A,B) = SIM^t(A,B) \cdot SConf_\beta(A,B).$$

The *Trust Set* of a member at some point in time is the subset of community members she trusts above some level. The idea behind the Trust Set concept is to allow every member to rely on members that provided ratings similar up to some degree α. The benefit of using Trust-Sets is in limiting the recommendation process to a smaller group of members that are better qualified for the task, while increasing the chance of getting more accurate results.

Definition 9. An α - *Trust Set* of member A denotes the set of all members whom A trusts with level α or more. The value of the α parameter depends on the domain and maturity of the community. We therefore use the term α-mature community to describe a community that requires α as the minimum value considered as trust. The α - *Trust Set* of member A at time t, denoted $TrustSet^t_\alpha(A)$, is defined as follows:

$$TrustSet^t_\alpha(A) = \{B|TM^t(A,B) \geq \alpha\}$$

3.3 Knots

A *knot* is a subset of community members identified as having overall strong trust relations among themselves. Every knot member should trust any other knot member (either directly or indirectly) above some threshold parameter. Two members A and B belong to the same knot if A has high enough direct trust in B (this implies that B is in A's trust set) or if A has high enough indirect trust in B (e.g., if A trusts C and C trusts B and by applying the transitive property of trust we conclude that A trusts B), and vice versa. knots are an extension of trust sets to create groups of members that can rely on each other's recommendations even if they did not rate the same experts. As will be discussed in section 3.5, knots have the ability of reducing the risk of relying on dishonest or biased recommendations, since the members that provide these recommendations are identified and excluded from the knot.

Instead of using trust propagation as in [5, 10, 7], we use the transitivity property to make sure there exists a predefined level of propagated trust among a knot's members. Highly trusted members are identified within each knot. Once a member A is added to a knot, it relies on the recommendations of these members even if A itself does not have high trust in them (either directly or indirectly).

The problem of identifying knots in a trust network is modeled as a graph clustering (GC) problem, where vertices correspond to individual items and edges describe relationships. Under this interpretation, a community is represented by a directed graph $G = (V, E)$, in which vertices represent members and edges represent the trust relations between the members represented by their end-point vertices. The weight on a directed edge from A to B is the level of trust A has in B and is computed by $TM^t(A, B)$. Since our model is time-dependant, this graph changes over time.

We define the edges with weight at least α as *Positive Edges*, and all other edges as *Negative Edges*. We use clustering algorithm to partition the graph into a collection of subgraphs that represent knots. More formally, we define a knot as a cluster of vertices, from each of which there exists a path of positive edges of length k or less (for some system parameter k) to any other, and in which the number of negative edges does not exceed some system threshold parameter (possibly zero).

We use an algorithm based on the notion of *distance-k cliques* as the initial clustering algorithm. A sub-graph is distance-k clique, if any two vertices in it are connected by a path of length k or less. In their paper [6], the authors present a heuristic algorithm for graph clustering using Distance-k cliques. Their work refers to an unweighted and undirected graph. We extend their algorithm to use edge weights as additional criteria.

The value of parameter α is a significant factor in our model. If the group of "negative" edges is relatively small, a higher value of α may be used for obtaining smaller sub-graphs with stronger connectivity. In the opposite case, if there are too many "negative" edges, resulting in a partition into many small sub-graphs, we may lower the value of α for obtaining bigger knots. If lowering the level below some predefined level of α is required in order to achieve the desired number of components, this indicates that the community is immature (i.e. not enough data is available) and no valuable partition can be obtained at this stage.

Knots should be constantly updated in order to identify un-trusted members and add new trusted candidates. New members are added to a knot if they are found to significantly contribute to it. We define the **strength** of an α-knot as the total weight of all edges in the sub-graph representing this knot. Positive edges contribute positive strength while negative edges contribute negative weight, proportional to their distance from the α level of trust. Knot strength is used for computing the global expert reputation, as discussed in section 3.4.2. For each vertex, we compute the value of a *contribution function* that measures the strength a vertex adds to the knot. This value is based on the ratio between the number of negative and positive edges connected to the vertex. The contribution function is used in the knot update process. The update process is triggered by the transactions performed in the system as follows. A transaction between member v and expert x, after which v rated x, updates the values of $TrustMember(v, u)$ and $TrustMember(u, v)$ for all members u who rated x in the current time interval (T_{now}). The value of $TrustSet^{t_{now}}(v)$ is also updated.

If v is not yet a member of a knot but has a trust set, it is added to the set of *un-clustered members*. If v is a member of a knot and its trust relations with members of the knot were modified, then this knot is reevaluated for checking whether there is a decrease in strength. If this is the case, then members with negative contribution may be removed from the knot and added to the set of un-clustered members. Finally, there is an attempt to add un-clustered members to knots to which they have the maximum positive contribution. A detailed description of the update algorithm is beyond the scope of this extended abstract and will be provided in the full paper.

3.4 Calculating Trust and Reputation

3.4.1 Reputation of members and experts

Local reputation is the reputation obtained based on information collected by the knot members, while global reputation is based on the complete data collected from the community. Formal definitions follow.

Definition 10. A *member's local reputation* is defined as the normalized sum of weights of the incoming edges of the vertex representing that member. Let $G_{KN_\alpha} = (V_{KN_\alpha}, E_{KN_\alpha})$ be the graph representing a knot of level α. Then the local reputation of member v is the relative portion of trust v gains in the knot and is defined as follows:

$$MLR^t(G_{KN_\alpha}, v) = \frac{\sum_{u \in V_{KN_\alpha}} TM^t(u, v)}{\sum_{(\forall u, k \in V_{KN_\alpha})} TM^t(u, k)}$$

Expert local reputation expresses the reputation of the expert within the knot. It is computed as the normalized weighted mean of all the ratings of the expert, where the weights are the local reputations of the rating members. This implies that members with higher local reputation contribute more to the final score of an expert. This is formalized by the following definition.

Definition 11. Let $TI \subseteq \{T_1, .., T_i\}$ be the set of time intervals for which member A rated expert x. Also let W_{T_j} denote the normalized weight of each time interval $T_j \in TI$ and let $DTE^t(A, x)$ denote the *direct trust* A has in expert x, calculated as the average of all ratings A gave x, weighted according to time interval weights, as follows:.

$$DTE^t(A, x) = \sum_{T_j \in TI} W_{T_j} \cdot R^{T_j}(A, x)$$

Then the local reputation of an expert x is defined as follows:

$$ELR^t(G_{KN_\alpha},x) = \frac{\sum_{(\forall v \in V_{KN_\alpha}, DTE^t(v,x) \neq \perp)} DTE^t(v,x) \cdot MLR^t(G_{KN_\alpha},v)}{\sum_{(\forall v \in V_{KN_\alpha}, DTE^t(v,x) \neq \perp)} MLR^t(G_{KN_\alpha},v)}$$

Global reputation is calculated based on all the ratings given to an expert within the community. In this computation, we take into account the local reputation as calculated within all knots, while the relative weight of each knot is a function of its strength within the community and the number of ratings used to calculate the local reputation of the expert within the knot. The *strength* of a knot containing a single member is defined as 0 and so it does not influence expert global reputation.

Using this method, vertices representing members that are knots of strength 0 (implying that no other member has trust in them) have no impact on the global reputation of experts. The real life meaning of this is that ratings given by new members will be disregarded until these members gain trust within the community. The global reputation of a new expert can be calculated after her first transaction, based on a rating provided by a single member, on condition that the member belongs to a knot (i.e., is she is trusted by a group of members). In this way, our model can prevent attempts by malicious experts to gain community reputation through friends that register as new members for that purpose.

As can bee seen from the above, an expert's reputation is composed of multiple scores. The expert's global reputation provides some general measure that assigns more weights to the ratings of trusted members and strong knots. For a node that belongs to a specific knot, however, the expert's local reputation within the knot is more useful.

3.4.2 Computing Expert Trust

TrustExpert - the extent by which a member trusts an expert - is used to assist a member in deciding with which expert to consult. We first consider the direct experience the member has with the expert. If there is no relevant direct experience, we turn to the members trust set. In case there is no information with respect to the expert there, we take the expert's local reputation within the knot of the member as the member's trust. Finally, if there is no local reputation for that expert within the knot, we turn to the whole community and use the global reputation score (see figure 1). A formal definition follows.

Definition 12. Let A and x respectively denote a member and an expert. Then the trust assigned by A to x in time t, denoted *TrustExpert*$^t(A,x)$, is defined as follows.

If A has direct (first hand) experience with x in the time interval [t-Tmax, t]:

$$TrustExpert^t(A,x) = TE^t(A,x) = DTE^t(A,x)$$

Else, if members of A's trust set have direct experience with x in $[t-Tmax,t]$:

$$TE^t(A,x) = \frac{\sum_{B \in TrustSet^t(A), DTE^t(B,x) \neq \perp} DTE^t(B,x) \cdot TM^t(A,B)}{\sum_{B \in TrustSet^t(A), DTE^t(B,x) \neq \perp} TM^t(A,B)}$$

Else, if no recent ratings exists within A's trust set w.r.t. x, or if A's trust set is smaller than some system threshold paramter:

$$TE^t(A,x) = ELR^t(G_{KN_\alpha(A)},x)$$

Finally, if A has no input from a trust set or a knot:

$$TE^t(A,x) = ExpertGlobalReputation^t(G_{community},x) = EGR^t(G_{community},x)$$

$$EGR^t(G_{community},x) = \frac{\sum_{i \in S} ELR^t(KN_i,x) \cdot Strength(KN_i) \cdot RatingPower(KN_i,x)}{\sum_{i \in S} Strength(KN_i) \cdot RatingPower(KN_i,x)}$$

Where S is the set of all knots of level α in which members rated x. $RatingPower$ (KN_i,x) is the number of ratings used to calculate the ExpertLocalReputation of x within knot KNi.

Fig. 1 Obtaining Trust in Expert

3.5 Resistance to Fraud and Malicious Member Behavior

One of the major benefits of the proposed model is its built-in ability to handle adversaries. Consider the two primary types of adversaries described by [13]: *selfish peers* and *malicious peers*. Selfish peers use the services of the community but do not contribute to the knowledge accumulated within it. The incentive provided by our model for not being selfish is that this allows a member to obtain more accurate information from members she trusts. Without providing ratings, a member cannot have a trust set nor can she belong to a knot (due to lack of trust in her). Thus, selfish members can only use the global and less accurate reputation data. In order to get the most out of the community services, one must provide ratings.

Consider a malicious member who wishes to harm the community (decrease the accuracy of the accumulated knowledge) by attempting to bias community ratings and members' reputation. Assume first that this member belongs to a knot. In order to join a knot, one must be trusted by a group of members. Since our model uses similarity as a measure of trust, if the malicious member's ratings deviate significantly from those of other knot members he is eventually removed from the knot. Thus, dishonest ratings will affect the knot for only a short period of time. Assume that the malicious member does not belong to any knot.In this case, the malicious member has no adverse effect on any community member, as the global reputation computation ignores ratings provided by her.

4 Model Evaluation

Our experiments are based on a simulation of our model using data from Movie-Lens [3]. The MovieLens data provided by the GroupLens project consists of over a million movie ratings submitted of 3883 movies by 6040 users. In reputation systems, all participants -both members and experts - are dynamic entities that may change over time. In the Movielens web-site, however, a movie is rated only once by a user. In the absence of a more suitable data-set, we used the MovieLens data for evaluating some aspects of our model. We plan to conduct a more comprehensive evaluation of our model once we are able to obtain a ratings database that better suites our model.

In our simulations, movies play the role of experts. We analyzed the data in order to understand the impact of the β parameter on the selection of the α parameter for trust sets. In addition, we simulated the trust a member has in an expert based on her own experience, her trust set and her knot and demonstrated the benefits of using a relatively small set of members. The MovieLens rating consists of a single integer in the range [1,5]. We normalized this range to [0,1] by linear scaling. In a 5 values rating scale, 20% error is measured for a one level difference from the member rating value. This explains the relatively high percentage error.

Prior to conducting our tests, a set of 20 movies was selected randomly and the ratings on these movies were excluded from the complete set of ratings. Three different values of the β parameter were examined: 0.6, 0.7 and 0.8. Trust sets of α level 0.7, 0.8 and 0.9 were produced for each of the three values of β. We analyzed the trust set for 150 members. The size of the trust set increased as we increased the β parameter. Increasing β results in assigning more weight to similarity and less weight to the experience factor. The reason for this is the large amount of experience in this community and the high variability of users' mutual experiences. On the other hand, the size of the TrustSets decreased as we required a higher level of trust by raising the α parameter value, as expected. The number of trust relations of level $\alpha = 0.9$ was about 2% of the number of trust relations of level 0.8 and about 0.5 percent of the number of trust relations of level 0.7. TrustSets of level 0.9 could not be produced for some of the members or were too small (5 members in average). A very large number of trust relations of level 0.7 resulted in very large trust sets (1400 members in average). For our evaluation, we chose to work with $\beta = 0.8$ and $\alpha = 0.8$, producing trust sets of 90 members on average. Trust sets corresponding to $\alpha = 0.7$ were used for comparison.

The set of tested members was constructed using three different types of users:low-raters, high-raters, and average-raters. The low-raters, high-raters, and average-raters are members that have low, high and average rating averages, respectively,

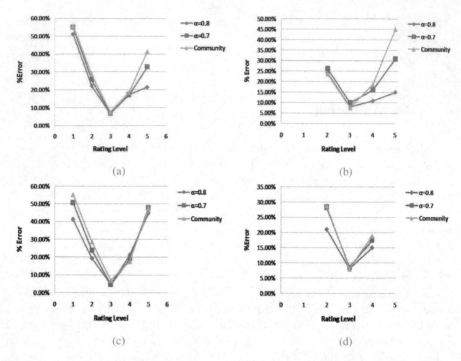

Fig. 2 Trust Sets Rating Error by member type: (a) All Members, (b) High Raters, (c) Low Raters, (d) Average Raters

and standard deviation smaller than 1. Our first goal was to evaluate the quality of the rating score derived by different levels of α trust sets. For each of the three types of users, we show the difference between the predicted rating of the trust set and the actual user rating on the pre selected movies. We found that, in general, trust sets of $\alpha = 0.8$ predict ratings better than trust sets of $\alpha = 0.7$ and that trust sets of $\alpha = 0.7$ predict ratings better than the overall community average. The average size of the $\alpha = 0.8$ trust sets was 75 while the average size of the $\alpha = 0.7$ trust sets was approximately 1400 (ranging from 261 to 2288). In addition, both trust sets yield better results than the average ratings of the overall community.

Figure 2(a) shows the average error-percentage for each of the 5 levels of ratings. It can be seen that, for ratings with high value, the number of errors is significantly reduced by the $\alpha = 0.8$ trust sets: it is reduced by 24% as compared with the average and by 14% as compared with $\alpha = 0.7$. For average-grade ratings, the improvement is less significant: more than 3% improvement for 4-ratings and less than 1% for 3-ratings as compared with the community average. For 1- and 2-ratings, the improvement was 5% and 6%, respectively. Splitting the data to the different groups of raters shows that, for the set of high raters, results improved as the ratings value increased: 26% better for ratings of 5 and 13% for ratings of 4, as compared with the community average. In the low rater set, we observe a similar phenomenon: 9%

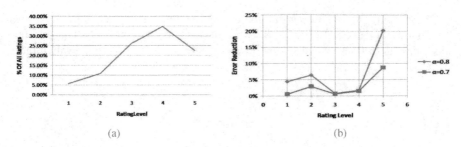

Fig. 3 (a) Distribution of ratings, (b) Error reduction by rating value

better for ratings of 2 and 13% better for ratings of 1. In the average raters set, the results are similar to the community average results: ratings of 5 are predicted 12% more accurately than the average community ratings. The other levels of rating are improved by only 1%-4%. In Figure 2(b),(c) and (d), we show the results for different types of users. The fact that low ratings are relatively rare in the data-set explains why the improvement is bigger on the high end of the rating scale than on the low end: only 5% of the ratings are of value 1 and approximately 10% of of value 2, while over 22% of the ratings are of value 5, as shown in figure 3(a). Figure 3(b) shows the average error reduction compared to the community average for each of the 5 levels of ratings.

A second goal of our experiments was to obtain the results for knots. The K parameter of clique distance was set to 6. We have examined three different types of knots, created around low raters, average raters and high raters. These consisted of 52, 101, and 119 users, respectively. The results for knots had correlation with the results for trust sets. In the high raters knot, the high ratings were predicted more accurately (around 9% improvement for ratings of 5 and 4% for ratings of 4). In the low raters knot, the low ratings were predicted with better accuracy (around 8% for ratings of 1 and 2).

5 Summary

In this paper, we presented a model for computing trust-based reputation for communities of strangers. The model uses the concept of knots, which are sets of members having high levels of trust in each other. We described algorithms for constructing and updating knots and presented a preliminary experimental evaluation which demonstrates the benefits of our knot-aware model.

In very large decentralized communities, the computation of reputation by aggregating the opinions of all community members may be a difficult task, mainly because data from all parts of the network needs to be collected in a secure and consistent manner. The knot-aware model is very suitable for such communities.

We are currently exploring distributed architectures and algorithms for implementing this model. In future work, we plan to investigate and evaluate different clustering algorithms. We also hope to conduct more comprehensive evaluation of the model by obtaining and using additional data-sets.

References

1. ebay, http://www.ebay.com/.
2. Experts exchange, http://www.experts-exchange.com/.
3. Grouplens, http://www.grouplens.org/.
4. Alfarez Abdul-Rahman and Stephen Hailes. Supporting trust in virtual communities. In *HICSS*, 2000.
5. Sudip Chakraborty and Indrajit Ray. Trustbac: integrating trust relationships into the rbac model for access control in open systems. In *SACMAT '06: Proceedings of the eleventh ACM symposium on Access control models and technologies*, pages 49–58, New York, NY, USA, 2006. ACM Press.
6. Jubin Edachery, Arunabha Sen, and Franz-Josef Brandenburg. Graph clustering using distance-k cliques. In *Graph Drawing*, pages 98–106, 1999.
7. R. Guha, Ravi Kumar, Prabhakar Raghaven, and Andrew Tomkins. Propagation of trust and distrust. In *Proceedings of WWW 04*, pages 403–412. ACM, ACM, May 2004.
8. Audun Josang and Roslan Ismail. The beta reputation system. In *15th Bled Electronic Commerce Conference e-Reality: Constructing the e-Economy*, June 2002.
9. Audun Josang, Roslan Ismail, and Colin Boyd. A survey of trust and reputation systems for online service provision.
10. Sepandar Kamvar, Mario Schlosser, and Hector Garcia-Molina. The EigenTrust Algorithm for Reputation Management in P2P Networks. In *Proceedings of WWW2003*. ACM, 2003.
11. M. Kinateder and K. Rothermel. Architecture and Algorithms for a Distributed Reputation System. In P. Nixon and S. Terzis, editors, *Proceedings of the First International Conference on Trust Management*, volume 2692 of *LNCS*, pages 1–16, Crete, Greece, May 2003. Springer-Verlag.
12. Evangelos Kotsovinos, Petros Zerfos, Nischal M. Piratla, and Niall Cameron. Jiminy: A scalable incentive-based architecture for improving rating quality.
13. Sergio Marti and Hector Garcia-Molina. Taxonomy of trust: Categorizing p2p reputation systems. *Computer Networks*, 50(4):472–484, March 2006.
14. L. Mui, M. Mohtashemi, and A. Halberstadt. A computational model of trust and reputation for e-businesses. In *HICSS '02: Proceedings of the 35th Annual Hawaii International Conference on System Sciences (HICSS'02)-Volume 7*, page 188, Washington, DC, USA, 2002. IEEE Computer Society.
15. Lars Rasmusson and Sverker Jansson. Simulated social control for secure internet commerce. In *NSPW '96: Proceedings of the 1996 workshop on New security paradigms*, pages 18–26. ACM, 1996.
16. Jordi Sabater and Carles Sierra. Review on computational trust and reputation models. *Artificial Intelligence Review*, 24(1):33–60, 2005.
17. Huirong Tian, Shihong Zou, Wendong Wang, and Shiduan Cheng. A group based reputation system for p2p networks. In *ATC*, pages 342–351, 2006.
18. B. Yu and M. Singh. An evidential model of distributed reputation management, 2002.
19. Giorgos Zacharia, Alexandros Moukas, and Pattie Maes. Collaborative reputation mechanisms in electronic marketplaces. *In Proceedings of the 32nd International Conference on System Sciences (HICSS'99)*, 8:8026, January 5–8 1999.

The North Laine Shopping Guide: A Case Study in Modelling Trust in Applications

Jon Robinson, Ian Wakeman, Dan Chalmers, and Anirban Basu

Abstract Facilitating navigation through commercial spaces by third party systems is a likely step in pervasive computing. For these applications to fully engage people they must build trust relationships in a natural manner. We hypothesize that the use of an explicit trust model in the design of the application would improve the rate at which trust is generated. To investigate this hypothesis, we have taken as a case study the design of a shopping guide for a local trading association. We have created an explicit trust model and incorporated this into our design. We have evaluated both our model and our application. The results of this confirmed our hypothesis and provided additional insight into how to model trust in the design of applications.

1 Introduction

We are moving towards a time when the environment around us is full of computing applications, most of which will be owned by third parties with whom we have no direct relationship. These applications will offer services such as providing navigational support through shopping arcades or reviews of the available amenities. For these applications to fully engage people, they must quickly build trust between users and the services they provide. The object of trust in this context is both the application and the service provider behind the application.

Jon Robinson
Department of Informatics, University of Sussex, UK, e-mail: J.R.Robinson@sussex.ac.uk

Ian Wakeman
Department of Informatics, University of Sussex e-mail: ianw@sussex.ac.uk

Dan Chalmers
Department of Informatics, University of Sussex e-mail: dc52@sussex.ac.uk

Anirban Basu
Department of Informatics, University of Sussex e-mail: ab25@sussex.ac.uk

Please use the following format when citing this chapter:

Robinson, J., Wakeman, I., Chalmers, D. and Basu, A., 2008, in IFIP International Federation for Information Processing, Volume 263; *Trust Management II*; Yücel Karabulut, John Mitchell, Peter Herrmann, Christian Damsgaard Jensen; (Boston: Springer), pp. 183–197.

The question arises about how to build applications which facilitate these trust relationships. We hypothesis that the use of an explicit trust model in the design of the application would improve the rate at which trust is generated. To investigate this hypothesis, we have taken as a case study the design of a shopping guide for a local trading association. We have investigated how to create an explicit trust model and how to incorporate this into our design where we only consider honest and non-malicious user feedback. We have then evaluated this model against the existing shopping guide which confirmed our hypothesis and provided additional insight into how to model trust in the design of applications.

Our contributions are to show how to create and make explicit a trust model within the design and to demonstrate how an explicit trust model improves applications.

In section 2 we examine the state of the art in trust models in consumer behaviour and e-commerce. Building on these models, we outline our trust model in section 3. We describe how we verify our trust model in section 3.1. In section 4 we discuss the implementation of the trust model within an application context. We provide an analysis of the trust building model and application in section 5. Finally, we conclude with a summary of our contribution in 6.

2 Consumer behaviour based models of trust

Consumer behaviour can be defined as [1]:

> the behaviour that consumers exhibit in searching for, purchasing, using, evaluating and disposing of products, services and ideas which they expect will satisfy their needs.

The Consumer Behaviour literature distinguishes between the behaviour of individuals and organisations. While organisational models such as the Webster-Wind Model of Organisational Buying Behaviour [11] and the Sheth Model Model of Industrial Buying Behaviour [12] can provide insight into model creation, our domain of interest is on an individual consumer, and we have investigated these models in greater detail.

Whilst there are a number of notable examples of consumer behaviour models available (Howard-Sheth Model of Buyer Behaviour [7], Engel-Kollat-Blackwell Model [14] and Sheth Model of family decision making [13]) the commonly accepted standard of understanding individual motivations for consumptions is the purchase decision process [1].

The purchase decision process provides us with a means to distinctly classify the tasks involved within the decision making process of a consumer. These tasks are:

- Problem recognition: when a consumer realises that there is some need for an item.
- Information Search: when the consumer finds additional information regarding the item. This can be based on previous experience (internal) or on external searches based on hunting for information from a variety of sources.

- Evaluation of alternatives: when the consumer has found a number of alternative brands, they evaluate each of the alternatives using the information at hand.
- Purchase: when the purchase of the item takes place once they have chosen a retailer and payment method.
- Post-Purchase evaluation: this happens after the purchase and is when the consumer decides if the purchase was successful or not.
- Divestment: the disposal of the product once they have finished using it.

We defer discussion of how these are integrated within our trust model until section 4. The final aspect regarding the divestment of the purchased item is not needed within our trust model as we are primarily interested in the processes leading up to this stage.

When exploring the literature for consumer behaviour, the notion of perceived risk was common place and acted as a central tenet for trust building systems in the e-commerce world. Perceived risk is based on the judgment that a consumer has on the severity of risk involved within a transaction. This is an important issue to take into consideration when designing a trust model as this can have a direct impact on how well the consumer trusts the information provided by our proposed model.

The literature identifies a number of different attributes that can affect the trust and perceived risk between a consumer and seller: benevolence; integrity; competence/ability; and predictability. Upon further inspection, these can be broken down to a number of trust attributes which we can use as the measurable attributes in our trust model as shown in table 1.

availability	consistency	discretion
fairness	loyalty	openness
promise fulfillment	receptivity	trustworthy intentions
intention to deliver	reputation	size
willingness to customize	trustee's promises	motives
moral integrity	goodwill	seals
re-embedding	web site design	professionalism
product reviews	price comparisons	

Table 1 Perceived Trust Attributes

The e-commerce literature also uses these models as a foundation for their discussion of trust models. For instance, Chen and Dhillon [2] propose the Path Model in which factors regarding the consumer, seller (in this case a firm), website and interactions act as inputs to the trust building attributes classified as competence, integrity and benevolence (which are commonly cited by others) to form a notion of overall trust which impacts on the consumers purchase decision.

Kim and Ahm [6] propose the Buyers Trust model where trust is formed through the transactions of market-makers and sellers based on a number of antecedents of trust for either. These are based on size, reputation, usability and security for the market-maker while expertise and reputation form the basis for a seller.

McKnight et al [3] propose the Trust Building Model where trust is formed out of a set of antecedent factors (in this case those that deal with the sellers perceived reputation and site quality) and factors that deal with structural constraints of the infrastructure or institution (such as the perceived risk of the web). These factors determine the level of trust the consumer has in the seller. This dictates the behaviour of the consumer and how trusting they are in following the seller's advice, allowing the seller access to personal information or how it impacts on their decision to purchase from the seller.

Lee and Turban [10] propose the Model for Consumers' Trust in Internet Shopping where factors regarding the trustworthiness of the seller (in this case a merchant on the Internet). Their model uses ability, integrity and benevolence coupled with trustworthiness of the medium in which the transaction takes place. These are supplemented with a set of contextual factors that focus on the security and effectiveness of third parties to produce a set of scores (trust propensities) which form the basis of the overall trust allocated to the operation.

Riegelsberger et al [8] provide a number of ways in which trust can be enhanced between a consumer and seller. They discuss how seals can be used as a way for identifying the authenticity of sellers (i.e. a seal could be used which allows the customer to be confident that they can trust the seller) to interacting with a human presence instead of a web page and how important the role of the interface and subsequent professional issues that arise are in the process of forming a trusting relationship. They also go on in [9] to outline a framework between interactions of a user and system and how trust can be formed based on a set of contextual and intrinsic properties.

3 Developing an application specific trust model

We are a building a kiosk system (using a touch screen connected to a PC) to help customers choose a route visiting shops through an area of Brighton called the North Laine. The North Laine is a popular local shopping area consisting of over 380 shops spread over an area of approximately 0.75 km square. Customers should be able to enter the goods they are looking for in order to identify appropriate shops and then to refine these according to their preferences. The "best" (as defined through our trust model) shops identified will be formed into a route through the area, limited by the time available for shopping.

Our approach to building trust has been to incorporate aspects of the consumer purchase buying model along with a number of criteria which we have identified as having an impact on a person's decision. The resulting trust model is shown in figure 1.

In accordance with the consumer behaviour model we have incorporated five main steps within our trust model:

• Problem Recognition: identifying which item or items the user is initially interested in purchasing.

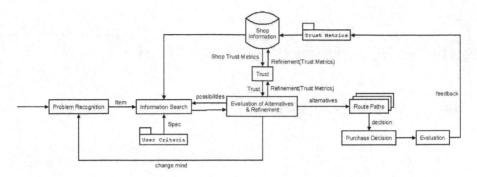

Fig. 1 The Trust Model

- Information Search: The process of considering what is available against the user's requirements. Additional information, such as the type of item, type of shop and the maximum distance to be traveled can be provided by the user to hone the results.
- Evaluation: The main interaction with our trust model occurs at this point. Based on the feedback given by previous users, the suggested shops will be ranked. This ranking process is discussed in more detail in section 4. The user would be able to decide at this point which shops to visit, and thus plan a route path.
- Route Paths / Purchase Decision: The user goes shopping.
- Post-Purchase Evaluation (feedback): Once the shopping expedition has been completed, the post-purchase evaluation stage provides the user with an opportunity to leave feedback regarding their shopping experience. This would be in the form of rating the experience based on each of the trust metrics which in turn would be used to update the trust model.

We identified 23 candidate criteria for our trust model by traversing the consumer behaviour and e-commerce literature. We also added more attributes to the ones identified in table 1 which were domain specific (i.e. quality, aftersales and satisfaction). We then gathered questionnaire data from 15 students about recent shopping excursions, including both good and bad experiences. Statistical analysis identified which criteria were strongly correlated allowing us to remove unnecessary criteria. We then verified our criteria using data from the Hardens Restaurant Guide [15]. This resulted in the nine attributes that have been chosen for our trust model:

- Availability: *The availability of the item.*
- Quality: *How good the item was.*
- Reputation: *The reputation of the shop that the item was bought from.*
- After Sales: *How good the after sales provided by the shop was if the customer had to return to the shop for any reason.*
- Discretion: *How well confidential details (for example credit card details) were handled.*
- Satisfaction: *How satisfied the customer was with the item that they bought.*

- Experience: *How the customer would rate the shopping experience.*
- Price: *How well the price compares with others.*
- Distance: *How far the customer is willing to travel to a particular shop.*

3.1 Verifying the Trust Model

To validate the trust attributes and to gather additional information about shopping habits, we produced a web-based questionnaire. The questionnaire had 164 participants start, of which 103 were fully completed. The purpose of the questionnaire was three fold:-

- gather details about the habits and demographics of the people shopping in the North Laine;
- provide "real" data to populate our system;
- and finally, to verify our trust model with data provided by the target users.

One of the key requirements of the study was to determine the relevance of each of the trust attributes. Participants were given the opportunity to rank the importance of each attribute using a range of scores from 1 (very important) to 5 (not important). The results are summarised in table 2.

	1(Very Important)	2	3	4	5(Not important/I don't know)
Quality	40.8%	32.0%	16.5%	5.8%	4.9%
Price	36.9%	37.9%	15.5%	4.9%	4.9%
Experience	11.7%	20.4%	26.2%	22.3%	19.4%
Distance	3.9%	15.5%	28.2%	26.2%	26.2%
Satisfaction	41.7%	45.6%	9.7%	1.9%	1.0%
Discretion	7.8%	7.8%	19.4%	20.4%	44.7%
After Sales	7.8%	12.6%	22.3%	24.3%	33.0%
Availability	26.2%	35.9%	13.6%	13.6%	10.7%
Reputation	12.6%	27.2%	20.4%	20.4%	19.4%

Table 2 Importance of trust attributes

The results in table 2 indicate that each trust attribute is at least somewhat important (score 1–3) to a significant proportion of people (35–97%). This indicates that each is important enough to justify its inclusion. No comments suggesting further attributes were made by any of the participants.

Because different people have differing interpretations of which attributes are important our model should provide a stronger sense of trust than a single summary rating the formative factors are clearly exposed.

A follow up question involved asking participants whether there were alternatives to the shops that they were they had visited (of which 48.5% said there were) and how these alternaitves fared in comparison based on each trust attribute. The results gained are summarised in table 3.

	Others Worse	Very Similar	Others Better, but less important
Quality	23.2%	69.6%	7.1%
Price	37.5%	48.2%	14.3%
Experience	22.2%	64.8%	13.0%
Distance (or time)	26.8%	62.5%	10.7%
Satisfaction	27.3%	65.5%	7.3%
Discretion	7.4%	81.5%	11.1%
After Sales	10.9%	69.1%	20.0%
Availability	32.7%	52.7%	14.5%
Reputation	18.9%	64.2%	17.0%

Table 3 Rating of alternatives

One of the most interesting aspects of the results in table 3 is that one third of the respondents did not consider it important if there were other shops which had better alternatives. From these results we can draw the conclusion that the model can be verified by as there was no dominant attribute and all attributes were relevant.

4 Design and Implementation

When examining the e-commerce world, we found that the perceived risk between the user and application gave rise to a number of issues to be addressed within our design of the kiosk system. For example, we have previously mentioned the notion of professionalism with respect to the interface acting as a trust building factor, separate from the trust model, that can positively impact on the user experience.

Some of these factors are not directly relevant to the kiosk application. For instance, the factors that deal with financial information would not be used within the system, but instead could form a logical association with one or more of the trust attributes, while personally identifiable information would not have any direct impact on the system. Similarly, we have not explored novel HCI approaches, the use of avatars, gestural input etc.

Egger [5] provides a trust model that incorporates pre-purchase knowledge (or in our case, the information gathering stage, to determine the item to purchase), interface properties and informational content which are aspects of the user interface that they base their trust model on. However, for our purposes, a more in-depth trust model is required which will drive the informational content within the application.

There is a growing body of literature which discusses trust in kiosk systems. However, these focus on the security aspects of trust, for instance in e-voting where the trust is used in authenticating that the user is who they say they are by consulting an authentication server, or by providing trust so that the user is confident in the handling of financial data (e.g. payment through credit cards). However, we have yet to find a kiosk system that incorporates a trust model within their design in the same way that we propose.

Our trust model is founded upon the consumer behaviour model and as such there are distinct phases in which the user must traverse when interacting with our kiosk. The first stage deals with the information gathering aspect of the model. Here, the user is provided with a set of categories of shops from which to choose the type of item that they are interested in. However, as the number of categories can be quite expansive, the user is provided with a more focused view of the types of shops that can be chosen from. This view provides a finer grained selection process which allows the user to identify shops selling a particular item for which they are interested in purchasing. Figure 2 highlights this process.

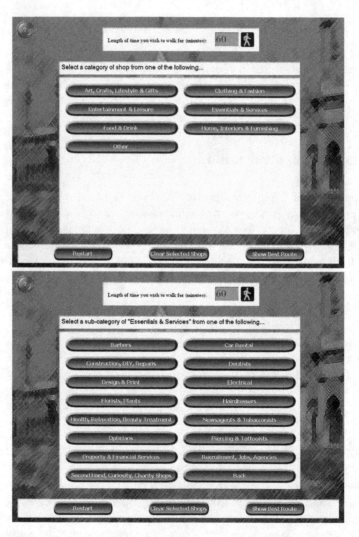

Fig. 2 Information Gathering Stage

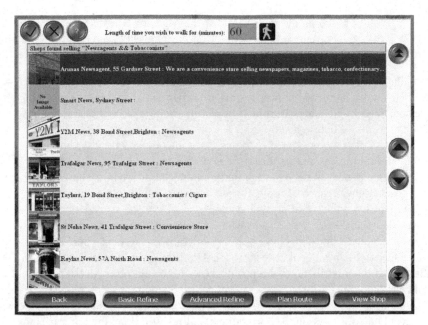

Fig. 3 Evaluation and Refinement Stage

Once the user has decided what type of item they are interested in purchasing the kiosk will present them with the shops that best match their requirements. Figure 3 shows the evaluation stage of the interface. It is at this stage that the trust model manifests itself within the user interface. The trust model uses as a measurable foundation, a set of nine trust attributes (see section 4) which are provided by previous peoples shopping experiences. The system calculates (using the following steps) a set of dynamic correlations between each of the trust attributes which forms the ranking order for the shops that are to be displayed.

1. For each attribute, work out the correlation between it and another to form a matrix of correlation co-efficients (Pearson Product-Moment Correlation) comparisons.
2. Filter out any duplicates to leave distinct correlations between all attributes.
3. Based on this set of correlations, order the attribute correlations depending on high(0.5 to 1.0), medium(0.3 to 0.49) and low(0 to 0.29) values to form a weighting.
4. The value of each of the attribute correlations for each shop is calculated based on the weightings found in step (3).

   • Any refinement of a trust attributes range is taken into account at this point. Rating scores that fall outside of the specified range are ignored. Based on this refined set of ratings, the overall value corresponding to the correlations for the shop are calculated.

5. Using values based on the weightings of the trust attributes combinations given
   in step (4), the shops are ordered from highest to lowest based on the summation
   of all weightings values.

As the trust model is dynamic, the correlations between each of the trust attributes
and their final relationship to how results are order can change over time. This provides the model with a high degree of flexibility, rather than pre-determining which
correlations to use before hand.

The shops that are presented to the user are thus ranked in order based on these
correlated rankings, such that those shops with a higher ranking will appear at the
top of the presented shops. As the more favorable shops are now shown to the user,
they have a higher chance of being chosen instead of ones with a lower ranking, and
thus further down the list of presented shops.

At this stage the user can accept what is presented and make their selection, or
they can refine the shops that have been provided by the system. There are two ways
in which a user can refine the trust model. The first is through directly altering the
influence of each attribute on the results extracted from the model. This would be
then be reflected in the restricted set of shops provided in the evaluation stage where
those shops with ratings that fall outside of the selected ranges will not be shown.
This would also impact on the correlations and resulting rankings of attributes and
consequently the ordering of the shops.

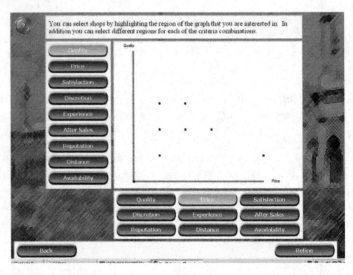

Fig. 4 Advanced Refinement

Another more advanced option for refinement has been provided in which the
user is provided with a scatter graph of the shops identified so far. Here, they are
able to change the trust attributes represented on the two axes. The user is able to
highlight regions of the graph that match the levels and trade-offs between attributes

which satisfy them. In this way the selection process is customised for each user and various ways of differentiating between results can be explored. For example, figure 4 shows the selection of shops based on a price / quality trade-off of "high price requires higher quality, highest price is limited". One of the aspects of the kiosk we are interested in exploring is how well these methods of refining the model are used by the user. This is discussed in more detail in section 5.

The feedback stage of the model allows the user to rate each of the trust attributes within the context of their shopping trip. This is accomplished by retrieving the shops details and filling out a small questionnaire where they can rate the attributes and also leave comments. At present we are not directly interested in the issues regarding abusive and malicious behaviour against this functionality, but instead have left this open to be re-addressed at a future date.

Once the user has selected a shop(s) and also possibly those for different types of items, they can then proceed to the route planning aspect of the kiosk. This provides the user with the most efficient path through all of the shops. Internally, a graph based representation of all shop locations based on their GPS coordinates and how they are connected together along the roads in the area, is maintained. When planning the most efficient route, the system will apply an algorithm based on the Traveling Salesman Problem to solve the best route to traverse each of the shops to be visited, just once. Once the path has been calculated it is provided to the user through the use of Google Maps to highlight their journey. On the information gathering and results sections of the kiosk, the user was able to specify the maximum walking time from the initial starting point. This would result in the kiosk precluding any shops that fall outside of this maximum walking distance. The route path would also take this into account, and thus, only the shops within the required walking time/distance would be provided.

5 Evaluation

When it came to evaluating the kiosk we used a group of sixteen students that represented the target users, comprising 7 native English speakers and 9 where English was their second language with varying fluency. They each undertook eight tasks that varied in complexity coupled with a follow up questionnaire. A control group of 3 native English speakers undertook the final task of planning a shopping route from an existing web-site.

We used a mock-up kiosk comprising a touch screen monitor on a stand to allow the correct orientation so that users could use it naturally. The eight tasks were designed to indicate how well participants would be able to interact with the kiosk for each function. The tasks were initially oriented towards providing the user with an introduction to each of the different aspects of the system. The final set of tasks dealt with using the system as a whole with the overall goal of defining a shopping route for several items from a varying number of shops.

When trying to characterise the types of metrics, we drew upon Nicholas et al [4]. Our primary metric was task time, although we had more detailed information through video and application logs which are still being analysed. The mean for each tasks execution time are shown in figure 5.

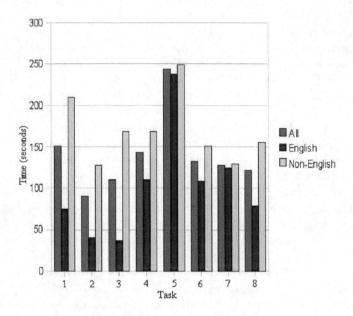

Fig. 5 Task Means

There are a number of points that we can extrapolate out of the evaluation timing results and post-evaluation questionnaire:-

1. Control Group

  • The control group performed the same final task as the other participants except it was completed using an existing on-line website. Analysis of the group showed that the task completion times were comparable to the primary group of participants. It was noted that due to the limited nature of the interface (a static web page) that participants relied on pen and paper to work out approximate distances and location relationships between each shop. However, this proved to be unsuccessful (within 1 to 2 minutes of starting the task) which resulted in participants selecting the first several shops on each page without applying any thought on the choices made.

2. English and Non-English participants

  • We observed that non-native English speakers (students that had only recently begun studying within the UK) had noticeably longer task times than native speakers in the early part of the study, as shown in figure 5. However, as they progressed through the study, using more of the features of the system, the times become comparable across these two groups. The times diverged again in the last task, however familiarity with the particular shops was a factor here. So, while there is a learning curve we believe that the concepts are not specific to English culture.

3. Participants' Opinions:

* The questionnaire focused on a number of points to gain information regarding the participants user experience. This incorporated asking questions regarding general interface design, and more explicitly, on each of the main areas of the system with respect to the tasks undertaken. With regards to the overall satisfaction of using the kiosk, 13% said that they were *very happy*, 81% said that they were *happy* while 6% gave an *average* score. In addition, when asked if they found choosing shops based on the trust model and subsequent route plan generation helpful, 68.75% said *yes*, 25% said *maybe* while 6.25% did not answer the question. Finally, when it came to finding out whether participants would use the kiosk if it was generally available, 68.75% said *yes*, 25% said *maybe* while 6.25% did not answer the question.
* From these results we can see that a high proportion of participants found the process of choosing shops based on what was returned from the trust model to be very helpful. We can also establish that the route planning aspect, coupled with the trust model proved to be high favorable between the participants, and given the opportunity, a high proportion would use the system irrespective of the language spoken. In each of these questions, no participant said they did not find the kiosk useful, but instead were all positive.

4. Ease of use:

* When asked to indicate how easy each task was (see table 4) and how intuitive it was to accomplish the task (see table 5).

Task	Very Easy	Easy	Average	Difficult	Very Difficult
Basic Refine	6.25%	50%	25%	18.75%	0%
Advanced Refine	0%	12.5%	25%	50%	12.5%
Feedback	25%	50%	25%	0%	0%

Table 4 Ease of use for tasks

Task	Very Intuitive	Intuitive	Average	Bad	Very Bad
Basic Refine	13%	50%	31%	6%	0%
Advanced Refine	0%	38%	38%	6%	19%
Feedback	31%	50%	13%	6%	0%

Table 5 Intuitiveness of tasks

- It can be seen that the basic refine and feedback aspects of the kiosk were easy to use as indicated in the high percentage of positive ratings. This was also reflected in the intuitiveness results for the same operations.
- The advanced refine option (using scatter graphs to refine the trust model) performed poorly as both types of participants found this functionality to be hard to understand with a high percentage of the participants not being able to complete the associated task. This also impacted on its lower intuitiveness scores.

6 Conclusion

The purpose of this work was to examine whether trust can be built between a user and third party application through both the interface and underlying trust model.

We have developed a model of consumer trust in shops which condenses the wide range of issues discussed in the literature into a process model and a nine attribute model of trust. We have verified that these attributes are all valid and reflect issues of significance to substantial proportions of our survey population. There was a range of importance attached to each attribute, no one attribute dominating shop selection, i.e. our subjects were not making decisions solely on price or quality etc. Hence, exposing all of our nine attributes allows a proper balance of these factors for a particular user, whereas a summary rating would fail for significant sections of the population.

We then applied this model in developing a kiosk system to support shop selection and route planning. In experiments with a prototype, using trust in selecting a sub-set of shops to visit was found to be quickly understood by all; and as quick as a control system while yielding a more informed selection of shops to visit.

So, we believe that exposing trust as a criteria in shop selection is practical and natural. We are further developing our application for a larger study.

6.1 Acknowledgments

Thanks to the Network Lab group for their help in participating in different studies and reviewing the paper. Also, thanks goes out to the participants of the questionnaires and evaluations.

References

1. G. Lancaster, L. Massingham, Essentials of Marketing, ISBN 0070841810, 1988.
2. S.C. Chen, G.S. Dhillon, Interpreting Dimensions of Consumer Trust in E-Commerce, Journal of Information Technology and Management, Vol 4 (2), pp 303–318, 2003.

3. D.H. McKnight, V. Choudhury, C. Kacmar, The impact of initial consumer trust on intentions to transact with a web site: a trust building model, Journal of Strategic Information Systems, Vol 11 (3-4), pp 297–323, 2002.
4. D. Nicholas, P. Huntington, P. Williams, P., Establishing metrics for the evaluation of touch screen kiosks, Journal of Information Science, Vol 27(2), pp 61–71, 2001.
5. F.N. Egger, F.N., "Trust me, I'm an online vendor": towards a model of trust for e-commerce system design, Conference on Human Factors in Computing Systems, pp 101–102, 2000.
6. M.S. Kim, J.H. Ahn, A model for buyer's trust in the e-marketplace, Proceedings of the 7th international conference on Electronic commerce, pp 195–200, 2005.
7. J.A. Howard, J.N. Sheth, The theory of buyer behavior, Wiley, 1969.
8. J. Riegelsberger, M.A. Sasse, "Trust Me, I'ma. com": Reassuring shoppers in electronic retail environments, Intermedia, 2000.
9. J. Riegelsberger, M.A. Sasse, J.D. McCarthy, The mechanics of trust: A framework for research and design, International Journal of Human-Computer Studies, Vol 62 (3), pp 381–422, 2005.
10. M. Lee, E. Turban, A Trust Model for Consumer Internet Shopping, International Journal of Electronic Commerce, Vol 6(1), pp 75-91, 2001.
11. F.E. Webster, Y. Wind, A general model for understanding organizational buying behaviour, Journal of marketing, Vol 36, pp 12–19, 1972.
12. J.N. Sheth, A model of Industrial Buyer Behaviour, Journal of Marketing, Vol 37, pp 50–56, 1973.
13. J.N. Sheth, "A theory of family buying decisions", in Sheth, J.N. (Eds),Models of Buyer Behavior, Harper & Row, New York, NY, pp.17-33, 1974.
14. J. Engel, R.D. Blackwell, D. Kollat, Consumer Behaviour, 3rd edition, New York: Holt, Rinehart, and Winston, 1979.
15. Hardens London Resturant Guide, www.hardens.com, 2007.

Cooperation in Growing Communities

Rowan Martin-Hughes

Abstract As communities grow in size over time from just a few people to hundreds and then thousands, members frequently find that they feel less involved, that the community lacks relevance, and that their trust in the community as a friendly place is gone. A prime example of this is online message boards or other communities developed around social interaction which are renowned for becoming bogged down in endless arguments and spamming as they increase in size. The same ideas apply to online trading systems such as eBay which require a far higher degree of trust and reliability. We follow a game theoretic model of frequent interactions over time between reactive agents to examine the conditions under which a population is likely to find a set of strategies which allow them to cooperate a sufficient percentage of the time to remain viable.

1 Introduction

Whether through a polite nod when passing on the street or through a more tangible exchange of items, people interact in many ways which have the potential to be mutually beneficial. These are transactions which have no inherent obligation for reciprocity but for which society has evolved strict laws, subtle peer pressure, or other mechanisms to encourage appropriate behaviour for the benefit of all. A society in which people feel confident that these potentially positive exchanges *will* take place is then by definition one in which there is a high degree of trust.

As the number of online and other long distance interactions increases we face many new challenges in maintaining a level of trust. A game theoretic consideration of this social shift would suggest to us that without repeated interaction the ability for one person to encourage pro-social behaviour in another through potential punishment is vastly diminished, and this reduction in consequences for anti-social

Rowan Martin-Hughes
The Australian National University, e-mail: rowan.martin-hughes@anu.edu.au

Please use the following format when citing this chapter:

Martin-Hughes, R., 2008, in IFIP International Federation for Information Processing, Volume 263; *Trust Management II*; Yücel Karabulut, John Mitchell, Peter Herrmann, Christian Damsgaard Jensen; (Boston: Springer), pp. 199–214.

behaviour may lead to undesirable outcomes. In thinking about online interactions specifically we can see a number of additional challenges as anonymity via cheap pseudonyms [8] is relatively easy to achieve and external judicial measures are often less readily available. The challenges are particularly clear when users are interacting at a distance, with the increased likelihood of added difficulty as differing cultural backgrounds make the probability of misunderstandings higher.

The question then is how critical each of these factors are to the emergence of trust from a community of users? We will approach this by simulating a group of agents and studying the conditions under which trust is able to emerge, thus demonstrating some broadly qualitative results.

2 Background

We begin by discussing a study by Lomborg [11] which showed how a community of agents playing the iterated Prisoner's Dilemma game could evolve over time from consisting of all defectors to a state where the average payoff more closely approached the ideal situation where cooperation is the norm, without any outside interference.

Early competitions between strategies consistently saw the tit-for-tat strategy outperforming others [2], but once we include noise tit-for-tat easily falls into a vicious cycle of defection, and these kinds of competitions did not allow much scope for the devlopment of different strategies over time and across the population as a whole.

Lomborg simulated reactive agents playing iterated Prisoner's Dilemma games and analysed the strategies being used as the population changed over time. Over long periods in which the average payoff remained stable at close to the payoff of mutual cooperation, the agents were seen to be playing a mix of strategies which conformed to a configuration made up of two broad types of strategy. These were desecribed as a *nucleus* of forgiving cooperative types, and a *shield* of strategies who would play cooperatively if their opponent did but who would aggressively punish any defectors. The resistance of this mixture of strategies to defection was due to the nucleus choosing to cooperate a vast majority of the time even under noisy conditions, while the shield was just sufficiently numerous and punitive against defection that an invading strategy involving unprovoked defection would recieve a lower payoff over time than a regular part of the population.[1]

With such a population breakdown, Lomborg found that the greatest vulnerability (aside from an overwhelming influx of defectors at once) was through complacency. At times where no invading strategies of defection exist the nucleus tended to grow at the expense of the shield, which left inadequate defence against an inevitable eventual threat.

---

[1] This phenomenom of the nucleus and shield was also observed in our system over long runs where the system was stable, with many agents using a highly cooperative strategy followed by a wide variety of (mainly slightly more zealous) variants on tit-for-tat.

This pattern has similarities with various models proposed in the field of psychology to describe the different social value orientations that people subscribe to. A review by Au and Kwong [1] describes a number of studies which indicate different breakdowns of prosocial (altruistic and cooperative) choices compared to individualistic or competitive choices. There does appear to be a great deal of variation within such studies though, which could be explained by the difficulty of measuring these distributions. A human playing what we call a nucleus strategy might show that in different ways depending on the phrase of the question and what game they feel they are playing - if they feel that they are being tested on their ability to cooperate with the experimenter in appropriately punishing a hypothetical defector then their response might be different to their choice in an open system where they have been wronged by another person and have to decide whether to seek justice.

It has been suggested that human emotions play a key role in ensuring that the appropriate balance of strategy types is maintained [16], and further evidence for this angle of investigation comes from neurological studies which showed reward centres in many people's brains were activated by punishing defectors [10]. These concepts and the way in which the number of people who act upon different strategies correlates with the mixture of agent strategies in Lomborg's model suggest that further examining the result of agents playing these types of games could supply useful feedback on describing and enforcing human social norms.

2.1 Trust

Reactive agents such as these are too simple to have notions of trust; they simply pursue what they believe is the most effective individual strategy at each point in time. From an outside perspective though we can describe this type of community as being trustworthy if cooperation is chosen regularly in the iterated Prisoner's Dilemma game.

This will occur when a majority of agents believe that a highly cooperative strategy will lead to the highest expected payoff. Thus a good measure for this notion of trust is the simple utilitarian measure of the average utility each agents gains over time by playing these games. An average payoff for agents which is close to the payoff for mutual cooperation will hence represent a trusting community while an average payoff approaching the payoff for mutual defection will show a system in which trust is almost entirely lacking.

3 The Model and Parameter Discussion

We are examining a society of simple agents of quite bounded decision making who try to maximise their utility over the course of many interactions with other agents. Such agents can be defined as playing transaction games wherein each agent has the possibility of spending some utility to give their opponent utility. In the generic form of such a game an agent has the choice of spending u_1 to give their opponent u_2, and likewise their opponent has the choice of spending u_3 to give the agent u_4 utility as shown in Table 1.

Table 1 The Transaction Game Payoffs

Agent/Opponent	Cooperates	Defects
Cooperates	$-u_1 + u_4 / -u_3 + u_2$	$-u_1 / u_2$
Defects	$u_4 / -u_3$	0/0

The meaning of the utility transfer is deliberately left quite open. Most obviously it may refer to an actual trade of goods for money, but it could equally be an exchange of ideas on a message board where each party has the option of trying to show themselves as being intellectually superior to the other or to be polite.

In an trading system such as eBay the use of a bidding system or other such mechanism generalised as *market forces* means that it makes sense for both agents to be considering this trade legitimately. Likewise in communications over a message board it is likely to cost relatively little effort to be polite (cooperate) than what the other person gains by feeling respected. Thus we can reasonably assume $u_1 < u_2$ and $u_3 < u_4$ is the standard situation leaving us with a (potentially asymmetric) Prisoner's Dilemma game.

With this we have sufficiently strong parallels to the model of Lomborg to consider the circumstances in such a modified community under which cooperation emerges to a satisfactory level. The main immediate difference is that most frequently the agents will only play once with other agents rather than iteratively, which makes the job of gaining cooperation dramatically harder. However, if they remember the actions their opponents took previously then over time they are still slowly playing iterated Prisoner's Dilemmas against each of the other agents.

Although it does not conform precisely to the structure of a transaction game, we use the same common formulation of the Prisoner's Dilemma as Lomborg, with payoffs given in Table 2.

Table 2 Default Payoffs

Agent/Opponent	Cooperates	Defects
Cooperates	3/3	0/5
Defects	5/0	1/1

3.1 Agents

Agents must be able to learn, innovate, have sufficiently complex strategic choices so as to have meaning while still being simple enough to model, and the system should include the possibility of noise. We use the same initial model of these factors as Lomborg did before describing how each of these and a number of other salient factors can be modified in more detail.

As a basis for this we follow Lomborg in defining the agents as Moore machines [4] who base their actions on a standard initial choice followed by actions dependent on the history of their opponent against them.

The reactive decision for each agent in a game is then based only on the most recent n moves of their opponent against them, giving them $\sum_{a=0}^{n} 2^a = 2^{n+1} - 1$ different situations for which they have a chosen action. For example if $n = 3$ there are 15 such situations as their opponent may have played 0, 1, 2, or 3+ times against them and could have any combination of cooperation or defection in each of those cases. Each agent thus has $2^{2^{n+1}-1}$ possible strategies, or 2^{15} in this case. The order in which this represents their response to the actions of the opposing agent is shown in Table 3. This equates to quite bounded rationality, but it will be seen later that manipulation of the other variables in the simulation can equate to greater deviousness of agents who may wish to be malicious.

Table 3 The opposing actions (least recent to most recent) which each point in an agent's strategy corresponds to. For readability, strategies will be broken down into segments corresponding to the number of moves their opponent has previously played. The classic tit-for-tat strategy is then represented by these types of agents as {C,DC,DCDC,DCDCDCDC}.

1	2	3	4	5	6	7	8	9	10	11	12	13	14	15
initial	D	C	DD	DC	CD	CC	DDD	DDC	DCD	DCC	CDD	CDC	CCD	CCC

As an example, consider the strategy {C,DC,CCCC,DDCCDDCC}. This agent cooperates first, then does whatever their opponent did the first time they played. The third time they play the same opponent they cooperate regardless and on the fourth and subsequent game they mimic the action of their opponent from two games previously.

3.2 Initial Conditions and Timeframe

The initial conditions we use involve all agents being in a state of defection. This is not something we are largely forced to accept in a real system, but it provides a consistent platform to compare parameters as well as the greatest challenge for such social solutions as our agents can find.[2] It can take a lengthy time period to escape

---

[2] If the parameters of the system show cooperation will develop and we already have cooperation then we expect it to be maintained over time, with perhaps small lapses which are quickly corrected

from this state of mutual defection to a more cooperative situation, and the time-frame of the simulations reflects this in being on a scale of hundreds of thousands of interactions.

In the real world we can assume that humans have developed mechanisms such that their original strategies on joining a group often closely mirror the kinds of strategies we develop over time, either through learning from previous similar communities or via an evolutionary explanation. Furthermore, it seems reasonable to assume that people can make individually more intelligent decisions than our reactive agents and are able to reason through this process themselves, thus choosing a strategy they feel will be in equilibrium after all of the people involved have gone through such deliberation. Due to these factors, the results obtained have little quantitative meaning in terms of the time taken to reach a given community state for instance, but the long term qualitative effects of changing the basis of the community remains relevant.

3.3 Number of Agents

The number of agents in a large-scale open system is by definition virtually unlimited, and if each agent by default interacts randomly with any other then most agents will only interact with other agents only once or twice if at all. Under these circumstances our Prisoner's Dilemma scenario is not iterated between pairs of agents at all and there is no ability to punish defection, so things do not tend to progress beyond the all defection stage.

Figure 1 shows how cooperation between agents decays to the mutual defection payoff of 1 as the population size approaches even the small number of 200 users.[3]

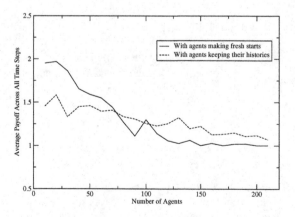

Fig. 1 This figure shows the way that it becomes more difficult for cooperation to flourish for any length of time even in small populations. It also compares the effect of agents maintaining their histories as opposed to letting them be cleared as discussed at the end of Section 3.6.

for. Conversely, if we find that our parameters show that cooperation will be highly unstable at best and we start with cooperative agents we expect that it is likely to degenerate.

[3] As a curious aside, we can see that cooperation is already scarce around 150 users which is Dunbar's Number [7], the number which anthropologist Robin Dunbar postulated as being where

Even at the very small population sizes we can see that the average payoff gained is a long way from the mutual cooperation payoff of 3. While these small populations are often in a cooperative state it requires little for them to temporarily fail and be dominated by defection again in an irregular cycle, as a sample run over a long time period with 25 agents shows in Figure 2.

3.4 Interaction Patterns

In many social interactions user activity is distributed according to a power law [13], and other aspects of network structure not covered by fully random interactions. Figure 3 shows some single sample runs of the average payoff in the system over time as we vary the frequency with which agents interact with the 10 agents to either side of them rather than with a random agent from the population at large.[4] With localised interaction eventually two agents willing to try cooperating will share a neighbourhood allowing them to outperform defectors [15], whereas without this property there are never enough repeated interactions between cooperators and the cooperators quickly switch back to a defector strategy.

Because of the poor performance of any system with a large population without this kind of property or a reputation system of the form described later, we assume that agents act according to a locally connected world in order to judge the effect of other parameters.

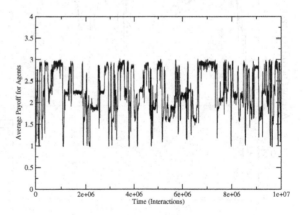

Fig. 2 A sample run over a long period of time with 25 agents, showing how cooperation is frequently found but rarely stable for any length of time.

---

a group of people loses social cohesion essentially because no one person is able to know all of the others.

[4] If we imagine all of the agents to be placed around a circle, then these agents show a regular social order in interacting with local "friends" some portion of the time and anyone else the rest of the time. When looking at actual people we may also be able to exploit the small-world properties [3] of infrequent long distance links to improve system efficacy.

3.5 *History*

Figure 4 shows sample runs where agents maintained a history size of 1, 3 or 5 past interactions with each other agent, and we can see how a short history translated into very quickly exploring the state space and finding a cooperative strategy, but also that it was completely unstable. With the limited strategies available to an agent with a history size of 1 this equates to essentially a cycle of dominant strategies across the agent population. Tit-for-tat fast becomes the dominant strategy, but is eroded over time by the equally good and more noise resistant cooperation strategy. This lasts until defection becomes the dominant strategic choice, quickly leading back to tit-for-tat replacing the now poorly performing cooperation strategies which results in defection performing poorly again as well. The dips that can be seen with the more complex strategies related to longer histories are examples of the same effect. Although it seems that a longer history size is likely to produce more consistent results, we used a history size of 3 for further tests due to the number of possible strategies with a large history size limiting our ability to closely observe strategic trends.

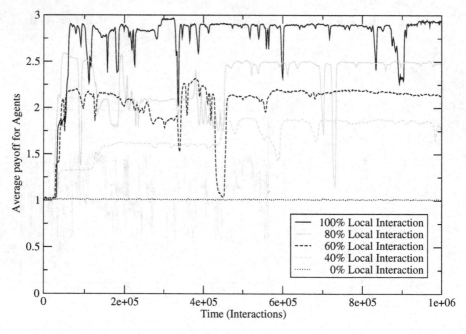

Fig. 3 A comparison of the average payoffs agents are able to recieve over time in a population of 1000 agents over 100000 time steps, given varying levels of local vs random interaction.

3.6 Innovation and Learning

In order to explore the space of possible strategies, agents modify their strategies on an infrequent basis. They may firstly innovate and make either a small adjustment to their current strategy, less commonly jump to a completely random new strategy, or still more rarely they may revert to the primal strategy of always defecting.

More frequently than innovating, the agents will demonstrate learning through imitation [5] in which they compare their performance to another randomly selected agent. If they feel they are being outperformed by the other agent then they will change their strategy to match that of the other agent. This seems sub-optimal because they could seek out the very best performing strategy at each point in time or indeed perform some kind of search to determine the optimal strategy given the state the other agents are in and their beliefs about the future, but these considerations can reasonably be described as too costly for our agents (as they are for humans in large populations) to determine.

The numbers used have little significance from a qualitative point of view, but every 10th time step 5% of the agents consider imitating a different strategy and 0.1% of the agents innovate. Of the agents who change strategies to something new, 90% simply invert one part of their current strategy, 9% choose a completely random strategy, and the remaining 1% revert to pure defection.

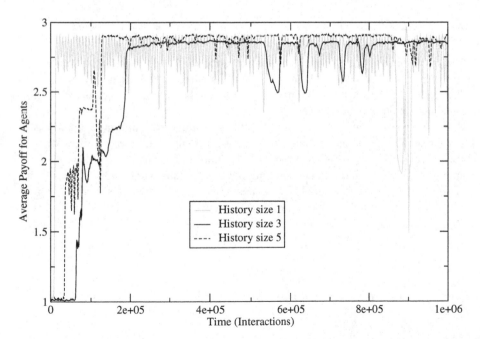

Fig. 4 This figure shows the differences between the amount of history used by agents when finding strategies for some single sample runs in a population of 1000 agents over a time period of 100000 interactions.

When agents decide to modify their strategy we find that we need to decide how they behave and are treated with respect to past actions. The first option is that they essentially start anew, forgetting the history of other players against them and being forgotten in turn as well as starting afresh in terms of their utility. This represents either a society willing to accept this, or the agent rejoining under a different name, or simply an agent leaving and being replaced. Alternatively, the agent may remember and be remembered, keeping their old utility and thus having their average payoff change slowly as they ease into the new strategy. This has the advantage of showing how an agent might modify their behaviour while still being observed, but it makes it difficult for agents to recognise whether the success of an agent belongs to their current strategy or a previous one, as well as making the initial part of the strategy less relevant over time.

Figure 1 shows how keeping the old history slightly dulls the ability of the population to find cooperative strategies in small populations, but also makes the presence of cooperation last for longer as the population grows. This seems to be as for a period after changing strategies to a more cooperative strategy even when it is unfavourable, other agents may emulate this if the previous strategy of defection was giving a higher payoff. In order to see the effects of other factors more clearly all agents clear their histories and start afresh, although in a real system there would be a mixture of these mechanisms.

3.7 Noise

We again follow Lomborg in considering the situation where the system is noisy but the agents do not know if their action has been misinterpreted. Hence when it occurs the payoffs stay the same as intended, but an agent has a small chance of putting the opposite action in their history.

Unsurprisingly noise makes the system less productive as in Figure 5, and based on this we globally assume a noise level of 0.01 although other combinations of conditions may allow us to tolerate higher levels of noise. A reduction in noise can occur in a trading system through encouraging better communication and more complete descriptions of items with photos. In a message board or comments system the goal of reducing communication difficulties is the same, so any structures which are able to discourage inflammatory comments on a general basis raising the tolerance for genuinely different opinions will have this kind of effect for instance.

3.8 Strategic Choice and the Folk Theorem

One of the randomly chosen strategies that can often be seen heading the list of worst performers early in a simulation run is {D,DD,DDDD,CDDDDDDD} which is comically awful in the way it angers everyone by defecting repeatedly but then curls up and plays dead under repeated punishment. While this seems a foolish choice under that state of the world, when playing against very forgiving opponents the rare apologetic confession after the opponent is sure they have to retaliate allows it to get away with more defections and a higher payoff in the long run.

In fact, by the Folk Theorem [9] every strategy has a counter strategy able to outperform it and thus invade the population over time. Without going into detail on this, the gist is that with the existence of credible threats as there is in the Prisoner's Dilemma *any* combination of strategies between fully rational players can be in equilibrium. Essentially this works because one player can always threaten the other with constant defection if they do not agree to play that strategy, which the other player can respond to in turn.

This vitally limits the possibility of stating some perfect population distribution which results in complete trustworthiness as any such society will be lacking a shield. Conversely, any society with an appropriate shield against defectors will see a constant dip in performance as agents in the shield will develop feuds over time due to noise. The important focus must remain on maintaining the conditions which allow trust to robustly return when defectors are able to invade in numbers for a period of time.

3.9 Frequency of Innovation and Imitation

Questions may arise as to why a successful agent changes strategy, or why a really unsuccessful agent may just keep on trying with a poorly performing strategy. Both of these see parallels in the bizarre behaviours that humans can exhibit at times, and they can also be seen as allegorical at times - a successful agent may simply leave the system and be replaced at the same time by some new strategy.

Of course, in a real trading system the payoffs for each individual transaction are unique, but for these agents it makes no practical difference over thousands of iterations to have individual payoffs instead of receiving an average every time as

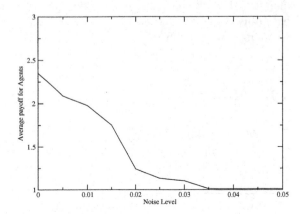

Fig. 5 This figure shows the debilitating effect of increased noise on a community of 1000 agents over a period of 100000 time steps.

we allow *market forces* or *social norms* to ensure that the payoffs are individually sensible. In the trading domain we have what seems to be another difficulty arising from a large population size. When many agents bid on a hypothetical auction the marginal benefit of cooperation to the buyer is likely to decrease, making them less likely to cooperate. However, it also *increases* the marginal benefit of cooperation to the seller, and as many trading systems are set up such that only the seller really has the opportunity to defect in a significant way,[5] this actually helps the chances of cooperation. In a truly competitive market where both buyers and sellers are competing, margins are likely to end up small and defection will thus in theory be more tempting.

The effect on the chances of cooperation as the relative payoffs change in this manner or some other manner has been studied for a long time beginning with Rapoport's index of cooperation $K = \frac{CvC-DvD}{DvC-CvD}$ based on the relative payoffs available to a player for the game with payoffs $\{CvD,DvD,CvC,DvC\}$ [14]. While this is not specifically useful aside from as a general guide, it is clear that an agent who receives payoffs of $\{0,1,300,301\}$ instead of $\{0,1,3,5\}$ will find it far easier to stay in a state of cooperation once they reach it. Even if such an agent only rarely plays an opponent who obliges them with cooperation, a frequent defector is unlikely to exist with a higher average payoff.

Unfortunately we also have to consider the problem of agents who are not honest traders, in that they agreed to the trading contract with no reason to carry it through in the first place. Whether by accident of timing or through intention to deceive from the beginning, their payoffs are likely to make defecting strictly optimal because the payoff for mutual cooperation will be lower than for mutual defection. We examine the effect of having a number of agents like this in the system in Section 4.

The complications that arise from either of these modifications are hard to gauge exactly, because in both cases the payoffs cease to be easily comparible between agents when they consider changing their strategy. More importantly from the perspective of evaluating the success of the system, it is hard to say what a good result is - some agents may simply have a higher capacity to gain utility and thus could be judged as more important, or equally we could compare the percentage of cooperation with no thought to the individual gains. When we add a second type of agents their payoffs are comparable so this philosophical question can be partially avoided, but utility comparisons between agents have long been a pitfall of game theoretic solutions to social problems.

4 Reputation Systems

The effectiveness of many systems is based around the ability to choose opponents and thus exclude players who defect, as the threat of being labelled as a defector and excluded is enough to make most rational agents cooperate. For instance, eBay's

---

[5] By virtue of up front payment from the buyer rather than simultaneous transaction.

reputation system is effective on the basis of allowing other people to avoid a player with a poor reputation rather than as a directly punitive action. Research on certain types of low cost items indicates that reputation can have a negligible effect on the sale price but a greater effect on the probability of a sale although other studies on different types of items found mixed results [6]. The moderation system used by Slashdot essentially does this also as poorly ranked post(er)s are simply unseen by most users and are thus not able to play the game of exchanging opinions.

An equivalent point of view is that essentially a reputation system forces each user to play a second parallel iterated game against *the system* which translates back into the original game as modified payoffs. Ideally this makes the payoffs for defection significantly lower and cooperation spreads far more easily.

In a previous paper [12], we discussed the different ways such as this and other social means that a rational agent might alter their payoffs in a transaction game, such that mutual cooperation becomes an equilibrium for them and most of their opponents. We also discussed the fact that we have to accept that some agents never have a reason to cooperate, such as the malicious agent recieving the irregular payoffs shown in Table 4. An agent like this may be a poster who joins a message board purely in order to push a very specific agenda, so any time their opinion is not being heard loudly they gain no utility from the game. We can see how reputation systems might have very little effect on this agent as a reduction in the payoff for mutual defection is liable to be irrelevant given the strict dominance of defection as a strategy in this game.

Table 4 Malicious Payoffs

Agent/Opponent	Cooperates	Defects
Cooperates	0/0	0/5
Defects	5/0	1/1

An obvious question that arises then is: if we have a global punishment scheme how resistant is a given population to some proportion of interlopers amongst the general population recieving payoffs according to Table 4? We assume that all agents still imitate others who they see as being successful because they individually assume that everyone is playing the same game, and that we have a reputation system which is capable of applying punishment to the extent of reducing a defector's payoff in half at the next time step after defection (with the same noise level as the agents have). The results of this as we vary the percentage of such malicious interlopers are then shown in Figure 6, in which agents interact randomly instead of locally.

Note that those with malicious payoffs are no longer playing a Prisoner's Dilemma game but rather a slightly weighted anti-coordination game, such that the symmetric mixed-strategy yielding optimal payoff is $\frac{3}{8}C + \frac{5}{8}D$ but which with the added punishment phase for defection is reduced back to $\frac{1}{2}C + \frac{1}{2}D$ yielding an expected payoff of $\frac{9}{8}$ which our community still manages to approach.

Likewise in the intermediate stages, if we were to assume that all agents were required to play the same mixed strategy then we could determine that without punishment for 20% interlopers the expected average payoff would be maximal at just over 2.4 with defection occuring in $\frac{5}{96}$ interactions. With punishment the average payoff becomes exactly 2.4 with all agents playing pure cooperation. Over the course of the simulation, we can see that this average payoff is frequently exceeded by virtue of the different types of agents playing individually appropriate strategies. Note that this means the malicious agents are still defecting on a regular basis, but the punishment system is enough to persuade the regular agents to not "stoop to their level" as they would do without it, instead maintaining cooperation the majority of the time.

5 Future Work

Future work could begin by analysing the most successful combinations of strategies which deter defection under the worst conditions of noise and having the global player play this as a mixed strategy against all players. This is likely to allow the relatively lowest level of punishment possible while still maintaining a degree of order. While we require something very closely approaching 100% accuracy in a

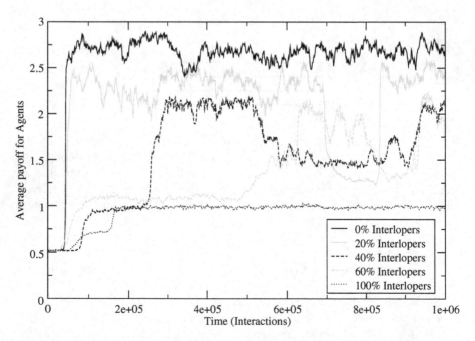

Fig. 6 Showing the effects of a varying percentage of interlopers once we have a global punishment system in place. With no global punishment system in place we gain no cooperation.

· trading system with tangible resources at stake all we need in a social community is for the overall order to be maintained with no dramatic loss of cooperation.

In application areas where the history of users can be followed by the system, allowing us to guess at the social roles each user is filling at a given point in time, it may make sense to implement a system which encourages the most effective ratio of those behaviours. This could be achieved with a sliding scale of incentives to punish transgressers and/or interact more locally, dependent on the current ratio of cooperation and the existing social roles.

In order to increase the relevance larger population sizes should also be explored, with a focus on adding agents to an existing system, and the rate at which we need to increase local interaction and/or punishments in order to maintain widespread cooperation despite the larger population.

6 Conclusions

We know from Lomborg's earlier results that agents are able to form combinations of strategies which play the iterated Prisoner's Dilemma cooperatively while being protected against invading strategies which might destabilise the system. Here we have examined the circumstances which can lead to the same development of effective global strategies even when agents are playing a far less iterated game.

With the population sizes studied, this is likely to be of more practical use in examining ways in which small communities should grow such that they do not collapse into defection rather than on the global trading systems we would like to focus on in future. In particular, with a recognition that some agents have very little cause to cooperate, it becomes apparent that the efficacy of an externally introduced reputation system does not require it to be strictly effective in punishing defectors in order to achieve the same long term results.

With the emphasis only on preventing a global collapse of trust rather than preventing every instance of defection, approaches which modify the variables of a system in such a way as to encourage the developments seen here are likely to be of use in lower security applications such as online social networks and services which require large scale collaboration without the resources to enforce strong punishments.

References

1. W. T. Au and J. Kwong. *Contemporary Psychological Research on Social Dilemmas.* Cambridge UP, 2004.
2. R. Axelrod. *The Evolution of Cooperation.* Basic Books, New York, 1984.
3. A.L.C. Bazzan, A.P. Cavalheiro Influence of Social Attachment in a Small-World Network of Agents Playing the Iterated Prisoner's Dilemma. *5th Workshop of Game Theoretic and Decision Theoretic Agents,* 2003
4. K. Binmore, L. Samuelson Evolutionary Stability in Repeated Games Played by Finite Automata. *Journal of Economic Theory,* 57(2):278-305, 1992.
5. R. Boyd, P.J. Richerson *Culture and the Evolutionary Process.* University of Chicago Press, Chicago, 1985
6. C. Dellarocas. The digitization of word-of-mouth: Promise and challenges of online feedback mechanisms. *Management Science,* 49(10):1407-1424, 2003.
7. R.I.M. Dunbar. Neocortex size as a constraint on group size in primates. *Journal of Human Evolution* 22:469-493, 1992.
8. Friedman, E. and Resnick, P. The Social Cost of Cheap Pseudonyms *Journal of Economics and Management Strategy,* 10 (2):173–199, 2001.
9. D. Fundenberg, E. Maskin. The Folk Theorem in Repeated Games with Discounting or with Incomplete Information. *Econometrica,* 54(3):533-554, 1986.
10. D. J.-F. de Quervain, U. Fischbacher, V. Treyer, M. Schellhammer, U. Schnyder, A. Buck, and E. Fehr. The neural basis of altruistic punishment. *Science,* 305:1254–1258, 2004.
11. B. Lomborg. Nucleus and shield: The evolution of social structure in the iterated prisoner's dilemma. *American Sociological Review,* 61(2):278–307, 1996.
12. R. Martin-Hughes, J. Renz Examining the Motivations of Defection in Large-Scale Open Systems. (to appear) *ACM Symposium on Applied Computing,* 2008.
13. M.E.J. Newman   The Structure and Function of Complex Networks.   *SIAM Review,* 45(2):167-256, 2003.
14. A. Rapoport A Note on the "Index of Cooperation" for Prisoner's Dilemma. *The Journal of Conflict Resolution,* 11(1, Law and Conflict Resolution):100-103, 1967.
15. B. Skyrms. *Evolution of the Social Contract.* Cambridge University Press, 1996.
16. E. Xiao, D. Houser Emotion Expression in Human Punishment Behavior *Proceedings of the National Academy of Sciences* Vol. 102(20), pp. 7398-7401, 2005.

A Model for Reasoning About the Privacy Impact of Composite Service Execution in Pervasive Computing

Roberto Speicys Cardoso and Valérie Issarny

Abstract Service composition is a fundamental feature of pervasive computing middleware. It enables users to leverage available computing power by using existing services as building blocks for creating new composite services. In open and dynamic environments, service composition must be flexible enough to admit realization by different executable workflows that have similar functionalities but that present different partitions of tasks among available services. This flexibility, however, raises new privacy issues e.g., a single service performing all tasks of a workflow has access to more data than different services executing parts of the workflow.

In this paper we propose a model that enables users to reason about the impact on privacy of executing a composite service. The model is based on an extension of Fuzzy Cognitive Maps, and considers the impact of the composition as a whole according to the partition of tasks. We introduce our extension called Fuzzy Cognitive Maps with Causality Feedback, describe how they can be used to model the relationship among different personal data and the privacy impact of their disclosure, and give an example of how the model can be applied to a composition scenario.

1 Introduction

In service-oriented pervasive computing environments, accessible resources and applications are modeled as services that users may combine to obtain new functionalities. There lies the greatest potential of service-oriented pervasive computing: clients can create innovative and unexpected applications by simply combining available services. Those composite services can be later reused to create yet more novel services, effectively enabling the user to leverage the existing pervasive computing power. Service composition is a key middleware functionality to realize

Roberto Speicys Cardoso · Valérie Issarny
INRIA Paris-Rocquencourt, 11 domaine de Voluceau, Le Chesnay Cedex France
e-mail: firstname.second_name@inria.fr

Please use the following format when citing this chapter:

Cardoso, R. S. and Issarny, V., 2008, in IFIP International Federation for Information Processing, Volume 263, *Trust Management II*; Yücel Karabulut, John Mitchell, Peter Herrmann, Christian Damsgaard Jensen; (Boston: Springer), pp. 215–230.

this scenario. Composition mechanisms must overcome challenges such as service heterogeneity and user mobility to enable effortless creation of services that are reliable, secure and that respect user-defined quality constraints. Many works proposed methods to improve service composition flexibility and to increase the probability of finding corresponding executable processes on dynamic environments [21, 19, 3].

An often neglected aspect of service composition is its impact over user privacy. In today's information society, personal information has become a valuable asset and many companies exist whose single purpose is to collect, combine and analyze personal data, threatening civil liberties and the citizen's right to privacy [16]. Pervasive computing environments are a valuable source of personal information since individuals are expected to use pervasive services to perform daily tasks and to generate a great quantity of virtual imprints that could be used to infer a number of intimate traits and beliefs. As a result, pervasive environments may become a notable target for privacy attacks and users need tools and models that allow them to identify risky situations and to avoid such attacks.

Companies offer identification services that explore data correlation to infer personal user details from apparently harmless data. For instance, even though one's gender, zip code and date of birth may not reveal much information individually, researchers affirm that between 63% [9] and 87% [23] of the American population can be uniquely identified when combining those three attributes. Some private data are also naturally conflicting and can expose crucial information when correlated. As an example, a customer may not feel comfortable to share the list of medicines he buys with his bank, since knowledge of this data could influence his bank's rates and terms for a personal loan. Such empirical studies and perceptions evidence the risks to privacy posed by entities that correlate different sources of personal data. When executing composite services and disclosing personal data to different providers, users must be aware of the privacy risks posed by their execution to decide whether or not to execute the service or to search for less invasive alternatives.

Existing research on privacy-enhanced workflow execution focuses mainly on more static and closed environments where workflows hardly ever change. Some solutions assume environments under a single administrative domain and propose mechanisms for specification of separation of duties in control flows [4, 13], while others enable specification of access control constraints on the data flow [6]. Pervasive computing environments, however, are more dynamic and hardly ever the exact user-defined workflow can be constructed with available services. A more suitable approach is based on a middleware component responsible for service composition, that separates or blends tasks of the original abstract workflow and creates different but functionally equivalent executable workflows using existing services. Specification of privacy constraints should be done independent of the composition workflow to cope with the dynamics of the environment.

In this paper, we introduce a model to reason about privacy when composing services in pervasive environments. The privacy consequences of disclosing personal data are modeled as an extension of Fuzzy Cognitive Maps (FCMs) [14]. This model can be later used to select the least privacy invasive executable workflow of a composite service and the privacy impact of reducing or increasing the precision of disclosed personal data. In Sect. 2 we give a brief introduction to Fuzzy Cognitive Maps and present our extension that allows the specification of FCMs with causality feedback. After that, in Sect. 3, we define how to model the privacy impact of independently disclosing atomic and composed personal information. Section 4 describes how to create Fuzzy Cognitive Maps with Causality Feedback that model the relationship among different personal information required for an executable workflow and how the model can be used to measure the privacy impact of its execution. In Sect. 5 we introduce an example scenario and show how to apply our model. Section 6 compares this work to related research and finally in Sect. 7 we draw some conclusions and discuss future work.

2 Fuzzy Cognitive Maps with Causality Feedback

In this section we quickly review the basics of Fuzzy Cognitive Maps, discuss its limitations and describe our extension called Fuzzy Cognitive Maps with Causality Feedback (FCM-CF). More details about FCMs can be found in [15].

2.1 Fuzzy Cognitive Maps

Fuzzy Cognitive Maps were proposed by Kosko [14] based on the work developed by Axelrod [2] on cognitive maps to model social knowledge. Cognitive maps are graphs that describe causality (edges) among varying concepts (nodes). A positive edge between two concepts means that increasing the first concept will result in increasing the second and conversely a negative edge indicates that increasing the first concept will cause a decrease on the second.

Kosko noticed that causality generally happens in degrees, and the traditional model of cognitive maps, where edges can assume only one value in $\{+, -\}$, was too rigid to represent real-world reasoning. To overcome this limitation he introduced fuzziness in cognitive maps, allowing the representation of causality with different levels (such as *a little*, *much* and *a lot*). Formally, an FCM is a fuzzy graph containing N nodes $C_1, ..., C_N$ representing concepts, and N^2 edges $W_{i,j}$ representing causality between concepts C_i and C_j. Concepts C_i are fuzzy sets and can assume values in the interval $[0, 1]$ while edges $W_{i,j}$ can represent positive or negative causality between concepts i and j receiving values in the interval $[-1, 1]$. The initial state of a FCM contains the initial values of each concept, $S(0) = \{C_1(0), ..., C_N(0)\}$. Figure 1 shows a FCM with 5 concepts (denoted by circles) and 8 edges (with causality values in boxes).

Fuzzy Cognitive Maps can be used to answer *what-if* questions related to the concepts represented. Given an initial state $S(0)$ and a matrix W containing the values of all edges $W_{i,j}$ between concepts on the FCM (where $W_{i,j} = 0$ means that there are no edges between concepts i and j), state $S(t)$ can be obtained by the matrix

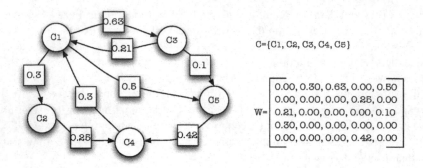

$C = \{C1, C2, C3, C4, C5\}$

$$W = \begin{bmatrix} 0.00, 0.30, 0.63, 0.00, 0.50 \\ 0.00, 0.00, 0.00, 0.25, 0.00 \\ 0.21, 0.00, 0.00, 0.00, 0.10 \\ 0.30, 0.00, 0.00, 0.00, 0.00 \\ 0.00, 0.00, 0.00, 0.42, 0.00 \end{bmatrix}$$

Fig. 1 A simple Fuzzy Cognitive Map with its set of concepts and its weight matrix

product $S(t-1) \times W$. To better represent learning, however, a sigmoid function is used to attenuate the new value of $C_i(t)$. Equation 1 is normally used to compute the next state of a concept on a FCM, where f is a sigmoid function such as arctangent. This operation is repeated until the map reaches a stable state (either $S(t) = S(t-1)$ or a cycle of states is detected).

$$C_i(t) = f\left(C_i(t-1) + \sum_{j=1}^{N} W_{j,i} C_j(t-1)\right) \tag{1}$$

FCMs proved to be a good abstraction to identify hidden patterns in causal relations and to simulate the global effects of changes in the values of some concepts. FCMs have been used to model causal relations in society [12], international politics [18], control engineering [22] and virtual worlds [7]. Researchers developed learning algorithms for FCMs that fine-tune edge weights to lead the FCM to certain pre-defined steady states [5]. However, FCMs have some weaknesses such as lack of support for time, conditional weights and non-linear weights [10].

2.2 Fuzzy Cognitive Maps with Causality Feedback

Despite their power, FCMs fail to capture an important notion of private information disclosure: when a personal attribute is disclosed to an entity, the privacy impact of disclosing other attributes to the same entity increases. There is a relation among concepts and causality that cannot be modeled by traditional FCMs. To enable the expression of such relations, we propose an extension to FCMs named Fuzzy Cognitive Maps with Causality Feedback, or FCM-CF.

A FCM-CF is the combination of two graphs. The first is a traditional FCM with N concepts $C_1, ..., C_N$ and N^2 edges $W_{i,j}$ representing causality between concepts C_i and C_j, where each C_i can assume values in the interval $[0, 1]$ and each $W_{i,j}$ can receive values in the interval $[-1, 1]$. The second graph represents causality feedback and has two sets of nodes: *source* nodes and *destination* nodes. Source nodes are the concepts C on the FCM and destination nodes are the edges W on the FCM. Edges $F_{i,jk}$ on the causality feedback graph can assume a value in $[-1,1]$ and always connect a source node C_i to a destination node $W_{j,k}$. As a result, a causality feedback graph CF=$(C \cup W, F)$ can have at most N^3 edges. Figure 2 shows a simple FCM-CF graph, where solid lines are edges on FCM while dashed lines are edges on CF.

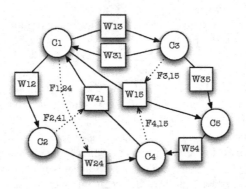

Fig. 2 An example of a Fuzzy Cognitive Map with Causality Feedback

The state of an FCM-CF at step t is composed of the values of its concepts and its weights on instant t, $S(t) = (C(t), W(t))$. Next state computation is a two-step process in FCM-CFs. Given a state $S(t)$, the values of $C(t)$ and $W(t)$ are fed into the CF graph to obtain the new matrix $W(t+1)$ that considers the causality increase on the FCM caused by the values of concepts. New values for W are computed using an equation similar to Eq. 1 as in traditional FCMs. After that, the new FCM= $(C(t), W(t+1))$ is used to compute $C(t+1)$. In summary, for each state containing the values of concepts and the weights on a FCM, first the edges of the FCM are updated according to the CF graph, and then the new concept values are obtained through the FCM.

3 Modeling the Privacy Impact of Information Disclosure

We propose a model based on FCM-CFs to enable individuals to measure the impact of disclosing personal information when executing composite services. Users first create an FCM-CF that represents the privacy impact of revealing each personal attribute to a different entity and afterwards they combine those graphs to model the effects of revealing subsets of data to the same entity. This final FCM-CF can be used to compare the privacy impacts of equivalent executable workflows featuring different service partitions or to simulate the effects on privacy when disclosing personal information with different levels of precision, as described in Sect. 4.

3.1 Characterizing Data Privacy Impact

There are two properties of private data that determine the privacy consequences of its disclosure: **identifiability** and **sensitivity**. Identifiability measures how easy it is to identify an individual after disclosure of a specific information; it is a metric related to the distribution of an attribute a with value v on a population U. We consider two metrics of identifiability: how much a user can be typically identified by the attribute a (I_a) and how much a particular user can be identified by a specific value v of attribute a (I_v). Definition of the value for I_v requires knowledge about the distribution of v on the population. When this distribution is unknown, I_a can be used as an approximation of I_v. Those values are expressed in the interval $[0,1]$ where 0 means that the attribute a or the value v are common to all members of the population U and do not allow to identify the user, and 1 means that the attribute a or the value v are exclusive to the user and can identify him uniquely. The value of I is the value of I_a if $I_v = 0$, or I_v otherwise.

Sensitivity, on the other hand, is a metric associated with the user perception of privacy. It measures how comfortable the user is when disclosing a particular attribute a with value v. We also consider two metrics for sensitivity, namely, the attribute sensitivity (S_a) that measures how sensible it is for the user to disclose attribute a in general, and the value sensitivity (S_v) that quantifies how embarrassed the user is to disclose value v of attribute a. Those values are also expressed in the interval $[0,1]$ where 0 means that the user does not see any issue when revealing attribute a or value v, and 1 means that the user is very embarrassed to reveal attribute a or value v. The data sensitivity S is also defined as S_a if $S_v = 0$, or S_v otherwise.

In many cases private information can be disclosed using different precision levels. For instance, when asked for his age, the user can disclose his exact age (e.g., 27 years old) or just his age range (between 20 and 30 years old). Each possibility represents different degrees of identifiability and sensitivity on the interval $[0,1]$. The values of I and S in this case may vary according to the precision of the information the user reveals. In other cases personal information can be decomposed into smaller components. As an example, a *complete name* contains a *first name* and a *last name*. The next section discusses how to combine information components to model the privacy impact on disclosing the complete information and how individuals can use the model to evaluate the different impacts on revealing subsets containing the information components.

3.2 Modeling Privacy Impact

The privacy impact of disclosing a specific personal information can be obtained from its identifiability and from its sensitivity as defined previously. Since sensitivity is a user-related metric, we give it a bigger weight than identifiability so that the user's perspective on privacy prevails. The sum of their weights does not have to be 1, the values only represent that identifiability has a positive effect slightly smaller than average (0.4) and that sensibility has a positive effect a little bigger than average (0.6) on the privacy impact of disclosing the information. The FCM-CF representing the privacy disclosure impact of an atomic personal attribute is described by Fig. 3 (I), where Ia is the identifiability of information a, Sa is its sensitivity and Pa is the privacy impact when the information a is disclosed. If information a has different levels of detail – e.g., location can be expressed in GPS coordinates, street name or city – this diagram can be used to measure the consequences of disclosing data using different resolutions. The values of Ia and Sa are fuzzy and may assume different degrees according to data resolution. For instance, identifiability of location in GPS coordinates may be closer to 1 while identifiability of location as a city name is much smaller. For each possible data resolution i corresponds a pair $\{Ia_i, Sa_i\}$. Variables Ia and Sa can be replaced by values Ia_i and Sa_i on the map to compute the privacy impact Pa_i of disclosing variable a with resolution i.

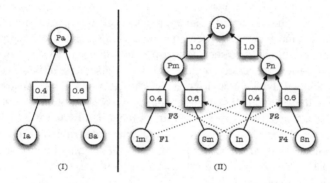

Fig. 3 An FCM-CF modeling the privacy impact of disclosing (I) an atomic personal information and (II) a composed personal information

Personal information can also represent a composition of other atomic information. Users can define the identifiability and sensitivity for each atomic attribute and create an FCM-CF that represents the impact caused by disclosure of all the attributes. Figure 3 (II) shows the FCM-CF of information o, which is composed by atomic informations m and n. This map shows how causality feedback is used to represent the relation between disclosure of different pieces of personal information. If information m is independent from n, or in other words, if knowledge of m does not affect knowledge of n, edges F_i have value 0 and the effect of disclosing m and n together (or o) is the same as disclosing each data separately. However, in many cases unveiling one personal information has consequences on further disclosures. For example, the privacy impact of disclosing a first name increases if the last name was already revealed to the same entity. Edges F_i can thus be used to represent the increase on privacy impact when both data are revealed. Their values are defined according to the strength of the relation between the information data types.

4 Privacy-Aware Selection of Pervasive Composite Services

After creating maps for all relevant personal information that the user may disclose, those maps can be combined to measure the privacy impact of service compositions. This section explains how the model is instantiated according to available service compositions and how the user can select the one that poses the smallest threat to his personal life.

4.1 Pervasive Service Composition

We assume a service-oriented pervasive computing environment, where services are described by their inputs, outputs and properties. Clients do not have any previous knowledge about the services available on a given environment, and find required functionalities by either discovering an appropriate service through the middleware **service discovery** mechanism or by composing existing services to obtain that functionality using the middleware **service composition** mechanism. Users are mobile and can play the roles of service providers, service consumers, or both.

In such open and dynamic environments, service composition must be flexible enough to take into account all services available at a given moment and to combine them in multiple ways to obtain the operations requested by the user. We suppose that clients describe service compositions by defining **abstract workflows**. An abstract workflow describes the process to obtain a certain functionality including its control and data flows. Abstract workflows can be built based on the user's past experiences creating composite services or using directions provided by other users or service providers. However, unlike a traditional workflow, an abstract workflow can be realized by different **executable workflows** [3]. The service composition mechanism may split an abstract task into different services, or merge different abstract tasks into a single executable service to obtain a composition that provides functionalities equivalent to the user-defined abstract workflow and that is achievable using available services.

Even though the process described by an abstract workflow and defined by its corresponding executable workflows are similar in terms of functionalities, the same is not true if we consider the user's perceived privacy impact. Although a user-defined abstract workflow may define that data about user's diseases and the user credit card number should be processed by different services, an executable workflow could merge those services in a composition that still provides the user-required functionality but that does not respect his privacy. As discussed in Sect. 1, data correlation is a big threat to privacy and users should be able to control which personal information can be accessed by a specific entity. However, executable workflows contain data flows that are not part of and cannot be predicted by the original abstract workflow, what makes specification of privacy constraints on abstract data flows not effective. These characteristics of service composition in open and dynamic environments require a flexible method for handling personal data disclosure that is not coupled to a particular workflow specification.

4.2 A Model for Reasoning about Privacy of Service Compositions

Ideally, the user wants to perform complex tasks without disclosing personal information to protect his privacy. However, privacy management involves a negotiation between user convenience and private information disclosure, and to obtain some specific outputs, certain private data may be necessary. A user who wants to buy a book and receive it at home will have to eventually disclose his home address. On the other hand, a service may ask the user to provide private data that is not required for the output, such as telephone, address and age to send an e-card[1]. Disclosure of personal data necessary to execute a task can be viewed as an acceptable risk, while transmission of unnecessary private data may be deemed inadmissible.

To model the compromise between revealing a private information and obtaining the composition functionality, we introduce the concept of **convenience**. Convenience is opposed to privacy, so the more convenient to the user it is to disclose a personal information, the smaller will be the privacy impact of its disclosure. Convenience has, thus, a weakening effect on the privacy consequences of personal data disclosure. Its value is fuzzy, and is related to the necessity of disclosing the information to obtain the desired output. It can be determined according to user experience (how many times that information was already requested to obtain the same output), recommendation (privacy activist groups may publish lists of abusive requests) or legislation (defining which categories of private data that merchants are allowed to require when providing a specific output).

Figure 4 shows an FCM-CF representing a service composition that requires three types of personal data. To model the privacy impact of the composition, a new concept P representing the total impact of executing the composition is created. The particular privacy impact of every information required to run the composition is connected to P with weight value 1. This is due to the fact that there is no attenuation on the disclosure privacy impact caused by their combination. Each information has its specific convenience factor C, that has an effect of -0.5 over its privacy impact. This weight corresponds to the notion that if an information has small identifiability, its disclosure does not trouble much the user and revealing it is highly convenient, then its privacy impact is close to 0.

Finally, the model requires weights for all dashed lines representing causality feedback. Identifiability of an information can only increase identifiability of another information, and sensitivity likewise. Causality feedback happens in service composition when related personal information is disclosed to the same service provider, and its value depends on the service composition being considered. If each data is disclosed to a different provider, the composition does not present causality

---

[1] www.netfuncards.com

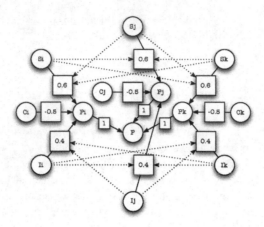

Fig. 4 An FCM-CF of a composition requiring three different atomic personal informations

feedback and the weight of all dashed arrows is 0. However, if the composition requires sending different information to the same provider, the CF edges relating those informations will have weights proportional to the privacy impact increase caused by their correlation. For instance, when the zip code and the gender of an individual are disclosed to the same entity, we can say that knowledge of the zip code greatly increases the identifiability of gender, while knowledge of the gender slightly increases the identifiability of zip code. Some service discovery protocols explicitly provide mechanisms for service provider description (such as the *bussinessEntity* field in UDDI [20]) and the model can use this information to define which causality feedback edges are active when evaluating a specific workflow. Other discovery protocols do not particularly support service provider specification, but this information could be extracted from data such as the service access point URL or external directories that categorize service providers.

Since only a few causality feedback edges are used to model the privacy impact of disclosing groups of personal data to the same provider, the resulting CF graph is very sparse which reduces the complexity of computing FCM-CF states. Also, since the resulting FCM-CF does not contain cycles, the map stabilizes after a few interactions. The value of outermost concepts never changes among interactions, so the edge values stabilize after one interaction. After two interactions the whole map reaches a stable state.

5 Application Example

To present how our model can be used to evaluate the privacy impact of executing different service compositions we introduce in this section a pervasive computing service composition scenario that can be realized by two possible executable work-flows.

William is passing his vacations at a city very distant from where he lives. Even though he suffers from a critical medical condition, due to advances in treatment he can lead an almost normal life. This morning, however, he is not feeling very well and he thinks it would be better to see a doctor. From his hotel room, he uses his smart phone to book a taxi that will take him to the nearest hospital that has a treatment center specialized on his condition. He uses a pervasive web service application provided by his personal doctor to help him to perform this task.

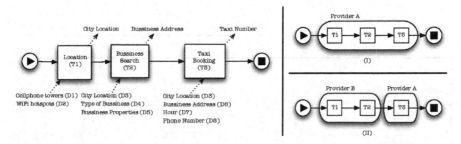

Fig. 5 Abstract workflow representing a composition and two possible executable workflows

The abstract composition workflow used by the application is depicted on the left side of Fig. 5. It uses the YAWL workflow notation [1] to represent the control flow, and incoming and outgoing dashed arrows to represent the data flow. It consists of three tasks: the first tries to locate the user based on information such as cellular phone towers and wireless hotspots nearby. The second task receives as input the user location and a type of business (in this case an hospital with a specific treatment center) and outputs the address of the closest establishment. Finally, the last task books a taxi based on the address of origin and destination, the time, and a phone number for confirmation. Figure 5 shows on the right side two possible executable workflows that provide the user-required functionality but present different privacy properties. Tasks inside the same capsule are executed by the same provider. Workflow (I) shows a situation where all the services are offered by the same entity, while workflow (II) represents an executable workflow where location-aware search is performed by one service provider and taxi reservation by another.

5.1 Building the Model

Two steps are necessary to model the privacy impact of composite service execution. First the user must create the model, and then instantiate it with information specific to the workflow. Model creation is independent of executable workflows and can be performed offline. It consists of defining the identifiability and sensitivity of each personal information that can be provided by the user, and the causality feedbacks that appear when different data is disclosed to the same entity. In this example, we will focus on the eight types of data required to execute the composition. Typical values are used for most of the data, except for the values "hospital" and the specific treatment center that have user-defined identifiability *medium* and *high*, and sensitivity *high* and *very high*. Typical values can be obtained from other users or from privacy activism groups, and can be related to particular inputs on service composition workflows by using ontologies (for instance to identify that *city location* is a type of *location*). Table 1 contains the values assigned to identifiability and sensitivity of each data.

Table 1 Definition of the identifiability and sensitivity of each personal data

Data	I_{a_i}	I_{v_i}	S_{a_i}	S_{v_i}
D_1	0.2	-	0.4	-
D_2	0.2	-	0.4	-
D_3	0.3	-	0.5	-
D_4	0.4	0.5	0.5	0.8
D_5	0.4	0.7	0.5	1.0
D_6	0.3	-	0.6	-
D_7	0.3	-	0.6	-
D_8	0.8	-	0.5	-

The weight of causality feedback edges can also be defined in advance. Afterwards, depending on the executable workflow under evaluation, those edges may receive the value 0 (for data disclosed to different entities) or the pre-defined value (for data disclosed to the same entity). Considering our scenario above, disclosure of the phone number greatly increases the identifiability of other personal data disclosed to the same entity. We define CF edges with value 0.7 from concept D_8 to the weights of all edges connecting data identifiability with its privacy impact.

5.2 Using the Model

The model above must be instantiated for each executable workflow under consideration. Model instantiation consists of the definition of convenience values C_i to each information according to the need to disclose it to obtain the desired output, and neutralization of CF edges connecting data that is not disclosed to the same entity on the executable workflow. In this example, all information required by the tasks is necessary to obtain the desired composition output, so all the convenience values are set to 1 in both model instances. Causality feedback edges, on the other hand, are different on both maps: the model for the first executable workflow will contain all causality feedback edges, since the same provider has access to the user's phone number and all other data the user provides, while on the second case the model instance will only have CF edges between the identifiability I_8 of data D_8 and the identifiability of other data accessed by the same entity, namely I_3, I_6 and I_7. Figure 6 shows both model instances.

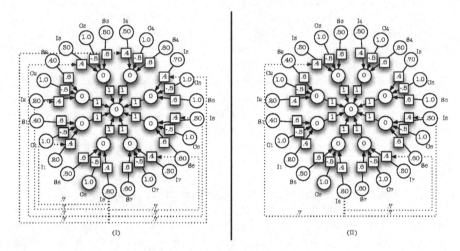

Fig. 6 Model instances corresponding to executable workflows (I) and (II)

Once values for all concepts are defined, we can iterate the FCM-CFs until they reach a stable state to compare the privacy impact of each executable workflow. The iteration begins by computing the new weights of all causality edges that are influenced by CF edges as explained in Sect. 2. In model (I) this results in changing the weight of all edges connecting the identifiability of an information to its privacy impact from 0.4 to 0.76. In model (II), only edges coming out from concepts I_3, I_6 and I_7 suffer causality feedback, so only their weights are updated to 0.76 while the others remain at 0.4. After updating the weights, the new state of the FCM-CF can be computed as in traditional FCMs. After two iterations the models reach a stable state, and the value of the total privacy impact concept (the innermost node of the graph) is 0.98 for executable workflow (I) and 0.71 for executable workflow (II). As a result, the user can compare the privacy impact of executing each workflow and select the second workflow since it is less privacy invasive.

6 Related Work

Many extensions to Fuzzy Cognitive Maps exist on the literature. The one that comes closer to represent the type of causality relations that we identified in personal information disclosure are Extended Fuzzy Cognitive Maps (E-FCMs) [10]. E-FCMs provide time support, weights $W_{i,j}$ can be any function on concept C_i (and no longer only a linear function as in traditional FCMs) and weights can be conditional (if C_m then $W_{i,j} = x$). However, E-FCMs do not provide features to express situations where concept C_k gradually affects the weight of $W_{i,j}$ as in FCM-CFs.

The idea of using information identifiability and sensitivity as metrics for privacy is shared by [11]. They propose a model to generate policies for attribute disclosure in access control based on factors such as attribute identifiability and sensitivity, inference rules and public knowledge. In order to compare different requests for personal information, they organize sensitivity on a lattice such that the sensitivity of revealing two attributes is always bigger than the sensitivity of revealing a single attribute. As a consequence, revealing data $\{D_1, D_2\}$ is always more sensitive than revealing only $\{D_1\}$ or only $\{D_2\}$, but $\{D_1, D_2\}$ and $\{D_1, D_3\}$ are incomparable since they are at the same level of the lattice. We believe that our model is better adapted to deal with real world situations where the privacy impact of disclosing groups of data must be compared e.g., the impact of disclosing {first name, gender} is smaller than the impact of disclosing {first name, last name}.

The results of research on workflow access control specification and separation of duty can help to increase the privacy of users executing composite services. The mechanism proposed by [6] enables specification of tuples <source, destination, message> on the abstract workflow that represent allowed messages between the source domain and the destination domain. In pervasive computing, however, a task on the abstract workflow may correspond to a composition of services on the executable workflow or a group of tasks on the abstract workflow may correspond to a single service on the executable workflow. Consequently, the source and destination of messages specified on the abstract workflow may be different than the ones found on the actual executable workflow. Specification of rules that account for all possible executable workflows originating from a service composition may be tiresome and error-prone. Definition of separation of duties for task execution [4, 13] may also help the user to avoid services to access conflicting data. Still, such solutions usually require that roles are well-defined among workflow participants and this is not always possible in open environments.

Finally, Falcone et. al. proposed the use of FCMs for modeling user trust decisions [8]. They categorize concepts that influence trust judgment into internal and external factors, and for each factor they identify four concepts that are sources of causality, namely, direct experience, categorization, reasoning and reputation. Their approach is complementary to ours since both models could be combined to enable users to compare executable compositions in terms of privacy and trust.

7 Conclusion and Future Work

In this paper we present a method for creating a model that allows users to reason about the privacy impacts of disclosing personal information. This model is specially valuable for users composing services in open and dynamic environments such as pervasive computing. In those environments, abstracts workflows defined in service compositions can be realized by functionally similar executable workflows whose control and data flow may be different from the ones the user specified. Tasks in the abstract workflow may be executed by a composition of services, or groups of abstract tasks may be realized by a single service, according to existing services on the environment. In those cases, users must be able to compare the privacy impact of possible executable workflows and select the one that presents the smallest risk.

Our model is based on an extension of FCMs called Fuzzy Cognitive Maps with Causality Feedback, or FCM-CFs for short. With FCM-CFs it is possible to model situations where an increase on a concept may strengthen the causality between two other concepts, which is common in personal data disclosure scenarios. We describe how FCM-CFs can be used to model the privacy impact of revealing a personal information based on its identifiability and its sensitivity. The user can later connect those models to each other, and according to available executable workflows, define weights to relevant edges and assign convenience values to information disclosure, to evaluate the privacy impact of their execution. Based on the model results, users can then select the least invasive executable workflow or simulate the impact of disclosing personal data using different resolutions.

Even though this work was inspired by pervasive computing scenarios where the user needs to protect his personal data from malicious services, the model can also be used in situations where a service that stores personal information must protect its data from malicious users performing consecutive accesses, e.g. a database server. In this case, client queries to the database could be represented by a workflow and the model could be used to measure the privacy impact of executing the complete query, complementing other approaches to database privacy protection such as the ones surveyed by [24]. We plan to investigate in the future how to successfully use our model in such scenarios. Also, we intend to expand the model to include other factors that are relevant to perform privacy-aware selection of executable workflows e.g., the service reputation on respecting the client's privacy or the trust that the service will use private data for the right purposes. We also plan to evaluate our model on real privacy-sensitive composition scenarios (such as hospitals) and to create techniques that enable fine-tuning of the weights defined based on known results, possibly using FCM learning algorithms [17, 5].

Acknowledgements This work is part of the IST PLASTIC project and has been funded by the European Commission, FP6 contract number 026955.

References

1. van der Aalst, W.M.P., ter Hofstede, A.H.M.: YAWL: Yet Another Workflow Language. Information Systems **30**(4) (2005)
2. Axelrod, R.: Structure of Decision: The Cognitive Maps of Political Elites. Princeton University Press (1976)
3. Ben Mokhtar, S., Georgantas, N., Issarny, V.: COCOA: COnversation-based Service COmposition in PervAsive Computing Environments. In: ICPS'06: Proceedings of the IEEE Interna-

tional Conference on Pervasive Services (2006)
4. Botha, R.A., Eloff, J.H.P.: Separation of Duties for Access Control Enforcement in Workflow Environments. IBM Systems Journal **40**(3) (2001)
5. Carlsson, C., Fullér, R.: Adaptive Fuzzy Cognitive Maps for Hyperknowledge Representation in Strategy Formation Process. In: Proceedings of International Panel Conference on Soft and Intelligent Computing (1996)
6. Chafle, G., Chandra, S., Mann, V., Nanda, M.G.: Orchestrating Composite Web Services under Data Flow Constraints. In: ICWS '05: Proceedings of the IEEE International Conference on Web Services (2005)
7. Dickerson, J.A., Kosko, B.: Virtual Worlds as Fuzzy Cognitive Maps. In: Proceedings of the IEEE Virtual Reality Annual International Symposium (1993)
8. Falcone, R., Pezzulo, G., Castelfranchi, C.: A Fuzzy Approach to a Belief-Based Trust Computation. In: Trust, Reputation, and Security: Theories and Practice (2003)
9. Golle, P.: Revisiting the Uniqueness of Simple Demographics in the U.S. Population. In: WPES '06: Proceedings of the 5th ACM Workshop on Privacy in Electronic Society (2006)
10. Hagiwara, M.: Extended Fuzzy Cognitive Maps. In: IEEE International Conference on Fuzzy Systems (1992)
11. Irwin, K., Yu, T.: An Identifiability-Based Access Control Model for Privacy Protection in Open Systems. In: WPES '04: Proceedings of the 2004 ACM Workshop on Privacy in the Electronic Society (2004)
12. Kang, I., Lee, S., Choi, J.: Using Fuzzy Cognitive Maps for the Relationship Management in Airline Service. Expert Systems with Applications **26**(4) (2004)
13. Knorr, K., Stormer, H.: Modeling and Analyzing Separation of Duties in Workflow Environments. In: Sec '01: Proceedings of the 16th International Conference on Information Security: Trusted Information (2001)
14. Kosko, B.: Fuzzy Cognitive Maps. International Journal of Man-Machine Studies **24**(1) (1986)
15. Kosko, B.: Neural Networks and Fuzzy Systems: A Dynamical Systems Approach to Machine Intelligence. Prentice-Hall International Editions (1991)
16. O'Harrow, Jr., R.: No Place to Hide. Free Press (2005)
17. Parsopoulos, K.E., Papageorgiou, E.I., Groumpos, P.P., Vrahatis, M.N.: A First Study of Fuzzy Cognitive Maps Learning Using Particle Swarm Optimization. In: CEC '03: The 2003 Congress on Evolutionary Computation (2003)
18. Perusich, K.: Fuzzy Cognitive Maps for Policy Analysis. In: Proceedings of the International Symposium on Technology and Society Technical Expertise and Public Decisions (1996)
19. Rajasekaran, P., Miller, J., Verma, K., Sheth, A.: Enhancing Web Services Description and Discovery to Facilitate Composition. In: SWSWPC '04: Proceedings of the First International Workshop on Semantic Web Services and Web Process Composition (2004)
20. Singh, M.P., Huhns, M.N.: Service-Oriented Computing - Semantics, Processes, Agents. John Wiley and Sons (2005)
21. Sirin, E., Hendler, J., Parsia, B.: Semi-automatic Composition of Web Services Using Semantic Descriptions. In: Web Services: Modeling, Architecture and Infrastructure Workshop in conjunction with ICEIS 2003 (2003)
22. Stylios, C.D., Groumpos, P.P.: Fuzzy Cognitive Maps in Modeling Supervisory Control Systems. Journal of Intelligent and Fuzzy Systems **8**(2) (2000)
23. Sweeney, L.: Uniqueness of Simple Demographics in the U.S. Population. Tech. Rep. LIDAP-WP4, Carnegie Mellon University, Laboratory for International Data Privacy, Pittsburgh, PA (2000)
24. Verykios, V.S., Bertino, E., Fovino, I.N., Provenza, L.P., Saygin, Y., Theodoridis, Y.: State-of-the-art in Privacy Preserving Data Mining. ACM SIGMOD Record **33**(1) (2004)

Protecting Location Privacy through Semantics-aware Obfuscation Techniques

Maria Luisa Damiani, Elisa Bertino, Claudio Silvestri

Abstract The widespread adoption of location-based services (LBS) raises increasing concerns for the protection of personal location information. To protect location privacy the usual strategy is to obfuscate the actual position of the user with a coarse location and then forward the obfuscated location to the LBS provider. Existing techniques for location obfuscation are only based on geometric methods. We state that such techniques do not protect against privacy attacks rooted in the knowledge of the spatial context. We thus present a novel framework for the safeguard of sensitive locations comprehensive of a privacy model and an algorithm for the computation of obfuscated locations

1 Introduction

Location-based services (LBS) and in particular GPS-enabled location services are gaining increasing popularity. Market studies [7] forecast that the number of GPS-enabled mobile devices, including personal navigation devices, cellular handsets, mobile PCs, and a variety of portable consumer electronics devices, will grow from 180 million units in 2006 to 720 million units in 2011.

Mobile users equipped with location-aware devices typically request a LBS service by forwarding to the service provider a query along with the user's position. The service provider then answers the query based on the position. Unfortunately, the communication of the user's position to the service provider raises strong pri-

Maria Luisa Damiani
DICO, University of Milan, Via Comelico 39, 20135 Milan(I), e-mail: damiani@dico.unimi.it

Elisa Bertino
Purdue University, West Lafayette (US) e-mail: bertino@cs.purdue.edu

Claudio Silvestri
DICO, University of Milan, Via Comelico 39, 20135 Milan(I), e-mail: silvestri@dico.unimi.it

Please use the following format when citing this chapter:

Damiani, M. L., Bertino, E. and Silvestri, C., 2008, in IFIP International Federation for Information Processing, Volume 263; *Trust Management II*; Yücel Karabulut, John Mitchell, Peter Herrmann, Christian Damsgaard Jensen; (Boston: Springer), pp. 231–245.

vacy concerns because it may result in the unauthorized dissemination of *personal location data*. Such data may in turn lead to the inference of sensitive information about individuals. For example the health status of a service user can be inferred from the nature of the clinics being visited.

Personal location data refers to the association (u, p) between user identifier u and position information p. Protecting *location privacy* means thus preventing u and p from being *both* disclosed without the consent of the user [2]. A well-known approach to the protection of location privacy is to deliberately degrade the quality of location information and forward to the LBS provider an imprecise position. Imprecision may however compromise the quality of service because the answer to the query may result too coarse. Therefore, the imprecise position must be defined at a resolution which is acceptable for the user. We refer to an imprecise user's position as *obfuscated location*.

In general, obfuscated locations are computed using techniques, such as (location) *k-anonymity* [6, 10, 8], based on geometric methods. We refer to these techniques as *geometry-based*. We claim that geometry-based obfuscation techniques do not protect against the following simple privacy attack.

Location privacy attack

Assume that John issues a LBS request from position p inside *hospital Maggiore* in Figure 1 (a). John however does not want to disclose the fact of *being inside* the hospital because that might reveal he has health problems. Now assume that location p is obfuscated by region q using some geometry-based technique (Figure 1 (b)). We can observe that if an adversary knows that John is in the obfuscated location q and q is entirely contained in the spatial extent of the hospital (the location of the hospital is publicly known), then such adversary can immediately infer that John is in the hospital. As a result, sensitive information is disclosed against the user consent. Note however that if John would be a doctor, such a privacy concern would not arise because the location would be related to the user's professional activity. We refer to this privacy attack as *spatial knowledge attack*.

The spatial knowledge attack arises because geometry-based obfuscation techniques do not consider the actual semantics of space, namely the spatial entities populating the reference space and their spatial relationships, in other terms the *spatial knowledge*. Therefore those technique are unable to protect against the inferences made by linking the geometric information with the location meaning which, depending on the perceptions of user, may represent sensitive information. The protection of location privacy thus calls for techniques able to take into account the qualitative context in which users are located as well as their privacy preferences.

To address those requirements, we propose a novel location obfuscation framework, that we refer to as *semantic-aware obfuscation system*. The main contribution

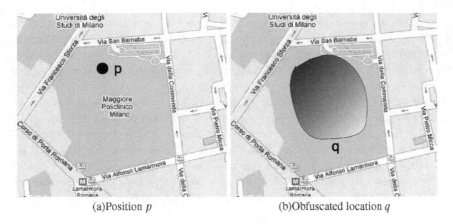

(a)Position p (b)Obfuscated location q

Fig. 1 Example of obfuscated location

of this paper is the definition of the core components of the obfuscation system, that is:

- a privacy model supporting the obfuscation of sensitive locations based on user preferences;
- an algorithm, called *SensFlow* (i.e. Sensitivity Flow), implementing the obfuscation strategy.

The remainder of the paper is structured as follows. Next section overviews related work. Then we present the outline of the approach and the privacy model. The *SensFlow* algorithm and two alternative approaches to space subdivision are discussed in the subsequent section. The final section reporting open issues and research directions concludes the paper.

2 Related work

Recent work on privacy models in LBS comprises two sets of approaches, focused respectively on the protection of location information and on the concept of *k-anonymity*.

Privacy models for the protection of location information

The problem is to how to process the query without knowing the exact location of the user. Atallah at al. [1] have proposed three methods of varying complexity to process nearest-neighbor queries such as *Where is the nearest hospital?* The simplest method is as follows: the client applies a geometric translation to the user's position and forwards the approximated position to the LBS provider. The database answers the query and returns an imprecise answer. The second method does not result in any accuracy loss but can potentially require more communication. The idea is to subdivide space in a grid of cells. The client queries the database with the tile that contains the client's location. The database answers the query with all spatial objects that are closest to at least one point in the query tile. Upon receiving these objects the client determines which of them is closest to the actual position. The third approach is more efficient and does not require any obfuscation of the user's position. The idea is to determine whether the user's position is contained in a cell of a space subdivision defined as Voronoi diagram without revealing to the database anything other than the Yes/No answer to the question. If the answer is Yes then the object associated with the cell is the one closest to the user. This mechanism, which uses a secure multi-part protocol [4], can be only applied whenever space is partitioned.

Another approach for processing nearest-neighbor queries is proposed by Duckham and Kulik [5]. In such approach the client obfuscates position p by supplying a set P of arbitrary positions including p. The database then answers the nearest-neighbor query by determining the objects that are closest to any point in P. Then, in the simplest case, the database returns the whole set of objects leaving the client to choose among them.

Protection of user identity through k-anonymity

A significant number of proposals are based on k-anonymity. The concept of k-anonymity has been originally defined for relational databases. A relational table T is *k-anonymous* when for each record there are at least (k-1) other records whose values, over a set of fields, referred to as *quasi-identifier*, are equal. A quasi-identifier consists of one or more attributes which, though not containing an explicit reference to the individuals identity, can be easily linked with external data sources and in this way reveals who the individual is. K-anonymity can be achieved by *generalization*, that is replacing a quasi-identifier attribute value with a less specific but semantically consistent value [13]. The concepts of k-anonymity are transposed in the LBS context as follows. The location attribute is treated as a quasi-identifier. Hence, a request is *location k-anonymous* if the user's location is undistinguishable form the location of other k-1 individuals. Finally a *generalized location* is a region containing the position of k individuals. Location generalization techniques generate obfuscated locations independent of the query type. The first technique has been proposed by Gruteser. The idea behind this scheme is to recursively subdivide space in quadrants of a *quadtree* [6]. The quadtree is then traversed top down, thus from the largest quadrant covering the whole space, until the smallest quadrant is found which includes the requester and other $k - 1$ users. Such a final quadrant constitutes the generalized location.

Another technique based on quadtrees has been proposed in the context of the Casper system [10]. A hash table allows one to directly locate the user. Such table contains the pointer to the lowest-level cell in the quadtree-based data structure in which each user is located and his *privacy profile*. A privacy profile is defined by the pair (k, A_{Min}) where k means that the user wishes to be k-anonymous, and A_{Min} is the minimum acceptable resolution of the generalized location. The location generalization algorithm works bottom-up: if a cell or combination of two adjacent cells does not satisfy privacy preferences, then the algorithm is recursively executed with the parent cell until a valid cell is returned. Kelnis et al. in [8] observe that location k-anonymity algorithms may compromise location privacy if an attacker knows the generalization algorithm, the value of k and the position of all users. Specifically, this happens when a generalized location can univocally associated with a user. To address this problem, Kelnis et al. present a new algorithm based on the use of a linear ordering of locations.

Recent work on relational data privacy has pointed out that k-anonymity does not ensure a sufficient protection against a number of privacy attacks. For example k-anonymity can generate groups of records that leak information due to the lack of diversity in the sensitive attribute. Such an information leak is called *homogeneity attack*. Against this attack, a possible counter-measure is *l-diversity*. The main idea behind l-diversity is the requirement that the values of the sensitive attributes must be *well represented* in each group [9]. In its simpler form, l-diversity means that each group should have at least l distinct values.

Another criticism against k-anonymity is that it does not take into account personal anonymity requirements on the acceptable values of sensitive attributes. To address this requirement, Xian and Tao [14] introduces the concept of *personalized anonymity*. The main idea is to organize the values of the sensitive attribute in a taxonomy and then let each user specify through a *guarding node* the most specific value of the attribute that the user wants to disclose. Interestingly, this approach attempts to protect the association between a user and the *meaning* of the sensitive attribute, which is close to what we propose. The approach of Xian and Tao, however, only works for categorical attributes.

3 Outline of the approach

The basic idea is to collect users' preferences about sensitive places and the desired degree of location privacy in *privacy profiles* and then carry out the process of location obfuscation in two steps. Such a process is described below. Consider a privacy profile v.

(1) The first step is to obfuscate the sensitive places specified in v based on the user's desired degree of privacy. This operation, that we call *obfuscated space generation*, results in the generation of a set of coarse locations hiding the actual extent of sensitive places in compliance with user preferences. We can abstractly think of obfuscated space generation as the function Obf:

$$Obf(v) = s$$

which maps profile v onto the set s of regions enclosing sensitive places.

(2) The second step is carried out upon a user's LBS request. Consider a user with privacy profile v in position p. The operation that we call *obfuscation enforcement* can be abstractly represented by the function Oe:

$$Oe(p,v) = q$$

mapping position p and profile v onto a location q where $q \in Obf(v)$ if p is contained in q and $q = p$ otherwise. As a result, when the location is obfuscated, an adversary cannot infer with certainty that the user is inside a sensitive (for the user) place. At most one can infer that the position *may be* in a sensitive place.

A naive implementation of the function Obf is to define, for each sensitive place, a region containing the place of interest. This solution has however important drawback: first if the sensitive place has a large extent, the obfuscated location may result too broad and thus compromise the quality of service. By contrast, if the obfuscated location is not large enough the probability of being located inside a sensitive place may be very high and thus obfuscation is ineffective. To overcome these drawbacks we subdivide sensitive regions in cells. Each cell has a sensitivity which depends on the user preferences in the privacy profile. Each cell is thus obfuscated separately through an *obfuscation algorithm*. To represent user preferences, we define a privacy model, called *obfuscation model*, centered on the following concepts.

- *Properties of places*. Places as classified into types. Users specify in their privacy profiles which types of places are *sensitive, non-sensitive* or *unreachable*. A place is sensitive when the user does not want to reveal to be in it; a place is unreachable when the user cannot be located in it; a place is non-sensitive otherwise.
- The *level of sensitivity* quantifies the degree of sensitivity of a region for a user. For example a region entirely occupied by a hospital has a high level of sensitivity, if hospital is sensitive for the user. We emphasize that the level of sensitivity depends on the extent and nature of the objects located in the region as well as the privacy concerns of the user.
- An *obfuscated space* is a set of obfuscated locations associated with a privacy profile. Specifically, the locations of an obfuscated space have a level of sensitivity less or equal than a sensitivity *threshold value*. The sensitivity threshold value is the maximum acceptable sensitivity of a location for the user. Since the threshold value is user-dependent, its value is specified in the privacy profile.

4 The obfuscation model

We first introduce the basic nomenclature used in the rest of the paper. A *position* is a point in a two-dimensional space S; *region* is a polygon; *location* broadly denotes a portion of space containing the user's position. Places are represented as *simple features*. A *feature* has an unique name, say *Milano*, and a unique *feature type*, say *City*. Furthermore, a feature has a spatial extent of geometric type [12] that, without significant loss of generality, consists of a region. Features extents are spatially dis-joint. Consider the case of two overlapping places, for example a restaurant within a park: the extent of the park feature must be defined in such a way that it does not contain the extent of the restaurant feature.

An advantage of our approach is that spatial features can be stored in commercial spatial DBMSs and easily displayed as maps. We denote with FT and F respectively the set of features types and the set of corresponding features. Hereinafter we refer to the pair (FT, F) as the *geographical database* of the application.

Sensitive and unreachable feature types

In a privacy profile a user specifies the feature types which are considered sensitive and unreachable. A feature type is *sensitive* when it denotes a set of sensitive places. For example if *Religious Building* is a sensitive feature type, then *Duomo di Milano*, an instance of Religious Building, is a sensitive feature. Instead a features type is *non-reachable* when it denotes a set of places which for various reasons, such as physical impediment, cannot be accessed by the user. For example, the feature type *MilitaryZone* may be non-reachable if the user is a common citizen. A feature type which is neither sensitive or unreachable is non-sensitive. In principle, a user can define multiple privacy profiles.

Quantifying the level of sensitivity of a region

We introduce first the concept of *sensitivity score* (simply score). The score of a feature type ft is a value which is assigned to ft to specify "how much sensitive" ft is for the user. For example the score of the *restaurant* feature type is typically lower than the score of *hospital* because an individual is usually more concerned with privacy of medical information than with information about his/her preferred restaurants. Formally, the score of feature type ft is defined by the function *Score(ft)* ranging between 0 and 1: value 0 means that the feature type is not sensitive or unreachable while a value 1 means that the feature type has the highest sensitivity. The concept of score captures the subjective perception of the degree of sensitivity. The score of each sensitive feature type is thus specified directly in the privacy profile. The score function is used for computing the sensitivity level of a region.

The *sensitivity level* (SL) of a region r, written as $SL_{Reg}(r)$, quantifies how much sensitive r is for the user. In particular, SL is defined as sum of the ratios of weighted sensitive area to the relevant area in the region. The *weighted sensitive area* is the surface in r occupied by sensitive features weighted with respect to the sensitivity score of each feature type. The *relevant area* of r is the portion of region not occupied by unreachable features.

To formally define SL, we introduce the following notation:

- E is the set of regions in the reference space

- (FT, F) is the geographical database, namely the set of features types and features
- $FT_{Sens} \subseteq FT$ is the set of sensitive feature types and $FT_{Nreach} \subseteq FT$ is the set of non-reachable features, with $FT_{Nreach} \cap FT_{Sens} = \emptyset$
- The functions: $Area_{Geo}(r)$ and $Area_{Fea}(r, ft)$ compute, respectively, the whole area of r and the area of r covered by features of type ft. In the latter case, only the portions of features which are contained in r are considered.

Definition 1 (Sensitivity level of a region). The sensitivity level of a region is defined by the function: $SL_{Reg} : E \rightarrow [0, 1]$ such that, given a region r:

$$SL_{Reg}(r) = \sum_{ft \in FT_{Sens}} Score(ft) \frac{Area_{Fea}(r, ft)}{Area_{Rel}(r)}$$

where $Area_{Rel}(r) = Area_{Geo}(r) - \sum_{ft \in FT_{Nreach}} Area_{Fea}(r, ft)$. If r only contains non-reachable features, we define $SL_{reg}(r) = 0$. $\diamond$

Example 1. Consider a space consisting of four regions c_0, c_1, c_2, c_3; the set of sensitive feature types is $FT_{sens} = \{ft_0, ft_1, ft_3\}$ and the set of non-reachable feature types is $FT_{Nreach} = \{ft_2\}$. Table 1 reports, for each feature type ft_i and region c_j, the area occupied by ft_i in c_j, with i, j ranging over $\{0, 1, 2, 3\}$. In addition, the row NS reports the non-sensitive area in each region. For example, region c_2 includes sensitive features (or portion) of type ft_0 and of type ft_3 both covering an area of 100 units; non-reachable features (or portion) of type ft_2 covering an area of 1000 units; and a non-sensitive area of 100 units. The row $Tot_{relevant}$ reports the *relevant* area in each region, that is the area not covered by unreachable features. For example the relevant area in region c_2 has an extent of 300 units. The last column on the right reports the sensitivity score assigned to each feature type.

$Area(c, ft)$	c_0	c_1	c_2	c_3	$Score(ft)$
ft_0	200	0	100	0	0.5
ft_1	100	0	0	100	0.7
ft_2	300	50	1000	400	0
ft_3	0	100	100	100	0.9
NS	0	0	100	0	-
$Tot_{relevant}$	300	100	300	200	-
SL_{reg}	0.57	0.9	0.47	0.8	-

Table 1 Area and sensitivity scores of feature types

The sensitivity level for regions c_0 and c_1 is:

- $SL_{reg}(c_0) = 0.5 \cdot \frac{200}{300} + 0.7 \cdot \frac{100}{300} = 0.57$
- $SL_{reg}(c_1) = 0.9 \cdot \frac{100}{100} = 0.9$.

It results that region c_1 is more sensitive than c_0. The motivation is that users located in region c_1 are certainly located in the extent of a feature of type ft_3, which has a high sensitivity score.

Obfuscated space

Finally we introduce the concept of obfuscated space. An obfuscated space is a space partition consisting of regions which are *privacy-preserving*. We say that a region r is privacy-preserving when the level of sensitivity of r, $SL_{Reg}(r)$ is equal or below a threshold value. The *threshold value* is the maximum acceptable sensitivity of locations for the user. Its value ranges in the interval $(0,1]$. A value equal to 1 means that the user does not care of location privacy in any point of space. We rule out the value 0 because it would be satisfied only if there were no sensitive locations (against the initial assumption). The threshold value is another parameter specified in the privacy profile. We formally define the notion of obfuscated space and of privacy profile in the definition below.

Definition 2 (Obfuscated space). Let (FT, F) be the geographical database. Moreover let:

- $FT_{Sens} \subseteq FT$ be a set of sensitive feature types.
- $FT_{Nreach} \subseteq FT$ be a set of non-reachable feature types.
- *Score* be the score function.
- $\theta_{sens} \in (0,1)$ be the sensitivity threshold value.

Then:

(1) An *obfuscated space OS* is a space partition such that:

$$\max_{c \in OS} SL_{Reg}(c) \leq \theta_{sens}$$

(2) The *privacy profile* associated with *OS* is the tuple

$$< FT_{Sens}, FT_{Nreach}, Score, \theta_{sens} >$$

Example 2. With reference to example 1, consider the profile:

- $FT_{Sens} = \{ft_0, ft_1, ft_3\}$ where ft_0 represents night clubs, ft_1 religious buildings and ft_3 clinics.
- $FT_{Nreach} = \{ft_2\}$ where ft_2 represents a military zone
- $Score(ft_0) = 0.5$, $Score(ft_1) = 0.7$, $Score(ft_2) = 0$, $Score(ft_3) = 0.9$
- $\theta_{sens} = 0.9$

Consider the four regions $\{c_0, c_1, c_2, c_3\}$ and the sensitivity level of each of them (reported in Table 1). It can be noticed that such value, in all cases, is less or equal than θ_{sens}. Thus, the set of regions is an obfuscated space.

5 Computing the obfuscated spaces

After presenting the privacy model, the next step is to define how to compute an obfuscated space. Our strategy consists of two main steps:

1. Specification of the initial partition. The reference space is subdivided in a set of small regions, referred to as cells, which constitute the initial partition denoted as C_{in}. The granularity of the initial partition, that is, how small the cells are, is application-dependent.
2. Iteration method. The current partition is checked to verify whether the set of cells is an obfuscated space. If not, it means that at least one cell is not privacy preserving. A cell c is thus selected among those cells which are not privacy-preserving and merged with an adjacent cell to obtain a coarser cell. The result is a new partition. This step is iterated until the solution is found, and thus all privacy preferences are satisfied or the partition degenerates into the whole space.

In the following we describe these two steps, starting from the latter.

5.1 The iteration method

Consider a partition $\mathscr{C}$ of the reference space. Given two adjacent cells $c_1, c_2 \in \mathscr{C}$, the *merge* of the two cells generates a new partition $\mathscr{C}'$ in which cells c_1 and c_2 are replaced by cell $c = c_1 \cup^S c_2$ with $\cup^S$ denoting the operation of spatial union. We say that partition $\mathscr{C}'$ *is derived* from partition $\mathscr{C}$, written as $\mathscr{C}' \succcurlyeq \mathscr{C}$. Consider the set $P_{\mathscr{C}_{in}}$ of partitions derived directly or indirectly from the initial partition $\mathscr{C}_{in}$ through subsequent merge operations. The poset $H = (P_{\mathscr{C}_{in}}, \succcurlyeq)$ is a bounded lattice in which the least element is the initial partition while the greatest element is the partition consisting of a unique element, that is, the whole space (called *maximal partition*).

It can be shown that an obfuscated space, if it exists, can be generated by progressively aggregating cells in coarser locations and thus by deriving subsequent partitions. The demonstration, that we omit, is articulated in two steps. First it is shown that the *SL* (i.e. sensitivity level) of the cell resulting from a merge operation is less or equal the sensitivity level of the starting cells. Then it is shown that the sensitivity level of the partition (i.e. the maximum sensitivity value of cells) resulting from subsequent merge operations is less or equal than the sensitivity level of the starting partition.

The algorithm

The algorithm computes the obfuscated space by progressively merging adjacent cells. In general, for the same privacy profile, multiple obfuscated spaces can be generated. We consider *optimal* the obfuscated space with the maximum cardinality, thus possibly consisting of the finest-grained regions. The problem of finding the optimal obfuscated space can be formulated as follows:

Given an initial partition $\mathscr{C}_{in}$, determine, if it exists, the sequence of merge operations such that the resulting partition $\mathscr{C}$ is the obfuscated space with the maximum number of cells

In this paper, we present an algorithm which computes an approximated solution to the problem. The idea is to progressively expand each cell which is not privacy preserving until a terminating condition is met. This approach raises a number of issues. The first issue is how to choose the cells to be merged. We adopt the following heuristic: we select the adjacent cell which determines the most sensible reduction of sensitivity of the aggregated cell. A second issue concerns the criteria for the expansion of cells. To address such issues, we have identified two basic strategies: the first strategy is to expand one over-sensitive cell (i.e. a non-privacy-preserving cell) at a time, until the level of sensitivity is below the threshold; the second strategy is to expand "in parallel" all cells which are over-sensitive. The second strategy is the one which has been adopted because it allows one to better control the size of the aggregated cells.

Insights on the *SensFlow* algorithm

We represent a space partition through a *Region Adjacency Graph* (RAG)[11]. In general a RAG is defined from a partition by associating one vertex with each cell and by creating an edge between two vertices if the associated cells share a common boundary. Within this framework, the edge information is interpreted as possibility of merging the two cells identified by the vertices incident to the edge. Such a merge operation implies to collapse the two vertices incident to the edge into one vertex and to remove this edge together with any double edge between the newly created vertex and the remaining vertices [3].

The input parameters of the algorithm are: 1) the initial RAG built on the initial partition; 2) the privacy profile. The algorithm returns an obfuscated space if it exists, an error otherwise. Starting from the RAG corresponding to the initial partition, the algorithm shrinks the graph by merging adjacent cells until all privacy constraints are satisfied or a solution cannot be found. At each iteration, the algorithm looks for non-privacy preserving cells; then each of such cells is merged with at most one adjacent cell. Among the cells in the neighborhood, merging is executed with the cell which determines the most significant reduction in the sensitivity of the resulting aggregated region. After the merge, the algorithm proceeds to scan the remaining cells, and the whole loop is repeated until no cell is modified. The complexity of the algorithm, evaluated with respect to the two key operations, that is (a) merge operations, (b) number of edges analyzed, is $O(n^2)$.

5.2 The specification of the initial partition

The above algorithm is applied to an initial space partition which is then mapped onto a graph. Now a key design issue is to define how to build the initial partition and how to specify sensitive and unreachable cells in such a partition. In other words, given a map of space, what kind of partition can be generated? And how can the sensitivity level of the initial partition be computed? We have investigated two approaches: a) To subdivide space into a regular grid of cells. Cells have thus equal shapes and sizes. b) To subdivide space into a set of irregular tiles based on a natural subdivision of territory. Each tile represents a real world entity, for example a census block.

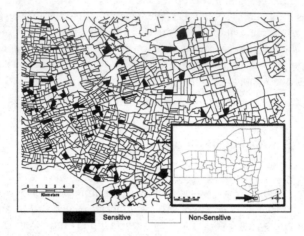

Sensitive   Non-Sensitive

Fig. 2 Sensitive cells in the initial partition

We now discuss the experiments carried out using these two approaches. The adopted software platform consists of a Java implementation of the *SensFlow* algorithm, the system Intergraph Geomedia for the visualization of spatial data and Oracle Spatial for the construction of the RAG.

We present first the experiment with the irregular tessellation of space. Seemingly the advantage of the irregular tessellation against grid is that tiles may represent physical entities. Therefore, since sensitive places, such clinics or religious places, have well-known boundaries, they likely correspond to tiles and thus can be more easily identified. Creating a space tessellation at very high resolution is, however, extremely costly. A more practical solution is to use publicly available datasets, albeit at lower resolution. A typical dataset representing a space partition is the US Census data.

We have thus run the algorithm on an initial partition obtained from US Census Block dataset. The data set consists of 15000 polygons representing Census Block Groups, that is, aggregation of census blocks. Each polygon is a cell of the partition. We assume:

- A unique feature type ft with $score = 1$ thus at the highest sensitivity.
- The density s of sensitive cells is a parameter of the experiment. For example $s=0.05$ means that 5% of cells contain sensitive features.
- The percentage of area which is sensitive in a cell is assigned randomly. Figure 2 shows a portion of the initial partition with $s = 0.05$: the black cells are sensitive, whereas the white cells are non-sensitive.

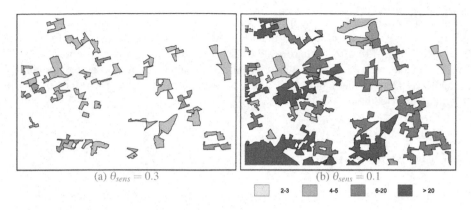

(a) $\theta_{sens} = 0.3$ (b) $\theta_{sens} = 0.1$

| | 2-3 | | 4-5 | | 6-20 | | > 20 |

Fig. 3 Visual representation of two obfuscated spaces relative to area in Figure 2 ($s = 0.05$)

The *SensFlow* algorithm has been run using different values of the sensitivity threshold. The experimental results are shown in the maps in Figure 3. The generalized regions are represented by polygons of different color, based on the number of aggregations: the color is darker for the more aggregated regions; white space denotes the original space. We can observe that the granularity of the obfuscated space is coarser for lower values of the sensitivity threshold.

The main limitation of this approach is that the publicly available data set is not sufficiently precise. Cells are generally too broad, especially in rural areas and that compromises the quality of service.

We have thus evaluated the grid-based approach to space subdivision. Space is subdivided into a grid of regular cells. Features do not have any physical correspondence with cells. Features are thus contained in a cell or overlap multiple cells. The sensitive area in the cell results from the spatial intersection of the feature extent with the cell. We have run the algorithm over a grid of 100 squared cells, assuming again a unique feature type with maximum score.

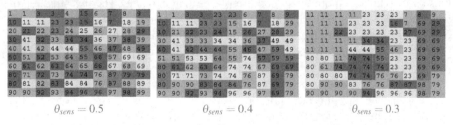

$\theta_{sens} = 0.5$ $\theta_{sens} = 0.4$ $\theta_{sens} = 0.3$

Fig. 4 Visual representation of the cell aggregation for different values of the sensitivity threshold θ_{sens}. Merged cells are indicated using both the same number and the same color

Figure 4 shows the obfuscated spaces generated for different values of the sensitivity threshold. The result is visualized as follows: adjacent cells which have not been merged are assigned different gray tones; merged cells have an identical gray tone and are labeled by the same number. We can observe how the granularity of obfuscated locations (i.e. a set of cells with identical label) changes for different values of θ_{sens}. From the experiments it turns out that the grid-based approach is more flexible because the granularity of partition can be defined based on application needs. On the other hand, the whole process of discretization of features in cells is much more complex.

6 Open issues and conclusions

In this paper we have presented a comprehensive framework for the protection of privacy of sensitive locations. Because of the novelty of the approach a number of important issues are still open, pertaining various aspects concerning: the privacy model, the computational complexity and the system architecture respectively. As concerns the privacy model, one could observe that the sensitivity of a place may vary depending on the context, such as time. Indeed in our approach the user is allowed to specify multiple profiles and thus, ideally, one could select the privacy profile based on the contextual conditions. Unfortunately this solution may result into an excessive burden for the user. Some mechanism for a context-driven selection of privacy profiles would thus be desirable. Another observation is that our privacy model requires detailed knowledge of the extents of sensitive places, while such a knowledge is difficult and costly to acquire. We believe that in the next few years high quality spatial data will become increasingly available under the push of the growing LBS market and thus the development of obfuscation services by LBS providers or third parties will become affordable. Our privacy model can be improved in several ways. First, we observe that the notion of threshold value may be not so intuitive for the user. As a consequence, the specification of the privacy profile may be complex. Second, in our model we assume that mobile users have equal probability of being located in any point outside an unreachable area, while that contrasts with the evidence that some areas are more frequented than others and thus an individual is more likely in those places than in others. The investigation of a probabilistic model is a major effort of the future activity.

A distinct class of issues are about the computational cost of obfuscated map generation. The present algorithm has a quadratic complexity. For an effective deployment of the system, a more efficient algorithm is needed. A related aspect is the development of a suitable platform for the experimental evaluation of the algorithms including a generator of initial partitions. Another major class of issues concerns the specification of a distributed system architecture. We envisage two main architectural solutions. The straightforward approach is to use a *trusted Obfuscation Server* as an intermediary between the client and the LBS provider. The TOS creates the obfuscated spaces and stores them along with the associated privacy profile in a local repository. At run time, the user's request is forwarded to the Obfuscation Server which applies the obfuscation enforcement. This scheme has a main drawback in that it requires a dedicated and trusted server. This may result into a bottleneck;

further the trustworthiness of the server is costly to ensure. To overcome this limitation, an alternative approach is to base the architecture on the following idea. The Obfuscator Server is still used but exclusively to generate obfuscated maps upon user's requests. Once generated, the map is then transferred back to the requesting client which stores it locally. Finally, the obfuscation enforcement is then carried out on the client. Because of the storage limitations of mobile devices, the generated map should be not only generated in an acceptable time for the user but also have a reasonable size.

Acknowledgements This work has been partially funded by the European Commission project IST-6FP-014915 "GeoPKDD: Geographic Privacy-aware Knowledge Discovery and Delivery (GeoPKDD)" (web site: http://www.geopkdd.eu), and by the US National Science Foundation grant 0712846 "IPS: Security Services for Healthcare Applications".

References

1. M. Atallah and K. Frikken. Privacy-preserving location-dependent query processing. In *ACS/IEEE Intl. Conf. on Pervasive Services (ICPS)*, 2004.
2. A. R. Beresford and F. Stajano. Location privacy in pervasive computing. *IEEE Pervasive Computing*, 2(1):46–55, 2003.
3. L. Brun and W. Kropatsch. Contains and inside relationships within combinatorial pyramids. *Pattern Recognition*, 39(4), 2006.
4. W. Du and M. J. Atallah. Secure multi-party computation problems and their applications: a review and open problems. In *NSPW '01: Proceedings of the 2001 workshop on New security paradigms*, pages 13–22, New York, NY, USA, 2001. ACM.
5. M. Duckham and L. Kulik. A formal model of obfuscation and negotiation for location privacy. In *Pervasive Computing*, volume 3468 of *Lecture Notes in Computer Science LNCS*, pages 152–170. Springer Berlin / Heidelberg, 2005.
6. M. Gruteser and D. Grunwald. Anonymous usage of location-based services through spatial and temporal cloaking. In *MobiSys '03: Proceedings of the 1st international conference on Mobile systems, applications and services*, pages 31–42, New York, NY, USA, 2003. ACM Press.
7. In-Stat. http://www.instat.com/press.asp?id=2140&sku=in0703846wt. Publication date: 5 November 2007.
8. P. Kalnis, G. Ghinita, K. Mouratidis, and D. Papadias. Preventing location-based identity inference in anonymous spatial queries. *IEEE Transactions on Knowledge and Data Engineering*, 19(12):1719–1733, 2007.
9. A. Machanavajjhala, J. Gehrke, D. Kifer, and M. Venkitasubramaniam. l-diversity: Privacy beyond k-anonymity. In *22nd IEEE International Conference on Data Engineering*, 2006.
10. M. F. Mokbel, C.-Y. Chow, and W. G. Aref. The new casper: query processing for location services without compromising privacy. In *VLDB'2006: Proceedings of the 32nd international conference on Very large data bases*, pages 763–774. VLDB Endowment, 2006.
11. M. Molenaar. *An Introduction to the Theory of Spatial Object Modelling for GIS*. CRC Press, 1998.
12. Open GIS Consortium. Open GIS simple features specification for SQL, 1999. Revision 1.1.
13. L. Sweeney. Achieving k-anonymity privacy protection using generalization and suppression. *Int. J. Uncertain. Fuzziness Knowl.-Based Syst.*, 10(5):571–588, 2002.
14. X. Xiao and Y. Tao. Personalized privacy preservation. In *SIGMOD '06: Proceedings of the 2006 ACM SIGMOD international conference on Management of data*, pages 229–240, New York, NY, USA, 2006. ACM.

Privacy2.0:
Towards Collaborative Data-Privacy Protection

Erik Buchmann, Klemens Böhm, Oliver Raabe

Abstract Data protection is challenging in scenarios where numerous devices collect personal data without drawing attention from the individual concerned, e.g., in Ubiquitous Computing applications, Sensor Networks or Radio Frequency Identification installations. Technical mechanisms for data protection force the individual to keep track of his personal data and require a thorough understanding of technology. Regulatory approaches cannot keep pace with the advent of new privacy threats. This paper proposes and describes a new multidisciplinary research direction for data protection: The idea is to use Web2.0 mechanisms which let users share their experiences, observations and recommendations regarding the privacy practices of service providers in an intuitive and flexible manner. We define an innovative framework at the logical level, i.e., identify the components of the architecture. The core of the framework is a folksonomy of tagged geo-locations, physical items and Internet addresses that might have an impact on privacy. Our framework envisioned helps the user to decide if a data collector handles personal information compliant with legal regulations and according to the user preferences. We find out which current technologies can be adapted to implement our framework, and we discuss design alternatives and new research directions.

1 Introduction

It has never been as simple as today to collect large volumes of personal data. In the near future, advances in the areas of Ubiquitous Computing [21], RFID [28] or Sensor Networks [14] will bridge the gap between the online and offline world and challenge data protection significantly [19]. Using current and novel information technologies in everyday life will shape the society of the future. If we do not find practical approaches for privacy protection, it might become as simple as using a search engine to assemble comprehensive personality profiles of individuals.

Erik Buchmann, Klemens Böhm
Institute for Program Structures and Data Organization, Universität Karlsruhe (TH), Germany,
e-mail: {buchmann | boehm}@ipd.uka.de

Oliver Raabe
Center for Applied Jurisprudence, Universität Karlsruhe (TH), Germany,
e-mail: raabe@ipd.uka.de

Please use the following format when citing this chapter:

Buchmann, E., Böhm, K. and Raabe, O., 2008, in IFIP International Federation for Information Processing, Volume 263, *Trust Management II*, Yücel Karabulut, John Mitchell, Peter Herrmann, Christian Damsgaard Jensen; (Boston Springer), pp. 247–262.

Current solutions for data protection divide into (1) legal norms and regulations and (2) technical mechanisms. Throughout the European Union, directives establish data protection as a fundamental human right [10]. However, the regulatory approach often results in a daunting number of norms that is unmanageable both for the persons concerned and for the data collectors. Further, there is a lack of legal certainty for new technologies which the legislator has not considered yet. Ensuring that regulations are met is particularly challenging in scenarios where the collection and processing of private data is *intransparent* to the individuals concerned [19]. This is the rule in most Ubiquitous Computing-, RFID- and Sensor Network scenarios. From a technical perspective, all current privacy-related approaches are *technology-centered, isolated* implementations and require a thorough understanding of the technology. For example, an entry 'X-No-Archive: Yes' in the header of Usenet messages prevents them from being filed. But it is hard to explain to persons without a technical background how to make use of such features. We expect that the situation will become worse with more sophisticated technology.

Intuitively speaking, one is neither interested in going through lawsuits nor in implementing technical mechanisms to enforce privacy. Instead of bothering with the details of technologies and regulations, the individual concerned simply wants to know: *"Can I trust a certain service provider to handle my personal information compliant with regulations and according to my preferences?"*. Since existing research does not directly address this demand, it is necessary to investigate new issues and directions for future research and development.

The core idea behind this paper is the deployment of Web2.0 technologies to support individuals in protecting their privacy. Web2.0 mechanisms like folksonomies, blogs and social network communities have become popular in the recent past. Our vision is to leverage them for data protection. This paper is the first step in the direction of a holistic Privacy2.0-framework that lets the individuals concerned share their experiences, observations and recommendations about privacy practices of service providers in an intuitive and flexible manner. We make the following contributions:

- We explain from an interdisciplinary point of view why existing solutions for data protection are not sufficient in current and future scenarios. We say why we think that social software mechanisms from the Web2.0 has the potential to overcome these limitations.
- We introduce a Privacy2.0 framework on the logical level based on social software mechanisms. It is flexible enough to meet individual privacy needs, and provides a holistic view on privacy threats coming from a broad range of technologies in the online and offline world, e.g., search engines, web shops, sensor networks or RFID-tagged products. We identify the components of our framework at the logical level.
- We review current technologies in order to find out which approaches can be adapted for an implementation of our framework, and we say which functionality is missing and requires further development. In addition, we discuss open issues for further research in multiple disciplines.

The remainder of this paper is organized as follows: The next section reviews technologies with an impact on privacy and solutions for data protection. Section 3 introduces the components of our framework, and in Section 4 we sketch an anonymous variant. Section 5 discusses applicability issues and outlines future work, followed by the conclusion in Section 6.

2 Privacy Threats

According to a recent survey of the IEEE Spectrum [15], more than 60% of 700 scientists interviewed expect that intelligent, interconnected devices performing individual-related services will have penetrated our daily lives in the next 10 years. In the following we will briefly overview prominent technologies that are relevant in this context, and we will explain how they affect privacy.

2.1 Future Technologies with an Impact on Privacy

A **Sensor Network** [17] consists of many sensor nodes equipped with sensing devices, radio transmitters and limited computational resources. By using self-organization technologies for sensing and network formation, sensor networks are able to fulfill complex measurement tasks in the fields of surveillance, border control or facility monitoring. The toll collect network, which operates approximately 2800 nodes[1], can be seen as a first large-scale sensor network in public spaces. Toll collect identifies trucks on German highways with an average capture rate of 99.75%[2]. Although toll collect's objective is to charge trucks for the use of highways, some parties have already demanded access this data for other purposes, e.g., civilian law enforcement.

The idea of **Radio Frequency Identification** (RFID) is to assign a globally unique identification number to physical objects for applications like object tracking or stock management [3]. The objects are labeled with a RFID tag containing a radio transmitter as well as very limited computing and storage capabilities. The tags can be read over a distance without requiring a straight line of sight. One of the most prominent RFID applications is to replace barcode-based processes, in particular at the points of sale of retailers [13]. Thus, RFID technology is about to enter public spaces at a large scale. But while barcodes contain only information about the product group and have to be visibly mounted and scanned, RFID labels can be embedded into products invisibly and be read without the knowledge of the individual concerned.

Ubiquitous Computing (Ubicomp) means equipping objects of everyday life (refrigerators, microwave ovens, etc.) with "intelligence" in order to ease repetitive tasks in household, business or medical care [29]. For instance, consider an Ubi-

---

[1] Bundesanstalt für Straßenwesen (BASt), 01/01/2008, http://www.mauttabelle.de

[2] Press release 14/12/07, "Truck toll in Germany: Three years", http://www.toll-collect.de

comp system that tracks the position of a certain user and reminds him of important appointments either via the handsfree set in his car, the hi-fi system in his living room or any other interconnected device with audio output in his vicinity. Ubicomp installations can monitor the behavior of their users around the clock.

As a cross-cutting service, the **Internet** enables a broad variety of devices and services to interact in order to drive highly personal, interconnected applications. When looking at today's Internet, privacy threats arise from an unmanageably large number of different technical protocols, services and service providers. On the Web, privacy-sensitive information can be gathered by using cookies, iframes, web-bugs, affiliation programs, services that require a personal login etc. The situation is expected to become even more unclear in the future [15].

Technologies like Sensor Networks, RFID or Ubicomp have a large impact on privacy, for the following reasons:

- They bridge the gap between the online and the offline world. Thus, the situation is not as simple as switching off the computer to leave the respective data-privacy issues behind.
- The technologies use networked devices to collect, transfer and process personal data in the background and without the assistance and the knowledge of the individual concerned. Thus, it is virtually impossible for each individual to keep track of all service providers which have his personal data.
- As the level of detail of the collected data is comprehensive, and personal data from multiple sources can be easily linked, the potential of any misuse of this information is huge.
- The applications outlined yield a clear benefit for their users. Thus, it is not an option to strictly avoid their use.

2.2 Solutions for Data Protection

In this subsection we will briefly outline the range of data-protection approaches.
Laws and Regulations. The European Union harmonizes the data-protection law of its members by issuing directives in sectors like e-commerce [12] or electronic communication [11]. However, the debates on transposing these directives into national law show that regulatory approaches have fundamental limitations. The legislator cannot predict new technologies. This involves periods of time without legal certainty, until regulations have been adopted for new privacy threats. Further, new technologies often result in a flood of new regulations. For example, German law contains approximately 1500 norms for data protection. But, to give an example, there still is no regulation for Peer-to-Peer Overlay Networks [25] where each peer can be a service provider which handles personal data. The regulatory approach is often ineffective in ensuring data protection: Service providers cannot find out which particular norms apply among a daunting but incomplete amount of regulations. Authorities are overloaded with an increasing number of regulations, and enforcing them requires a fundamental understanding of the technical background.

In consequence, it is *intransparent* for the individual if a service provider handles personal data with care or not, even if appropriate regulations exist.

Technical Mechanisms. The number of privacy enhancement technologies available is large. For example, epic.org lists approximately 200 privacy tools, and vunet.com finds about 100 commercial privacy suites. Nevertheless, existing technical mechanisms cannot ensure data protection for the majority of people, for various reasons. For example, P3P-enabled web servers [5] inform the web browser of the user about the privacy policy of the service provider, and let the browser reject cookies which pose a privacy threat according to the user preferences. But understanding the impact of cookies on privacy and therefore setting the preferences accordingly requires a thorough understanding of the Internet protocols. Finally, P3P cannot express all details required from EU privacy regulations, and addresses only a tiny fraction of privacy threats in the Internet (cf. [9]). Other technical mechanisms face similar problems. k-anonymity [27] handles the problem that anonymized micro-data, e.g., from surveys or field studies, can be linked with public data to obtain personal profiles. However, it turned out that it is even challenging for experts to anonymize personal data properly [24]. This does not mean that it is not important to develop such mechanisms. The finding simply indicates that it cannot be left to the individual to use a large number of specific privacy techniques efficiently.

Other Mechanisms. Considering that both legal and technical mechanisms are not sufficient to ensure data protection, recent political debates suggest the legislator to focus on self-regulation, education and training [4]. Privacy seals are one approach for self-regulation. They certify that service providers follow specific privacy guidelines [1]. Thus, privacy seals signalize trust in the data-handling practices of the provider audited. However, as long as the prerequisites to obtain a seal are unclear for the most of the public, the significance of privacy seals is limited.

3 A Collaborative Framework for Data Protection

We have shown that all available technical solutions for data protection are technology-centered, isolated mechanisms which require thorough knowledge from the individuals, and we have explained the fundamental problems of regulatory approaches. Before proposing our novel *collaborative* framework for data protection, we will introduce the requirements for data-protection mechanisms in current and future scenarios, as we see them. The requirements rely on the assumption that the user does not want to deal with technical and legal details; instead, he simply wants to know which service he can commit personal information to.

(R1) One Mechanism for All Data-Privacy Issues.   From the user perspective it is not sufficient to develop isolated technical mechanisms tailored to specific privacy threats. Instead, the user requires a *holistic* view of all possible threats. It should indicate if it is safe to entrust personal data to a particular service. It should be independent from the technologies and protocols used by the service.

Obviously, one typically cannot foresee new data-privacy threats. This calls for flexible and adaptive mechanisms.

(R2) Privacy Self-Protection.   Currently, the authorities are overloaded with the enforcement of a daunting number of regulations, and new technologies often result in a lack of legal certainty. Furthermore, most existing technical privacy mechanisms have to be implemented at the data collector, and it is impossible for the majority of people to assess their effectiveness. Thus, from the perspective of the individuals concerned, data protection currently is a matter of trust in the willingness and ability of the data collectors to care for the privacy of their customers. But, according to our perception, individuals want powerful tools which put data protection in their hands.

(R3) Intuitive Use.   The widespread use of information technology in public spaces makes data protection a concern for broad parts of the society. In consequence, it is of utmost importance that a privacy measure is applicable without requiring a special training or in-depth knowledge from its user. Otherwise, the result could be a two-tier society where the educated part of the population is able to keep its privacy while the other one is not.

(R4) Individual Preferences.   As [7, 6] have shown, the desired level of privacy varies at large scale. While some persons are willing to provide private information to a significant extent just for comfort or gaming, others request a considerable compensation for their private data. Thus, it is important to support an individual not only according to existing norms and regulations, but also by representing his preferences. In line with the requirement 'Intuitive Use', this calls for a set of basic preference templates, e.g., "discreet", "standard" and "communicative". Individuals then may adapt these templates.

3.1 Overview

The vision behind the framework proposed is to use modern Web2.0 techniques for data protection. The framework lets individuals share their experiences with the data-handling practices of service providers, and it provides a warning before someone reveals personal information against his preferences. As observations by privacy activists and committees for data protection show[3], attentive persons can detect many privacy violations, and they are willing to communicate their findings. Sharing data-privacy issues would put pressure on services which violate the privacy of their consumers and lets society enforce social standards for data protection. Thus, a privacy framework based on Web2.0 allows the individuals concerned to supervise the data collectors and to put data protection in their own hands.

We describe our logical framework as it could be implemented at a *trusted third party*. The framework stores the pseudonyms of its users, which could have an impact on their privacy. In Section 4 we will sketch an alternative Peer-to-Peer realization that provides complete anonymity.

---

[3] See http://www.trust-us.ch, http://www.ccc.de/club/archiv, http://netzpolitik.org for examples.

Fig. 1 Overview of the Privacy2.0 Framework

Figure 1 provides an overview of our logical framework. Its core component is the **PrivacyTagger**, a user-managed taxonomy of data-privacy issues. It stores tuples of the form (*privacy threat, user pseudonym, label*), and it lets the users intuitively label privacy-threatening Internet-service providers, geographical locations or objects referenced by RFID tags. For example, one could tag a certain geographical position with the labels "video", "surveillance" and "no privacy policy". The **TagMiner** component extracts the semantics of the labels provided, i.e., it tries to identify labels with the same meaning. For example, the labels "worse policy" and "spammer" provide the same negative assessment. In order to find out if the privacy threats identified by one particular user are relevant for another one, the **PreferenceMatcher** computes the similarity of two users, based on the tagged objects and the tags they have created. The **ThreatTaxonomy** component determines similar services, locations and objects. Finally, social software systems require a minimum number of active users to become operational. Thus, the **IncentivesManager** motivates the users to create useful and reliable labels, e.g., by providing better service for dependable users.

In the following, we will explain the functionality of each component, and we will provide a discussion of design alternatives, implementation issues and technology available.

G	Geographic locations
P	Physical objects
I	Internet-services
O	Privacy issues referenced by the tags
U	Pseudonyms of users who provided the tags
T	Tags

Table 1 Symbols used to describe the framework.

3.2 The PrivacyTagger Component

The PrivacyTagger lets the users gather information on the data-privacy practices of a wide range of service providers in the online and offline world collaboratively. We propose a *folksonomy* [22] ("folk taxonomy") as the basis infrastructure for this component. *Social tagging* means that the users can label privacy threats with schema-free *tags*, e.g., "spammer" or "good privacy policy". Technorati and Flickr[4] are prominent examples of social tagging. The tags can be arbitrarily chosen; the users do not need to agree on global standards. Since tags consist of only a few letters each, it is possible to support a wide range of end-user devices. Even the 160 letters allowed in an SMS would be sufficient to generate tags en route with a cellphone. More systematically, folksonomies are in line with our requirements: They make no restrictions regarding the tags and objects tagged (R1), help the users protecting their privacy by making privacy violations transparent (R2), and their use is intuitive (R3). Note that R4 is addressed by other components.

A folksonomy typically is a tripartite network [20] described by (*object, user, tag*)-tuples. Let O be the set of objects that can be referenced, e.g., the URL of a web shop or the location of a surveillance camera which might have an impact on privacy. U is the set of users who provide the tags. T stands for the set of all tags (Table 1 contains all symbols used). Thus, the PrivacyTagger component stores the records $(O, U, T) = \{(o_1, u_1, t_1), \cdots, (o_n, u_n, t_n)\}$ where $o \in O$, $u \in U$, $t \in T$. Since Requirement R1 calls for holistic mechanisms, we have to ensure that our framework can address a broad range of privacy threats. For this reason, we propose to let the users tag geographic locations (G), physical items (P) and Internet services (I). The range of taggable objects is $dom(O) = dom(G) \cup dom(P) \cup dom(I)$. $dom(G) = (latitude, longitude, height)$ describes geographic locations. Internet services are referenced by its uniform resource locator (URL), and RFID labels[5] can identify physical objects. Extending the framework for other privacy threats simply requires extending $dom(O)$.

Due to its simple structure, the implementation of a folksonomy is straightforward. Alternatively, one can adapt open-source implementations like Scuttle[6].

---

[4] http://www.technorati.com, http://www.flickr.com/tags

[5] Each RFID label stores a globally unique EPC-ID, cf. http://www.epcid.com.

[6] http://sourceforge.net/projects/scuttle

3.3 The ThreatTaxonomy Component

The ThreatTaxonomy component computes the similarity of privacy threats o_a, o_b which are represented differently in the PrivacyTagger component. There are many reasons why similar threats can have different representations. For example, the accuracy of civilian Global Positioning System (GPS) receivers used to tag geographic locations is typically about 15 meters. Further, one company might be represented in the Internet, e.g., with a web shop, at certain geographic locations, e.g., outlets in shopping malls, and with RFID-tagged objects, e.g., bonus cards. In order to provide a holistic view on all privacy issues (Requirement R1), our framework has to identify similar privacy threats. Thus, the ThreatTaxonomy implements the function $tt(o_a, o_b) = x$ with $x \in [0, 1]$, where $x = 1$ refers to exactly the same and $x = 0$ to completely different privacy threats.

The similarity between differently represented objects can be computed in numerous ways; it has to be investigated which method is adequate for an implementation of our logical framework. For example, an inspection of the commercial register provides a taxonomy of the corporate structure and interconnected companies. Based on the accuracy of GPS receivers, two locations could be distinguished as follows:

$$tt(g_a, g_b) = \begin{cases} 1 & \text{if } distance(g_a, g_b) \le 2 \cdot 15m \\ 0 & \text{otherwise} \end{cases}$$

It is also possible to infer similar privacy threats from the PrivacyTagger data. The records $\{(o_1, u_1, t_1), \cdots, (o_n, u_n, t_n)\}$ can be regarded as a graph structure $S = (V, E)$ where the set of vertices is $V = O \cup U \cup T$, and each record (o, u, t) constitutes three undirected edges $\{(o, u), (u, t), (t, o)\} \in E$. Now a wide range of well-known graph-based measures can be used to determine the similarity of two privacy threats o_a, o_b, e.g., the number of disjoint paths or the structural equivalence. See [26] for a comparison of graph-based distance measures that could be applied in our context.

Finally, it would be feasible to employ a second folksonomy to let the users create a taxonomy of similar privacy threats.

3.4 The TagMiner Component

Folksonomies can be intuitively used (cf. Requirement R3), but this might result in less accurate tags. According to [16], the tags provided by typical users can be, amongst other challenges:
- ambiguous, imprecise or inexact,
- misspelled or language dependent,
- homonymous, synonymous or consisting of singular and plural forms,
- consisting of compound tags and separators.

The TagMiner component extracts the meaning from the tags provided. In the context of this framework it is sufficient to learn if a certain user finds a particular privacy issue either threatening or not. Thus, TagMiner implements the function $tm(t) = x$ with $x \in \{positive, negative\}$.

A realization of the TagMiner component could use information-retrieval and knowledge-discovery mechanisms, e.g., rely on existing work in the area of opinion extraction [8, 18]. Opinion extraction aims to find out if customers like a certain product or not from, say, textual product reviews provided at shopping portals like Ciao.com. In order to extract the opinion from a text, complex preprocessing steps are required to identify the "opinion words" and to consider the order of words in a sentence. Opinion extraction on folksonomies should be slightly easier, because the tags are always descriptive [16] and do not require such preprocessing. However, the tags are not necessarily expressed in natural language but contain special characters and separators, which might stress existing opinion-extraction techniques.

3.5 The PreferenceMatcher Component

The preferences of different users regarding the desired level of privacy vary significantly. This has an influence on the tags the users generate. For example, while one user labels a web shop with "bad privacy policy", a less suspicious user might come up with "acceptable" for the same issue (cf. Requirement R4). Because it is important to know if the tags from one user can serve as a recommendation for another one, the PreferenceMatcher determines the similarity between two users.

For this reason, the PreferenceMatcher stores a set of preferences of all users $\{\pi_1, \cdots, \pi_n\}$. Based on the preferences π_a, π_b of two users a, b, the Preference-Matcher computes the function $pm(\pi_a, \pi_b) = x$ with $x \in [0, 1]$. $x = 0$ means that two users have complementary preferences, while $x = 1$ stands for users with equal attitudes regarding data protection.

It remains to be discussed how the preferences π_u of user u should be represented. Identifying the *real* preferences of individuals is challenging: Since privacy is a highly emotional topic, observations show that persons are rarely able to estimate their desired level of privacy exactly [6]. In order to approach this problem, we define the preference of each user u as a set of $(object, tag)$-pairs, i.e., $\pi_u = \{(o_1, t_1), \cdots, (o_m, t_m)\}$. As a starting point, each new user chooses a set of popular objects and tags π^t with $\forall (o, t) \in \pi^t : o \in O \land t \in T$. As the user subsequently labels new objects, these join his preferences, i.e., $\pi_u = \pi^t \cup \{(\hat{o}, \hat{t}) \mid (\hat{o}, u, \hat{t}) \in (O, U, T)\}$. Since the choice of tags and tagged threats represent the opinion of the user, newly created tags refine the preferences towards his real objectives.

The folksonomy can be represented as a graph structure $S = (V, E)$ where the set of vertices is $V = O \cup U \cup T$, and each record (o, u, t) constitutes three undirected edges $\{(o, u), (u, t), (t, o)\} \in E$ (cf. Subsection 3.3). The preferences of each user u form a subgraph of $S' = (V', E')$, i.e., $\forall (o, t) \in \pi_u : o \in V' \land \{(o, u), (u, t), (t, o)\} \in E'$ and $S' \subseteq S$. Thus, the PreferenceMatcher can determine the similarity of two users by finding overlapping subgraphs [30] or the distance between subgraphs [26] in the graph structure.

3.6 The IncentivesManager Component

People participate in social software systems like folksonomies for various reasons: for personal use, to express their opinion, to attract attention, for self presentation issues, or to play and compete with others (cf. [22] for an exhaustive description). The purpose of the IncentivesManager component is to achieve *incentive compatibility* between the individuals participating and the global objectives of the framework envisioned. The IncentivesManager has to motivate the users to:

- **participate.** A social framework for data protection becomes effective only if a *sufficient number of attentive users* observes and labels privacy threats.
- **tag the right objects.** As research has pointed out, tags in a folksonomy usually follow a power-law distribution [16]: Few popular objects are tagged frequently, while most objects are labeled with a few tags at most. However, Requirement R2 targets at a sufficient number of tags on less popular privacy threats, too.
- **provide high-quality tags.** The description of the TagMiner component lists a number of issues like ambiguous or misspelled tags the framework has to deal with. In order to facilitate this, the IncentivesManager should motivate the users to *create tags carefully* right from the start.

Research in the area of social networking provides a number of incentives mechanisms possible. Examples are a ranking of the most active users or comfort features for users who have provided reliable information. As another example, [2] introduces a social psychology approach to motivate the members of a film community (MovieLens) to review particular movies. The participants received emails emphasizing that the receiver has been chosen because he provides better reviews than others, and that his review would be useful for many people. [2] shows that this approach motivates to participate in a way an operator has devised a priori. At this point, we do not impose any restriction on the incentive mechanisms, except that they have to follow the Requirements R1–R4.

3.7 The Privacy2.0 Framework

Having introduced the components of our framework, we can now specify how the framework decides if it is safe for a certain user to commit his personal data to a service provider. The provider is identified by a particular physical object, geographic location or Internet address. Formally, the framework requires a possible privacy threat q with $dom(q) \in dom(o), o \in O$ and the requesting user u as input. Based on the folksonomy (O, U, T) and the user preferences $\{\pi_1 \cdots \pi_n\}$, the framework computes $f(q, u) = x$ with $x \in \{true, false, unknown\}$. The value *unknown* is returned if the folksonomy does not contain tags related to q. A return value *true* means that q identifies a service provider in the folksonomy, and the privacy practices of the service provider match the preferences of user u. Otherwise, *false* is returned.

To ease the presentation, we divide the computation into three steps. First the TagMiner partitions the (O, U, T)-tuples stored in the PrivacyTagger component into two sets of $(object, tag)$-pairs with positive (M^{pos}) and negative (M^{neg}) tags:

$$M^{pos} = \left\{ (\hat{o}, \hat{u}) \mid (\hat{o}, \hat{u}, \hat{t}) \in (O, U, T) \;\wedge\; tm(\hat{t}) = positive \right\}$$

$$M^{neg} = \left\{ (\hat{o}, \hat{u}) \mid (\hat{o}, \hat{u}, \hat{t}) \in (O, U, T) \;\wedge\; tm(\hat{t}) = negative \right\}$$

Second, we find out if q refers to a privacy issue that is threatening for the user or not. Therefore, we compute a score over each pair $(\hat{o}, \hat{u}) \in M^{pos}, M^{neg}$. The Threat-Taxonomy component computes a measure that quantifies the similarity between the threat in question q and a threat $\hat{o}$ that has been tagged before. The Preference-Matcher provides a measure for the similarity of the current user u and the user $\hat{u}$ who provided the tag. One way to compute the score is to sum the products of these values:

$$score = \sum_{(\hat{o}, \hat{u}) \in M^{pos}} tt(\hat{o}, q) \cdot pm(\pi_u, \pi_{\hat{u}}) - \sum_{(\hat{o}, \hat{u}) \in M^{neg}} tt(\hat{o}, q) \cdot pm(\pi_u, \pi_{\hat{u}})$$

Finally, the framework returns *unknown* to the user if there is no privacy threat similar to q in the folksonomy. It returns *true* if the score is positive and *false* otherwise.

$$f(q, u) = \begin{cases} unknown & \text{if } \forall o \in O : tt(q, o) = 0 \\ true & \text{if } score > 0 \\ false & \text{otherwise} \end{cases}$$

Note that we have kept the framework simple on purpose to ease presentation. It has to be investigated if more elaborate methods result in an increased utility. For example, the score could outweigh negative tags to reflect that false positives are more problematic than false negatives. Further, the score could weigh the tags of the questioner higher than the tags provided by others. Another extension could provide an aging mechanism to remove outdated privacy issues. It requires a prototypical implementation and user studies to investigate the effect of these extensions.

4 Anonymity vs. Pseudonymity

The framework proposed so far requires unique identifiers for the users. Although pseudonyms are well-suited as identifiers, knowledge of all (o, u, t) records of a certain user actually is a privacy threat. In the following we discuss how the framework must change in order to provide full anonymity.

In its anonymity-preserving variant, the PrivacyTagger component stores $(object, tag)$ records, i.e., $(O, T) = \{(o_1, t_1), \cdots, (o_n, t_n)\}$. Because it is possible to infer the user identity based on his IP address and the queries he issues, PrivacyTagger should store these records in a Peer-to-Peer data structure (see [23] for an overview), where the records are distributed among many peers, and communication can be encrypted. Without knowing the set of users U and their preferences π_u, the framework is restricted to compute $f(q)$ based on the similarity between the threat q and the set of already tagged threats O:

$$M^{pos} = \{o \mid (o,t) \in (O,T) \wedge tm(t) = positive\}$$

$$M^{neg} = \{o \mid (o,t) \in (O,T) \wedge tm(t) = negative\}$$

$$f(q) = \begin{cases} unknown & \text{if } \forall o \in O : tt(q,o) = 0 \\ true & \text{if } \sum_{o \in M^{pos}} tt(o,q) - \sum_{o \in M^{neg}} tt(o,q) > 0 \\ false & \text{otherwise} \end{cases}$$

After having sketched an anonymous privacy framework, we compare it with the pseudonymous variant. We see two reasons why the framework should be implemented using pseudonyms:

- Not knowing which user has assigned a tag to a privacy issue would degrade the service quality. It is impossible to provide incentives for the users, i.e., amount and quality of the anonymous tags would be worse in comparison to a pseudonymous implementation. Further, it is not possible to compute the similarity between the current user and the user who provided a certain tag. Thus, the decision of the anonymous framework relies solely on the accumulated opinions and the experiences of the majority of users. While the framework would represent the joint privacy standards of the society, it cannot consider individual preferences.
- The framework can be used to assess itself, i.e., the users are free to generate tags on the URL of a service that implements the framework. To provide an extreme example, immediately after a new user has specified his preferences, a warning could appear that he should delete his profile and log off. However, the framework does not require to disclose any personal information. Given that a responsible and dependable provider implements the framework, such extreme cases should not happen.

It is up to future research to find out if the concerns regarding a pseudonymous privacy mechanism outweigh its increased usefulness, as compared to an anonymous variant.

5 Discussion

The benefits of the Privacy2.0 framework envisioned are broad. It promises to produce a new level of transparency on privacy violations. While it is hard for the individual to estimate if a certain provider meets a daunting number of regulations and follows acceptable privacy standards, our framework profits from the observations and experiences of a community of users. Due to the flexibility of the underlying folksonomy infrastructure, the framework addresses a wide range of privacy threats and user preferences without forcing the users to master the details of a large number of isolated data-protection techniques. By providing transparency for the data handling practices of service providers, the framework fits into the EU directive [10] and could be a cornerstone of self-regulation approaches for data protection.

Legal Aspects of our Framework. Because our framework does not restrict the tags generated, users are free to provide slander, gossip or negative opinions without any reason. This raises legal challenges for a trusted third party which operates an implementation of the framework. As an instance for the situation in the EU, we will briefly summarize recent developments in Germany.

Reviews on the eBay platform[7] are similar in length and nature to the tags in our framework. Thus, the legal risks of the framework can be derived from judicial decisions on eBay lawsuits. On April 3, 2006, the Higher Regional Court of Oldenburg has decided on the legitimacy of negative reviews (file reference 13 U 71/05). Specifically, the court has defined under which premises a few words constitute an untrue claim of fact which violates the personal rights of the individual concerned. Another relevant decision comes from the Higher Regional Court of Koblenz at July 12, 2007 (file reference 2 U 862/06). The court has specified the borderline between claims of fact that can be verified, subjective expressions of opinion, value judgments and illegal abusive criticism. However, an in-depth investigation of the legal issues cannot be performed solely on the framework, but requires a concrete implementation of the components and of the score function.

Directions for Future Research. The framework presented tries to establish a new research direction in the field of data protection with a focus on society. From this point of view, both technical and legal measures for data protection are of utmost importance: Since it cannot be guaranteed that users detect all privacy threats, the framework proposed complements existing legal and technical methods, but does not want to replace them. In that sense our framework uses collaborative mechanisms to observe and communicate if a service provider implements appropriate and effective techniques.

As a consequence, research on the framework calls for multidisciplinarity. Computer scientists would explore efficient and effective technologies for the infrastructure. Sociologists would investigate how interactions between people of different cultures, social classes, gender etc. influence the use of the framework proposed. Since both privacy threats and privacy techniques affect the behavior of the users, research in technology assessment is needed to estimate the impact of an implementation of the framework on society. There are open questions regarding data-privacy legislation, liability for misuse, copyright etc. which require the attention of jurists. Finally, economists have to investigate the relationships between pricing and the handling of private data in the presence of a mechanism that makes privacy violations public.

An evaluation of the framework must reflect this multidisciplinary alignment and therefore consider different perspectives. The technical point of view requires to prove that the basic infrastructure is effective and scales well in a global setting

---

[7] http://www.ebay.com

where many people issue large numbers of queries in parallel. One option to evaluate the social and legal aspects is to initiate and supervise a public discourse in collaboration with privacy activists and media partners. Field tests with a prototypical implementation in a supervised environment can provide insight in the behavior of the users and of individuals concerned, the quality of the tags and the applicability of the framework components in isolation.

6 Conclusion

The integration of current and future technologies in the everyday life will shape the society of the future not only because of its benefits, but also due to significant new challenges with regard to data protection. Current solutions for data protection require time and effort from the user. In the presence of many networked devices to collect, transfer and process personal data, these solutions cannot ensure privacy.

The objective of this paper is to propose investigating the deployment of Web2.0 technologies to support individuals in protecting their privacy. To this end, we have specified a framework based on a folksonomy of tagged geo-locations, physical items and Internet addresses with an impact on privacy. It lets the users share observations and experiences on data-privacy issues. By comparing possible privacy threats to the user preferences, the framework helps the user to decide if a particular data collector handles personal information with care and according to his preferences.

A broad variety of technology needed to implement the framework is currently being researched or developed. Future research issues are multidisciplinary and involve computer science, social science, economic science and jurisprudence.

References

1. Beatty, P., Reay, I., Dick, S., Miller, J.: P3P Adoption on E-Commerce Web sites: A Survey and Analysis. IEEE Internet Computing (IC) **11**(2), 65–71 (2007)
2. Beenen, G., et al.: Using Social Psychology to Motivate Contributions to Online Communities. In: Proceedings of the ACM Conference on Computer Supported Cooperative Work (CSCW'04) (2004)
3. Chawathe, S.S., et al.: Managing RFID Data. In: Proceedings of the 30st International Conference on Very Large Data Bases (VLDB'04) (2004)
4. Concil of the European Union: European Policy Outlook RFID (draft version). Working document for the expert conference "RFID: Towards the Internet of Things" (2007)
5. Cranor, L., et al.: The Platform for Privacy Preferences 1.0 (p3p1.0). W3C Recommendation, Available at http://www.w3.org/TR/P3P/ (2002)
6. Cvrcek, D., Kumpost, M., Matyas, V., Danezis, G.: A study on the value of location privacy. In: Proceedings of the 5th Workshop on Privacy in the Electronic Society (WPES'06) (2006)
7. Danezis, G., Lewis, S., Anderson, R.: How Much is Location Privacy Worth? In: Proceedings of the 4th Workshop on Economics of Information Security (WEIS'05) (2005)

8. Dave, K., Lawrence, S., Pennock, D.M.: Mining the Peanut Gallery: Opinion Extraction and Semantic Classification of Product Reviews. In: Proceedings of the 12th International World Wide Web Conference (WWW'03) (2003)

9. Electronic Privacy Information Center: Pretty Poor Privacy: An Assessment of P3P and Internet Privacy. Available at http://www.epic.org/reports/prettypoorprivacy.html (2000)

10. European Parliament and the Council of the European Union: Directive 95/46/EC on the protection of individuals with regard to the processing of personal data and on the free movement of such data. Official Journal L 281, 11/23/1995, p.31. (1995)

11. European Parliament and the Council of the European Union: Directive 2000/31/EC on certain legal aspects of information society services, in particular electronic commerce, in the Internal Market. Official Journal L 178, 07/17/2000 p.1–16 (2000)

12. European Parliament and the Council of the European Union: Directive 2002/58/EC concerning the processing of personal data and the protection of privacy in the electronic communications sector. Official Journal L 201, 31/07//2002 p.37–47 (2002)

13. Gaukler, G.M., Seifert, R.W., Hausman, W.H.: Item-Level RFID in the Retail Supply Chain. Production and Operations Management 16, 65–76 (2007)

14. Gehrke, J., Madden, S.: Query Processing in Sensor Networks. IEEE Pervasive Computing 03(1), 46–55 (2004)

15. Gorbis, M., Pescovitz, D.: Bursting Tech Bubbles Before They Balloon. In: IEEE Spektrum (2006)

16. Guy, M., Tonkin, E.: Folksonomies: Tidying Up Tags? D-Lib Magazine 12(1) (2006)

17. Haenselmann, T.: An FDL'ed Textbook on Sensor Networks. Published under GNU FDL at http://www.informatik.uni-mannheim.de/~haensel/sn_book (2005)

18. Hu, M., Liu, B.: Mining and Summarizing Customer Reviews. In: Proceedings of the 10th Conference on Knowledge Discovery and Data Mining (KDD'04) (2004)

19. Klüver, L., et al.: ICT and Privacy in Europe – A Report on Different Aspects of Privacy Based on Studies Made by EPTA Members in 7 European Countries. Available at DOI: http://dx.doi.org/10.1553/ITA-pb-a44s (2006)

20. Lambiotte, R., Ausloos, M.: Collaborative Tagging as a Tripartite Network. Available at http://arxiv.org/abs/cs.DS/0512090 (2005)

21. Langheinrich, M.: A Privacy Awareness System for Ubiquitous Computing Environments. In: Proceedings of the 4th International Conference on Ubiquitous Computing (UbiComp'02), pp. 237–245 (2002)

22. Marlow, C., et al.: HT06, Tagging Paper, Taxonomy, Flickr, Academic Article, ToRead. In: Proceedings of the 17th ACM Conference on Hypertext and Hypermedia (Hypertext'06) (2006)

23. Milojicic, D.S., Kalogeraki, V., Lukose, R., Nagaraja, K., Pruyne, J., Richard, B., Rollins, S., Xu, Z.: Peer-to-Peer Computing. Tech. Rep. HPL-2002-57, HP Labs (2002).

24. Ninghui, L., Tiancheng, L., Venkatasubramanian, S.: t-Closeness: Privacy Beyond k-Anonymity and l-Diversity. Proceedings of the 23rd International Conference on Data Engineering (ICDE'07) (2007)

25. Raabe, O., Dinger, J., Hartenstein, H.: Telekommunikationsdienste in Next-Generation-Networks am Beispiel von Peer-to-Peer-Overlay-Systemen. In: Kommunikation und Recht (2007)

26. Schenker, A., et al.: Comparison of Distance Measures for Graph-Based Clustering of Documents. In: Proceedings of the 4th International Workshop on Graph Based Representations in Pattern Recognition (GbRPR'03) (2003)

27. Sweeney, L.: k-Anonymity: A Model for Protecting Privacy. International Journal of Uncertainty, Fuzziness and Knowledge-Based Systems 10(5), 557–570 (2002)

28. Wang, F., Liu, P.: Temporal Management of RFID Data. In: Proceedings of the 31st International Conference on Very Large Data Bases (VLDB'05), pp. 1128–1139 (2005)

29. Weiser, M.: The Computer for the 21st Century. ACM SIGMOBILE Mobile Computing and Communications Review 3(3) (1999)

30. Yan, X., Yu, P.S., Han, J.: Substructure Similarity Search in Graph Databases. In: Proceedings of the 24th International Conference on Management of Data (SIGMOD'05) (2005)

Automatic verification of privacy properties in the applied pi calculus*

Stéphanie Delaune, Mark Ryan, and Ben Smyth

Abstract We develop a formal method verification technique for cryptographic protocols. We focus on proving observational equivalences of the kind $P \sim Q$, where the processes P and Q have the same structure and differ only in the choice of terms. The calculus of ProVerif, a variant of the applied pi calculus, makes some progress in this direction. We expand the scope of ProVerif, to provide reasoning about further equivalences. We also provide an extension which allows modelling of protocols which require global synchronisation. Finally we develop an algorithm to enable automated reasoning. We demonstrate the practicality of our work with two case studies.

1 Introduction

Security protocols are small distributed programs that aim to provide some security related objective over a public communications network like the Internet. Considering the increasing size of networks and their dependence on cryptographic protocols, a high level of assurance is needed in the correctness of such protocols. It is difficult to ascertain whether or not a cryptographic protocol satisfies its security requirements. Numerous protocols have appeared in literature and have subsequently been found to be flawed [13, 14, 5]. Typically, cryptographic protocols are expected to achieve their objectives in

Stéphanie Delaune
LSV, ENS Cachan & CNRS & INRIA, France, e-mail: delaune@lsv.ens-cachan.fr

Mark Ryan · Ben Smyth
School of Computer Science, University of Birmingham, UK, e-mail: {B.A.Smyth, M.D.Ryan}@cs.bham.ac.uk

* This work has been partly supported by the ARA SESUR project AVOTÉ and the EPSRC projects *Verifying anonymity and privacy properties* (EP/E040829/1) & *UbiVal* (EP/D076625/1).

Please use the following format when citing this chapter:

Delaune, S., Ryan, M. and Smyth, B., 2008, in IFIP International Federation for Information Processing, Volume 263; *Trust Management II*, Yücel Karabulut, John Mitchell, Peter Herrmann, Christian Damsgaard Jensen; (Boston: Springer), pp. 263–278.

the presence of an attacker that is assumed to have full control of the network (sometimes called the Dolev-Yao attacker). He can eavesdrop, replay, inject and block messages. The attacker can also modify them by performing cryptographic operations when in possession of the required keys. Furthermore the attacker may be in control of one or more of the protocol's participants. With no more than the abilities listed, and irrespective of the underlying cryptographic algorithms, numerous protocols have been found to be vulnerable to attack. Formal verification of cryptographic protocols is therefore required to ensure that cryptographic protocols can be deployed without the risk of damage.

Traditionally cryptographic protocols have been required to satisfy secrecy and authentication properties [6]. These requirements have been successfully verified by modelling them as reachability problems. Current research into applications such as electronic voting, fair exchange and trusted computing has resulted in a plethora of new requirements which protocols must satisfy (e.g. [11, 4]). Some of these properties cannot easily be expressed using traditional reachability techniques but can be written as equivalences. For example, the privacy, receipt-freeness and coercion-resistance properties of electronic voting protocols can be expressed using equivalences (see [12, 7]).

We focus on proving equivalences of the kind $P \sim Q$, where the processes P and Q have the same structure and differ only in the choice of terms. For example, the secret ballot (privacy) property of an electronic voting protocol can be expressed as

$$P(skva, v_1) \mid P(skvb, v_2) \sim P(skva, v_2) \mid P(skvb, v_1)$$

where P is the voter process with two parameters: its secret key ($skva$, $skvb$) and the candidate for whom he wish to cast their vote (here v_1, v_2). Historically many applications of equivalences to prove security requirements of cryptographic protocols have relied upon hand written proofs [12, 7]. Such proofs are time consuming and error prone. Accordingly, we direct our attention to automated techniques. The calculus developed by Blanchet et al. makes some progress in this direction [3]. However, the method developed for proving observational equivalence is not complete and is unable to prove certain interesting equivalences.

Contribution. We build upon [3] to provide reasoning about further equivalences (see Section 2). We also extend the syntax to allow the modelling of a new class of processes which require global synchronisation. Finally we develop an algorithm to enable automated reasoning about security requirements. The focus of our work is to model the privacy properties increasingly found in cryptographic protocols (Section 3). We demonstrate the practical application of our contribution with case studies (Sections 4 and 5). Using our approach we provide the first automated proof that the electronic voting protocol due to Fujioka, Okamoto & Ohta (FOO) [10] satisfies privacy. As a second case study we provide a formal methods proof that the Direct Anonymous Attestation (DAA) [4] protocol also satisfies privacy (the DAA authors provided a provable security proof). An extended version of this paper [9] and our ProVerif source code are available at http://www.cs.bham.ac.uk/~bas/.

Related work. Kremer & Ryan [12] have previously demonstrated the electronic voting protocol FOO satisfies fairness, eligibility and privacy. The first two properties were verified automatically using ProVerif, and the third relied on a hand proof. Backes *et al.* [2] model a variant of DAA and provide some proofs. We observe that their model is not accurate with regards to DAA due to some subtleties in their formalisation. Nevertheless their idea of modelling synchronisation by private channel communication influenced the design of our translator.

2 Calculus of **ProVerif**

The process calculi of Blanchet *et al.* [3], used by the tool ProVerif, is a variant of the applied pi calculus [1], a process calculi for formally modelling concurrent systems and their interactions. In this paper we use the phrase *calculus of ProVerif* to mean the calculus defined in [3], and *ProVerif software tool* to refer to the software tool developed in accompaniment of [3].

2.1 Syntax and informal semantics

The calculus assumes an infinite set of *names* and an infinite set of *variables*. It also assumes a *signature* Σ, i.e. a finite set of *function symbols* each with an associated arity. A function symbol with arity 0 is also called a *constant*. We distinguish two categories of function symbols: *constructors* f and *destructors* g and we use h to range over both. We use standard notation for function application, i.e. $h(M_1, \ldots, M_n)$. Destructors are partial, nondeterministic operations, that processes can apply to terms. They represent primitives that can visibly succeed or fail, while constructors and the associated equational theory apply to primitives that always succeed but may return "junk". The grammar for terms/term evaluations is given below.

$M, N ::=$	term	$D ::=$	term evaluation
a, b, c	name	M	term
x, y, z	variable	$\text{choice}[D, D']$	choice term eval.
$\text{choice}[M, M']$	choice term	$h(D_1, \ldots, D_n)$	function eval.
$f(M_1, \ldots, M_n)$	constructor		

We equip the signature Σ with an *equational theory*, say E, i.e. a finite set of equations of the form $M_i = N_i$, where M_i and N_i are terms without names. The equational theory is then obtained from this set of equations by reflexive, symmetric and transitive closure, closure by substitution of terms for variables and closure by context application. We write $M =_E N$ (resp. $M \neq_E N$) for equality (resp. inequality) modulo E.

Processes are built up in a similar way to processes in the pi calculus, except that messages can contain terms/term evaluations (rather than just names). In the grammar described below, M and N are terms, D is a term evaluation, a is a name, x a variable and t an integer.

$P, Q, R ::=$	processes
null	null process
$P \mid Q$	parallel composition
$!P$	replication
new $a; P$	name restriction
let $x = D$ in P else Q	term evaluation
in$(M, x); P$	message input
out$(M, N); P$	message output
phase $t; P$	weak phase

We note that the ProVerif software tool allows the definition of a single main process which in turn may refer to subprocesss of the form "let $P = Q$." The tool also permits the use of comments in the form *(* comment *)*.

The choice operator allows us to model a pair of processes which have the same structure and differ only in the choice of terms and terms evaluations. We call such a pair of processes a *biprocess*. Given a biprocess P, we define two processes fst(P) and snd(P) as follows: fst(P) is obtained by replacing all occurrences of choice$[M, M']$ with M and choice$[D, D']$ with D in P. Similarly, snd(P) is obtained by replacing choice$[M, M']$ with M' and choice$[D, D']$ with D' in P. We define fst(D), fst(M), snd(D) and snd(M) similarly.

As usual, names and variables have scopes, which are delimited by restrictions and by inputs. We write $fv(P)$, $bv(P)$ (resp. $fn(P)$ and $bn(P)$) for the sets of free and bound variables (resp. names) in P. A process is *closed* if it has no free variables (but may contain free names). A *context* $C[\_]$ is a process with a hole. We obtain $C[P]$ as the result of filling $C[\_]$'s hole with P. An *evaluation context* C is a closed context built from $[\_]$, $C \mid P$, $P \mid C$ and new $a; C$. We sometimes refer to contexts without choice as *plain contexts*.

The major difference between the syntax of the applied pi calculus and the calculus of ProVerif, is the introduction of the choice operator. In addition there are some minor changes. For instance, communication is permitted on arbitrary terms, not just names. Function symbols are supplemented with destructors. Active substitutions are removed in favour of term evaluations. The syntax does not include the conditional "if $M = N$ then P else Q", which can be defined as "let $x = equals(M, N)$ in P else Q" where $x \notin fv(P)$ and *equals* is a destructor with the equation $equals(x, x) = x$. We omit "else Q" when the process Q is *null*. Finally the calculus of ProVerif does not rely on a sort system. We believe that processes written in the calculus of

ProVerif, can be mapped to semantically equivalent processes in the applied pi calculus and vice-versa, although proving this remains an open problem. This can easily be extended to biprocesses.

2.2 Operational semantics

The operational semantics of processes in the calculus of ProVerif, are defined by three relations, namely *term evaluation* $\Downarrow$, *structural equivalence* $\equiv$ and *reduction* $\rightarrow$. Structural equivalence and reductions are only defined on closed processes. We write $\rightarrow^*$ for the reflexive and transitive closure of $\rightarrow$, and $\rightarrow^* \equiv$ for its union with $\equiv$. The operational semantics for the calculus of ProVerif differ in minor ways from the semantics of the applied pi calculus. *Structural equivalence* is the smallest equivalence relation on processes that is closed under application of evaluation contexts and some other standard rules such as associativity and commutativity of the parallel operator. *Reduction* is the smallest relation on biprocesses closed under structural equivalence and application of evaluation contexts such that

RED I/O $out(N, M); Q \mid in(N', x); P \rightarrow Q \mid P\{^M/_x\}$
                   if $\mathsf{fst}(N) = \mathsf{fst}(N')$ and $\mathsf{snd}(N) = \mathsf{snd}(N')$

RED FUN 1   let $x = D$ in P else $Q \rightarrow P\{^{\mathrm{choice}[M_1, M_2]}/_x\}$
                   if $\mathsf{fst}(D) \Downarrow M_1$ and $\mathsf{snd}(D) \Downarrow M_2$

RED FUN 2   let $x = D$ in P else $Q \rightarrow Q$
                   if there is no M_1 such that $\mathsf{fst}(D) \Downarrow M_1$ and
                   there is no M_2 such that $\mathsf{snd}(D) \Downarrow M_2$

RED REPL $!P \rightarrow P \mid !P$

2.3 Extension to processes with weak phases

Many protocols can be broken into phases, and their security properties can be formulated in terms of these phases. Typically, for instance, if a protocol discloses a session key after the conclusion of a session, then the secrecy of the data exchanged during the session may be compromised but not its authenticity. To enable modelling of protocols with several phases the calculus of ProVerif is extended [3]. The syntax of processes is supplemented with a phase prefix "phase $t; P$", where t is a non-negative integer. Intuitively, t represents a global clock, and the process "phase $t; P$" is active only during phase t. However, it is possible that *not* all instructions of a particular phase are executed prior to a phase transition. Moreover, parallel processes may only communicate if they are under the same phase.

Example 1. Let P = phase 1; out(c, a) | phase 2; out(c, b). The process P can output b without having first output a.

The semantics of processes are extended to deal with weak phases (see [3]).

2.4 Observational equivalence

The notion of observational equivalence was introduced by Abadi & Fournet [1], subsequently Blanchet, Abadi & Fournet [3] defined strong observational equivalence. This paper will use strong observational equivalence, henceforth we shall use observational equivalence to mean strong observational equivalence. We first recall the standard definition of observational equivalence. We write $P \downarrow_M$ when P emits a message on the channel M, that is, when $P \equiv C[\text{out}(M', N); R]$ for some evaluation context $C[\_]$ that does not bind $fn(M)$ and $M =_E M'$.

Definition 1 ([3]). *Observational equivalence* $\sim$ is the largest symmetric relation $\mathcal{R}$ on closed processes such that $P \mathcal{R} Q$ implies:

1. if $P \downarrow_M$ then $Q \downarrow_M$;
2. if $P \to P'$ then there exists Q' such that $Q \to Q'$ and $P' \mathcal{R} Q'$;
3. $C[P] \mathcal{R} C[Q]$ for all evaluation contexts C.

Intuitively, a context may represent an attacker, and two processes are observationally equivalent if they cannot be distinguished by any attacker. Given a biprocess P, we say that P satisfies observational equivalence when we have that $\text{fst}(P) \sim \text{snd}(P)$.

A reduction $P \to Q$ for a biprocess P implies the corresponding processes have reductions $\text{fst}(P) \to \text{fst}(Q)$ and $\text{snd}(P) \to \text{snd}(Q)$. However, reductions in $\text{fst}(P)$ and $\text{snd}(P)$ do not necessarily correspond to any biprocess reduction. When such a corresponding reduction does exist the processes $\text{fst}(P)$ and $\text{snd}(P)$ satisfy uniformity under reduction (UUR):

Definition 2 ([3]). A biprocess P satisfies *uniformity under reduction* if:

1. $\text{fst}(P) \to Q_1$ implies that $P \to Q$ for some biprocess Q with $\text{fst}(Q) \equiv Q_1$, and symmetrically for $\text{snd}(P) \to Q_2$;
2. for all plain evaluation contexts C, for all biprocess Q, $C[P] \to Q$ implies that Q satisfies UUR.

Blanchet *et al.* [3] have shown that if a biprocess P satisfies uniformity under reductions then P satisfies observational equivalence. The ProVerif software automatically verifies whether its input satisfies uniformity under reduction and thus enables us to prove observational equivalence in some cases.

2.5 Limitations of the calculus

There are trivial equivalences (see Example 2 described below) which the calculus of ProVerif is unable to prove since the definition of observational equivalence by uniformity under reductions is too strong. We overcome this problem with *data swapping*.

Example 2. The equivalence out(c, a) | out$(c, b) \sim$ out(c, b) | out(c, a) holds trivially since the processes are in fact structurally equivalent. But the corresponding biprocess out$(c, \text{choice}[a, b])$ | out$(c, \text{choice}[b, a])$ does not satisfy uniformity under reductions and therefore the equivalence cannot be proved by ProVerif.

Moreover, the phase semantics introduced by the calculus of ProVerif [3] are insufficient to model protocols which require synchronisation, as the phase semantics do not enforce that all instances of a phase must be completed prior to phase progression. We solve this problem with the introduction of *strong phases*.

Both of these problems are encountered when modelling cryptographic protocols from literature. As case studies we demonstrate the suitability of our approach by modelling the privacy properties of the electronic voting protocol FOO [10] and Direct Anonymous Attestation (DAA) [4].

3 Extending the calculus

To overcome the limitations stated in the previous section, we extend the calculus with strong phases and data swapping.

3.1 Extension to processes with strong phases

Similarly to weak phases the syntax of processes is supplemented with a strong phase prefix "strong phase t; P", where t is a non-negative integer. A strong phase represents a global synchronisation and t represents the global clock. The process strong phase t; P is active only during strong phase t and a strong phase progression may only occur once all the instructions under the previous phase have been executed.

Example 3. Consider our earlier example (Example 1) with the use of strong phase. Now, the process

$$\text{strong phase } 1; \text{out}(c, a) \mid \text{strong phase } 2; \text{out}(c, b)$$

cannot output b without having previously output a.

3.2 Extension to processes with data swapping

Let us first consider the background to our approach. Referring back to Example 2 we recall the biprocess $Q = \text{out}(c, \text{choice}[a, b]) \mid \text{out}(c, \text{choice}[b, a])$ which does not satisfy UUR. We note that $\text{fst}(Q) = \text{out}(c, a) \mid \text{out}(c, b)$ and $\text{snd}(Q) = \text{out}(c, b) \mid \text{out}(c, a)$. Since $\text{out}(c, b) \mid \text{out}(c, a) \equiv \text{out}(c, a) \mid \text{out}(c, b)$ it seems reasonable to rewrite $\text{snd}(Q)$ as $\text{out}(c, a) \mid \text{out}(c, b)$, enabling us to write Q as $\text{out}(c, \text{choice}[a, a]) \mid \text{out}(c, \text{choice}[b, b])$ which is semantically equivalent to $\text{out}(c, a) \mid \text{out}(c, b)$. Our new biprocess satisfies uniformity under reduction, and thus observational equivalence. It therefore seems possible (under certain circumstances) to *swap* values from the left to the right side of the parallel operator. Sometimes the swap is not done initially but instead immediately after a strong phase. To specify data swapping we introduce the special comment *(**swap*)* in process descriptions, which can be seen as a *proof hint*. Returning to our example, we would rewrite Q as

$$Q' = \textit{(**swap*)}\, \text{out}(c, \text{choice}[a, b]) \mid \textit{(**swap*)}\, \text{out}(c, \text{choice}[b, a])$$
$$= \text{out}(c, \text{choice}[a, a]) \mid \text{out}(c, \text{choice}[b, b]).$$

3.3 Automated reasoning with ProVerif

To allow automated reasoning we describe a translator which accepts as input processes written in our extended language. It will also include a single main process and subprocesses of the form "let $P = Q$", subject to the following restrictions.

1. The commands strong phase t; and *(**swap*)* can only appear in a single subprocess defined using the let keyword (not in the main process);
2. The subprocess defined using the let keyword that contain strong phases and data swapping must be instantiated precisely twice in the main process. Moreover, it must be of the form let $P = \alpha$, where α is a process that is sequential until its last strong phase, at which point it is an arbitrary process. Formally α is given by the grammar below:

$$\alpha := R \mid \text{new } a; \alpha \mid \text{in}(M, x); \alpha \mid \text{out}(M, N); \alpha \mid \text{let } x = D \text{ in } \alpha \mid \text{strong phase } t; \alpha$$

where R is an arbitrary processes without data swapping and strong phases;
3. We further require that *(**swap*)* may only occur at the start of a subprocess definition or immediately after a strong phase.

The translator outputs processes in the standard language of ProVerif, which can be automatically reasoned about by the software tool. The pseudocode of our algorithm is presented in Figure 1.

Step one of our translator makes the necessary modifications to subprocesses. It defines each strong phase as an individual subprocess. Step two handles the main process which combines the subprocesses defined in step one in such a way that preserves notion of strong phases. The other parts of the translator's input are copied to the output verbatim. We demonstrate its application with several toy examples (see Section 3.4) and two case studies (see Sections 4 & 5).

Step 1: We replace any subprocess declaration of the form

    let $P = \alpha_0$; strong phase 1; α_1; strong phase 2; α_2; ...; strong phase n; α_n.

with the declarations

    let $P_0 = \alpha_0$; out(pc, M_0).
    let $P_1 = \alpha_1$; out(pc, M_1).
    $\vdots$
    let $P_{n-1} = \alpha_{n-1}$; out(pc, M_{n-1}).
    let $P_n = \alpha_n$.

where M_i is a term consisting of a tuple containing each bound name in $\alpha_0, \alpha_1, \ldots, \alpha_i$ and the free variables in $\alpha_{i+1}, \alpha_{i+2}, \ldots, \alpha_n$.

Step 2: We replace instance declarations in the main process of the form

$$\text{let } \tilde{x} = \tilde{N} \text{ in } P \mid \text{let } \tilde{x} = \tilde{N}' \text{ in } P$$

with

    new pc_0; new pc_0'; new pc_1; new pc_1'; ...; new pc_{n-1}; new pc_{n-1}'; (
      let $\tilde{x} = \tilde{N}$ in let $pc = pc_0$ in $P_0|$
      let $\tilde{x} = \tilde{N}'$ in let $pc = pc_0'$ in $P_0|$
      in(pc_0, z_0); in(pc_0', z_0'); (* start strong phase 1 *) (
       let $M_0 = z_0$ in let $pc = pc_1$ in $P_1|$
       let $M_0 = z_0'$ in let $pc = pc_1'$ in $P_1)|$
      $\vdots$
      in(pc_{n-1}, z_{n-1}); in(pc_{n-1}', z_{n-1}'); (* start strong phase n *) (
       let $M_{n-1} = z_{n-1}$ in $P_n|$
       let $M_{n-1} = z_{n-1}'$ in $P_n)$
)

If α_0 starts with (**swap*), we further modify the above description, by replacing

    let $\tilde{x} = \tilde{N}$ in   *with*   let $\tilde{x} = $ choice$[\tilde{N}, \tilde{N}']$ in
    let $\tilde{x} = \tilde{N}'$ in   *with*   let $\tilde{x} = $ choice$[\tilde{N}', \tilde{N}]$ in

Similarly, if α_i starts with (**swap*) and $1 \leq i \leq n$, we further modify the description

    let $M_i = z_i$ in   *with*   let $M_i = $ choice$[z_i, z_i']$ in
    let $M_i = z_i'$ in   *with*   let $M_i = $ choice$[z_i', z_i]$ in

---

Fig. 1 Translator algorithm

3.4 Examples

Example 4. We begin by returning to our trivial observational equivalence:

$$out(c, a) \mid out(c, b) \sim out(c, b) \mid out(c, a).$$

As the definition of observational equivalence by UUR is too strong, the calculus, and therefore the software tool, are unable to reason about such an equivalence. Using our data swapping syntax, the biprocess encoding the previous equivalence is given below.

```
let P = (**swap*) out(c,x).
process let x = choice[a,b] in P| let x = choice[b,a] in P
```

Our translator gives us the following biprocess, which ProVerif can successfully prove.

```
let P = out(c,x).
process let x = choice[choice[a,b],choice[b,a]] in P|
        let x = choice[choice[b,a],choice[a,b]] in P
```

Example 5. We consider the observational equivalence shown below:

$$out(c, a); \text{strong phase } 1; out(c, d) \mid out(c, b); \text{strong phase } 1; null$$
$$\sim \quad out(c, a); \text{strong phase } 1; null \mid out(c, b); \text{strong phase } 1; out(c, d)$$

The pair of processes are both able to output a and b. We then have a synchronisation and obtain the process $out(c, d) \mid null \sim null \mid out(c, d)$. To allow ProVerif to prove such an equivalence we provide our translator with the following input:

```
let P =out(c,x); strong phase 1; (**swap*) if y=ok then out(c,d).
process let x = a in let y = choice[ok,ko] in P|
        let x = b in let y = choice[ko,ok] in P
```

Our translator produces the biprocess described below.

```
let P1 = out(c,x); out(pc,y).
let P2 = if y = ok then out(c,c).
process new pc0; new pc1;(
    let x = a in let y = choice[ok,ko] in let pc = pc0 in P1|
    let x = b in let y = choice[ko,ok] in let pc = pc1 in P1|
    in(pc0,y0); in(pc1,y1);(
        let y = choice[y0,y1] in P2|
        let y = choice[y1,y0] in P2))
```

Example 6. As our final example we consider the following equivalence:

$$out(c, a_1); \text{strong phase } 1; out(c, a_2) \mid out(c, b_1); \text{strong phase } 1; out(c, b_2)$$
$$\sim \quad out(c, a_1); \text{strong phase } 1; out(c, b_2) \mid out(c, b_1); \text{strong phase } 1; out(c, a_2)$$

This is similar to Example 5 with two outputs after the strong phase. Again, thanks to our translator, we are able to conclude on such an example.

4 E-voting protocol due to Fujioka *et al.*

In this section, we study the privacy property of the e-voting protocol due to Fujioka *et al.* [10]. In [12], it is shown that this protocol provides fairness, eligibility and privacy. However, the proof of privacy given in [12] is manual: ProVerif is unable to prove it directly.

4.1 Description

The protocol involves voters, an administrator and a collector. The administrator is responsible for verifying that only eligible voters can cast votes and the collector handles the collecting and publishing of votes. The protocol requires three strong phases.

In the first phase, the voter gets a signature on a commitment to his vote from the administrator, i.e. $m = sign(blind(commit(v, k), r), ska)$ where k is a random key, r is a blinding factor and ska is the private key of the administrator. At the end of this first phase, the voter unblinds m and obtains $y = sign(commit(v, k), ska)$, i.e. the signature of his commitment. The second phase of the protocol is the actual voting phase. The voter sends y to the collector who checks correctness of the signature and, if the test succeeds, enters (ℓ, x, y) onto a list as an ℓ-th item. The last phase of the voting protocol starts, once the collector decides that he received all votes, e.g. after a fixed deadline. In this phase the voters reveal the random key k which allows the collector to open the votes and publish them. The voter verifies that his commitment is in the list and sends ℓ, r to the collector. Hence, the collector opens the ballots.

4.2 Modelling privacy in applied pi

Privacy properties have been successfully studied using equivalences. In the context of voting protocols, the definition of privacy is rather subtle. We recall the definition of privacy for electronic voting protocols given in [12]. A voting protocol guarantees ballot secrecy (privacy) whenever a process where Alice votes for candidate v_1 and Bob votes for candidate v_2 is observationally equivalent to a process where their votes are swapped, i.e. Alice votes v_2 and Bob votes v_1. We denote their secret keys $skva$ and $skvb$ respectively. In [12],

```
let V =
  new k; new r;
  let x = commit(v,k) in
  out(c,(pk(skv),sign(blind(x,r),skv)));
  in(c,m2);
  let y = unblind(m2,r) in
  if checksign(y,pka) = x then
  strong phase 1; (**swap*)
  out(c,y);
  strong phase 2;
  in(c,(l,yprime));
  if yprime = y then out(c,(l,k)).

process
  new ska; new skva; new skvb;
  let pka = pk(ska) in
  out(c,(ska,pka,pk(skva),pk(skvb)));(
    (let (skv,v) = (skva,choice[v1,v2]) in V)|
    (let (skv,v) = (skvb,choice[v2,v1]) in V))
```

Process 1 FOO model (extended syntax)

they rely on hand proof techniques to show privacy on FOO. Our modelling of FOO in the applied pi is similar to the one given in [8]. The underlying equational theory is the same as in [12].

The main process given in Process 1 models the environment and specifies how the other processes are combined. To establish privacy, we do not require that the authorities are honest, so we do not need to model them and we only consider two voter processes in parallel. First, fresh private keys for the voters and the administrator are generated. The corresponding public keys are then made available to the attacker. We also output the secret key of the administrator. This allows the environment to simulate the administrator (even a corrupted one) and hence we show that the privacy property holds even in the presence of a corrupt administrator.

The process V given in Process 1 models the role of a voter. The specification follows directly from our informal description. Note that we use the strong phase command to enforce the synchronisation of the voter processes. As mentioned initially in [12], the separation of the protocol into strong phases is crucial for privacy to hold. We also provide a data swapping hint to allow our translator to produce an output suitable for automatic verification using ProVerif.

4.3 Analysis

We use our translator to remove all instances of strong phases and handle data swapping. Our translator produces Process 2, which is suitable for automatic

```
let V1 =
 new k; new r;
 let x = commit(v,k) in
 out(c,(pk(skv),sign(blind(x,r),skv)));
 in(c,m2);
 let y = unblind(m2,r) in
 if checksign(y,pka) = x then out(pc,(y,k)).

let V2 =
 out(c,y); out(pc,(y,k)).

let V3 =
 in(c,(l,yprime)); if yprime = y then out(c,(l,k)).

process
 new ska; new skva; new skvb;
 let pka = pk(ska) in
 out(c,(ska,pka,pk(skva),pk(skvb)));
 new pc1; new pc2; new pc3; new pc4;(
  (let (skv,v)=(skva,choice[v1,v2]) in let pc=pc1 in V1)|
  (let (skv,v)=(skvb,choice[v2,v1]) in let pc=pc2 in V1)|
  (in(pc1,(y1,k1)); in(pc2,(y2,k2)); (*strong phase 1*) (*swap*)(
   (let (y,k)=choice[(y1,k1),(y2,k2)] in let pc=pc3 in V2)|
   (let (y,k)=choice[(y2,k2),(y1,k1)] in let pc=pc4 in V2)))|
  (in(pc3,(y3,k3)); in(pc4,(y4,k4)); (*strong phase 2*)(
   (let (y,k)=(y3,k3) in V3)|
   (let (y,k)=(y4,k4) in V3))))
```

Process 2 Translated FOO model (ProVerif syntax)

verification using ProVerif. Hence, using our approach, we provide the first automatic and complete proof that this protocol satisfies privacy.

5 Direct Anonymous Attestation (DAA)

The Direct Anonymous Attestation (DAA) scheme provides a means for remotely authenticating a trusted platform whilst preserving the user's privacy [4]. In [15], two of the authors have shown that corrupt administrators are able to violate the privacy of the host. Using our extended calculus we are now able to provide a formal and automatic proof that the rectified protocol proposed in [15] satisfies its privacy requirements. We start with a short description of the protocol (for a more complete description, see [4, 15]).

5.1 Description

The protocol can be seen as a group signature scheme without the ability to revoke anonymity and an additional mechanism to detect rogue members. In broad terms the *host* contacts an *issuer* and requests membership to a group. If the issuer wishes to accept the request, it grants the host/TPM an *attestation identity credential*. The host is now able to anonymously authenticate itself as a group member to a *verifier* with respect its credential.

The protocol is initiated when a host wishes to obtain a credential. This is known as the join protocol. The TPM creates a secret f value and a blinding factor v', where $f = hash(hash(\text{DAASeed}\|hash(PK_I'))\|\text{cnt}\|0)$. The value DAASeed is a secret known only to the TPM, cnt is a counter used by the TPM to keep track of how many times the Join protocol has been run and PK_I' is the long term public key of the issuer. The inclusion of PK_I' prevents cross issuer linkability [15]. The TPM then constructs the blind message $U := blind(f, v')$ and $N_I := \zeta_I^f$, where $\zeta_I := hash(0\|bsn_I)$ and bsn_I is the basename of the issuer (see [15] for further discussion on DAA basenames). The U and N_I values are submitted to the issuer I. The issuer creates a random nonce value n_e, encrypts it with the public key PK_{EK} of the host's TPM and returns the encrypted value. The TPM decrypts the message, revealing n_e, and returns $hash(U\|n_e)$. The issuer confirms that the hash is correctly formed. The issuer generates a nonce n_i and sends it to the host. The host/TPM constructs a signature proof of knowledge that the messages U and N_I are correctly formed. The issuer verifies the proof and generates a blind signature on the message U. It returns the signature along with a proof that a covert channel has not been used. The host verifies the signature and proof and the TPM unblinds the signature revealing a secret credential v (the signed f).

Once the host has obtained an anonymous attestation credential from the issuer it is able to produce a signature proof of knowledge of attestation on a message m. This is known as the sign/verify protocol. The verifier sends nonce n_v to the host. The host/TPM produce a signature proof of knowledge of attestation on the message $(n_t\|n_v\|b\|m)$, where n_t is a nonce defined by the TPM and b is a parameter. In addition the host computes $N_V := \zeta^f$, where $\zeta := hash(1\|bsn_V)$ and bsn_V is the basename of the verifier. Intuitively if a verifier is presented with such a proof it is convinced that it is communicating with a trusted platform and the message is genuine.

5.2 Modelling privacy in applied pi

The DAA protocol satisfies privacy whenever a process where Alice interacts with the verifier is observationally equivalent to when Bob interacts with the verifier. For privacy we require that both Alice and Bob have completed the join protocol.

Signature and equational theory. The DAA protocol makes extensive use of signature proofs of knowledge (SPK) to prove knowledge of and relations among discrete logarithms. We will discuss our formalism with an example. The signature proof of knowledge $SPK\{(\alpha, \beta) : x = g^\alpha \wedge y = h^\beta\}(m)$ denotes a signature proof of knowledge on the message m that x, y were constructed correctly. This leads us to define function spk/3 to construct an SPK. The first argument contains a tuple of secret values known to the prover α, β. The second argument consists of a tuple of the values on which the prover is claiming to have constructed correctly x, y, such that $x = g^\alpha$ and $y = h^\beta$. Finally the third argument is the message m on which the prover produces a signature on. Verifying the correctness of a SPK is specific to its construction, thus we must require a function checkspk for each SPK that the protocol uses. To verify the SPK produced in the aforementioned example the verifier must be in possession of the SPK itself and x, y, g, h, m. We define the equation: $checkspk(spk((\alpha, \beta), (g^\alpha, h^\beta), m), g^\alpha, h^\beta, g, h, m) = ok$. A verifier can now check a SPK using an if statement.

Modelling the DAA protocol. As in FOO, the main process (see [9]) models the environment and specifies how the other processes are combined. First, fresh secret keys for the TPMs, the issuer and the verifier are generated using the restriction operator. We also generate two DAASeed values. The public keys are then sent on a public channel, i.e. they are made available to the intruder. We also output the secret key of the verifier and issuer since the privacy property should be preserved even if they are corrupt. Next we input the basenames bsn_I, bsn_V of the issuer and verifier. Then we instantiate two instances of the DAA protocol with the necessary parameters.

Our encoding of the DAA protocol (see [9]) follows directly from our informal description. Note that we use the strong phase and data swapping commands introduced by our extension to the calculus to ensure synchronisation. The two instances of the DAA processes must first execute all instructions of DAAJoin before moving onto DAASign. The separation of the protocol into strong phases is crucial for privacy to hold.

5.3 Analysis

We use our translator to remove all instances of strong phases from our encoding and produce code suitable for input to ProVerif. Our translator produces a process (see [9]) which permits the automatic verification of the privacy property using ProVerif. We are also able to detect the vulnerability in the original DAA protocol and prove the optimisation presented in [15].

6 Conclusion

In this paper we have extended the class of equivalences which ProVerif is able to automatically verify. More specifically we are able to reason about processes which require data swapping and/or strong phases. Using the approach developed we are able to automatically verify the privacy properties of the electronic voting protocol FOO and the Direct Anonymous Attestation scheme. In future work, we would like to generalise our translation algorithm and provide a formal proof of the correctness of our translator. Moreover we plan to automate the swapping procedure.

References

1. Abadi, M., Fournet, C.: Mobile values, new names, and secure communication. In: POPL'01: Proc. 28th ACM Symposium on Principles of Programming Languages, pp. 104–115. ACM Press, New York, USA (2001)
2. Backes, M., Maffei, M., Unruh, D.: Zero-knowledge in the applied pi-calculus and automated verification of the direct anonymous attestation protocol. In: IEEE Symposium on Security and Privacy, Proceedings of SSP'08 (2008). To appear
3. Blanchet, B., Abadi, M., Fournet, C.: Automated verification of selected equivalences for security protocols. Journal of Logic and Algebraic Programming **75**(1), 3–51 (2008)
4. Brickell, E., Camenisch, J., Chen, L.: Direct Anonymous Attestation. In: CCS '04: 11th ACM conference on Computer and communications security, pp. 132–145. ACM Press, New York, USA (2004)
5. Chadha, R., Kremer, S., Scedrov, A.: Formal Analysis of Multi-Party Fair Exchange Protocols. In: R. Focardi (ed.) 17th IEEE Computer Security Foundations Workshop, pp. 266–279. IEEE, Asilomar, USA (2004)
6. Clark, J., Jacob, J.: A Survey of Authentication Protocol Literature (1997). URL http://www.cs.york.ac.uk/~jac/papers/drareviewps.ps
7. Delaune, S., Kremer, S., Ryan, M.: Coercion-Resistance and Receipt-Freeness in Electronic Voting. In: CSFW '06: Proc. 19th IEEE workshop on Computer Security Foundations, pp. 28–42. IEEE (2006)
8. Delaune, S., Kremer, S., Ryan, M.D.: Verifying privacy-type properties of electronic voting protocols. Research report, Laboratoire Spécification et Vérification, ENS Cachan, France (2008)
9. Delaune, S., Ryan, M., Smyth, B.: Automatic verification of privacy properties in the applied pi calculus (extended version) (2008). URL http://www.cs.bham.ac.uk/~bas/
10. Fujioka, A., Okamoto, T., Ohta, K.: A Practical Secret Voting Scheme for Large Scale Elections. In: ASIACRYPT '92: Proceedings of the Workshop on the Theory and Application of Cryptographic Techniques, pp. 244–251. Springer, London (1993)
11. Hirt, M., Sako, K.: Efficient receipt-free voting based on homomorphic encryption. In: Eurocrypt, *LNCS*, vol. 1807, pp. 539–556 (2000)
12. Kremer, S., Ryan, M.D.: Analysis of an Electronic Voting Protocol in the Applied Pi Calculus. In: ESOP'05: Proc. of the European Symposium on Programming, *LNCS*, vol. 3444, pp. 186–200 (2005)
13. Lowe, G.: An attack on the Needham-Schroeder public-key authentication protocol. Information Processing Letters **56**(3), 131–133 (1995)
14. Mukhamedov, A., Ryan, M.D.: Fair Multi-party Contract Signing using Private Contract Signatures. Information & Computation (2007). Preprint
15. Smyth, B., Ryan, M., Chen, L.: Direct Anonymous Attestation (DAA): Ensuring privacy with corrupt administrators. In: ESAS'07: 4th European Workshop on Security and Privacy in Ad hoc and Sensor Networks, *LNCS*, vol. 4572, pp. 218–231 (2007)

Place and Time Authentication of Cultural Assets *

Leonardo Mostarda, Changyu Dong, and Naranker Dulay

Abstract This paper proposes a place and time authentication system for cultural assets. We develop a protocol that combines traditional cryptographic techniques with place and time information to generate a *secure* tag for each cultural asset. We model the attacker capabilities and show that our secure tag helps ensure the authenticity of works of art. Our system has been deployed and validated in Italian and Greek museums in the context of CUSPIS project.

1 Introduction

Art appreciation dates back more than two-thousand years when Roman sculptors produced copies of Greek sculptures for religious inspiration or simply for aesthetic enjoyment. Over the years art has become a commercial commodity and unauthorised copying an illegal but highly profitable business. Counterfeit cultural assets are sold in auctions and even exhibited around the world. The trade in counterfeit artworks and antiques is a six billion dollar per year business and the largest crime after drug and gun trafficking [1]. For instance in Operation "Canale", the Italian police sequestered 20,000 pieces of paintings and graphics works. Of all the pieces, 17,000 of them were imitations and ready to be sold. In 2006 about 2,000 Italian and French exhibitions were visited by 44 million people with an average fee of 6.3 euros per person [2]. It has been estimated that five percent of such profits have been made by exhibitions of counterfeit cultural assets.

Leonardo Mostarda, Changyu Dong and Naranker Dulay
Department of Computing, Imperial College London, London, UK SW7 2AZ e-mail: {lmostard,cd04,nd}@doc.ic.ac.uk

* This research was supported by the UK EPSRC, research grants EP/D076633/1 (UBIVAL) and EP/C537181/1 (CAREGRID). The authors would like to thank our UBIVAL and CAREGRID collaborators and members of the Policy Research Group at Imperial College for their support.

Please use the following format when citing this chapter:

Mostarda, L., Dong, C. and Dulay, N., 2008, in IFIP International Federation for Information Processing, Volume 263; *Trust Management II*; Yücel Karabulut, John Mitchell, Peter Herrmann, Christian Damsgaard Jensen; (Boston: Springer), pp. 279–294.

The main reason for the increase in criminal activity is the inadequacy of countermeasures. Traditionally, the authenticity of a cultural asset is provided by a paper certificate issued by a recognised authority such as a museum. The experts from the authority examine the provenance, i.e. the documented history of the asset, the style of the artist, and they use forensic methods (e.g. carbon dating [3], thermoluminescence [4] and statistical analysis of digital images [5]) to verify the authenticity of the cultural asset. If they believe this asset is authentic, they sign a certificate containing details of the cultural asset.

The main problem with paper certificates is obvious: the certificates can be forged or duplicated and then presented with counterfeit works of art that are shown in an exhibition or sold in an auction.

This paper describes a novel place and time authentication system to detect counterfeit cultural assets. The system generates a tag for each cultural asset that holds the location where, and the time when, the cultural asset can be shown, as well as a cultural asset description, for example, a picture or text signed by an authenticator. Visitors to an exhibition, or potential buyers at an auction can read the cultural asset's tag and use location and time data to check the authenticity of the asset. The digital signature is used to ensure the integrity of the tag data and the authenticator's identity. Although a valid tag can still be copied by an attacker, its use in a different place and time is detectable. To mitigate the tag duplication and reuse problem in the same place and time, the authentication process provides a history-based check and also signed descriptive information for users to check. The history based check analyses each new tag to determine if it is a previously verified tag or if it is a duplicated tag, while the descriptive information can include photos of the asset and place in the tag.

In this paper we formalise the place and time authentication system and establish a threat model. We then show that the system ensures the authenticity of cultural assets. The system has been validated in the context of the CUSPIS European project [6]. For outdoor use, it uses EGNOS, the European Geostationary Navigation Overlay Service, a precursor of the Galileo satellite infrastructure[7]. For indoor use it requires users to check location information stored in RFID and graphical bar codes that users download and run on their mobile device (e.g. PDA or smart phone). It should be pointed out that the approach is independent of the location service, for example, we could use cell-tower or wifi access-point triangulation for indoor applications.

The paper is organized as follows. In Section 2, we describe the use cases, the threat model and the system requirements. In Section 3, we provide an overview of the place and time authentication system. In Section 4, we define the formal model of our system and provide security proofs. In Section 5, we evaluate the implementation of the system. Finally, sections 6 and 7 discuss related work and provide conclusions.

2 Use cases and system requirements

In this section, we motivate our approach with two use cases, highlight potential attacks and outline the overall requirements of the system.

2.1 Use cases

We consider two different but similar scenarios, namely exhibitions and auctions. Figure 1 shows the entities involved and their relations. An entity is represented either as a stylized person or as an object. A line connecting two entities models some relationship between them.

Fig. 1 The entities involved in the use cases

The following entities are involved: (i) a cultural asset; (ii) the owner of the cultural asset; (iii) a qualified organisation that authenticates the asset, e.g. a museum or a research institute; (iv) an official department that manages the qualification of (iii); (v) an exhibitor/dealer; (vi) an end user.

A cultural asset is a valuable object with social or artistic significance. For example, an ancient Roman sculpture or a Picasso painting. The owner can be a person or an organisation e..g museum. In the exhibition case, the exhibitor hires the cultural asset from the owner; in the auction case, the owner sells the cultural asset through a dealer. In both cases, the cultural asset needs to go through an authentication process. The authentication is performed by a qualified organisation. The qualification of such organisations is managed by an official department. For instance, in Greece and Italy, the ministries of cultural heritage manage such qualifications. The qualification is granted based on the speciality, the technical strength and the reputation of the organisation. The qualification aims to provide some guarantee on the trustworthiness of authentication results. The same organisation can have different qualifications related to different types of cultural assets that they can authenticate. After authenticating a cultural asset, the organisation generates a certification vouching for the authenticity of the cultural asset.

If the cultural asset is to be exhibited, then it must be transported to the exhibition site and remains there until the end of the exhibition. After the exhibition, the cultural asset must be returned to the owner. If the cultural asset is to be sold in an auction then it must be kept securely by the organisation. After the auction, if someone buys it, it must be securely transferred to the buyer; if the auction fails, it must be returned to its owner. The reason why the cultural asset is kept securely by the organisation during the auction is that otherwise the owner and dealer could collude and send a counterfeited asset to the auction and keep the original one.

Among all the entities involved, (iii) and (iv) can usually be trusted. The organisation that provides authentication of cultural assets is unlikely to cheat because this will damage its reputation and it can be held liable if found providing false results. The official department has the ultimate responsibility of protecting the authenticity of the cultural assets and is the one motivated most to fight counterfeit cultural assets. The owner and the exhibitor/dealer are not trusted because they can benefit from counterfeiting the assets. The cultural asset itself is a passive object in the system. The end user is normally the victim of counterfeit cultural assets and in need of protection.

2.2 Threats and potential attacks

In the scenarios described above, we highlight the following attacks to the traditional certification system:

- Certificate forgery. The attacker can forge a cultural asset and a certificate from an authority which claims it is an unrevealed work of a famous artist or a newly discovered antiquity.
- Certificate modification. The attacker can modify a certificate to claim it has a higher value.
- Swapping. The attacker who has a cultural asset and its certificate, counterfeits the asset and swaps the real one with the fake one.
- Certificate reuse. The attacker who has a certificate for a cultural asset issued by an authority counterfeits the asset and reuses the certificate.
- Certificate duplication. The attacker duplicates a certificate for a cultural asset issued by an authority, counterfeits the asset and uses the duplicated certificate.
- Certificate replication. The attacker who has the cultural asset obtains different valid certificates and uses them in counterfeit ones.

2.3 System requirements

The goal of our place and time authentication system is to stop the illegal profits made from counterfeit cultural assets. We propose the use of digital tags to prevent counterfeit cultural assets entering circulation through auctions and detect them from being shown in exhibitions. The high level requirements of the digital tags are:

- Providing authentication. End users must be convinced they are viewing or buying an authentic cultural asset after they verify its tag.

- Non-forgeable. No one can forge a tag and claim it was generated by a trusted entity.
- Integrity. After being generated, no one can modify the contents of the tag.
- Non-reusable. The tag can be used only once.
- Anti-duplication. It should be hard to duplicate the tag or use the duplicated tags without being detected.
- Tag uniqueness. For each cultural asset there must be exactly one valid tag at the same time.
- Off-line operation. Most of the operations should be able to be performed off-line without recourse to online services.

We emphasise that conventional digital certificates/credentials are non-forgeable and can provide integrity, but they can be easily duplicated and reused. Therefore, as shown in the following sections, our digital tags use place and time information to address the aforementioned problems.

3 Overview of approach

In this section we show how our place and time authentication system can be added to the cultural asset life cycle in order to enhance security. Our approach is composed of the following phases: (i) certification; (ii) tag generation and revocation; and (iii) authentication.

3.1 Certification phase

In the certification phase organisations that claim to be qualified to check assets (e.g. a museum) interact with an official department (i.e., a government authority) in order to obtain a digital qualification. This certification phase is composed of two basic steps: (i) qualification; and (ii) certificate generation. In the first step the organisation gets in touch with the certification authority, fills on some forms and proves its identity. The certification authority conducts a comprehensive evaluation of the technical and nontechnical merits of the organisation to establish the extent to which the organisation's ability in authenticating cultural assets meets its set of specified requirements. If the organisation qualifies, the certification authority generates a certificate for it. The certificate (see Figure 2) is an X509 v3 digital certificate [8]. This certificate is identified by a serial number and contains: the issuer (e.g., the certification authority) information, the subject (e.g., the organisation) information, the period of validity, the public key of the organisation and the issuer signature. Moreover, the extensions field can contain additional accreditation constraints, e.g. the organisation is approved to authenticate certain types of cultural assets. The related private key must be kept safely. [2] For instance in the CUSPIS project the certification authorities are the Italian and Greek Ministries of Cultural Heritage. Certificates have been released to Roman museums and to the National Museum of Athens.

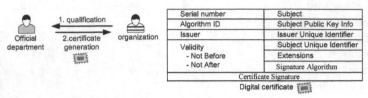

Fig. 2 The certification phase

3.2 Tag generation and revocation phases

In Figure 3 the tag generation revocation phases.

Fig. 3 The tag generation phase

In the tag generation phase an qualified organisation checks a cultural asset, if it is "authentic", the organisation generates a place and time based tag (GD) for it. A GD (see Figure 3) contains the following fields: (i) a Unique Code (UC); (ii) the organisation certificate (C); (iii) the destination area (DA); (iv) the starting time (ST); (v) the end time (ET); (vi) extensions; (vii) the organisation signature (S).

The UC field is an identifier that uniquely identifies the cultural asset. The field C contains the digital certificate of the organisation which is generated in the certification phase (see section 3.1). The destination area field (DA) defines the location where the cultural asset will be exhibited/sold. The starting and end time denote the period in which the cultural asset will be exhibited or the period of the auction. The extensions fields contains information for users to uniquely identify the cultural asset, e.g., a description, a picture of the asset and place, the owner, the cultural asset origin and so on. The organisation signature (S) is a standard digital signature of the GD that is generated using the organisation's private key.

---

[2] In the CUSPIS project, the private keys are generated by the certification authorities and sealed into a tamper-proof device which is delivered securely to the organisations.

The GD can be stored and attached to the cultural asset in different ways. For instance, in the CUSPIS project, we use both RFID tags [3] and graphical bar code (e.g., a shot code and QR code) tags to store the GD. The end user can read the RFID tags with a PDA or take a picture of the graphical bar code with a mobile device in order to obtain the GD.

The tag revocation phase is undertaken by an owner that wishes to withdraw its cultural asset from an exhibition/auction. To this aim the owner shows its GD to the organisation that reads it, verifies the signature S and checks the owner identity. If the GD is successfully verified then the organization updates the revocation list of the exhibition/auction where the cultural asset was destined for. In our implementation revocation lists are updated through a trusted logically centralised web site.

Organisations must take further measures to avoid a replication attack. A replication attack can result as a consequence of users asking for a new GD without revoking the old one. For instance if an owner has a two year tag, GD, for his cultural asset and he has lent it to an exhibition. Now suppose that the exhibitor uses the cultural asset to obtain a new tag, GD1, counterfeits the cultural asset and sells it to an auction. Then we are in a situation where two valid tags, at the same time, are used. Our approach is to require that organisations update and use a logically centralised data base of GDs. After an organisation authenticates a cultural asset it must query the DB with asset information [4]. In the case that a valid GD is currently issued then the organisation requires that the owner performs a revocation process. We emphasise that this is not the only solution to deal with the replication attack. For instance, if we assume that we have only short term GDs there is no need for both database and revocation lists.

Although cultural asset authentication requires organisations to have "cumbersome" tools, update a logically centralised DB and have specialised skills [10, 3, 4, 5], users can easily read all GDs and perform off line authentication with simple widespread devices (e.g., PDA).

3.3 The Authentication phase

In the authentication phase (see Figure 4), the end user reads a GD and verifies the authenticity of the related cultural asset. To this end the user employs mobile device (e.g. a PDA) equipped with a verification component, a positioning component, two revocation lists and a time component. The main steps performed in the verification process are *replication checking, digital certificate verification, GD digital signa-*

---

[3] We used RFID tags with 128KB of memory that maintain full compatibility with the EPC standard [9].

[4] In our current implementation, cultural asset search is performed based on the cultural asset type, period, weight and author. However, other techniques such as fingerprinting [10] are available to produce a unique ID for each cultural asset.

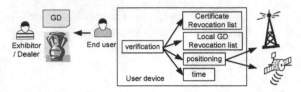

Fig. 4 The authentication phase

ture verification, place and time verification, object verification, and *duplication checking.*

In the *replication checking* step, the verification component verifies that the GD is not present in the GD revocation list [5]. The GD revocation list can be downloaded from a trusted web site and installed prior to the verification. In particular, if a user has decided the places he wishes to visit (cities/museums/auctions), only the revocation lists for those places need to be downloaded.

In the *digital certificate verification* step the verification component reads the certificate (C) contained in the GD tag and performs the usual verification on digital certificates [8]. The public key of the certification authority and revocation lists can be downloaded from a trusted web site and installed prior to the verification.

In the *GD digital signature verification* step, the verification component reads the signature field (S) from the GD and verifies it by using the public key retrieved from the certificate (C).

In the *place and time verification* step, the verification component contacts the positioning component and the time component to get the user's current position and time. It is worth noting that the positioning component and the time component must ensure the correctness of the information they provide, this can be done by signal authentication and cross-checking. For instance, in the CUSPIS project, the Authentication Navigation Messages (ANM) service [11] provided by Galileo satellite systems could be used for providing reliable position information. The verification component verifies that the current user position is inside the destination area (DA) contained in the GD tag. Moreover, it verifies that the current time is greater than the start time (ST) and less than the end time (ET).

In the *object verification* step, the verification component verifies that the characteristics of the cultural asset and place meet the identification information contained in the extension field of the GD. The end user is involved in this step. The verification component presents the identification information to the end user and the end user provides the verification result.

If any of the steps fail, then the authentication fails. Otherwise, the verification component checks the authentication history in the period of this exhibition tour / auction to see whether the GD has been duplicated, i.e. to perform a *duplication checking* step.

---

[5] The search inside the revocation lists is performed based on the GD digital signature S, the UC code and the owner

In the exhibition case, the authentication history is a sequence of (GD, POS) tuples where GD is a verified tag and POS is the user position when this tag was read. Suppose that a user is verifying a tag GD at the position POS, and a tuple (GD, POS') is in the authentication history (i.e., the tag GD has already been visited). Then when POS is sufficiently far from POS' the verification component concludes that the tag has been duplicated. As we are going to see in Section 5 the notion of sufficiently far is strictly related to the technologies used to implement the system.

In the auction case, the authentication history is just a sequence of verified GDs, this is because in the auction, the cultural assets are presented one after another and the user does not change the position. If any in the sequence is the same as the one being verified, a duplication is detected. When the verification component detects a duplication, it raises an alarm and marks both as duplicated.

If all the steps succeed, then the authentication succeeds and the end user can be assured that the cultural asset is not counterfeited.

4 Security analysis

In this section, we provide a formal model of the system and discuss the security of our authentication system. Since the system is designed for special use cases, we do not intend to, and believe it would be difficult to, prove it is secure in a general settings. The security analysis in this section is bound to a specific context and certain assumptions, for example, in the analysis, we do not consider any attacks at the physical level, e.g. theft, destruction etc.

4.1 Modeling

The system is modeled as a tuple $(\mathbf{A}, \mathbf{A'}, \mathbf{I}, \mathbf{C}, \mathbf{O}, \mathbf{P}, \mathbf{T}, \mathbf{CERT}, \mathbf{GD})$ whose elements are disjointed sets described as follows:

- $\mathbf{A}$ is the set of all cultural assets. $\mathbf{A'}$ is the set of counterfeit assets. $counterfeit$: $\mathbf{A} \to 2^{\mathbf{A'}}$ is a partial function. For a cultural asset $a \in \mathbf{A}$, $counterfeit(a) \in 2^{\mathbf{A'}}$ are the counterfeit items of a. $\mathbf{A^0}$ is defined as $\mathbf{A} \cup \mathbf{A'}$. $\mathbf{I}$ is the set of all identifiers. We also define a surjection mapping function $ID : \mathbf{A^0} \to \mathbf{I}$, such that for all $a, b \in \mathbf{A}, a \neq b$ if and only if $ID(a) \neq ID(b)$ and for all $a, b \in \mathbf{A^0}, ID(a) = ID(b)$ if and only if we can find $x \in \mathbf{A}$ such that $a, b \in (x \cup counterfeit(x))$. Loosely speaking, this means that each real cultural asset has a unique identifier and the counterfeit items can be identified as the real asset.
- $\mathbf{C}$ is the set of all certification authorities in our system, i.e. the official departments. $\mathbf{O}$ is the set of all qualified organisations. Let $\mathbf{E} = \mathbf{C} \cup \mathbf{O}$, a function $pk : \mathbf{E} \to \{0,1\}^k$ defines the public key for each entity in $\mathbf{E}$, where k is a security parameter.

- **P** is the set of places. Function $in : \mathbf{P} \times \mathbf{P} \to boolean$ returns true if and only the first places lies within the second place.
- **T** is the set of times. Two times are comparable such that $t_1 < t_2$ and $t_2 > t_1$ if and only if t_1 is a time point before t_2, $t_1 = t_2$ if they refer to the same time point. $\leq, \geq$ are defined as abbreviations.
- **CERT** is the set of all valid certificates. Functions $subject : \mathbf{CERT} \to \mathbf{O}$, $issuer : \mathbf{CERT} \to \mathbf{C}$, $spk : \mathbf{CERT} \to \{0,1\}^k$ are defined to return the subject, the issuer and the subject public key field in the certificate. Function $certSig : \mathbf{CERT} \to \{0,1\}^m$ returns the signature of the certificate.
- **GD** is the set of all GDs created by the organisations. Function $getCert : \mathbf{GD} \to \mathbf{CERT}$ extracts the certificate embedded in the GD. Function $da : \mathbf{GD} \to \mathbf{P}$ returns the destination area. $validity : \mathbf{GD} \to (\mathbf{T}, \mathbf{T})$ returns the $(start, end)$ time period. $idInfo : \mathbf{GD} \to \mathbf{I}$ returns the identification information of the cultural asset stored in the extension field. Function $GDSig : \mathbf{GD} \to \{0,1\}^m$ returns the signature of the GD.
- For every public key key, key^{-1} denotes the related private key. Function $sign : \{0,1\}^* \times \{0,1\}^k \to \{0,1\}^m$ generates a signature over a message using a private key. Function $checkSign : \{0,1\}^* \times \{0,1\}^m \times \{0,1\}^k \to boolean$ checks the validity of a signature. $checkSign(m, sig, key) = true$ if and only if $sig = sign(m, key^{-1})$. We assume the cryptographic schemes are perfect. We also assume that each private key is only known by its owner.

With the model, we can formalise the authentication process in section 3.3 as shown in Fig. 5.

1.	authentication$((a, gd), t, p, history)$	19.	$(t_1, t_2) = validity(gd)$;
2.	Output:	20.	$area = da(gd)$;
3.	$true$ or $false$	21.	**IF** $t_1 \leq t \leq t_2$ and $in(p, area)$
4.	Function:	22.	$id = idInfo(gd)$;
5.	**IF** $gdRevoked(gd)$	23.	**IF** $id = ID(a)$
6.	return $false$;	24.	**FOR EACH** (gd_i, p_i) in history
7.	**ENDIF**	25.	**IF** $gd = gd_i$ and $p \neq p_i$
8.	$cert = getCert(gd)$;	26.	$alarm()$;
9.	$cSig = certSig(cert)$;	27.	return $false$;
10.	$issuer = issuer(cert)$;	28.	**ENDIF**
11.	$key = pk(issuer)$;	29.	**ENDFOR**
12.	**IF** $certRevoked(cert)$	30.	$history = history \| (gd, p)$;
13.	return $false$;	31.	return $true$;
14.	**ENDIF**	32.	**ENDIF**
15.	**IF** $checkSign(cert, cSig, key)$	33.	**ENDIF**
16.	$skey = spk(cert)$;	34.	**ENDIF**
17.	$gdSig = GDSig(gd)$;	35.	**ENDIF**
18.	**IF** $checkSign(gd, gdSig, skey)$	36.	return $false$;

Fig. 5 Algorithm for the authentication process

4.2 Proof sketch

For the sake of presentation, here we only sketch the proofs informally. The goal of authentication in our system is: given an asset a and a GD gd, current time t and place p, an authentication history in the period of the exhibition/auction *history*, decide whether the asset is real, i.e. $a \in \mathbf{A}$. It is clear that t, p and *history* come from trusted sources and the attacker can manipulate the (a, gd) tuple. Let "real asset" denote $a \in \mathbf{A}$, "fake asset" denote $a \in \mathbf{A}'$, "matched tag" denote $gd \in \mathbf{GD}, ID(a) = idInfo(gd)$, "unmatched tag" denote $gd \in \mathbf{GD}, ID(a) \neq idInfo(gd)$, "fake tag" denote $gd \notin \mathbf{GD}$. Then there are six cases for the (a, gd) tuple: (i) a is a real asset and gd is a matched tag; (ii) a is a real asset and gd is a unmatched tag; (iii) a is a real asset and gd is a fake tag; (iv) a is a fake asset and gd is a matched tag; (v) a is a fake asset and gd is a unmatched tag; (vi) a is a fake asset and gd is a fake tag. Obviously, our authentication system is secure if the system returns *true* only in case (i).

Now we will prove that our system is secure by enumerating all the possible attacks and show that they are either infeasible or not sensible.

It is easy to see that cases (iii) and (vi) are not possible. Under the assumption that the cryptographic schemes are perfect and only the owner knows the private key, the attacker cannot produce a valid signature for the forged or modified tag. The authentication returns *false* in such cases. It is also easy to see that cases (ii) and (v) are not possible because the authentication will return *false* in the object verification step.

Before going into case (iv), let's explain the intuitions of using position and time in our authentication system. The reason why we include position and time information is to limit the reuse/duplication of the tags. The underlying assumption of the traditional certificate authentication is that the certificate is unique and is bound to the cultural asset. Unfortunately, in real life, the assumptions rarely hold. First of all, certificates can be duplicated, especially digital ones. Secondly, there is no way to bind the certificate to the asset directly, it can only be bound to the identification characteristics of the asset. This indirect binding makes the traditional system much weaker. For a cultural asset, the identity is easy to forge. The attacker can create a counterfeit item with the same appearance as the real asset. Then he can bind a recycled real certificate or a duplicated certificate to the counterfeit item in order to sell/exhibit them. Since the reuse/duplication can happen across a vast geographical-time space, the user cannot effectively track the usage of the certificate and detect the reuse/duplication. In our system, by using position and time as constraints, the tag is only valid in a specific area and a specific time period, so the attacker cannot use it or the duplicated ones in other places or other time. If the attacker reuses the tag or uses the duplicated ones within the valid place-time space, the reuse/duplication can be easily detected by the end user.

Returning to case (iv), given (a, gd), if the gd is issued to be used in another time or area, the place and time verification step will fail so it will be impossible to reuse a tag for other purposes. If the exhibitor/dealer uses a valid gd and binds it to different assets in the same exhibition/auction, the end user can detect it because the same gd will appear several times in the authentication history. Another possibility of case (iv) is that a valid *gd* is bound to a counterfeit item, but this *gd* is used only once in the exhibition/auction. In the exhibition case, the only entity who can do so is the exhibitor, but it is not sensible for the exhibitor to do so because if the tag is valid, it means the exhibitor has paid for the loan of the real asset and has permission to exhibit it in the exhibition. The exhibitor gains no advantage by exhibiting a counterfeit item while holding the real one. In the auction case, if the tag is valid, the asset bound to it must be real because the asset bound to the tag is authenticated and kept securely by a trusted party.

5 Implementation evaluation

Fig. 6 A Roman sculpture exhibited in Villa Adriana

Our system has been implemented and validated in the context of the CUSPIS European project [6]. The Italian and Greek ministries of cultural heritage took the role of official departments. Qualified organisations were the National Museum of Athens and Roman museums. Exhibitions were organised in Villa Adriana (a roman villa), in the National Museum of Athens and in several places located in Rome.

In the case of Villa Adriana (an open space area) each cultural asset was equipped with an RFID device where the related GD is written. The destination area written inside the GD is an ordered list of points (i.e., a polygon) where each point is a couple of numbers (i.e., longitude and latitude). For instance the area $\{(41.94231, 12.77278), (41.94222, 12.77538), (41.94139, 12.77529), (41.94142, 12.77267)\}$ identifies the location of a Roman sculpture inside Villa Adriana. Each user employs a mobile device equipped with both an RFID reader and a Galileo receiver. The mobile device reads the RFID information, a local key store, the Galileo time-positioning information, the authentication history and automatically checks the cultural assets authenticity. In particular the history authentication is used to check duplication as described in Section 5 by taking into account the range of our RFID tags. If the user reads the same tag GD in two different positions POS and POS' then when they differ more than the RFID radius range a duplication is found. It is worth noticing that within the RFID radius range the same GD will be quickly detected.

In Figure 6 we show part of Villa Adriana where the aforementioned sculpture is located. The sculpture's RFID is physically bound to its basement. On the left side of the picture we show the graphical user interface where the map of the villa is shown. This map shows the location of all cultural assets and the current user position. It is worth noticing that if the sculpture had been non-authentic a warning message would have been shown on the mobile device.

In the case of indoor exhibitions we have written a GD on a graphical code located next to its cultural asset. The destination area is encoded as a mail address (Roman temporary exhibition, via Dante Alighieri, n 34B, floor 2). People can take a picture of the code and receive all location and time information on their device. It is worth noting that in this case that the location verification is not automatic, a user has to read and validate the location data.

In Figure 7 we show the graphical user interface of the indoor visit. It displays two paintings exhibited in Florence. In this case information was stored in graphical codes located next to the paintings. A camera was used to retrieve the data and a component of the PDA was installed to verify the authenticity of all information. Note that a user can use the images to visually verify that the paintings are the ones to be authenticated.

Several GDs for different cultural assets were loaned to several museums [12]. In each museum mobile devices were used to locally perform the authentication of cultural assets in an efficient and fast way. Moreover, GDs with some variations have been used to transport and track cultural assets during their journey.

Our system has minimal cost for both organizations and for end users. Organizations require a normal PC and our implementation to generate the GD. When GDs are written as graphical bar codes the museum needs only to buy the kit and they can easily print the code on a piece of paper. When GDs are written to RFIDs the organization must add the cost of the RFIDs. Users require a cellphone with RFID/GPS capability and a camera when GDs are stored as a graphical bar code.

6 Related work

In this section we overview the related work in the area. We include systems supporting exhibitions; some because they present approaches to discourage imitations of valuable assets, others because they use place and time data for authentication purposes. We also consider RFID and graphical bar code technologies since they share our counterfeiting and integrity problems.

Fig. 7 A picture displayed on the indoor visit

Systems with auto-localization functionalities are now available to help people visiting museums avoid traditional audio/visual pre-recorded guides. For instance, MAGA [13] is a user friendly virtual guide, that provides cultural asset information on PDAs. The interaction between the application running on the PDA and the environment is triggered by the detection of both passive and active RFID tags. A passive RFID is used to hold unique ID for the cultural asset. The ID is passed to the server application via a Wi-Fi connection in order to retrieve cultural asset information. The active RFID holds the cultural asset data directly and allows offline operation without an online server connection. Mobile applications have also been experimented with in [14, 15] where mobile devices perform local and remote connections to get cultural asset information. Although the aforementioned systems improve the user experience in museum visits they do not address security concerns. Cultural asset information received on a user mobile device can be easily copied and used for counterfeit assets.

ETG (Traceability and Guarantee Label) [16] presented recently in Vicenzaoro Winter adds to a traditional bar code an encrypted one that contains asset information signed with the producer's private key. Although the digital signature it provides data integrity it does not protect against the duplication attack since all encrypted data can be reused and copied.

RFID technology shares many of the counterfeiting and integrity problems [17]. Passive RFID have been successfully applied to identify, catalogue and track valuable assets [18, 19]. They bring real-time, read/write data tracking and process history useful for producers and users. However, passive RFIDs containing non-encrypted information are not useful for authentication and integrity purposes. To solve this problem two companies, Texas Instruments and VeriSign Inc., have proposed a 'chain-of-custody' approach [20]. Their model involves managing a PKI infrastructure and signing the RFID information with private keys in order to provide the integrity service. However, digital signatures do not confer cloning resistance to tags. They prevent forging of data, but not copying of data. A solution to cloning and corruption of passive RFIDs can be offered by active ones [17, 21, 22]. They offer anti-cloning mechanisms and hold private keys to perform authentication and establish encrypted communication. However, advanced RFIDs still allow certain attacks. Although anti-cloning RFIDs cannot be duplicated, they can be reused. And since they can be physically handled by an adversary, they can be breached with appropriate technologies. They also require dedicated devices and exclude other kinds of storage (e.g, graphical bar codes).

Counterfeiting and authentication of assets is so important that international organizations are trying to address it. For instance the EPC global standard for RFID technologies proposes global object naming services [23] that provide each object a with a unique ID. A centralised database stores asset information that can be used to authenticate and verify the product authenticity. However, this centralised DB poses scalability problems, requires a user to establish a remote connection and still require time-space information to avoid duplication of asset information. In our approach although organizations coordinate to maintain a logically centralised data base of GDs, users perform offline GD verification thus scalability is enhanced.

In [24] intrusion detection techniques are applied to detect cloned data. This approach is prone to false alarms that are not allowed in our system implementation (especially in the case of auctions). False alarm rate is reduced in the approach presented in [25] where they provide a probabilistic based approach for location based authentication. They use past location of products as location-based information for counterfeit asset detections. However, our system starts from different assumptions in fact very often previous locations of a cultural asset is unavailable but where it will be exhibited is known a priori. Since we are dealing with high valuable objects no false alarm is permitted. Moreover, we have introduced different security measures (especially in the same destination area) to ensure security properties.

In [26] location information is used to address the forgery of origin information and the transport problems of assets [26]. Each asset is equipped with a tag that contains origin and tracking information signed with the producer private key. Tags can be read by users for origin information and a centralised DB is used for asset authentication. In our system we perform off line authentication verifications. We add the concept of time and authentication history to address the problem of duplication in the same area. Moreover, our approach is formally described and security properties are formally verified.

7 Conclusion and future work

Our place and time based system provides novel authentication and integrity services for cultural assets. Its main contribution is the combination of both place and time information as well as traditional security mechanisms to generate a place and time based tag for each cultural asset. This tag avoids duplication, reuse and modification of key cultural asset information. Moreover, it prevents the introduction of counterfeit cultural assets in the market. Our approach has been implemented and deployed in several museums where its performance has been validated by several users. As future work we are extending and generalising the use of place and time information to authenticate other kinds of assets (e.g., jewels, watches and wines).

References

1. Jacob, J.: Counterfeited arthow to keep it out of your collection:. Chub collectors (2002)
2. Center of Stuy TCI: Dossier of MUSEUM 2006 (2006) www.touringclub.it/ricerca/pdf/DOSSIER_MUSEI_2007.pdf.
3. BBC on line resource.: Radiocarbon Dating (2002) www.bbc.co.uk/ dna/h2g2/A637418.
4. Minnesota State University. : Thermoluminescence (2002) www.mnsu.edu/emuseum/ archaeology/dating/ thermoluminescence.html.
5. Klarreich, E.: Con artists: Scanning program can discern true art. science news **166** (2004) 340
6. European Commision 6th Framework Program - 2nd Call Galileo Joint Undertaking: Cultural Heritage Space Identification System (CUSPIS), (www.cuspis-project.info)
7. official web page of Galileo: (www.galileoju.com)
8. Stallings, W.: Cryptography and network security: Principles and Practice. Fourth edn. (2006)
9. web page on EPCglobal organization: (http://www.epcglobalinc.org/home)
10. James D. R. Buchanan and Russell P. Cowburn and Ana-Vanessa Jausovec and Dorothee Petit and Peter Seem and Gang Xiong and Del Atkinson and Kate Fenton and Dan A. Allwood and Matthew T. Bryan: 'Fingerprinting' documents and packaging. Nature **436** (2005)
11. Pozzobon, O., Wullems, C., Kubic, K.: Secure tracking using trusted gnss receivers and galileo authentication services. Journal of Global Positioning Systems **3** (2004) 200–207
12. (CUSPIS official home page, TITLE = CUSPIS demnonstration and performance avaluation report, p..w.)
13. Augello, A., Santangelo, A., Sorce, S., Pilato, G., Gentile, A., Genco, A., Gaglio, S.: Maga: A mobile archaeological guide at agrigento, (University of Palermo, *ICAR_CNR)
14. Pilato, G., Augello, A., Santangelo, A., Gentile, A., Gaglio, S.: An intelligent multimodal site-guide for the parco archeologico della valle dei templi in agrigento. In: Proc. of First European Workshop on Intelligent Technologies for Cultural Heritage Exploitation, at The 17th European Conference on Artificial Intelligence. (2006)
15. Park, D., Nam, T., Shi, C., Golub, G., Loan, C.V.: Designing an immersive tour experience system for cultural tour sites. In chi '06 extended abstracts on human factors in computing systems edn. ACM Press, 1193-1198, Montral, Qubec, Canada, April 22 - 27 (2006)
16. (web page of Italia Oggi journal) http://www.italiaoggi.it/giornali/ giornali.asp? codiciTestate=45&argomento=Circuits.
17. Juels, A.: Rfid security and privacy: A research survey. IEEE Journal on Selected Areas in Communication. (2006)
18. Caputo, T.: Rfid technology beyond wal-mart. WinesandVines (2005)
19. web page of the TagStream Company: (http://www.tagstreaminc.com)
20. Texas Instruments and VeriSign, Inc.: Securing the pharmaceutical supply chain with RFID and public-key infrastructure technologies., (Whitepaper, www.ti.com/ rfid/ docs/ customer/ eped-form.shtml)
21. Juels, A., Weis, S.A.: Authenticating pervasive devices with human protocols. In Shoup, V., ed.: CRYPTO. Volume 3621 of Lecture Notes in Computer Science., Springer (2005) 293–308
22. Tuyls, P., Batina, L.: Rfid-tags for anti-counterfeiting. In Pointcheval, D., ed.: CT-RSA. Volume 3860 of Lecture Notes in Computer Science., Springer (2006) 115–131
23. EPC global standard powered by GS1.: Object Naming Service (ONS) 5 Version 1.0, (Whitepaper, www.epcglobalinc.org/ standards/ Object_Naming_Service_ONS_Standard_Version_1.0.pdf EPCglobal Ratified Specification Version of October 4, 2005)
24. Mirowski, L.: Detecting clone radio frequency identifications tags. Bachelor's Thesis, School of Computing, University of Tasmania (2006)
25. Lehtonen, M., Michahelles, F., Fleisch, E.: Probabilistic approach for location-based authentication. In: 1st International Workshop on Security for Spontaneous Interaction IWSSI 2007. (2007)
26. Mostarda, L., Tocchio, A., Inverardi, P., Costantini, S.: A geo time authentication system. In proceeding of IFIPTM 2007 (2007)

A Lightweight Binary Authentication System for Windows

Felix Halim, Rajiv Ramnath, Sufatrio, Yongzheng Wu, Roland H.C. Yap

Abstract The problem of malware is greatly reduced if we can ensure that only software from trusted providers is executed. In this paper, we have built a prototype system on Windows which performs authentication of all binaries in Windows to ensure that only trusted software is executed and from the correct path. Binaries on Windows are made more complex because there are many kinds of binaries besides executables, e.g. DLLs, drivers, ActiveX controls, etc. We combine this with a simple software ID scheme for software management and vulnerability assessment which leverages on trusted infrastructure such as DNS and Certificate Authorities. Our prototype is lightweight and does not need to rely on PKI infrastructure; it does however take advantage of binaries with existing digital signatures. We provide a detailed security analysis of our authentication scheme. We demonstrate that our prototype has low overhead, around 2%, even when all binary code is authenticated.

1 Introduction

Malware such as viruses, trojan horses, worms, remote attacks, are a critical security threat today. A successful malware attack usually also modifies the environment (e.g. file system) of the compromised host. Many of the system security problems such as malware stem from the fact that untrusted code is executed on the system. We can mitigate many of these problems by ensuring that code which is executed only comes from trusted software providers/vendors and the code is executed in the correct context. In this paper, we show that this can be efficiently achieved even

Felix Halim, Yongzheng Wu, Roland H.C. Yap
School of Computing, National University of Singapore, e-mail: {halim, wuyongzh, ryap}
@comp.nus.edu.sg

Rajiv Ramnath, Sufatrio
Temasek Laboratories, National University of Singapore, e-mail: {tslrr, tslsufat@nus.
edu.sg}

Please use the following format when citing this chapter:

Halim, F., Ramnath, R., Sufatrio, Wu, Y. and Yap, R.H.C., 2008, in IFIP International Federation for Information Processing, Volume 263;
Trust Management II, Yücel Karabulut, John Mitchell, Peter Herrmann, Christian Damsgaard Jensen; (Boston: Springer), pp. 295–310.

on complex operating systems such as Windows. Our system provides two guarantees: (i) we only allow the execution of binaries (in the rest of the paper, we refer to any executable code stored in the file system as a *binary*) whose contents are already known and trusted — we call this *authenticating binary integrity*; and (ii) as binaries are kept in files, the pathname of the file must match its content — we call this *authenticating binary location*. Binary integrity authentication ensures that the binary has not been tampered with, e.g. cmd.exe is not a trojan. Binary location authentication ensures that we are executing the correct executable content. A following extreme example illustrates location authentication. Suppose the binary integrity of the shell and the file system format executables are verified. If an attacker swaps their pathnames, then running a shell would cause the file system to be formatted. In this paper, we refer to *binary authentication* to mean when both the binary's data integrity and location are verified.

Most operating systems can prevent execution of code on the stack due to buffer overflow, e.g. NX protection. Combining stack protection with binary authentication makes the remaining avenues for attack smaller and more difficult. Binary authentication is also beneficial because it is even more important for the operating system to be protected against malicious drivers and the loading of malware into the kernel.

Most work on binary integrity authentication is on Unix/Linux [1, 2, 3]. However, the problem of malware is more acute in Windows. There are also many types of executable code, e.g. executables (.exe), dynamic linked libraries (.dll), ActiveX controls, control panel applets, and drivers. In this paper, we focus on mandatory binary authentication of all forms of executables in Windows. Binaries which fail authentication cannot be loaded, thus, cannot be executed. We argue that binary authentication together with execute protection of memory regions (e.g. Windows data execution prevention) provides protection against most of the malware on Windows.

A binary authentication needs to be flexible to operate under different scenarios. Our prototype signs binaries using a HMAC [4] which is more lightweight than having to rely on PKI infrastructure, although it can also make use of it. The authentication scheme additionally allows for other security benefits. Not only is it important to authenticate software on a system but one also needs to deal with the maintenance of the software over time. Nowadays, the number of discovered vulnerabilities grows rapidly [5]. This means that binaries on a system (even if they are authenticated) may be vulnerable. This leads to a vulnerability management and patching problems. We propose a simple software ID system leveraging on the binary authentication infrastructure and existing infrastructures such as DNS and certificae authorities to handle this problem.

Windows has the Authenticode mechanism [6]. In Windows XP version and earlier, it alerts the users of the results of signature verification under a few situations. However, it is not mandatory, and can be bypassed. The Windows Vista UAC mechanism makes use of signed binaries but it only deals with EXE binaries. It is also limited to privilege escalation situations. One common drawback of existing Windows mechanisms is that they do not authenticate the binary location. Moreover, requiring PKI infrastructure and certificates, we believe, is too heavy for a general purpose mechanism.

The main contribution of this paper is that we believe that it provides the first comprehensive infrastructure for trusted binaries for Windows. This is significant given that much of the problems of security on Windows stems from inability to distinguish between trusted and untrusted software. It provides mandatory authentication for the full range of binaries under Windows, and goes beyond authenticated code in XP and Vista. We also protect driver loading which gives increased kernel protection. Our scheme provides mandatory driver authentication which 32-bit Windows does not, and can be integrated with more flexible policies which 64-bit Windows does not support. We also analyze the security of our system. Our benchmarking shows that the overhead of comprehensive binary authentication can be quite low, around 2%, with a caching strategy.

2 Windows Issues

We discuss below the complexities and special problems of Windows which make it more difficult to implement binary authentication than in other operating systems such as Unix. Windows NT (Server 2000, XP, Server 2003, Vista) is a microkernel-like operating system. Programs are usually written for the Win32 API but these are decomposed into microkernel operations. However, Windows is closed source — only the Win32 API is documented and not the microkernel API. Our prototype makes use of both the documented and undocumented kernel infrastructure. However, it is not possible to make any guarantees on the completeness of the security mechanisms (which would also be a challenge even if Windows was open source). Some of the specific issues in Windows which we deal with are:

- **Proliferation of Binary Types:** It is not sufficient to ensure the integrity of EXE files. In Windows, binaries can have any file name extension, or even no extension. Some of the most common extensions include EXE (regular executables), DLL (dynamic linked libraries), OCX (ActiveX controls), SYS (drivers) and CPL (control panel applets). Unlike Unix, binaries cannot be distinguised by an execution flag. Thus, without reading its contents, it is not possible to distinguish a binary from any other file.
- **Complex Process Execution:** A process is created using CreateProcess() which is a Win32 library function. However, this is not a system call since Windows is a microkernel, and in reality this is broken up at the native API into: NTCreateFile(), NTCreateSection(), NTMapViewOfSection(), NTCreateProcess(), NTCreateThread(). Notice that NTCreateProcess() at the microkernel level performs only a small part of what is needed to run a process. Due to this, it is more complex to incorporate mandatory authentication in Windows.
- **DLL loading:** To load a DLL, a process usually uses the Win32 API, LoadLibrary(). However, this is broken up in a similar way to process execution above.
- **Execute Permissions:** Many code signing systems, particularly those on Linux [1, 3], implement binary loading by examining the execute permission bit in the

access mode of file open system-call. The same mechanism, however, does not work in Windows. Windows programs often set their file modes in a more permissive manner. Simply denying a file opening with execute mode set when its authentication fails, will cause many programs to fail which are otherwise correct on Windows. Instead, we need to properly intercept the right API(s) with correctly intended operation semantics to respect Windows behavior.

Compared to other open platforms, Windows potentially also makes the issue of locating vulnerable software components more complicated. A great deal of binaries created by Microsoft contain an internal file version, which is stored as the file's meta-data. The Windows update process does not indicate to the user which files are modified. Moreover, meta data of the modified file might still be kept the same. Thus, it is difficult to keep track of files changes in Windows. More precisely, one cannot ensure whether a version of a program P_i remain vulnerable to an attack A. It is rather difficult for a typical administrator who examines vulnerability information from public advisories to trace through the system and pinpoint the exact affected components. Our software naming scheme, associates binaries with their version and simplifies software vulnerability management.

3 Related Work

Tripwire [9] is one of the first to do file integrity protection but is limited as it in user-mode program and checks file integrity off-line. It does not provide any mandatory form of integrity checking and there are many known attacks such as: file modification in between authentication times, and attacks on system daemons (e.g. cron and sendmail) and system files that it depends on [10, 11].

There a number of kernel level binary level authentication implementations. These are mainly for Unix such as DigSig [1], Trojanproof [2] and SignedExec [3], which modify the Unix kernel to verify the executable's digital signature before program execution. DigSig and SignedExec embed signatures within the the the elf binaries. For efficiency, DigSig employs a caching mechanism to avoid checking binaries which have been verified already. The mechanism is similar to ours here but we need to handle the problems of Windows. It appears that DigSig provides binary integrity authentication but not binary location authentication.[1] In this paper, we examine the implementation issues and tradeoffs for Windows which is more complex and difficult than in Unix.

Authenticode [6] is Microsoft infrastructure for digitally signing binaries. In Windows versions prior to Vista, such XP with SP2, it is used as follows:

1. During ActiveX installation: Internet Explorer uses Authenticode to examine the ActiveX plugin and shows a prompt which contains the publisher's information including the result of the signature check.

---

[1] Mechanisms based solely on signatures embedded in the binaries do not have sufficient information for binary location authentication.

2. A user downloads a file using Internet Explorer: If this file is executed using the Windows Explorer shell, a prompt is displayed giving the signed the publisher's information. Internet Explorer uses an NTFS feature called Alternate Data Streams to embed the Internet zone information –in this case, the Internet– into the file. The Windows Explorer shell detects the zone information and displays the prompt. This mechanism is not mandatory and relies on the use of zone-aware programs, the browser and GUI shell cooperating with each other. Thus, it can be bypassed.

Since Authenticode runs in user space, it can be bypassed in a number of ways, e.g. from the command shell. It is also limited to files downloaded using Internet Explorer. Only the EXE binary is examined by Authenticode, but DLLs are ignored. One possible attack is then to put malware into a DLL and then execute it, e.g. with `rundll32.exe`. Furthermore, Authenticode relies heavily on digital certificates. Checking Certificate Revocation Lists (CRL) may add extra delay including timeouts due to the need to contact CA. In some cases, this causes significant slowdown.

The latest Windows Vista improves on signed checking because User Account Control (UAC) can be configured for mandatory checking of signed executables. However, this is quite limited since the UAC mechanism only kicks in when a process requests privileged elevation, and for certain operations on protected resources. UAC is not user friendly since there is a need for constant interactive user approval. Vista does not seem to prevent the loading of unsigned DLLs and other non EXE binaries. The 32-bit versions of Windows (including Vista) do not checked whether drivers are signed. However, the 64 bit versions (XP, Server 2003 and Vista) require all drivers to be signed (this may be too strict and restrict hardware choices).

The closest work on binary authentication in Windows is the Emu system in by Schmid et al. [13]. They intercept process creation by intercepting the NtCreateProcess system call. It is unclear whether they are able authenticate all binary code since trapping at NtCreateProcess is not sufficient to deal with DLLs. No performance benchmarks are given, so it is unclear how if their system is efficient.

4 Binary Authentication and Software IDs

We want a lightweight binary authentication scheme which can work under many settings without too much reliance on other infrastructure. Furthermore, it should help in the management of binaries, and incurs low overhead. Management of binaries includes determining which binaries should be authentic, dealing with issues arising from disclosed vulnerabilities, and software patching.

4.1 Software ID Scheme

We complement binary authentication with a software ID scheme meant to simplify binary management issues. The idea is that a *software ID* associates a unique string to a particular binary of a software product. The software ID should come either from the software developer or alternatively be assigned by the system administrator. The key to ensuring unique software_ID, even among different software developers, lies on the standardized format of the ID. We can define software_ID as follows:

Software_ID ::= ⟨ opcode_tag || vendor_ID || product_ID || module_ID || version_ID⟩. [2]

Here, || denotes string concatenation. Opcode_tag distinguishes different naming convention, eg. *Software_ID* and *Custom_ID* defined below.

Ideally, we want to be able to uniquely assigning vendor_IDs to producers of software which can make the software_ID unique. This problem in practice might not be as difficult as it sounds since it is similar to domain name registration or the assignment of Medium Access Control (MAC) addresses by network card manufacturers. One can leverage on existing trust infrastructures to do this. For example, the responsibility for unique and well known software_IDs can be assigned to a Certificate Authority (CA), which then define the vendor_ID as ⟨ CA_ID || vendor_name ⟩. Alternatively, one might be able to use the domain name of the software developer as a proxy for the vendor_ID.

A software_ID gives a one to one mapping between the binary and its ID string. This is useful for dealing with vulnerability management problems [15]. Suppose a new vulnerability is known for a particular version of a software. This means that certain binaries, providing that they correspond to that software version may be vulnerable. However, there is no simple and standard way of automatically determining this version information. Once we have software_IDs associated with binaries then one can check the software_ID against vulnerability alerts. The advisory may already contain the software_ID. Automatic scanners can then be used to tie-in this checking with the dissemination of vulnerability alerts to automatically monitor/manage/patch the software in an operating system. General management of patches in an operating system can also be done in much the same way.

In the case where no software_ID comes with a software product, one can alternatively derive one. It can be constructed, for instance, using the following (coarse-grained) string naming:

Custom_ID ::= ⟨ opcode_tag || *hash*(vendor_URL + product_name + file_name + salt) ⟩.

The salt expands the name space to reduce the risk of a hash function collision.

---

[2] Module_ID suffices to deal with software versioning. Having a separate version_ID, however, is useful to easily track different versions (or patched versions) of the same program.

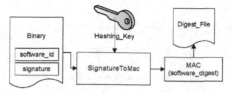

Fig. 1 SignatureToMac: Deriving the MAC

4.2 Binary Authentication System Architecture

In the following discussion, we assume here that binaries already come tagged with a software_ID. During the binary authentication set-up, preferably done immediately after the targeted binary installation, we generate the MAC values for each binary. In the case where binaries are digitally signed by its developer, then we verify the signature and then generate the MAC for each binary. Thus, only one public-key operation needs to be done at install time. We choose to use a keyed hash, the HMAC algorithm [4], so there is a secret key for the administrator. This is mainly to increase the security of the stored hashes. To authenticate binary integrity for any future execution of the code, only the generated HMAC needs to be checked. In what follows, we mostly write MAC which already covers the choice of HMAC.

One way of storing the generated MAC is by embedding it into the binary. However, doing so may interfere with file format of the signed binaries and may also have other complications. We instead use an authentication repository file which stores all the MAC values of authenticated binaries with their pathnames. During the boot-up process, the kernel creates its own in-memory data structures for binary authentication from this file. We ensure that the repository file is protected from further modification except under the control of the authentication system to add/remove binaries.[3] We can also customize binary authentication on a per user basis rather than system-wide which is a white-list of binaries approved for execution. In the case, when the initial binary does not have a digital signature, then the administrator can still choose to approve the binary and generate a MAC for it.

There are two main components of the system: the **SignatureToMac** and **Verifier**. The SignatureToMac maintains the authentication repository, *Digest_file*, consisting of ⟨path, MAC⟩ tuples. The Verifier is a kernel driver which makes use of *Digest_file* and decides whether an execution is to be allowed.

4.2.1 SignatureToMac

Once software is installed on the system, Fig. 1 shows how SignatureToMac processes the binaries:

---

[3] Further security can be achieved by integrating binary authentication with a TPM infrastructure. We do not do so in the prototype as that is somewhat orthogonal.

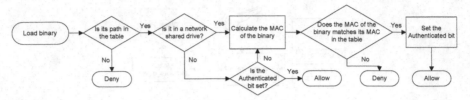

Fig. 2 Verifier: The Verifier in-kernel authentication process

1. Checks the validity of the binary's digital signature. If the signature is invalid, then report failure.
2. It consults the user or system administrator whether the software is to be trusted or not (this is similar to the Vista UAC dialog but only happens once). Other policies (possibly mandatory) can also be implemented.
3. It generates the MAC of the binary (including software_ID string) using a secret key, *Hashing_key*, to produce *software_digest*. The *Hashing_key* is only accessible by the authentication system, e.g. obtained on bootup.
4. It adds an entry for the binary as a tuple ⟨*path name*, *software_digest*⟩ into the *Digest_file* repository and informs the Verifier. The repository is protected against modification. Note that because the entries are signed, the repository can be read for other uses, e.g. version control and vulnerability management.

4.2.2 Verifier

The Verifier performs mandatory binary authentication — it denies the execution of any kind of Windows binary which fails to match the MAC and pathname. There are two general approaches for the checking. One is *cached MAC* which avoids generating the MAC for previously authenticated binaries. The other is *uncached MAC* which always checks the MAC. As we will see, they have various tradeoffs. The cached MAC implementation needs to ensure that binaries are unmodified. Hence, the Verifier monitors the usage of previously authenticated files on the cache, and removes them from the cache if it can be potentially modified.

The core data structure of the Verifier component can be viewed as a table of tuples in the form ⟨*Kernel_path*, *FileID*, *MAC*, *Authenticated_bit*⟩ representing the allowed binaries. It is indexed on *Kernel_path* and *FileID* for fast lookup. The fields are as follows:

- The *Kernel_path* is Windows kernel (internal) pathname representation of a file. In Window's user space, a file can have multiple absolute pathnames, due to: (i) 8.3 file naming format, e.g. "C:\Program Files\" and "C:\progra~1\" are the same; (ii) symbolic links (reparse points is similar); (iii) hard links; (iv) volume mount points; or (v) the SUBST and APPEND DOS commands. The *Kernel_path* is a unique representation for all the possible pathnames. When the system loads ⟨*path name, software_digest*⟩ from *Digest_file* during the startup, *path name* is converted to *Kernel_path* since all subsequent checks by Verifier in the kernel all use the latter.

- The *FileID* is a pair of ⟨*device_name, NTFS_object_ID*⟩. The *device_name* is a Windows internal name to identify a disk or partition volume. For instance, the device name `HarddiskVolume1` usually refers to `C:\`. The *NTFS_object_ID* is a 128-bit length number uniquely identifying a file in the file system volume (this is not the same as Unix inode numbers) The Verifier uses the *FileID* to identify the same file given more than one hard link. This prevents an attacker from creating a hard link for modifying a binary without invalidating the binary cache. The *FileID* values will be queried from the system and filled into the table during system boot.
- The *MAC* is same as a *software_digest* entry in *Digest_file*. Our prototype implements the HMAC-MD5 [4], HMAC-SHA-1 and HMAC-SHA-256 [16] hash algorithms.[4]
- The *Authenticated_bit* remembers whether the binary has been previously authenticated. It is initially set to false, and set to true after successful authentication.

Fig. 2 shows the authentication process when a binary executes/loads:

1. It checks if the binary's *Kernel_pathname* exists in the table. If not, then deny the execution and optionally log the event. A notification is accordingly sent to the user.
2. It the file is on a network shared drive, goto step 4. The MAC is always recomputed as we cannot keep track of modification to files on network shares.
3. If the *Authenticated_bit* is set go to step 7.
4. It performs MAC algorithm operation on the binary.
5. If the resulting MAC doesn't match with the *MAC* stored in the table, execution is denied.
6. It sets the *Authenticated_bit* of the binary.
7. It passes the control to the kernel to continue the execution.

To control binary execution, we intercept the section creation action (`NtCreate-Section()` system call) which is better than:

- Intercepting file opening (`NtCreateFile()` and `NtOpenFile()`). This would need to authenticate any file opened with with execute access mode. As discussed in Sec. 2, however, this introduces unnecessary overheads and can cause some correct programs to fail if the files do not pass authentication. There are also technical difficulties to distinguish between process creation and regular file IO operations, which is not always easy given its microkernel nature.
- Intercepting process creation (`NtCreateProcess()`). This method is not effective for our purpose. Firstly, we cannot use it to control `DLL` loading. Secondly, it is more difficult to get the pathname of the binary because process creating is broken down into microkernel operations.

---

[4] Due to recent concerns which show weaknesses and attacks against MD5 [17], we also have stronger hash functions, namely SHA-1 and the stronger SHA-256.

It turns out that since all code from any kind of binary needs to have a memory section to execute, it suffices to intercept `NTCreateSection()`.

The cached MAC verifier needs to ensure that binaries which have been already authenticated are not modified. However, the uncached verifier will not need to perform file monitoring. A binary with pathname P is considered modified, if the following occurs:

- P is created: Hence, we monitor system call `NtCreateFile()` and `NtOpenFile()`.
- P is opened with write access mode: the previous two system calls are also intercepted for this purpose. [5]
- Another file is renamed to P: We monitor file renaming (`NtSetInformationFile(FileRenameInformation)`) system call.
- A drive containing P is mounted: We monitor drive mounting `IRP_MJ_VOLUME_MOUNT`.

Note that we do not need to monitor file deletion since we only care about executing correct files but not missing files. The details of file modification monitoring are given in Fig. 3.

Upon modification of P, we reset the *Authenticated_bit* of binary P, and update the *FileID* in the table if it is changed. Should FAT file system be used, pathname is used to identify the binary as *FileID* is not supported but neither are hard and soft links. Since *FileID* is optional and can be removed, we monitor *FileID* removal (`NtFsControlFile(FSCTL_DELETE_OBJECT_ID)`) and deny the removal if the *FileID* is in the table. Dut to the semantics of NTFS, our use of *FileID* can coexist with other applications using it.

If additional hardware and infrastructure is available to support secure booting, such as the Trusted Platform Module (TPM) initiative, the system can benefit from increased security. Offline attacks would have to first attack the TPM. The Hashing_key can also be stored securely by the TPM.

4.3 Security Analysis

The security of binary authentication relies on the strength of the chosen hash functions (MD5, SHA-1, SHA-256) as well as the HMAC algorithm. Thus, we assume that any change in a binary can be detected through a changed MAC.

In our authentication on binary with digital signature, the subsequent invocations using MAC verification is sufficient to ensure the authenticity of the binary. In other words, MAC authentications "*preserve*" the previously established properties of binary authentication derived from digital signature. A subtlety comes when the

---

[5] An alternative way is to monitor the file (block) writing operation (`NtWriteFile()`). However, it is less efficient because file block writings take place more frequently than file openings as one opened file for modification might be subject to multiple block writings. Furthermore, it cannot capture file-memory mapping.

```
procedure UponModification (FilePath)
  if (FS is NTFS)
     FileID := GetFileID(FilePath) # FileID can be NULL
     if (FilePath is in the table)
        Entry := LookupTableByPath(FilePath)
        if (FileID == NULL)
           # this can happen when the file is deleted and created again.
           # generate a new FileID and update the table
           Entry.FileID := CreateFileID(FilePath)
        else if ( FileID != Entry.FileID in the table)
           # this can happen when the drive is unmounted,
           # id changed off-line and re-mounted
           Entry.FileID := FileID
        end if
        Entry.Authenticated := false
     else if ((FileID != NULL) AND (FileID is in the table))
        Entry := LookupTableByID(FileID)
        Entry.Authenticated := false
     end if
  else if ((FS is FAT) AND (FilePath is in table))
     Entry := LookupTableByPath(FilePath)
     Entry.Authenticated := false
  end if
end procedure
```

Fig. 3 Pseudo code of file modification monitor

certificate expires or is revoked at some point in time after SignatureToMac. We view that the question of whether one should keep trusting the binary for execution depends on one's level of trust on certificate expiration/revocation. If the certificate expiration or revocation means that the public key must no longer be used, but the fact that *previously established* goodness binary properties still hold, then we can keep trusting the binary for execution (as long as we still believe the issuer).

Here we discuss some possible attacks to the authentication system. All the attacks except the last two target the caching system. More precisely, the attacker attempts to modify an already authenticated binary without causing the *Authenticated_bit* to be set to false.

- **Manipulating symbolic links:** The attacker can use the path S which is a symbolic link of an authenticated P to indirectly modify P and subsequently execute P. However, the modified file will not be executed successfully, because Windows kernel resolves symbolic links to real paths. More precisely, the symbolic link S is resolved to the real path P. As a result, the *Authenticated_bit* of P will be set to false. When P is executed, its MAC will be recalculated and it will not pass the authentication.
- **Manipulating hard links:** The attacker can create a hard link H on an already authenticated file P and then modifies the file using path H. This attack will not succeed because we use *FileID* to identify files. H has the same *FileID* as P, thus the *Authenticated_bit* will be set to false. Note that this attack will not succeed in FAT file system either, even though we cannot use *FileID*. This is because hard link is not supported in FAT.
- **Manipulating FileID:** Recall that *FileID* consists of *device_name* and *NTFS_object_ID*. The latter is optional and thus can be removed. The attacker can re-

move the *NTFS_object_ID*, and then performs the previous attack. We handle this attack by denying *NTFS_object_ID* removal on authenticated files. This is implemented by monitoring the file system control event `FSCTL_DELETE_OBJECT_ID`

- **Remote File Systems:** Since we cannot keep track of modification on a network shared file system, we do not cache the authentication. More precisely, the MAC of the binary is always calculated upon loading. Same applies to removable media such as floppy in which we can not keep track of modification of files.

- **TOCTTOU:** TOCTTOU stands for Time-Of-Check-To-Time-Of-Use. It refers to a race condition bug of an access control system where the resource is changed during the time of checking the resource to the time of using the resource. In the binary authentication context, the binary may be modified after the time it is authenticated and before the time it is executed. However, we observed that all binaries are exclusive-write-locked when it is opened. That means binaries cannot be modified from the time it is opened to the time it is closed. Also note that the file is authenticated after it is opened and before it is executed. As a result, binaries cannot be modified during TOCTTOU.

  When the binary is in a network shared volume, i.e. SMB share, and the write-lock is not properly implemented in the SMB server, an attacker is able to modify the binary after authentication. However, we have observed that both Windows and Samba implement write-lock properly. Thus the attack is only possible when the SMB server is compromised. One way to prevent this is to disallow binary loading from SMB share.

- **Driver Loading:** The binary authentication system authenticates all binaries including kernel driver. This means all drivers are authenticated thus driver attacks such as kernel rootkits and malware drivers can be prevented.

- **Offline Attack:** Offline attack means modification of the file system when Windows is not in control. For example, boot another OS or remove the disk drive for modification elsewhere. Such an attack will require physical access to the machine. Offline attack can corrupt data or change programs/files and affect the general functioning and we cannot prevent that. What we can do is to ensure the integrity of executable code and other data loaded in memory for processes.

  We assume that the kernel is still secure, i.e. authentication occurs early in the boot. We also assume that kernel functioning is not impaired, e.g. deleting some system files does not cause the kernel to have an exploitable vulnerability.

  Since the hashing_key is not stored in the machine, it is not available to the attacker. The attacker can still change the digest file and the binaries, however, MACs of modified binaries cannot be produced without the hashing_key. Thus modified binaries cannot be executed when the system is online.

5 Empirical Results

Our authentication system can detect when a modified binary is loaded or run from the wrong pathname. In this section, we examine the three factors which impact on system performance: (i) Verifier checking upon binary loading (execution); (ii) file modification monitoring; and (iii) binary set-up during the SignatureToMac process. The first two above are the most important as they directly affect user's waiting time for process execution and affect overall system operation. The tests here are meant to determine the worst case overhead as well as average overheads.

The benchmarks are run on a Core 2 Duo with 2GB of ram running Windows XP with SP2. Each benchmark is run five times. As we want to investigate the effect of the cached Verifier, each benchmark is run with caching and without caching. When caching is enabled, we ignore the result of the first run because the overhead of authentication overhead is already shown in the uncached case. Even if we count the first run, its impact will be very small because some of the microbenchmarks run for 10K times, so the authentication overhead becomes negligible.

To see the difference of using different hashing algorithms, we implement and benchmark three algorithms: MD5, SHA-1 and SHA-256. Only MD5 and SHA-256 are shown in Table 1 as the results of SHA-1 are always between these. When caching is enabled, results of different hashing algorithms are not distinguished (shown as Cached-MAC in the table), because binaries are not require MAC checking during the benchmark. The reason is that the first run is ignored, and the binaries are not modified during the benchmark.

To see the difference with digital signature based authentication system, we also compare the performances of our scheme against the Microsoft official Authenticode utility called Sign Tool [18], and another Sysinternals (now acquired by Microsoft) Authenticode utility Sigcheck [19]. Note that two tools are user-mode programs. They are there to illustrate the difference between non-mandatory strategies used with Authenticode with our in-kernel mandatory authentication.

The first two benchmarks investigate system performance under two scenarios:

1. **Micro-benchmark:** The micro-benchmark aims to measure the worst case performance overhead incurred by the scheme. Note that this is primarily intended to measure the authentication cost but not other overhead, which is done by the last file modification microbenchmark. Here, we have two micro-benchmark scenarios.

   a. **EXE Loading:** This executes the noop.exe program, a dummy program that immediately exits, for 10K times. This scenario measures the overhead for authenticating the EXE file. The benchmark program first calls CreateProcess(), and waits for the child process' termination using the WaitForSingleObject() function. We use different binary sizes (40KB, 400KB, 4MB and 40MB, only the 40K and 40MB results are displayed) for noop.exe to see how executable size impacts performance.

   b. **Loading DLL:** The second scenario executes the load-dll.exe program for 100 times. This scenario is used to find out how the number of loaded DLLs impacts the performance. Program load-dll.exe loads 278 standard Microsoft DLLs with a total file size of ~75MB. The size of the load-dll.exe itself is 60KB. Note that in Windows, the bulk of code is

Authentication System	Micro-Benchmark						Macro-Benchmark	
	noop 40K		noop 40M		load-dll		build	
	time	slowdown	time	slowdown	time	slowdown	time	slowdown
Clean	22.76	–	30.07	–	45.32	–	66.26	–
EXE Only:								
Signtool	2822	11637%	4850	16033%	73.49	62.16%	97.00	46.39%
Sigcheck	1720	7457%	5629	18623%	62.82	38.62%	110.5	66.72%
Uncached-MD5	25.96	14.08%	2150	7052%	45.34	0.05%	70.85	6.93%
Uncached-SHA256	30.29	33.07%	9005	29851%	45.34	0.05%	71.79	8.35%
Cached-MAC	23.20	**1.93%**	30.63	**1.88%**	45.33	**0.02%**	67.62	**2.06%**
All Binaries:								
Signtool	11867	52043%	14030	46565%	16018	35244%	–	–
Sigcheck	4283	18772%	6186	20478%	12548	27587%	–	–
Uncached-MD5	26.10	14.67%	3881	12811%	128.8	184.1%	79.31	19.69%
Uncached-SHA256	30.42	33.67%	9302	30839%	201.3	344.0%	91.80	38.55%
Cached-MAC	23.25	**2.14%**	30.58	**1.72%**	45.35	**0.07%**	67.88	**2.45%**

Table 1 Benchmark results showing times (in seconds) and slowdown factors. The worst slowdown factors for each benchmark scenario are shown with underline, whereas the best are in bold. We define $slowdown_x = (time_x - time_{clean})/time_{clean}$.

often in DLLs which is why the EXE file may be small, e.g. Open Office has over 300 DLLs.

2. **Macro-benchmark:** The macro-benchmark measures overhead under a typical usage scenario. Our benchmark is to create the Windows DDK sample projects using the build command. In each test run, 482 C/C++ source files in 43 projects are built. This benchmark is chosen as it is deterministic, non-interactive, creates many processes and uses many files.

We benchmark Sign Tool and Sigcheck in the following fashion. We first sign noop.exe and load-dll.exe using Sign Tool's signing operation. We then measure the execution time of authenticating and executing the two programs. For the macro-benchmark, we replace each development tool in the DDK (i.e. *build.exe, nmake.exe, cl.exe* and *link.exe*) with a wrapper program which first authenticates the actual development tool and then invokes it. For the micro-benchmark, we consider two settings: (i) EXE only; and (ii) all binaries (EXE + DLL). The macro-benchmark, however, only tests the EXE case. This is because, during the macro-benchmark, many programs are invoked, and each program each invocation may dynamically load a different set of DLLs. Thus, it is hard to keep track of what DLLs are loaded, and it is unfair to simulate with all DLLs used.

The results are given in Table 1 but we have not shown "noop 400K" and "noop 4M" because they are bounded by the results of "noop 40K" and "noop 40M". Other results not shown are that the overhead is approximately linear with respect to the file size, e.g. the results of the All-binaries/Uncached/SHA-256 benchmarks are 40K:30.42s, 400K:85.43s, 4M:598.0s, 40M:9302s.

We can see that the overhead of Signtool and Sigcheck makes it unusable if DLLs are to be checked (352x slower on load-dll). If only EXE are checked, then at least 40% overhead and based on the `load-dll` benchmark, one could expect about an order of magnitude worse if all DLLS are checked. Of course, using these tools would incur additional overhead from creating a process and the main purpose is just to show the difference between what can be done in user-mode versus in-kernel. We can see that all the uncached-MD5/SHA256 are considerably faster than `Signtool` and `Sigcheck`.

Authenticating only `EXE`, the difference between uncached has overheads around 8% while cached brings this down to very small, around 2%x and almost neglible in the `load-dll` benchmark (0.02%). Note that as uncached overhead is quite small, the results are dominated by non-determinism in timing measurements. Moving to all DLLs (`EXE + DLL`), we can see the effect of Windows programs using many DLLs (more code in `DLL` than `EXE`). The overhead incurred by caching is still small while uncached can grow to between 20-40% depending on the hash algorithm. Note that the uncached overhead is applicable for files which cannot be cached.

The final microbenchmark investigates the tradeoffs between cached and un-cached verification. Caching means that MAC verification is amortized over exe-cutions but has added overhead from monitoring file modification, while uncached is the opposite. Our micro-benchmark opens a file for writing 100K times to measure the worst case overhead incurred by file modification monitoring. We have 3 experiments: (i) a clean system without binary authentication; (ii) binary authentication with cache and the modified file is a binary; and (iii) binary authentication with cache and the modified file is not a binary.

The results for the file modification micro-benchmark show that for binary authentication with a cache, it doesn't matter whether the file being written to is a binary or not. Both cases incur about 60% overhead compared to a clean system. Since binary authentication with no-cache has no overheads for file modifications, this means that under some usage scenarios where file modification is very high, the uncached strategy may be preferable over cached even when Verifier overhead is higher.

6 Conclusion

We have shown a comprehensive system which authenticates both content and path-name for Windows to ensure that only trusted binaries are executed. Unlike other operating systems, Windows poses significant challenges. We show that it is possi-ble to ensure that only trusted binaries can be loaded from files for execution. This can also be combined with a simple software ID scheme which simplifies binary version management, and dealing with vulnerability alerts and patches. Our system is lightweight and integrates well with PKI and trust mechanisms without having to rely on them. The overheads of our prototype are quite low when caching is is used. In the case of workloads with heavy file modifications, an uncached strategy might be preferable. The overheads are still low in this case, since the system overhead will be dominated by I/O rather than binary authentication, so the overall binary authentication would still be low as a percentage of overall system overhead. In summary, although this is a prototype, it significantly adds to the security of any Windows system but at the same time is sufficiently flexible so that it can be tailored for different usage scenarios.

References

1. A. Apvrille, D. Gordon, S. Hallyn, M. Pourzandi and V. Roy, "DigSig: Run-time Authentication of Binaries at Kernel Level", *Usenix LISA*, 2004.
2. M.A. Williams, "Anti-Trojan and Trojan Detection with In-Kernel Digital Signature testing of Executables", NetXSecure NZ Ltd.. http://www.netxsecure.net/downloads/sigexec.pdf, 2002.
3. L. v. Doorn, G. Ballintijn, and W. A. Arbaugh, "Signed Executables for Linux", *Technical Report CS-TR-4256* University of Maryland, 2001.
4. H. Krawczyk, M. Bellare and R. Canetti, "HMAC: Keyed-Hashing for Message Authentication", *RFC 2104*, 1997.
5. CERT, "Vulnerability Remediation Statistics", http://www.cert.org/stats/vulnerability_remediation.html, 2007.
6. R. Grimes, "Authenticode", Microsoft Technet, http://www.microsoft.com/technet/archive/security/topics/secaps/authcode.mspx?mfr=true.
7. Microsoft TechNet, "KnownDLLs", http://www.microsoft.com/technet/prodtechnol/windows2000serv/reskit/regentry/29908.mspx.
8. "Microsoft Security Advisor Program: Microsoft Security Bulletin (MS99-006)", http://www.microsoft.com/technet/security/bulletin/ms99-006.mspx.
9. G.H. Kim and E.H. Spafford, "The Design and Implementation of Tripwire: A File System Integrity Checker", *ACM CCS*, 1993.
10. E.R. Arnold, "The Trouble With Tripwire", http://www.securityfocus.com/infocus/1398, 2001.
11. M. Slaviero, J. Kroon and M. S. Olivier, "Attacking Signed Binaries", *Proc. of the 5th Annual Information Security South Africa Conference (ISSA)*, 2005.
12. B. Acohido, "Security feature in Microsoft's new Windows could drive users nuts", USA Today, http://www.usatoday.com/tech/products/2006-05-15-vista-security_x.htm?POE=TECISVA, 2006.
13. M. Schmid, F. Hill, A.K. Ghosh, and J.T. Bloch, "Preventing the Execution of Unauthorized Win32 Applications", *DARPA Information Survivability Conf. & Exposition II (DISCEX)*, 2001.
14. S. Patil, A. Kashyap, G. Sivathanu, E. Zadok, "I3FS: An In-Kernel Integrity Checker and Intrusion Detection File System", *USENIX LISA*, 2004.
15. Sufatrio, R. Yap and L. Zhong, "A Machine-Oriented Integrated Vulnerability Database for Automated Vulnerability Detection and Processing", *USENIX LISA*, 2004.
16. D.E. Eastlake and T. Hansen, "US Secure Hash Algorithms (SHA and HMAC-SHA)", RFC 4634, 2006.
17. X. Wang, H. Yu, "How to Break MD5 and Other Hash Functions", Eurocrypt '05, LNCS 3494, Springer, 2005.
18. "Sign Tool", http://msdn2.microsoft.com/en-us/library/8s9b9yaz(vs.80).aspx.
19. "Sigcheck", http://www.microsoft.com/technet/sysinternals/Security/Sigcheck.mspx.

Towards Standards-Compliant Trust Negotiation for Web Services

Adam J. Lee and Marianne Winslett

Abstract Web services are a powerful distributed computing abstraction in that they enable users to develop workflows that incorporate data and information processing services located in multiple organizational domains. Fully realizing the potential of this computing paradigm requires a flexible authorization mechanism that can function correctly without a priori knowledge of the users in the system. Trust negotiation has been proposed as a viable solution to this problem, but doing so within the framework provided by existing web services standards remains an unsolved problem. In this paper, we show how existing web services standards can be extended to enable fully standards-compliant support for trust negotiation. We also show that it is possible to compile trust negotiation policies specified using the WS-SecurityPolicy standard into a representation that is suitable for analysis by CLOUSEAU, a highly-efficient trust negotiation policy compliance checker. Lastly, we show that the TrustBuilder2 framework for trust negotiation can be parameterized to act as a trust engine that can be used by the WS-Trust standard to facilitate these negotiations.

1 Introduction

Web services and other service oriented architectures stand poised to usher in a new era of distributed computing. Standards such as WSDL [8] and UDDI [20] enable entities to describe and deploy computational services that can be searched for, discovered, and utilized by other entities. Furthermore, languages such as BPEL4WS [7] can be used to describe potentially complex workflows that utilize data and computational services spread across multiple administrative domains. Fully realizing the potential of this computing paradigm requires a flexible autho-

Adam J. Lee and Marianne Winslett
Department of Computer Science, University of Illinois at Urbana-Champaign, 201 N. Goodwin Ave., Urbana, IL 61801, e-mail: {adamlee, winslett}@cs.uiuc.edu

Please use the following format when citing this chapter:

Lee, A. J. and Winslett, M., 2008, in IFIP International Federation for Information Processing, Volume 263; *Trust Management II*; Yücel Karabulut, John Mitchell, Peter Herrmann, Christian Damsgaard Jensen; (Boston: Springer), pp. 311–326.

rization mechanism that can function correctly without a priori knowledge of the users in the system, as this would allow for the discovery and composition of new services at runtime. Unfortunately, existing web services security mechanisms are largely identity-based; this requires that a user be, in some sense, "hard-wired" into every administrative domain that they wish to access services from. This severely hinders the full potential of the web services model.

Trust negotiation [21] has previously been proposed as an appropriate authorization model for use in a web services context. In trust negotiation, resources are protected by attribute-based access policies. Entities use digital credentials issued by third-party attribute certifiers (e.g., professional organizations, employers, government bodies, etc.) to prove various characteristics about themselves and their surrounding environment. Because these attributes might also be considered sensitive, they can optionally be protected by release policies constraining the individuals to whom they can be disclosed. As such, a trust negotiation session evolves into a bilateral and iterative exchange of policies and credentials with the end goal of developing new trust relationships on-the-fly. Because these types of systems allow resource administrators to specify the *intension* of a policy, rather than its logical *extension* (i.e., an explicit access control list), authorized entities can gain access to available resources without requiring that their identity be known a priori.

The decentralized and expressive nature of trust negotiation makes it a natural fit for web services computing environments. As a result, previous research has explored this connection to some extent [4, 10]. While this work has made important contributions to the fields of trust negotiation and authorization architectures for web services, it has not addressed one important consideration: compliance with existing web services standards. There are currently a myriad of security-oriented standards in the web services domain that aim to enable many advanced security features. Rather than further cluttering this space with yet other standards, it is important to consider how existing standards might be used to support more advanced authorization paradigms, such as trust negotiation. In this paper, we consider exactly this problem. Specifically, we make the following contributions:

- We show how the existing token-based security model described by the WS-SecurityPolicy [16] standard can be used to specify trust negotiation policies. We then describe a standards-compliant *claims dialect* that can be used in conjunction with WS-SecurityPolicy to enable the specification of more expressive authorization policies.
- We propose extensions to WS-Trust's challenge/response framework [17] that can be used to facilitate trust negotiation sessions in a fully standards-compliant manner. These extensions do not limit the strategies, policies, or credential types that can be used during the trust negotiation process.
- We present a procedure for compiling trust negotiation policies specified using the WS-SecurityPolicy standard into a format suitable for analysis by CLOUSEAU [13], a highly efficient and language-agnostic policy compliance checker for trust negotiation systems.

- We show that the TrustBuilder2 framework for trust negotiation can be param-eterized to act as a trust engine—as defined by WS-Trust—that is capable of driving standards-compliant trust negotiation sessions.

The rest of this paper is organized as follows. In Section 2 we discuss related efforts in using trust negotiation within a web services context, as well as overview important web services security and trust standards. Section 3 describes how trust negotiation policies can be specified using the WS-SecurityPolicy standard. In Section 4, we show how to execute trust negotiations through extensions to the WS-Trust standard. Section 5 focuses on systems issues, including a correct and complete compilation procedure that enables policies specified using WS-SecurityPolicy to be translated into a format suitable for analysis by the CLOUSEAU compliance checker. We further describe how the TrustBuilder2 framework for trust negotiation can be parameterized to function as the trust engine used by WS-Trust during these negotiations. We then present our conclusions in Section 6.

2 Related Work

In this section, we provide background information on a number of relevant web services security standards, as well as discuss related work involving the use of trust negotiation in the web services domain.

2.1 Web Services Security Standards

At their most basic level, web services are nothing more than software components that communicate with one another by sending XML messages enclosed in SOAP envelopes. Each of these envelopes consists of a header containing routing information and other meta-data, as well as a body that encapsulates the "payload" of the message. Since these messages are often routed over public networks, such as the Internet, they are susceptible to observation and tampering by unauthorized entities. The WS-Security standard [18] defines a number of useful primitives that can help protect against these types of threats. This standard defines an optional security header that can be used to transport key material, message authentication codes, and various types of security tokens that can be used to authenticate users or protect the confidentiality or integrity of messages.

In order to take full advantage for the security features enabled by WS-Security, service administrators need some means of defining the security requirements for a web service. The WS-SecurityPolicy standard [18] defines *policy assertions* that allow administrators to place constraints on the types of authentication tokens that need to be presented to gain access to a service, the portions of incoming and outgoing messages that need to be encrypted or authenticated, suites of cryptographic algorithms that are supported, and other security-relevant properties of their service.

The basic policy structures and connectives defined by WS-Policy [19] are then used to combine these policy assertions into comprehensive *security policies*.

The final web services standard that we will leverage in this paper is WS-Trust [17]. Properly exchanging and using the types of security tokens defined in the WS-Security standard requires that each party involved can assess the trustworthiness of each security token that it acquires. WS-Trust leverages the security primitives defined in WS-Security along with additional extensions to enable services to carry out protocols designed to issue, renew, and validate security tokens, as well as broker trust relationships. In Section 4, we will describe how the negotiation and challenge extensions to WS-Trust can be used to carry out trust negotiation sessions in a standards-compliant manner.

2.2 Trust Negotiation for Web Services

While much research effort has been placed into the foundations of trust negotiation—such languages for expressing resource access policies (e.g., [2, 3, 9, 15]), protocols and strategies for conducting trust negotiations (e.g., [4, 11, 12, 23]), and logics for reasoning about the outcomes of these negotiations (e.g., [6, 22])—only a few research groups have investigated the applications of trust negotiation within the web services domain.

Bertino et al. describe Trust-$\mathcal{X}$ [4], an XML-based framework for supporting trust negotiations in peer-to-peer systems. In Trust-$\mathcal{X}$, each user creates an $\mathcal{X}$-profile that stores $\mathcal{X}$-TNL certificates [3] describing their attributes, uncertified declarations containing information about the user (e.g., preferences, phone numbers, or other such information), and $\mathcal{X}$-TNL policies to protect their sensitive resources. Since these data are all specified using XML, they can be queried or constrained using standard query languages, such as XQuery [5]. To allow users to optimize various aspects of the trust negotiation process, Trust-$\mathcal{X}$ supports a variety of interchangeable trust negotiation strategies. Another particularly innovative feature of the Trust-$\mathcal{X}$ framework is its support for *trust tickets*, which are receipts that attest to the fact that a user recently completed some negotiation with another party that be presented within some limited lifetime to bypass redundant portions of future negotiations. Although Trust-$\mathcal{X}$ makes heavy use of XML, it was not designed specifically for the web services environment. In particular, the authors do not specify how these trust negotiations might be carried out within the framework provided by other web services protocols and standards.

In [10], Koshutanski and Massacci describe a trust negotiation framework designed for web services. This framework facilitates the composition of access policies across the constituent pieces of a workflow, the discovery of credentials needed to satisfy these policies, the management of the distributed access control process, and the logic to determine what missing credentials must be located and provided to satisfy a given policy. This work operates at the business process level by determining and satisfying the composite access control policy for a workflow prior to its execution; as a result, existing web services security standards are not used. Furthermore, policies are represented using a datalog-based language, rather than an existing standards-compliant language.

3 Specifying Trust Negotiation Policies

During a trust negotiation session, attribute-based policies are used to describe the characteristics of the entities authorized to access a given resource. Digital credentials are then used to satisfy these policies; in a web services context, these credentials can be represented using the formats specified in WS-Security and its extensions. In this section, we address the problem of representing trust negotiation *policies* for web services. We first show that policy assertions defined in WS-SecurityPolicy can be used to specify basic trust negotiation policies, and then present a standards-compliant claims dialect that extends WS-SecurityPolicy to enable the specification of more expressive trust negotiation policies.

3.1 Basic Policy Specification

WS-SecurityPolicy takes a token-based approach to security, in that policies identify specific *security tokens* that must be presented in order to gain access to a particular service. The WS-SecurityPolicy specification defines policy assertions that can be used to require the use of Kerberos tickets, SAML assertions, and X.509 certificates, as well as other security token formats. As an example, the following policy assertion requires the use of an X.509 certificate issued by the Better Business Bureau's (fictitious) security token service:

```
<sp:X509Token xmlns:sp="..." xmlns:wsa="...">
  <sp:IssuerName>C=US/O=Better Business Bureau/CN=sts.bbb.org</sp:IssuerName>
</sp:X509Token>
```

Trust negotiation policies are typically more complicated than this, however, as they can include *multiple* attribute constraints. Requiring the use of multiple security tokens can be accomplished through the use of the basic policy connectives defined by WS-Policy. WS-Policy defines the ExactlyOne and All connectives, which require that either *one* or *all* subclauses of a particular clause in a policy be satisfied in order for that clause of the policy to be satisfied. Although these two connectives can be used to express any arbitrary policy structure, the WS-Policy specification recommends that policies be expressed in disjunctive normal form (DNF).

Combining the security token policy assertions from WS-SecurityPolicy with the policy connectives defined in WS-Policy allows us to specify a range of interesting trust negotiation policies. For example, consider a service that wishes to be protected by a policy requiring that users present X.509 certificates issued by the registrar of State University and the ACM; this would indicate that authorized users of the

```
<wsp:Policy xmlns:wsp="..." xmlns:sp="...">
  <wsp:ExactlyOne>
    <wsp:All>
      <sp:X509Token xmlns:wsa="...">
        <sp:IssuerName>
          C=US/O=State University/OU=Registrar/CN=sts-reg.stateu.edu
        </sp:IssuerName>
      </sp:X509Token>
      <sp:X509Token xmlns:wsa="...">
        <sp:IssuerName>
          C=US/O=ACM/CN=sts.acm.org
        </sp:IssuerName>
      </sp:X509Token>
    </wsp:All>
  </wsp:ExactlyOne>
</wsp:Policy>
```

Fig. 1 An example trust negotiation policy requiring users to present X.509 certificates from the State University registrar, as well as the ACM.

service need to be students of State University and members of the ACM. Assuming that State University's registrar and the ACM each run an online security token service (STS) that manages the credentials issued within their respective domains, Figure 1 illustrates how such a policy could be written in a standards-compliant manner.

3.2 Encoding Advanced Attribute Constraints

While the above, strictly token-based approach to trust negotiation policy specification works in some circumstances, it is inadequate for others. For example, consider complex credentials such as driver's licenses that contain information about the type of vehicles the bearer is authorized to drive and the date of birth of the bearer, or employee IDs that indicate the employee's rank, department, and year of hire. The policies used in the previous section can only determine whether an entity has an employee ID or driver's license, but cannot constrain the attribute fields—also known as claims—encoded in the certificate.

The authors of the WS-SecurityPolicy and WS-Trust standards recognize that placing constraints on the claims encoded in a security token is an important aspect of security policy specification. As such, these standards define an optional Claims element that can be included in the security token policy assertions that make up a given security policy. These standards do not specify the contents of given Claims element; to allow for maximum extensibility, third parties can define claims *dialects* that specify the format and contents of these elements.

To facilitate the use of more expressive—yet standards-compliant—trust negotiation policies within the WS-SecurityPolicy framework, we have developed one such claims dialect. Our claims dialect allows policy writers to place an arbitrary number of (attribute name, comparison operator, value) constraint triples on the claims encoded in a security token. This format was chosen because it is sufficiently ex-

Element	Description
/cl:Claim	This element is used to encode a constraint on some claim encoded in the security token to which it refers. These constraints take the form of (attribute, operation, value) triples.
/cl:Claim/cl:Attribute	The name of the attribute or claim to which this constraint refers.
/cl:Claim/cl:Op	The operation portion of a constraint triple. Acceptable values for this field are EQ, GT, LT, GTEQ, and LTEQ. These values denote "equals," "greater than," "less than," "greater than or equal to," and "less than or equal to," respectively.
/cl:Claim/cl:Value	The value field of the constraint triple.
/cl:Ownership	This element is used to indicate whether proof of ownership of the security token to which it refers needs to be demonstrated when the token is disclosed.
/cl:Ownership/@Status	This optional attribute may be set to either true or false depending on whether proof of ownership is required. If this attribute is not present, a default value of true is assumed.

Table 1 Descriptions of the elements making up our claims dialect.

pressive to represent instances of the constraint checking problem. For example, the constraint triple (License Type, EQ, CDL) would require that the "License Type" field of a particular driver's license security token be set to the value "CDL." Furthermore, our claims dialect provides a mechanism through which policy writers can require not only the disclosure of a particular security token, but also a demonstration of proof-of-ownership. This enables explicit differentiate between credentials that must be *owned* by the individual requesting access to a particular service and other supporting credentials that must be presented. The XML elements defined by this claims dialect are summarized in Table 1; a more detailed treatment of this claims dialect can be found in the XML schema defining the dialect (see Appendix A of [14]).

Figure 2 contains a more complex version of the policy presented in Figure 1. This version of the policy leverages our claims dialect to restrict service access to *graduate* students of State University who have been members of the ACM *since at least 2006*. The use of the Ownership element inside each of the Claims elements requires that proof of ownership be demonstrated for both tokens.

4 Trust Negotiation Using WS-Trust

Now that we have described how trust negotiation policies can be specified in a standards-compliant manner, we must show how trust negotiation *protocols* can be executed within the framework provided by existing web services standards.

4.1 WS-Trust Basics

As described in Section 2, the WS-Trust standard focuses on the brokerage of trust relationships between entities in a web services environment. In the trust model articulated in the WS-Trust standard, trust relationships are represented as security tokens. For example, if Alice runs a web service that she would like to allow Bob's

```
<wsp:Policy xmlns:wsp="..." xmlns:sp="...">
  <wsp:ExactlyOne>
    <wsp:All>
      <sp:X509Token xmlns:wsa="...">
        <sp:IssuerName>
          C=US/O=State University/OU=Registrar/CN=sts-reg.stateu.edu
        </sp:IssuerName>
        <wst:Claims Dialect="http://dais.cs.uiuc.edu/claim.xsd">
          <cl:Claim>
            <cl:Attribute>Type</cl:Attribute>
            <cl:Op>EQ</cl:Op>
            <cl:Value>Graduate Student</cl:Value>
          </cl:Claim>
          <cl:Ownership Status="true"/>
        </wst:Claims>
      </sp:X509Token>
      <sp:X509Token xmlns:wsa="...">
        <sp:IssuerName>
          C=US/O=ACM/CN=sts.acm.org
        </sp:IssuerName>
        <wst:Claims Dialect="http://dais.cs.uiuc.edu/claim.xsd">
          <cl:Claim>
            <cl:Attribute>MemberSince</cl:Attribute>
            <cl:Op>LTEQ</cl:Op>
            <cl:Value>2006</cl:Value>
          </cl:Claim>
          <cl:Ownership Status="true"/>
        </wst:Claims>
      </sp:X509Token>
    </wsp:All>
  </wsp:ExactlyOne>
</wsp:Policy>
```

Fig. 2 A more complex example trust negotiation policy that makes use of our claim dialect.

friends to use, she would protect her web service with a WS-SecurityPolicy policy requiring a security token issued by Bob. This type of token would serve as formal proof of the fact that Bob is friends with a certain individual. The WS-Trust standard then goes on to define the protocols that can be used to issue, renew, revoke, and check the validity of security tokens; later in this section, we will show that the token issuance protocol described by WS-Trust can be extended to enable native support for trust negotiation. As a means of introduction to this protocol, we now discuss an example execution of the basic protocol.

Figure 3 illustrates how the scenario described in our previous example might make use of the WS-Trust standard to control access to Alice's web service. When a user Charlie tries to access Alice's service, he is returned a WS-SecurityPolicy policy indicating that he must present a security token that identifies him as a friend of Bob's before he can access the service in question. Charlie does not have such a token, so he contacts Bob's STS and sends a SOAP message containing a RequestSecurityToken element indicating that he would like to be issued a security token identifying him as a friend of Bob's. This message includes a copy of Charlie's public key certificate—which is attached as described in the WS-Security standard—and is digitally signed to ensure its authenticity. Bob's STS then checks to see if Charlie is on the access control list (ACL) containing the names of Bob's friends. Since Charlie is on this list, the STS generates a security token for Charlie,

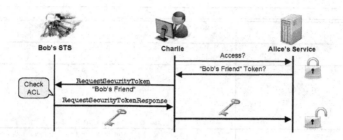

Fig. 3 An example of the WS-Trust token issuance mechanism.

embeds the token in a `RequestedSecurityTokenResponse` element, and includes this element in the body of a SOAP message. This message is then signed, encrypted, and returned to Charlie, who can then use the encapsulated token to access Alice's service.

4.2 Trust Negotiation Extensions to WS-Trust

Since the issuance of a security token might not always fit within a single request and response, WS-Trust includes a *negotiation and challenge framework* that enables support for more complex token issue protocols. After a requestor discloses an initial `RequestSecurityToken` message, this framework allows the requestor and STS to send any number of `RequestSecurityTokenResponse` messages containing arbitrary XML structures to one another before the final `RequestSecurityTokenResponse` message containing a new security token is disclosed (or a fault is generated). While these extensions were intended to support basic challenge/response protocols and legacy key exchange protocols, they can also be used to support trust negotiation.

Table 2 describes the `TNInit` and `TNExchange` XML elements that we have defined to encapsulate trust negotiation sessions within the WS-Trust negotiation and challenge framework. The `TNInit` element is exchanged by participants during the first round of the negotiation and contains information used to parameterize the negotiation that is about to take place. The remaining rounds of the negotiation consist of exchanges of `TNExchange` elements containing `PolicyCollection` and `TokenCollection` elements describing the policies and credentials being disclosed, respectively. Policies are encoded as described in Section 3, while security tokens are contained in `Token` elements that include a token type descriptor (in the form of a URI), the token itself (encoded as described in the WS-Trust specification), and an optional proof of ownership.

The above two-phase negotiation process enables support for an arbitrary array of trust negotiation protocols within the WS-Trust framework. Since the entities participating in the negotiation use the exchange of `TNInit` objects to choose which negotiation strategies and security token formats will be supported, the security token and policy exchanges that take place during the later phase of the negotiation

Element	Description
tn:TNInit	This element is used to encapsulate initialization information that needs to be passed between negotiation parties.
tn:TNInit/tn:SignatureMaterial	This holds one party's contribution to the signature challenge used when proving token ownership.
tn:TNInit/tn:StrategyFamily	This element identifies one strategy family [23] supported by the sending entity. This element may occur multiple times in the first TNInit element, indicating that multiple strategy families are supported. The TNInit element returned by the second negotiation participant must include exactly one copy of this element, which indicates the strategy that was chosen for use during this negotiation.
tn:TNInit/tn:TokenFormat	This element identifies one security token type supported by the sending entity. This element may occur multiple times, indicating that multiple security token formats are supported.
tn:TNExchange	This element is used to encapsulate all information transferred during one exchange of a trust negotiation session.
tn:TNExchange/tn:TokenCollection	This element contains one or more tn:Token elements embodying the security tokens disclosed during a single trust negotiation exchange.
tn:TNExchange/tn:PolicyCollection	This element contains one or more wsp:Policy elements embodying the trust negotiation policies disclosed during a single trust negotiation exchange.
tn:Token	This element encapsulates information describing a single security token that is being disclosed.
tn:Token/wst:TokenType	This element contains a URI describing the type of security token being disclosed.
tn:Token/wst:RequestedSecurityToken	The security token being disclosed is encoded in this element, which is defined in the WS-Trust specification.
tn:Token/tn:OwnershipProof	This optional element contains a Base64-encoded representation of a response to a proof of ownership challenge for this security token.

Table 2 Descriptions of the elements making up our extensions to the WS-Trust negotiation and challenge mechanism.

can occur in accordance with these initial choices. Furthermore, the schema defining the TNInit and TNExchange elements[1] can itself be easily extended to include support for the exchange of data items other than policies and security tokens (e.g., proof fragments [1, 22], uncertified claims [4, 6], or trust tickets [4]). Another benefit of this method of supporting trust negotiation is that the tokens issued by the STS function in many ways like the "trust tickets" described by Bertino et al. in [4]. That is, after a *single* successful trust negotiation, a service requestor can access the protected web service *many times* within the lifetime of the token issued by the STS.

4.3 An Example Standards-Compliant Trust Negotiation Session

In Figure 4, we see that Charlie is attempting to access a web service that uses trust negotiation authorization controls. Upon requesting access to the service, Charlie is told that he must present a security token issued by State University's STS in order to access the service. He contacts the STS and sends a SOAP message containing a RequestSecurityToken element indicating that he needs a security token to access the protected web service. The STS returns a SOAP message containing RequestSecurityTokenResponse element that initiates a trust negotiation

---

[1] Please see Appendix B of [14].

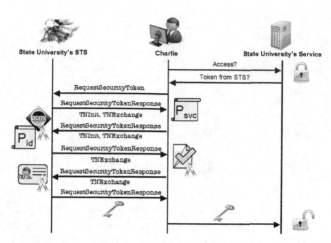

Fig. 4 An example illustrating the use of extensions to the WS-Trust negotiation and challenge framework to facilitate trust negotiation sessions.

with Charlie. This element contains a `TNInit` element containing initialization information for the trust negotiation session, as well as a `TNExchange` element containing a `PolicyCollection` element that includes the policy from Figure 2. Recall that this policy requires users to prove that they are graduate students at State University *and* that they have been a member of the ACM since at least 2006.

Upon receiving this message, Charlie creates a new SOAP message to the STS consisting of a `RequestSecurityTokenResponse` message containing a `TNInit` element to finalize the negotiation parameters, as well as a `TNExchange` element. The `TNExchange` contains a `TokenCollection` element that includes a copy of his ACM membership token (and its corresponding proof of ownership) and a `PolicyCollection` element containing a single `Policy` element requiring that the STS prove that it is certified by State University. This message is then sent to the STS, which returns another SOAP message to Charlie containing a `RequestSecurityTokenResponse` with an embedded `TNExchange` element containing a `TokenCollection` element that includes the requested security token (and its corresponding proof of ownership). This message satisfies Charlie, who then discloses his Student ID token, which identifies him as a graduate student of State University. At this point, the STS returns a SOAP message containing the final `RequestSecurityTokenResponse` element, which includes a new security token indicating that Charlie has satisfied the web service's policy. Charlie then discloses this token to the web service and is granted access.

5 Systems Considerations

We now focus on the *systems* aspects of the trust negotiation process. We first show that policies expressed as in Section 3 can be compiled into a format suitable for

```
;; This policy is satisfied by graduate students at State University
;; who have been members of the ACM since at least 2006.
(defrule rule-service-access
   (credential (id ?istud) (issuer ?issstud) (owned true) (map ?mstud))
   (credential (id ?iacm) (issuer ?issacm) (owned true) (map ?macm))
   (test (eq ?issstud "C=US/O=State University/OU=Registrar/CN=sts-reg.stateu.edu"))
   (test (eq "Graduate Student" (?mstud get "Type")))
   (test (eq ?issacm "C=US/O=ACM/CN=sts.acm.org"))
   (test (<= (?macm get "MemberSince") 2006))
=>
   (assert (satisfaction (resource-name server)
            (credentials ?istud ?iacm))))
```

Fig. 5 The policy presented in Figure 2 specified using CLOUSEAU's policy syntax.

analysis by CLOUSEAU, an efficient trust negotiation policy compliance checker. This not only reduces implementation overheads, but also establishes CLOUSEAU as a *general-purpose* compliance checker capable of analyzing both Datalog-based and industry-standard policy languages. We then show that the TrustBuilder2 framework for trust negotiation can be parameterized to function as a trust engine capable of driving these types of negotiation sessions.

5.1 Efficient Policy Compliance Checking

Given a policy p and a set of security tokens S, a *policy compliance checker* finds one or more minimal subsets of S that can be used to satisfy p. We call such minimal subsets *satisfying sets* of security tokens. Compliance checkers are used to find sets of local security tokens that can be disclosed to satisfy a remote policy, as well as to determine whether the security tokens disclosed by a remote party can be used to satisfy some local policy. Before the techniques outlined in this paper can be put to use, we require a compliance checker capable of analyzing policies written using the WS-Policy and WS-SecurityPolicy standards.

CLOUSEAU is an optimized policy compliance checker designed for trust nego-tiation systems [13]. Internally, CLOUSEAU represents policies as sets of *patterns* placing constraints on the collection of security tokens that must be presented to access a given resource. When invoked, CLOUSEAU translates the provided set of security tokens into an abstract *object* representation and then leverages efficient pattern matching algorithms to determine the collection of *all* satisfying sets of secu-rity tokens. Space limitations prevent a full discussion of the format of the constraint patterns analyzed by CLOUSEAU, so we instead refer interested readers to [13] for more details. As an introduction to CLOUSEAU's policy syntax, Figure 5 shows the policy presented in Figure 2 specified using this syntax.

In [13] the authors describe a compilation procedure for translating role-based policies written in the RT_0 and RT_1 policy languages [15] into the intermediate pol-icy representation analyzed by CLOUSEAU. We now describe such a compilation procedure that can be used to translate policies specified as in Section 3 into a for-mat suitable for analysis by CLOUSEAU. This translation is actually quite natural, as the token-based approach to trust and security embodied by WS-Trust maps directly onto the intermediate policy language used by CLOUSEAU.

In presenting the following compilation procedure, we assume that policies are expressed in DNF, as recommended by [19]. That is, we assume that policies are a collection of n All clauses, each identifying one satisfying set of security tokens for the policy. The ith such All clause in the policy should be processed as follows. First, a new rule will be created for this All clause:

```
(defrule rule-<i>
```

In the above rule, the <i> will be replaced with a counter indicating which All clause the rule represents. Assume this All clause has m Token elements. The kth such element will be processed as follows. First, a constraint will be added to the policy requiring that this token be presented:

```
(credential (id ?id-<k>) (issuer ?iss-<k>) (owned ?o-<k>) (map ?m-<k>))
```

If this Token's Claims element or IssuerName element specifies that the token must be issued by some specific issuer, <issuer>, the following test will be added to rule-<i>:

```
(test (eq ?iss-<k> <issuer>))
```

If this Token's Claims element contains the assertion <Ownership Status="true">, then the following test will be added to rule-<i>:

```
(test (eq ?o-<k> true))
```

For all other constraint triples encoded in the Claims element of this token, the following test will be inserted. Note that <op> is either eq, <, >, <=, or >= depending on whether the operation encoded in the constraint tuple is EQ, LT, GT, LTEQ, or GTEQ. Similarly, <name> and <value> are placeholders for the attribute name and constraint value identified in the constraint triple.

```
(test (<op> (?m-<k> get <name>) <value>))
```

After each Token element in the ith All clause has been processed as above, rule-<i> will be terminated as follows:

```
=>
   (assert (satisfaction (resource-name rule-<i>)
          (credentials ?id-1 ... ?id-<m>))))
```

This process then repeats for each other All clause defined by the policy. We now present the following theorem regarding the correctness and completeness of this compilation procedure, the full proof of which can be found in [14]:

Theorem 1. *Assume that a trust negotiation policy p specified using the WS-Policy and WS-SecurityPolicy specifications is compiled using the above procedure into a* CLOUSEAU *policy p'. Given the policy p' and a set of security tokens S, the satisfying sets $s_1, \ldots, s_n$ returned by* CLOUSEAU *are exactly the subsets of S that satisfy the original policy p.*

5.2 TrustBuilder2 as a WS-Trust Trust Engine

The WS-Trust standard defines a *trust engine* as "a conceptual system that evaluates the security-related aspects of a message" [17]. Revisiting the basic WS-Trust token issuance example from Section 4.1, the trust engine would have been responsible for checking to see that Charlie was on Bob's list of friends. To execute the more complex example from Section 4.3, a more powerful trust engine would be required. This trust engine would need to determine which policies and/or security tokens should be disclosed at each round of the negotiation as a function of the existing negotiation state and the policies and/or security tokens that were received during the previous round. We now argue that in the future such a trust engine could—with minimal effort—be implemented using TrustBuilder2, an extensible open-source framework for trust negotiation.[2]

To substantiate this claim, we must show that TrustBuilder2 can analyze policies specified using WS-Policy and WS-SecurityPolicy, and that it is at least as extensible as the trust negotiation extensions to WS-Trust described in Section 4. Recall from Section 5.1 that trust negotiation policies specified using WS-Policy and WS-SecurityPolicy can be compiled into a format that is analyzable by the CLOUSEAU compliance checker. Since TrustBuilder2 supports CLOUSEAU natively, it can analyze policies specified as described in Section 3. In Section 4.2, we showed that the extensibility afforded by our extensions to WS-Trust comes from two sources: the ability to support arbitrary trust negotiation strategies and security token formats, and the ability to extend the TNExchange element to transport trust negotiation evidence other than policies and security tokens.

The TrustBuilder2 framework makes use of an extensible data type hierarchy that users can extend to add support for new security token formats, policy languages, or trust negotiation evidence types (e.g., trust tickets, etc.). Additionally, the primary components of a trust negotiation system—including strategies—are represented as abstract interfaces that can be extended or replaced by users of the system. TrustBuilder2 also leverages a two-phase negotiation model in which participants first exchange InitBrick data structures allowing them to establish a mutually-acceptable system configuration. The remaining rounds of the negotiation involve the exchange TrustMessage objects that encapsulate the policies, security tokens, and other forms of evidence exchanged during the negotiation; note that this mirrors the exchange of TNInit and TNExchange elements described in Section 4.2. As a result, each message exchange during our trust negotiation extensions to WS-Trust can be translated in a one-to-one fashion into an object that can be parsed TrustBuilder2. TrustBuilder2 can then examine the state of the negotiation, determine the next step, and generate an appropriate response. This response can then be translated into the XML elements described in Section 4.2 and transmitted.

---

[2] TrustBuilder2 is available for download at http://dais.cs.uiuc.edu/tn.

6 Conclusions

Web services are a promising distributed computing paradigm, but fully unlocking their potential requires flexible authorization techniques that can function correctly without a priori knowledge of the users in the system. In this paper, we have shown that the adoption of *trust negotiation* within this realm can occur within the framework provided by existing web services security standards. In particular, we showed that after defining a rudimentary claims dialect—which is fully-compliant with the WS-Trust standard—the WS-Policy and WS-SecurityPolicy standards can be used to define a range of expressive trust negotiation policies. We also showed that WS-Trust's negotiation and challenge framework can be extended to act as a standards-compliant transport mechanism within which trust negotiation sessions can occur.

We also examined the systems aspects of this process and showed that trust negotiation policies specified using the WS-Policy and WS-SecurityPolicy standards can be complied into a format that is suitable for analysis by CLOUSEAU, an efficient policy compliance checker for trust negotiation systems. This not only eases the development of trust negotiation solutions for the web services domain, but shows that it is possible to design a *single* compliance checker—namely CLOUSEAU—that is capable of analyzing Datalog-style policy languages, as well as other industry standard policy languages. Furthermore, we show that the TrustBuilder2 framework for trust negotiation can be parameterized to act as a trust engine, as described by the WS-Trust standard, that can be used to drive these interactions.

Acknowledgments. This research was supported by the NSF under grants IIS-0331707, CNS-0325951, and CNS-0524695 and by Sandia National Laboratories under grant number DOE SNL 541065.

References

1. Bauer, L., Garriss, S., Reiter, M.K.: Distributed proving in access-control systems. In: Proceedings of the IEEE Symposium on Security and Privacy, pp. 81–95 (2005)
2. Becker, M.Y., Sewell, P.: Cassandra: Distributed access control policies with tunable expressiveness. In: Proceedings of the Fifth IEEE International Workshop on Policies for Distributed Systems and Networks, pp. 159–168 (2004)
3. Bertino, E., Ferrari, E., Squicciarini, A.C.: $\mathcal{X}$-TNL: An XML-based language for trust negotiations. In: Proceedings of the Fourth IEEE International Workshop on Policies for Distributed Systems and Networks (POLICY), pp. 81–84 (2003)
4. Bertino, E., Ferrari, E., Squicciarini, A.C.: Trust-$\mathcal{X}$: A peer-to-peer framework for trust establishment. IEEE Transactions on Knowledge and Data Engineering 16(7), 827–842 (2004)
5. Boag, S., Chamberlain, D., Fernandez, M.F., Florescu, D., Robie, J., Simeon, J., (Editors): XQuery 1.0: An XML Query Language. W3C Recommendation (2007). http://www.w3.org/TR/xquery/
6. Bonatti, P., Samarati, P.: Regulating service access and information release on the web. In: Proceedings of the Seventh ACM Conference on Computer and Communications Security (CCS), pp. 134–143 (2000)

7. Business process execution language for web services version 1.1. Web page (2007). `http://www.ibm.com/developerworks/library/specification/ws-bpel/`

8. Christensen, E., Curbera, F., Meredith, G., Weerawarana, S.: Web services description language (WSDL) 1.1. W3C Note (2001). `http://www.w3.org/TR/wsdl`

9. Herzberg, A., Mass, Y., Michaeli, J., Naor, D., Ravid, Y.: Access control meets public key infrastructure, or: Assigning roles to strangers. In: Proceedings of the IEEE Symposium on Security and Privacy, pp. 2–14 (2000)

10. Koshutanski, H., Massacci, F.: Interactive access control for web services. In: Proceedings of the 19th IFIP Information Security Conference (SEC), pp. 151–166 (2004)

11. Koshutanski, H., Massacci, F.: An interactive trust management and negotiation scheme. In: Proceedings of the Second International Workshop on Formal Aspects in Security and Trust (FAST), pp. 139–152 (2004)

12. Koshutanski, H., Massacci, F.: Interactive credential negotiation for stateful business processes. In: Proceedings of the Third International Conference on Trust Management (iTrust), pp. 257–273 (2005)

13. Lee, A.J., Winslett, M.: Towards and efficient and language-agnostic compliance checker for trust negotiation systems. In: Proceedings of the Third ACM Symposium on Information, Computer and Communications Security (ASIACCS 2008) (2008)

14. Lee, A.J., Winslett, M.: Towards standards-compliant trust negotiation for web services (extended version). Tech. Rep. UIUCDCS-R-2008-2944, University of Illinois at Urbana-Champaign Department of Computer Science (2008)

15. Li, N., Mitchell, J.C., Winsborough, W.H.: Design of a role-based trust-management framework. In: Proceedings of the 2002 IEEE Symposium on Security and Privacy, pp. 114–130 (2002)

16. Nadalin, A., Goodner, M., Gudgin, M., Barbir, A., Granqvist, H., (Editors): WS-SecurityPolicy 1.2. OASIS Standard (2007). `http://docs.oasis-open.org/ws-sx/ws-securitypolicy/200702/`

17. Nadalin, A., Goodner, M., Gudgin, M., Barbir, A., Granqvist, H., (Editors): WS-Trust 1.3. OASIS Standard (2007). `http://docs.oasis-open.org/ws-sx/ws-trust/200512/`

18. Nadalin, A., Kaler, C., Monzillo, R., Hallam-Baker, P., (Editors): WS-Security Core Specification 1.1. OASIS Standard (2006). `http://www.oasis-open.org/committees/download.php/16790/wss-v1.1-spec-os-SOAPMessageSecurity.pdf`

19. Schlimmer, J., (Editor): Web Services Policy 1.2 - Framework (WS-Policy). W3C Member Submission (2006). `http://www.w3.org/Submission/WS-Policy/`

20. OASIS UDDI Specifications TC. Web page. `http://www.oasis-open.org/committees/uddi-spec/`,

21. Winsborough, W.H., Seamons, K.E., Jones, V.E.: Automated trust negotiation. In: Proceedings of the DARPA Information Survivability Conference and Exposition, pp. 88–102 (2000)

22. Winslett, M., Zhang, C., Bonatti, P.A.: PeerAccess: A logic for distributed authorization. In: Proceedings of the 12th ACM Conference on Computer and Communications Security (CCS 2005), pp. 168–179 (2005)

23. Yu, T., Winslett, M., Seamons, K.E.: Supporting structured credentials and sensitive policies through interoperable strategies for automated trust negotiation. ACM Transactions on Information and System Security 6(1) (2003)

Assigning Responsibility for Failed Obligations

Keith Irwin, Ting Yu and William H. Winsborough

Abstract Traditional security policies largely focus on access control. Though essential, access control is only one aspect of security. In particular, the correct behavior and reliable operation of a system depends not only on what users are permitted to do, but oftentimes on what users are required to do. Such obligatory actions are integral to the security procedures of many enterprises. Unlike access control, obligations assigned to individual users are often unenforceable, that is, the system cannot ensure that each obligation will be fulfilled. Accurately determining who was at fault when obligations are not met is essential for responding appropriately, be it in terms of modified trust relationships or other recourse. In this paper, based on a formal metamodel of obligations, we propose an approach for fault assessment through active online tracking of responsibilities and dependencies between obligations. We identify and formalize two key properties for the correct assessment of fault, and design responsibility assignment and fault assessment algorithms for a concrete yet general access control and obligation system.

1 Introduction

A security policy defines the correct behavior of an information system. Today, a majority of techniques, literature, and infrastructure in security policy management focus on access control. Though essential, access control is only one aspect of security. In particular, the correct behavior and reliable operation of a system relies not only on what users are permitted to do, but oftentimes on what users are required to do. Such obligatory actions are integral to the security procedures of many enterprises. For instance, when an employee leaves a firm, it is usually very important that the employee's computer accounts and physical access be deactivated. Obligations are also essential to privacy policies. Enterprises that collect or use the private information of individuals must abide by laws that require certain actions, such as deleting data after a certain period of time. Finally, oblgations are often key elements of contracts and other agreements.

Keith Irwin and Ting Yu
North Carolina State University, e-mail: {kirwin, tyu}@ncsu.edu

William H. Winsborough
University of Texas at San Antonio, e-mail: wwinsborough@acm.org

Please use the following format when citing this chapter:

Irwin, K., Yu, T. and Winsborough, W. H., 2008, in IFIP International Federation for Information Processing, Volume 263; *Trust Management II*; Yücel Karabulut, John Mitchell, Peter Herrmann, Christian Damsgaard Jensen, (Boston: Springer), pp. 327–342.

Recently, we have witnessed an increasing trend to express obligations explicitly as part of security policies [5, 10, 14, 18, 19]. Obligation policies have different properties from access control policies. In particular, obligations assigned to individual users, though monitorable (i.e., a system can determine whether and when an obligation is fulfilled), are, in general, not enforceable (i.e., the system cannot ensure that an obligation is always fulfilled). Thus, the handling of failed obligations is an indispensable part of obligation management. Besides conducting necessary actions to compensate for failed obligations, a system should appropriately assign culpability to responsible parties. In this paper, we call this process *fault assessment*.

Fault assessment can be significant for several reasons. It may be a simple question of evaluating the performance of employees at their assigned tasks. However, an obligation failure may result in the violation of a contract, which may lead to sanctions against the responsible party or the organization he represents. Even when an agreement does not rise to the level of a legal contract, failing to meet one's obligations has and should have consequences for one's reputation and the level of trust that others place in one.

At a first sight, the solution to the fault assessment problem seems straightforward. Indeed, in many cases, if a user does not complete her obligation, she is to blame for the failure. On the other hand, it is common that one or more obligations provide necessary privileges or resources to enable the fulfillment of other obligations. For example, in work-flow systems, frequently one user's obligation can be fulfilled only if some other users first complete their obligations, thus making the necessary resources available. A dependency between two obligations occurs if one user is obligated to grant an authorization necessary to enable another user to fulfill his obligation. Fairness requires that if a user cannot fulfill an obligation due to a lack of sufficient privileges or necessary resources, the user should not be considered to be at fault. A lack of privileges may be caused by other users failing to fulfill their obligations. Clearly, in such cases, fault assessment requires analyzing and maintaining the dependencies between obligations, which is a non-trivial task.

In this paper, we propose an active approach to fault assessment through online tracking of responsibilities and dependencies between obligations. The contributions of this paper include:

- Instead of relying on postmortem analysis of the dependency between failed obligations, we propose a framework that allows a system to dynamically observe dependencies at the time when obligations are assigned to users and assign responsibility at that point. We show that such online responsibility tracking significantly reduces the complexity of fault assessment of failed obligations.
- Fault assessment is often application or policy dependent. Instead of advocating a single solution, we identify and formalize two key properties for responsibility tracking based on a metamodel of obligation and access control systems. We argue that any responsibility tracking algorithm should satisfy these two properties in order to achieve correct blame assignment.
- We present an algorithm that computes fault assessment when given a set of failed obligations and their resposibility graph maintained by a system.

- We further instantiate the metamodel and study fault assessment in a concrete access control and obligation system based on an access-matrix model. We show that obligation dependency can be efficiently identified in this system. We propose a generalized obligation responsibility-tracking algorithm, and prove that it satisfies the key properties for responsibility tracking that we identify in the contribution mentioned above.

The rest of the paper is organized as follows. In section 2, we discuss work closely related to this paper. In section 3 and 4, we briefly describe the construction of a metamodel of access control and obligation systems, and introduce the concept of accountability, a security objective for obligation systems. The fault assessment problem and the two properties for responsibility tracking are articulated in section 5. Our discussion of fault assessment in a concrete obligation and access control system is presented in section 6. We conclude in section 7.

2 Related Works

Obligations are common features of security policies in a variety of application domains. For example, due to requirements from laws and other regulations, enterprise privacy policies often include obligations regarding the handling of private information collected from individuals. Typical examples concern the retention and deletion of customers' personal and transactional information, notification when such information is shared with other parties, and auditing after access to private information [12, 13]. Obligations are also integral to the security policies of cross-domain data sharing, since data sharing and handling contracts between autonomous entities, such as responsive forwarding and nondisclosure agreements and usage notification, are often specified in the form of obligations [17].

Several policy languages have been proposed that support the specification of obligations in security policies. XACML [18] and KAoS [19] both have a limited model of obligations. Specifically, they model obligations assigned to a system and cannot describe user obligations, i.e., obligations assigned to ordinary users who are not always trusted to fulfill obligations. Ponder [5], SPL [14], and Rei [10] all support the specification of user obligations.

To the best of our knowledge, Bettini et al. [1] were the first to investigate the analysis of obligations in the context of access control. They studied the problem of choosing appropriate policy rules to minimize the provisions and obligations that a user incurs in order to take a certain action. However, they assume actions in obligations are not subject to access control, and thus they can always be fulfilled. Bettini et al. [2, 3] further extended their work to place under policy control the handling of obligation violations.

Heimdall [6] is a prototype obligation monitoring platform which tracks pending obligations. It detects when obligations are fulfilled or violated. This requires the modeling of time constraints in obligations, which are explicitly supported in its policy language xSPL. Sailer and Morciniec [15] propose a means of using a third party to monitor obligation compliance in contracts in a web services settings.

Hilty, et al. [8] describe how to formally model obligation policies and how to enforce obligation policies which might initially appear to be unable to be monitored. Their work is complimentary to ours.

Responsibility assignment is also related to auditing systems, which collect audit data and analyze them to discover security violations [16]. Most works in auditing target intrusion detection, which is distinct from the problem addressed in this paper.

Obligations and contracts are central concepts in collaborative multi-agent systems. Deontic logic [11] is commonly used to express the agreed obligations among agents. Works in this area typically do not concern the interaction between obligations and access control. Instead, they focus on expressing the dependencies between obligations, assuming such dependencies have already been identified [4, 7]. In this paper, we formalize the key properties for correct identification of dependencies between obligations.

3 Metamodel

We now present a highly abstract model of an obligation system, which we call a metamodel. Any concrete model instantiates one or more of its features. This metamodel was first presented in [9] and more detail can be found there.

We model an obligation as a tuple $obl(s, a, O, t_s, t_e)$, in which $[t_s, t_e]$ is the time interval during which subject s is obliged to take action a and O is a finite sequence of zero or more objects that are parameters to the action. An obligation system consists of the following components:

- $\mathscr{T}$: a countable set of time values.
- $\mathscr{S}$: a set of subjects.
- $\mathscr{O}$: a set of objects with $\mathscr{S} \subseteq \mathscr{O}$.
- $\mathscr{A}$: a finite set of actions that can be initiated by subjects. Each action is a function that takes as input the current system state (defined just below), the subject performing the action, and a finite sequence of zero or more objects. It outputs a new system state.
- $\mathscr{B} = \mathscr{S} \times \mathscr{A} \times \mathscr{O}^* \times \mathscr{T} \times \mathscr{T}$: a set of obligations that can be introduced to the system. Given an obligation $b \in \mathscr{B}$, we use $b.s$ to refer to the subject, $b.a$ for the action, $b.O$ for the objects that are parameters to the action, and $b.t_s$ and $b.t_e$ to refer to the start and end times.
- $\mathscr{ST} = \mathscr{T} \times \mathscr{FP}(\mathscr{S}) \times \mathscr{FP}(\mathscr{O}) \times \Sigma \times \mathscr{FP}(\mathscr{B})$: the set of system states. Here, we use $\mathscr{FP}(\mathscr{X}) = \{X \subset \mathscr{X} | X \text{ is finite}\}$ to denote the set of finite subsets of the given set. We use $st = \langle t, S, O, \sigma, B \rangle$ to denote systems states, where t is the time in the system, S and O are the subjects and objects currently in the system, B is the set of pending obligations, and σ is a fully abstract representation of all other features of the system state. Σ, the domain of abstract states, is possibly

infinite[1]. We use $st_{cur} = \langle t_{cur}, S_{cur}, O_{cur}, \sigma_{cur}, B_{cur} \rangle$ to denote the current state of the system.

- $\mathscr{P}$: a set of policy rules. Each policy rule specifies an action that can be taken, under what circumstances it may be taken, and what obligations (if any) results from that action. Each policy rule p has the form $p = a(st, s, O) \leftarrow cond : F_{obl}$ in which $a \in \mathscr{A}$ and $cond$ (denoted by $p.cond$) is a predicate in $\mathscr{S} \times \mathscr{T} \times \Sigma \times \mathscr{O}^* \rightarrow \{true, false\}$, indicating that subject s is authorized to perform action a on objects O at time t with the system in state σ if $cond(s, t, \sigma, O)$ is true. F_{obl} is an *obligation function*, which takes the current state of the system σ, the current time, the subject s, and the arguments O as its input and returns a finite set $B \subset \mathscr{B}$ of obligations resulting from the action. Obligations in B may not be incurred by the same subject who performed the action.

We assume that actions scheduled for a given time can be finished in a single clock tick, and their effect will be reflected in the state of the next clock tick.

Suppose a (finite) set of actions are attempted at the same time, $t = i$, in state st_i. We denote such a set by $AP \subset \mathscr{S} \times \mathscr{A} \times \mathscr{O}^*$. ($AP$ stands for action plan.) The order in which the elements of AP are executed is given by a fixed, arbitrary total order over $\mathscr{S} \times \mathscr{A} \times \mathscr{O}^*$. This means that two actions, if present in AP, will be executed in the same order regardless of other actions that may or may not be in the set. Let us assume $|AP| = n$ and $ap_0, ap_1, \ldots, ap_{n-1}$ enumerates AP in the order mentioned above.

Given st_i and AP, we let the function $\mathsf{apply}(AP, st_i) = st_{i+1}$ in which st_{i+1} is obtained by ordering and applying the actions. Details of how this would be carried out can be found in the previous paper. This defines the *transition* from st_i to st_{i+1} determined by AP. Given st_i, AP, and $ap \in AP$, we let $\mathsf{permitted}(ap, AP, st_i) = true$ if ap is permitted when it is attempted. Otherwise, $\mathsf{permitted}(ap, AP, st_i) = false$.

An *obligation-abiding* transition corresponds to the system evolution where subjects take actions (*i.e.*, contribute actions to AP) only to fulfill their obligations. A sequence of valid obligation-abiding transitions corresponds to the situation where subjects are diligent and always fulfill their obligations. An obligation-abiding transition is *valid* if no pending obligations in st_i become violated in st_{i+1}.

4 Accountability

Since obligations are unenforceable, a system can never guarantee that an obligation will be fulfilled. What a system *can* seek to ensure is that all obligations *could* be fulfilled if the obligated user is diligent. Roughly speaking, what we want is that the only reason that an obligation will go unfulfilled is due to negligence on the part of a user, not because of insufficient privileges or resources.

If performing a requested action would cause some user to incur an obligation they could not fulfill, the system should deny that action. Conversely, if the user will

---

[1] Σ would certainly be instantiated in any concrete model.

have sufficient privileges to fulfill the obligation, then the system should allow the requested action. However, it is not obvious what the appropriate behavior should be if the ability of the user to perform the obligation depends on whether or not other actions are taken which change his privileges.

In [9], we propose a concept we call *accountability* as a more satisfactory obligation-security notion. Intuitively, if all users will have sufficient privileges and resource to carry out their obligations provided every other user diligently carries out his or her obligations (and no other actions are performed), then we say the system is in an *accountable state*. Starting from an accountable state, if no actions are initiated other than existing obligations being diligently carried out, then the first obligation that becomes violated must be due to lack of diligence on the part of the obligated subject, and that subject should be assigned the blame.

Notice that if at some point the system is in an accountable state and then transitions to a new state through diligent obligation fulfillment, the new state is also accountable. However, when actions are requested that are not required by an existing obligation, to remain in an accountable state, the system needs to analyze the would-be effect of the action on accountability. Once the system determines whether the resulting state will be accountable or not, it can permit or deny the action accordingly.

Definition 1. Let st be a system state with time $st.t = t$ and pending obligations $st.B = \{b_1, \ldots, b_n\}$. We say st is a *type-1 undesirable state* if there exists $B' \subseteq \{b \in st.B | b.t_s \leq t \leq b.t_e\}$ and, letting $AP' = \{(b.s, b.a, b.O) | b \in B'\}$, there exists $ap \in AP'$ such that $\mathsf{permitted}(ap, AP', st) = \{false\}$.

A state is type-1 undesirable if a subject cannot fulfill an obligation although the current time is within the time window of the obligation.

Definition 2. A state st is *strongly accountable* if there exists no sequence of valid obligation-abiding transitions that lead st to a type-1 undesirable state.

5 Fault Assessment

An aspect of obligation systems which we wish to automate is the assessment of fault. When an obligation failure occurs, we wish to know which party is at fault for that failure. The first question to examine is whether or not the user to whom the obligation was assigned possessed the necessary privileges and resources to carry out the obligation. If he did, then he is at fault for the failed obligation. If, however, he did not, it is likely that someone else is at fault.

One possibility is that the fault lies with the system. If an obligation is assigned to a user who is unable to fulfill it, this may be because the system failed to adequately ensure that needed permissions would be available to the user. However, if the system achieved an accountable state at some point between the assignment of the obligation and the obligation failure, then we know that this cannot be the case.

Instead, the fault lies with one or more other users for failing to fulfill their own obligations. We do not, however, assume that the system achieves an accountable state all the time. Because of the nature of obligations, we do assume that the system is making some attempt to achieve an accountable state, but the fault analysis does not depend on such a state ever being achieved.

Failing to fulfill an obligation can potentially result in other users lacking needed privileges. As such, a single failure can sometimes result in a cascade of obligation failures and some of the failures can have quite serious consequences. However, modeling and understanding the dependencies between different obligations turns out to be quite difficult.

In traditional (that is, non-automated) obligation systems, the assignment of fault for failures is often carried out by examining the events surrounding the failures and doing a postmortem analysis. Such an analysis often factors in a variety of facts concerning responsibility such as who was assigned a task, who was able to do it, and what communication there was concerning the task. Ideally we would do a similar postmortem analysis in our automated system. But simple information about which obligations were assigned to which users is not going to be sufficient. Given a series of failed obligations, an automated tool may be able to determine which obligations, had they been fulfilled, would have satisfied the preconditions of other failed obligations. However, this information alone is not adequate to determine where the fault lay.

Example 1. Let us consider, for instance, a situation in which there are three users, Alice, Bob and Carol, such that each of these users has an obligation, and Carol cannot fulfill her obligation unless at least one of Alice and Bob fulfills theirs. If neither Alice nor Bob fulfill their obligations and, as a result, Carol fails hers, are Alice and Bob both equally at fault? The answer depends on further information of the circumstances. If Alice's job was specifically to make sure that Carol has what she needs, but Bob's task only enabled Carol as an incidental side-effect, then the responsibility would fall more on Alice. If, instead, Alice was known to be very busy and Bob was given the task in order to ensure that it got done even if Alice could not do it, then the responsibility would fall more on Bob. Further, if Bob had told Alice that he would do it and that she did not have to worry about Carol failing if Alice failed her obligation, then clearly the fault in Carol's failure would be Bob's. As such, it is clear that issues of responsibility and fault are more complex than simply determining if an action will cause a precondition to be satisfied.

Any postmortem analysis of the responsibility for failures would need to include information about the policies, intents of the policies, communication between parties, and other factors. Such analysis is certainly possible, but it would be very difficult, if not impossible to automate.

As such, we instead propose solving the basic problem of determining responsibility by tracking responsibility in an active, on-line fashion rather than attempting to determine it after the fact. Because responsibility is tied into the intent behind the assignment of obligations, we propose a policy-driven system for responsibility tracking. Instead of attempting to discover, afterwards, who could have prevented the situation, we propose to keep track ahead of time of what the consequences of an obligation failure are.

What we propose is a module in an obligation management system which keeps track of which obligations bear responsibility for which other obligations. Essentially, the module will keep a directed graph of responsibility, indicating which obligations are responsible for which other obligations. As obligations are fulfilled and discharged, and as other circumstances change, this module should update the graph to reflect changes in responsibility.

The responsibility information in the module will serve as a means of determining fault both after the fact and before the fact. For example, users can consult the module to better understand the implications of their actions, in case there are circumstances where they only have time to fulfill one of the obligations assigned to them.

Because, as we demonstrated above, there are a variety of different possible intents behind the assignment of obligations, we wish to allow for a policy which describes what the assignment of responsibility should be. In other words, this policy specifies, given an obligation b, what other obligations are considered responsible to provide the necessary privileges and resources to b.

Such a responsibility assignment policy is application specific. In practice, we would like to have policies that consist of one general rule and some special-case exceptions. That way, instead of having to imagine every possible situation and write a policy for it, the administrator could choose a default policy and then worry about specifying more specific policy rules only for exceptional cases. For example, if both obligations b_1 and b_2 provides the same needed privileges for obligation b, the administrator may determine that in general the early one of b_1 and b_2 is responsible for b. The administrator may further specify the special situations where this general rule does not apply.

5.1 Desirable Properties

Although we have argued that fault assessment is not simply about knowing which obligations enable which other obligations, the dependencies between obligations play an important role in determining fault. Intuitively, if two obligations are entirely independent of each other, then the failure of one should not be blamed on the failure of the other in any circumstance. Similarly, if one is completely, directly, and solely dependent on another obligation, then clearly the failure of the later one should be blamed on the failure of the earlier one.

These two properties effectively form an upper and lower bound for dependency relationships between pairs of obligations. We do not expect that the majority of pairs of obligations will have one of these two properties. Rather we expect that most will live in the great grey area in the middle, where responsibility is unclear. This is why we later describe the specifics of a policy-driven fault assessment engine. But for pairs of obligations which do have one of these two properties, obviously our system should properly assign responsibility or the lack of it. We say a responsibility assignment policy is *valid* if the above two properties are preserved. As such, we aim to formalize the two properties so that we can prove that a given policy is valid. For this purpose, we introduce the following notations to facilitate our discussion.

Let us assume that we have some set of obligations B, a start time, t_0, and a set of possible future times, T, such that for all $t \in T, t > t_0$. For convenience below we augment each obligation $b = obl(s,a,O,t_s,t_e) \in B$ with a version of the function permitted, denoted b.permitted, that is specialized to b. The type of this function is b.permitted : $\mathscr{FP}(\mathscr{S} \times \mathscr{A} \times \mathscr{O}^*) \times \mathscr{ST} \to \{true,false\}$. Given a set of actions AP to be executed in state st such that $(b.s, b.a, b.O) \in AP$, b.permitted$(AP, st) =$ permitted$((b.s, b.a, b.O), AP, st)$.

Definition 3. A *schedule* of obligations in B is a function $H : B \to T \bigcup \{null\}$ in which $H(b) = t$ means that b is performed at time t. If $H(b) = null$ for some obligation $b \in B$, this means that in schedule H, b is not fulfilled.

We also define a helper function $AP(H,t) = \{b | H(b) = t\}$. In our obligation system, all transitions are deterministic. As such, given a start state, st_0 at some time t_0, any schedule H over B uniquely defines a sequence of states $st_H(t)$, defined by letting the action plan at any time t be the set of actions associated with the obligations in $AP(H,t)$. Note that if an action plan includes obligations whose conditions are not met, the system will reject them, and as such, they will not affect future system states.

A schedule is considered to be *valid* for B, st_0, and t_0 if for all $b \in B$, $(b$.permitted$(AP(H,H(b)), st_H(H(b))) = true$ and $b.t_s \leq H(b) \leq b.t_e)$ or $H(b) = null$. Intuitively, in a valid schedule, the action of each obligation is authorized to be performed at the scheduled time.

Given two schedules, H_1 and H_2, where H_1 is defined over some set of obligations B_1 and H_2 is defined over some $B_2 \subseteq B_1$, we define $H_1 \sim H_2$ to be the schedule H' such that $H'(b) = H_2(b)$ when $b \in B_2$ and $H'(b) = H_1(b)$ otherwise. For example, suppose we have two schedules $H_1 = ((b_1, 10), (b_2, 20), (b_3, 30), (b_4, 40))$ and $H_2 = ((b_2, 35), (b_3, 25))$. Then $H_1 \sim H_2 = (((b_1, 10), (b_3, 25), (b_2, 35), (b_4, 40))$.

Also for convenience, we denote by $H^{B,t}$ the schedule defined over B such that $H^{B,t}(b) = t$ for all $b \in B$. That is, given a set of obligations B, $H^{B,t}$ is the schedule that says that all the obligations in B happens at time t.

5.1.1 Not Responsible For

The first property we call *not responsible for*, which captures the concept that obligations are completely unrelated to each other.

Formally, we say an obligation b_1 is *not responsible for* another obligation b_2 at some time t_0, if given any valid schedule H over B such that

1. $H(b_1) \neq null$; and
2. for $H' = H \sim H^{\{b_1\},null}$, it is the case that for all t', $b_2.t_s \leq t' \leq b_2.t_e$, $\neg b_2$.permitted$(AP(H,t'), st_H(t')) \vee b_2$.permitted$(AP(H,t'), st_{H'}(t'))$.

To summarize, b_1 is not responsible for b_2 if there is no valid schedule H in which b_1 happens, such that b_2 can happen in H, but such that b_2 cannot happen if H is modified so that b_1 does not occur. Specifically, we compare H to a schedule just like H except that we remove b_1 from it, which means that b_1 does not occur and neither does any obligation whose condition is invalidated by the removal of b_1 from the schedule. So, if there exists any schedule for which whether or not b_1 happens has a negative outcome on whether or not b_2 can happen, then we do not say anything about b_1's responsibility for b_2. But if no such schedule exists, then we say that b_1 is not responsible for b_2.

5.1.2 Definitely Responsible For

There also exists the converse idea. If an obligation is always fundamental to another obligation, then clearly it should be responsible for that obligation.

Formally, we say that an obligation b_1 is *definitely responsible for* another obligation b_2, if both of the following hold:

1. For all valid schedule H defined over B such that $H(b_1) \neq null$, let $H' = H \sim H^{\{b_1\}.null}$. Then for all t' such that $b_2.t_s \leq t' \leq b_2.t_e$, $b_2.\mathsf{permitted}(st_{H'}(t'), AP(H', t'))$ is false.
2. There exists some valid schedule H defined over B where $H(b_1) \neq null$, such that for all t' such that $b_2.t_s \leq t' \leq b_2.t_e$, $b_2.\mathsf{permitted}(st_H(t'), AP(H, t'))$ is true.

To summarize in a plainer language, an obligation b_1 is definitely responsible for another obligation b_2 if there is no way that b_2 can happen when b_1 does not happen, and there is at least some case in which b_2 can happen when b_1 does. The second condition is needed because we do not want to blame b_1 for b_2 in circumstances in which there is no way that b_2 can occur.

5.2 Fault Assessment

Because we wish to discover who was at fault when an obligation failure occurs, we need to keep track of which obligations are responsible for enabling which other obligations. In order to do so, we represent responsibility using a directed graph. Each node in the graph corresponds to an obligation. There is an edge in the graph from obligations b_1 to obligation b_2 if and only if b_1 is considered to be responsible for b_2.

If our assignments of responsibility are reasonable, then it should be the case that any obligation depends only on obligations which are before it. It is worthwhile to note that if this property holds, then it will be the case that our graph is acyclic. This is a desirable property since if our graph contains cycles, we could wind up blaming an obligation's failure for causing itself to fail, which is not quite sensible.

When there is an obligation failure, we can then use this graph to determine who was responsible for the failure. In order to do so, we use an algorithm which traces backwards following the links of responsibility in reverse, in order to figure out which failed obligations are to blame for this failure.

The algorithm uses a working set, K, which contains obligations which are potentially at fault and produces an output set, L, of obligations which are at fault. The initial failed obligation is designated as b. The algorithm assumes the existence of sufficient logs to check things such as what the system state, st, was at different times, which we will designate as $st(t)$, and whether or not particular obligations were carried out. The action plan which was executed at any particular time t is represented as $AP(t)$.

1. $K := \{b\}, L := \emptyset$
2. If K is empty, terminate.
3. Select an obligation b' from K, $K := K - \{b'\}$
4. Using the system logs, check when b'.permitted was true.

   a. If
      b'.permitted$(st_t, AP(t) \bigcup \{b'\})$
      is true for all t such that $b'.t_s \leq t \leq b'.t_e$, then
      $L := L \bigcup \{b'\}$ and go to step 2.

5. Let F be the set of all obligations which have edges which point to b' and which failed.
6. $K := K \bigcup F$
7. Goto step 2.

In essence, we simply move backwards through the graph, looking at each obligation which could be responsible. For each obligation, if its condition was true, then it must be the case that it was simply not done by the user to which it was assigned. As such, we need not seek anyone further to blame for it. However, if its condition was false, then the access control policy would prevent it from happening, thus it is not the fault of the user to which the obligation was assigned. Instead, we must look to the obligations which are responsible for that obligation and see which of those failed, and in turn determine who was at fault for those.

It should be noted that it is possible that in some case the algorithm above could return an empty, L set, indicating that no one is to blame. For instance, if an obligation did not have the permissions it needed to happen, but all of the other obligations responsible for it occurred. At first, this could be seen as a failing of the analysis, but instead it is an indicator which tells us that the system made a mistake. Most likely this will occur when there is an obligation in the system which is simply not able to be completed.

Even if a system strives to maintain an accountable state, it may be the case that obligation failures push it out of that state. And then difficult decisions may need to be made weighing the goal of returning to accountability against the overall goals of the obligation policies. This may potentially result in the assignment of obligations which cannot be fulfilled or obligations which interfere with the fulfillment of other obligations.

An empty L set could also indicate that the responsibility analysis has not identified all obligations which should have been considered responsible. As we will outline in the next section, the assignment of responsibility is a task which depends on the specifics of a system, and as such cannot be described only in terms of the meta-model. Generally speaking, we expect that responsibility assignment will not be algorithmically difficult, but there are theoretical systems for which it could be quite difficult. As such, there may be some situations where responsibility assignment would be approximated, resulting in occasional mistakes in exchange for greater efficiency.

5.3 Responsibility Assignment

Given a set of obligations, we wish to analyze them and form some assignment of responsibility. There is a great deal of flexibility in assigning the responsibility, but there are three properties which the assignment should meet. The first one is that no obligation should depend on an obligation which comes after it. The second two are based on our properties above. If, at the time that we are assigning responsibility, b_1 is not responsible for b_2 according to the definition presented in the previous section, then b_1 should not be assigned responsibility for b_2. If, at the time that we are assigning responsibility, b_1 is definitely responsible for b_2 according to the definition presented in the previous section, then b_1 should be assigned responsibility for b_2.

However, the reverse may not be true as it is possible that for one obligation there is no obligation definitely responsible for it. For instance, in example 1, since both Alice's and Bob's obligations can enable Carol's, according to our definition, neither of them are definitely responsible for Carol's obligation. In this situation, depending on the policy, the system may choose one of Alice's and Bob's obligations to be responsible for Carol's.

As a result, there are likely many different ways to assign responsibility which meet all three of the properties outlined above. In this paper we are going to present an algorithm which can be adjusted to form a variety of different basic policies. Unfortunately, the first step of this algorithm is not something which can be generally applied to any system which fits the meta-model. Instead, if must be done in a system-specific way and there do exist specific systems for which the step cannot be done. However, it is our belief that the step can be accomplished in many practical systems in reasonable time. To back-up our argument, we describe how to perform this step in a concrete example system in the next section.

This first step is as follows: given a set of outstanding obligations B and a particular obligation b, find a set of subsets of B, which we will call $N(b)$, that has the following properties:

1. In any schedule for which at least one member of each set occurs, then b will be permitted.

2. There exists a schedule in which all the obligations from any one set do not occur, but all other obligations occur, in which b is not permitted.

Intuitively, each set in $N(b)$ is a set of obligations which collectively supply some needed permission or resource. Once we have a set of subsets of B which has such a property, then we are going to choose precisely one member of each subset to be considered responsible. Because there may be some subsets which overlap, it should be noted that the number of subsets only forms an upper bound for the number of responsible obligations. There are a number of different ways in which the particular member can be selected, and these reflect different policies, as we discuss later.

However, whatever choice we make, our choice will satisfy the three properties outlined earlier. The proofs that this is the case have been omitted for reasons of space. However, this still leaves the question of how efficiently $N(b)$ can be found. As the determination of $N(b)$ is system specific, we cannot argue that it will be efficient in all systems, however we believe that it will be able to be computed efficiently in many real-world systems. In section 6, we demonstrate a system in which it is possible to follow our algorithm because the $N(b)$ can be computed efficiently.

As we have shown above, in our algorithm there is a lot of room for flexibility concerning how we select the specific obligation which is considered to be responsible. So long as at least one obligation from every set in $N(b)$ is selected, then the system is guaranteed to satisfy the principles outlined. As such, we can use any policy we want to select the obligations, for example, oldest obligation, smallest covering set, or highest ranking user, and still be guaranteed that the properties will hold.

6 A Concrete Example

Lets us now consider how fault assessment would work in a more concrete system. Specifically, we will use a system based on the Access Matrix Model. We first introduced this system in [9], but we will summarize it here.

In our concrete model, Σ, the set of abstract states, is instantiated to be $\mathcal{M} = 2^{\mathcal{S} \times \mathcal{O} \times \mathcal{R}}$, the set of permission sets, in which $\mathcal{R}$ is a set of access rights subjects can have on objects. We denote permission sets by M and individual permissions by $m = (s, o, r)$. Each permission is a triple consisting of a subject, an object, and an access right, and signifies that the subject has the right on the object.

Actions are also modified so as to operate on permission sets. Each action $a \in \mathcal{A}$ performs a finite sequence of operations that each either add or remove a single permission from the permission set ($grant(m)$ and $revoke(m)$). Clearly, a subject or an object with no associated permissions has no effect on the system, so we assume that in every state st, an object or a subject exists in $st.O$ and/or $st.S$ if and only if it occurs in some permission in the permission set $st.M$.

Policy rule conditions consist of a Boolean combination of permission tests ($m \in M_{cur}$ or $m \notin M_{cur}$) expressed in conjunctive normal form.

6.1 Responsibility Assignment

In order to run the responsibility assignment algorithm for an obligation b, we need to be able to compute $N(b)$. Here we present the algorithm for doing so. Our condition for a given obligation is in conjunctive normal form. Each conjunct (that is, each disjunction) logically corresponds to a set in $N(b)$, and that is, in fact, how we build our sets.

For each conjunct, which we consider to be a set of permissions, we first check to see if the conjunct is guaranteed to be true under any schedule. If it is, then it does not need a set. The first step is to see if any permission and its opposite are both tested for in our conjunct. If they are, then we are done, since $m \vee \neg m$ is a tautology. Assuming that this isn't the case, then we have some distinct set of permission tests.

In what follows, we treat each permission test as being a positive test. We do this without loss of generality since we can convert any negative test to a positive test by reversing its presence in the current state (that is, adding it if it is not there and removing it if it is) and changing all grants into revokes and vice versa. So, for simplicity, we treat all tests in a given conjunct as positive, and hence represent the tests as a set of permissions, $M = \{m_1, ..., m_n\}$, but it is not the case that we are actually assuming them to be positive.

Since each test is distinct from the others, our conjunct is only guaranteed to be true if at least one of the needed permissions already exists in the system, and no existing obligation can remove it without adding another permission we need. So, in order to find this, we simply check our needed permissions against existing permissions in the system. If none of our needed permissions are already present, then we know that the truth of our conjunct cannot be guaranteed, so we move to the next step which is described in the next paragraph. If we find some of our needed permissions to be present, then we check for obligations which would revoke them which come before b or overlap b. If we do not find any such obligations, then we know that our conjunct is true, and hence, does not need a set in $H(b)$, and we move on to the next conjunct. If we do find any such obligations which do this then we have to examine whether or not they grant another permission which we need. If they do not, then we know that our conjunct is not guaranteed to be true, and we go to the next step. If they do, then we have to repeat these checks for the new permission, considering potential revoking obligations which overlap with our granting obligations or which fall between them and b. If we do not find any sequence of obligations which can result in needed permissions being revoked without corresponding ones being granted, then we are not guaranteed, and we continue to the next step, constructing our set for $N(b)$.

Given our set of obligations B and our set of needed permissions, we first exclude any obligations which overlap with or come after b. We then define an output set, which we'll call N' and a candidate set which we'll call C. Both sets are initially empty. Then we examine each obligation which grants a needed permission. If no obligation which revokes that same right overlaps it or comes after it, then we add the obligation to N'. If not, then we examine the obligations that might revoke the right it needs. If all such obligations also grant a right needed, then we add our obligation to C, and note which obligation or obligations interfere with it (that is, overlap it or come afterwards and revoke the granted permission).

Once we have completed this process for all permissions, we revisit our candidate set. If there are any obligations in C which are being interfered with by obligations which are not in $C \bigcup N'$, then remove we them from C. We repeat this process until all obligations which remain in C are interfered with only by other obligations in $C \bigcup N'$. Then our final set is $C \bigcup N'$.

We know that any set created using this process has the two needed properties. Firstly, we know that if any one obligation occurs in our set occurs, then our condition will be satisfied. Secondly, we know that if all the other obligations happen and all of the ones in the set fail to occur, then there is a schedule for which the condition for b will not be satisfied. This schedule is the one in which any grants in obligations which we did not select happen prior to the revokes. We know that this is a valid schedule because every grant which came after the last revoke is in our set and because when a system is strongly accountable, any two overlapping obligations must be able to happen in either order.

7 Conclusion

In this paper, we introduce the problem of blame assignment in obligation management, and discuss why straightforward approaches to blame assignment are not feasible. We present an alternate general approach to blame assignment and formalize two properties which any blame assignment algorithm should meet. We further present a general algorithm for assigning blame, and prove that it has the requisite properties. We presented a number of different specific policies which could be used with the general algorithm, and demonstrate that the algorithm was workable on at least some realistic real-world systems by demonstrating how it would work on one particular system which instantiates the metamodel.

This work is part of a larger project to develop a comprehensive study of obligation-management systems. Assuming users are diligent, we already know how, in certain kinds of systems, to preserve accountability. With this paper we also know how to assign blame when users are not diligent. In the future we plan, among other things, to study methods of restoring the system to an accountable state when users are not diligent.

References

1. C. Bettini, S. Jajodia, X. S. Wang, and D. Wijesekera. Provisions and obligations in policy management and security applications. In *VLDB*, Hong Kong, China, Aug. 2002. IEEE Computer Society Press.

2. C. Bettini, S. Jajodia, X. S. Wang, and D. Wijesekera. Obligation monitoring in policy management. In *IEEE International Workshop on Policies for Distributed Systems and Networks (POLICY 2003)*, Lake Como, Italy, June 2003. IEEE Computer Society Press.
3. C. Bettini, S. Jajodia, X. S. Wang, and D. Wijesekera. Provisions and obligations in policy rule management. *J. Network Syst. Manage.*, 11(3):351–372, 2003.
4. H. Chockler and J. Halpern. Responsibility and Blame: A Structural-Model Approach. *Journal of Artifical Intelligence Research*, 22:93–115, 2004.
5. D. Damianou, N. Dulay, E. Lupu, and M. Sloman. The Ponder Policy Specification Language. In *2nd International Workshop on Policies for Distributed Systems and Networks*, Bristol, UK, Jan. 2001. Springer-Verlag.
6. P. Gama and P. Ferreira. Obligation policies: An enforcement platform. In *6th IEEE International Workshop on Policies for Distributed Systems and Networks (POLICY 2005)*, Stockholm, Sweden, June 2005. IEEE Computer Society.
7. D. Grossi, F. Dignum, L. Royakkers, and J. Meyer. Collective Obligations and Agents: Who Gets the Blame? In *International Workshop on Deontic Logic in Computer Science*, Madeira, Portugal, May 2004.
8. M. Hilty, D. A. Basin, and A. Pretschner. On obligations. In *ESORICS*, pages 98–117, 2005.
9. K. Irwin, T. Yu, and W. Winsborough. On the Modeling and Analysis of Obligations. In *ACM Conference on Computer and Communications Security (CCS)*, Alexandria, VA, Oct. 2006.
10. L. Kagal, T. W. Finin, and A. Joshi. A policy language for a pervasive computing environment. In *IEEE International Workshop on Policies for Distributed Systems and Networks (POLICY 2003)*, Lake Como, Italy, June 2003. IEEE Computer Society.
11. P. McNamara. Deontic Logic, 2006. Stanford Encyclopedia of Phylosophy. Available at http://plato.stanford.edu/entries/logic-deontic/.
12. M. C. Mont. A System to Handle Privacy Obligations in Enterprises. Technical Report HPL-2005-180, HP Labs - Research, 2005. Available at http://www.hpl.hp.com/techreports/2005/HPL-2005-180.html.
13. M. C. Mont and R. Thyne. A Systemic Approach to Automate Privacy Policy Enforcement in Enterprises. Technical Report HPL-2006-51, HP Labs - Research, 2006. Available at http://www.hpl.hp.com/techreports/2006/HPL-2006-51.html.
14. C. Riberiro, A. Zuquete, P. Ferreira, and P. Guedes. SPL: An Access Control Language for Security Policies and Complex Constraints. In *Network and Distributed System Security Symposium (NDSS)*, San Diego, CA, Feb. 2001.
15. M. Sailer and M. Morciniec. Monitoring and execution for contract compliance. Technical Report TR 2001-261, HP Labs, 2001.
16. R. Sandhu and P. Samarati. Authentication, Access Control, and Audit. *ACM Computing Survey*, 28(1), Mar. 1996.
17. V. Swarup, L. Seligman, and A. Rosenthal. Specifying Data Sharing Agreements. In *IEEE Workshop on Policies for Distributed Systems and Networks (POLICY)*, London, Ontario Canada, June 2006.
18. X. TC. Oasis extensible access control markup language (xacml). *http://www.oasis-open.org/committees/xacml/*.
19. A. Uszok, J. M. Bradshaw, R. Jeffers, N. Suri, P. J. Hayes, M. R. Breedy, L. Bunch, M. Johnson, S. Kulkarni, and J. Lott. Kaos policy and domain services: Toward a description-logic approach to policy representation, deconfliction, and enforcement. In *IEEE International Workshop on Policies for Distributed Systems and Networks (POLICY 2003)*, Lake Como, Italy, June 2003. IEEE Computer Society Press.

Role- and Relationship-Based Identity Management for Private yet Accountable E-Learning

Mohd Anwar and Jim Greer

Abstract In every communicative context, each participant assumes some kind of role and negotiates some type of relationship with their counterparts. In the e-learning domain, the roles (e.g. instructor, learner, marker, administrator, etc.) for participants are well structured and relationships (e.g. one-to-one, one-to-many, hierarchical, etc.) among roles are relatively predictable. This paper proposes role-based and relationship-based identity management in the e-learning domain to enable participants to enjoy a desired amount of privacy and to hold participants accountable for their actions. In this approach, a role-based identity hides an actor in the crowd of actors with same roles, and a relationship-based identity allows an actor to disclose information appropriate for a respective relationship. Moreover, public roles (e.g. instructor in a course, disciplinary committee in a department, etc.) are assigned guarantor privileges to sanction foul acting and to facilitate usage control over disclosed information.

1 INTRODUCTION

Historically, privacy is a relatively minor concern in a close knit group like a learning community, where each participant carries one embodied identity. The bodily presence works as the guarantee of authenticity of a participant, which makes the participant more trustworthy and accountable towards other participants. On the other hand, since the participants in e-learning may not carry their embodied identities, identity thefts, social engineering attacks, or man-in-the-middle attacks

Mohd Anwar
ARIES Laboratory, Computer Science, University of Saskatchewan, Saskatoon, SK, CANADA
e-mail: mohd.anwar@usask.ca

Jim Greer
ARIES Laboratory, Computer Science, University of Saskatchewan, Saskatoon, SK, CANADA
e-mail: jim.greer@usask.ca

Please use the following format when citing this chapter:

Anwar, M. and Greer, J., 2008, in IFIP International Federation for Information Processing, Volume 263; *Trust Management II*; Yücel Karabulut, John Mitchell, Peter Herrmann, Christian Damsgaard Jensen; (Boston: Springer), pp. 343–358 are more likely to happen in e-learning environments. Even though privacy issues in e-learning are very different from a traditional classroom [1], classroom-based views about privacy are often extrapolated to e-learning. As a result, actors in an e-learning environment retain little privacy and are susceptible to threats ranging from annoying spam attacks to more serious identity frauds.

The realization that online learning brings together participants with a wide range of goals, attitudes and ethical stances, raises concerns about the safety of participants who fail to protect their privacy. E-learners are becoming more perceptive about the privacy implications of their online activities. Borcea et al. point out that privacy requirements are obviously important for e-learning, since they establish an unbiased environment without prejudice or favoritism [2]. A learner should be able to act under different pseudo-identities or, when possible, anonymously. The separation of activities from identity encourages learners to be unrestricted and allows them to learn without pressure.

For reasons similar to those in other domains, privacy is very valuable in the e-learning domain. Privacy protects learners from being mis-defined and judged out of context [4]. For example, the conversation between two co-learners is less guarded than that of the conversation between a learner and an instructor. It may be inappropriate for an instructor to judge a learner based on the learner's conversation with their co-learners in a discussion forum. Westin identifies the following four functions that privacy performs for us: Personal Autonomy, Emotional Release, Self-Evaluation, and Limited and Protected Communications [10]. We see these functions as equally important for the participants in e-learning. Privacy provides autonomy to learners while a threat to autonomy puts an individual under the control of those who know that individual's secrets. Privacy provides moments of "off stage," when the individual can be tender, angry, irritable, frustrated, or dream-filled. In the learning process, it is natural for a learner to be sometimes frustrated, overwhelmed, or dissatisfied with learning objects or instructors. These moments of "off stage". may emerge in conversations among a group of close friends or in a personal blog. Privacy is essential for carrying on self-evaluation and other reflective activities. Learners should be able to play with their seminal or inchoate ideas and verify them with trusted peers or mentors without fear of being ridiculed. Learners should have opportunities to share confidences and intimacies with their trusted colleagues— a close friend, a graduate supervisor, etc. As in any online domain, concerns for privacy of its participants are growing in the e-learning domain. However, in online learning, little consideration is given to privacy and security. Privacy-related research for the e-learning domain is inadequate, and the majority of approaches aim at addressing only learners' privacy. An e-learning system involves participants of various roles designed to participate in various types of relationships in various contexts, including peer coaches, markers, tutors, and other learning support staff. Therefore, privacy concerns of every participant are important and need to be addressed. In that vein, a role-based or a relationship-based solution can cater to privacy needs for participants of any role or relationship.

Each context explicitly or implicitly manifests some purpose for its participants. Based on the purpose, a participant assumes an appropriate role or engages in a relationship. A role can be defined as an expected behaviour attached to the position of an individual in a community. For example, in a learning community, an individual in a teaching role is expected to set learning objectives, give lectures, evaluate students' performance, etc. Likewise, an individual in a basic learner role is expected to enroll in a course and undertake course related activities like attending lectures, asking questions, participating in course evaluation, etc. A relationship is a specific connection manifested in individualized interaction between two roles. For example, in an advisor-advisee relationship, a teacher engages in personalized communication with a student for guiding the student during their academic career. Or, an individual in a student role may engage in a peer relationship with a lab-partner drawn from individuals of the same role (student) in a specific course context.

In the e-learning domain, the number of contexts including the number of roles and relationship types (among roles) for each context are relatively few, and information sharing needs for each role or relationship can be anticipated. As a result, a role- and relationship-based identity management approach effectively partitions an identity into multiple partial identities for the purpose of various contexts, roles, and relationships. Partitioning of identity contributes to information parsimony which, in turn, contributes to privacy. For example, a graduate student holds multiple partial identities based on the role they play: a student, a tutor, an instructor or a marker. In the context of a course in which a student acts in a teaching role, their student id number may be extraneous information whereas in the context of a course in which that student acts in a registrant role, their employee id may be irrelevant.

In a role-based identity, say "student", each actor sharing this role would be identified only by their role (e.g. SomeStudent). A role-based identity allows a participant to be indistinguishable from the other participants of the same role. A relationship-based identity, on the other hand, has one or more of the actors identifiable by a pseudonym rather than by their true identity (e.g. Student23 or Henry). This allows one participant to hold a privacy-preserving relationship with another participant. Since, in every context, each role-based identity (e.g. SomeStudent) serves an actor's purpose in a specific role (e.g. student), and each relationship-based identity (e.g. Student23) serves an actor's purpose in a specific relationship (e.g. lab-partner), any disclosed information is only associable to an identity during the duration of its pertinent role or relationship. When a piece of information is no longer associable to an identity, in effect, that piece of information expires. For example, student23 may accidentally reveal to his lab-partner Bob that he is diagnosed to have HIV. As soon as Bob's relationship with his lab-partner ends, the lab-partner's relationship-based identity with pseudonym student23 expires and this information is no longer associable to an identity. At that point, Bob only knows that some student of his class has HIV. However, privacy without accountability is counter-productive. When innocuous behaviours or relatively minor offenses of an individual ought to be forgotten, their malicious behaviours or serious offenses ought to be tracked. For that reason, public roles (e.g. instructor in a course, disciplinary committee in a department, etc.) are assigned guarantor privileges to connect pseudonyms with actual identities, to sanction foul acting and to authorize usage control over disclosed information.

2 ROLES, RELATIONSHIPS, AND CONTEXTS IN E-LEARNING ENVIRONMENT

Participants of an e-learning system assume following basic kinds of roles: learner, instructor, instructional support, and administrator. In various contexts, each participants of an e-learning environment engages in the following type of relationships: one-to-one, one-to-many, many-to-many, and hierarchical. In a one-to-one relationship, two participants want to be identifiable to each other and distinguishable from other participants. In a one-to-one relationship, the participants share personal information warranted by the role and purpose of the one-to-one relationship. In a one-to-many relationship, a participant wants to communicate with a group of actors in the same manner. In a one-to-many relationship, for example, an instructor in a course wants to inform all the course registrants about course materials. For this kind of purpose, the entire class usually carries a group identity. A many-to-many relationship can be broken into two one-to-many relationships: in a student-instructor many-to-many relationship, a student enrolls in multiple courses and an instructor teaches multiple courses in a semester. A hierarchical relationship serves to define a hierarchy. For example, a student in a marker role grades other students' work. An instructor working as a department head supervises other instructors.

In e-learning, one context cascades into another more finely-grained context attaching a dimension of direction to a role. The roles acting on the most generic context are omni-directional: the most public presentation of the self of a participant. On the other hand, the roles acting on the most specific context are uni-directional: the most private presentation of the self of a participant. In every context, participants of different roles form various types of relationships among themselves. Each context and all the roles or relationships therein have temporal dimensions. For example, when a student enrolls in a course, their role as a registrant of that course or their relationship with the TA for the evaluation context ends as the course ends. The notion of a relationship is dynamic as it evolves from one interaction to the next.

3 ROLE-BASED AND RELATIONSHIP-BASED IDENTITY MANAGEMENT IN E-LEARNING

In this paper, we employ a purpose-based and recursive notion of context in the e-learning domain (shown in Figure 1). For a well-defined purpose, each participant creates a context by assuming some type of role and negotiating some type of relationship. Each context exists until its underpinning purpose is achieved. Since each role or relationship is contextual, any role or relationship is not valid any longer than that of the relevant context. A context may spawn another more granular context, which in turn may spawn yet another context and so on. A context rewinds all its descendant contexts before it comes to an end. A participant in a context may use either their context-specific temporal (i.e. until the context lives) identity or more generic identity from any of its progenitor contexts. For example, in a Computer Science course context, a student may use their context-specific role-based identity of type "course registrant", or the student may choose to use more generic role-based identity of type "CMPT-major" from the degree context (i.e. progenitor of the course context).

In building a role and relationship-based identity management system, we have identified the following tasks: identifying relevant roles for different contexts, crafting role-based identities to be used by each participant of a role, allowing each participant to assume multiple roles as they qualify and to switch between roles, facilitating the creation of relationship-based identities for roles to build justifiable relationships, and allowing a guarantor to link historical data to its owner to make them accountable for their actions. As depicted in the Figure 2 and 3 below, a representative system should facilitate the creation of a context for a purpose (e.g. a course context for the offering of a course CMPT111), roles for various job functions in a context (e.g. a registrant role in the context of Course- CMPT111), and relationships for various job functions among roles (e.g. a supervisor-supervisee relationship between an instructor and a marker role).

After authentication, the system generates a context hierarchy for a user, in which each context-node corresponds to the affiliation of the user in a context. Once roles are identified (i.e. a set of tasks expected of a role to perform in a given context is grouped under a role name), a role-based identity creation involves assigning a user to a pertinent role, generating a role-term pseudonym for the user on the assumption of a role, and creating an identity dataset consisting of only role-specific information. Based on their assumed role within a context, the system should allow one user to choose an appropriate relationship with another user, help a user create a relationship-specific identity dataset, and generate a relationship-term pseudonym for the user to be used in a relationship. For providing awareness cues to a user, the system should display the hierarchy of contexts relevant to them together with their assumed roles and relationships therein.

Even though a role-based identity from one context can be used to all the descendant contexts, a relationship-based identity in one context is irrelevant in another context. For example, instead of using her context-specific pseudonym as a registrant of a course, registrant43, a student may choose to appear as cs37, revealing her affiliation to Computer Science department. Other enrollees of that course would not know whether cs37 is a co-registrant in the respective course, an instructor of this course, or a student in the department who may or may not be enrolled in that course. When cs37 seeks technical writing help from the learning centre and creates a relationship-based identity with a writing help, she reveals more personal information. Due to the temporal dimension of role or relationship, any information released under a role or relationship ought to be virtually unusable for the counterpart when the respective role or relationship expires. Anytime, a participant fears a privacy threat in a relationship-based identity, the participant may abandon their respective relationship-based pseudonymous identity and take refuge in their role-based identity. The participant can negotiate a new relationship at any time and craft a new relationship-based identity.

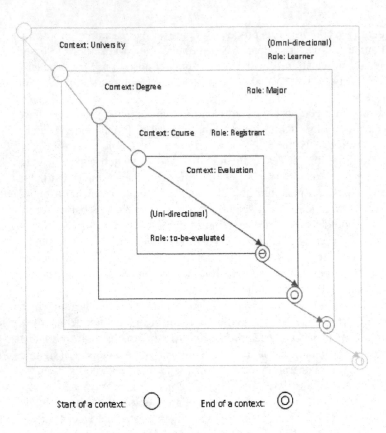

Context: University

(Omni-directional)
Role: Learner

Context: Degree   Role: Major

Context: Course   Role: Registrant

Context: Evaluation

(Uni-directional)

Role: to-be-evaluated

Start of a context: ◯   End of a context: ◎

Fig. 1 Contexts of Various Granularities

Ideally, a relationship-based identity is constrained by the purpose of a relationship, which in turn is constrained by the context of the relationship and contextual
roles of the participants involved in that relationship. A relationship should not blow
the cover of a role, and the identity revealed in a relationship in one context should
not be linkable to another context. Since all the participants in the same role carry
the same role-based identity, the role-based identity approach provides a degree of
anonymity to the participants of a role.

The creation and maintenance of so many role- and relationship- based identities
may seem like daunting tasks for users. However, in an e-learning environment, contexts, roles, and relationships are relatively predictable and well-defined. For each
user account, the system performs context and role assignments providing a default
role-based identity for each role that the user may partake in. The system also enables users to engage in likely relationships (determined by their assumed roles in
respective contexts) and provides relationship-based identities. To help users manage their identities, the system provides awareness to users through visualization
of contexts, roles, relationships and pseudonyms of them and their partners. Addi-

tionally, the system enforces expiration of context, role, or relationship and tracks information for a cause, which is deemed justifiable by a guarantor.

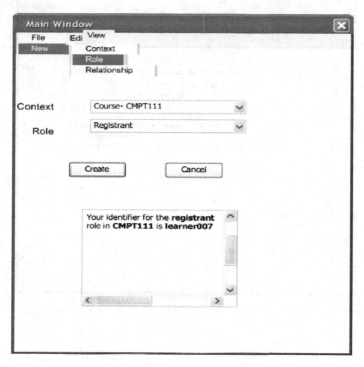

Fig. 2 A Prototype of Role and Relationship Based Identity Management Client

3.1 Example Scenarios

When Alice appears in the freshman orientation of Computer Science Department, her freshman-student role is revealed to the articipants of the program. She may share some comments with the participant sitting next to her. When Alice chooses to befriend that individual, who introduces himself as Bob, she reveals her name to him. Alice and Bob can both uniquely distinguish each other from other freshman Computer Science students. The friendship of Alice and Bob is an example of a relationship. Since one body presents one identity in the physical world, it is hard for Alice to be indistinguishable from other students to Bob. In the disembodied online world, Alice can hide herself in the crowd of fellow students just by choosing her role based pseudonym, A032 (or Abigail or any other unique identifier), and as such have an identity that persists for some time but also remains become indistinguish-

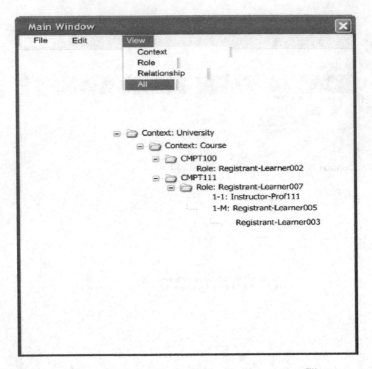

Fig. 3 A Prototype of Role and Relationship Based Identity Management Client

able from other students to Bob. Alice may even renegotiate her relationship with Bob and befriend Bob as A99 (or Antionette).

As shown in Figure 3, a context spawns more granular contexts. For example, Alice wants to go to a college to attain a bachelor's degree. Upon admission, she begins a student context assuming a student role. Her role as a student is the beacon of her identity to the members of the college community. Any member of the college community should at least recognize her as a student of the respective college. As Alice registers in a course for the purpose of fulfilling the course requirements for the degree, she creates another context assuming a role of a registrant (e.g. registrant56). To earn credits from the course, she has to participate in various course-related activities. By participating in each activity, Alice creates even more granular contexts. Each activity may consist of various parts and each part may require building relationships with other actors. Therefore, a context can be presented by an assumed role and relationships built by a participant for a specific purpose. A relationship-based identity (and associated identifier) has to expire by latest the end of the respective role under which the relationship has been initiated. For example, when Alice and Bob want to partner with each other for the group project4 in a course CMPT111, they need to be personable to each other and share each other's schedule, contact information, etc. At the end of the project4, this relationship and the relationship-based identity should expire.

An entity in hierarchical relation may be subjected to prejudice or vindictiveness by the other entities, and therefore, the participants have to be provided with disjoint identities in similar contexts. For example, a 3rd year student Bob bears grudge against a 2nd year student Alice for making derogatory comments about Bob's presentation in the course they took together in the past. As a marker for a course that Alice is currently taking, Bob may act on that grudge against Alice. To prevent this type of situation, Alice's identity from one context (a course) has to be non-linkable to the identity from another related type of context (another course).

3.2 Features of a Role and Relationship Based Identity Management

The privacy solution provided by the proposed role and relationship based identity management is two-fold: on one hand, the role-relationship initiation feature contributes to privacy by constructing contextual identity. On the other hand, forgetting of disclosed information is enforced by the following features: disavowing a relationship, temporal aspect of role and relationship, expiration of context, and disclosure/obligation management. The model also enforces accountability by holding an actor responsible for foul acting through guarantor administered investigation and sanction.

Role-relatonship Initiation: Users are granted membership into roles based on their affiliation to a context in the domain. By taking on an assigned role, an actor assumes an identity warranted by the role. For the purpose of the assumed role, an actor may engage in one of the system-defined relationships and assume an identity warranted by the relationship. By partitioning an identity based on role and relationship, a role/relationship identity management (RRIM) system can provide privacy and restrict information linkage attacks. A role-based identity also provides anonymity for users by making them indistinguishable from other users of the same role.

Disavowing a Relationship: When a relationship is or appears to be privacy threatening for a participant, they can disavow the relationship and disappear in one of their role-based identities. Once returned to a role-based identity, a participant cannot be re-identified to their forgone relationship-based identity. For example, assuming a role-based identity (and corresponding identifier) as a registrant in a course, a learner is known to his fellow learners as a course-mate. Later on, the learner may negotiate a one-to-one relationship with another learner and subsequently choose a relationship-based identity (uni-directional identifier). As time progresses, the relationship may turn out to be disadvantageous for one of the learners and the valuable information released may appear to be at risk. Or, one learner may realize the disclosure of some critical information is extraneous for the respective context. In that situation, the learner could shed their relationship-based identity and put on a role-based identity from the current or any of the ancestor contexts (a registrant of the course or a Computer Science major) and negotiate another rela-

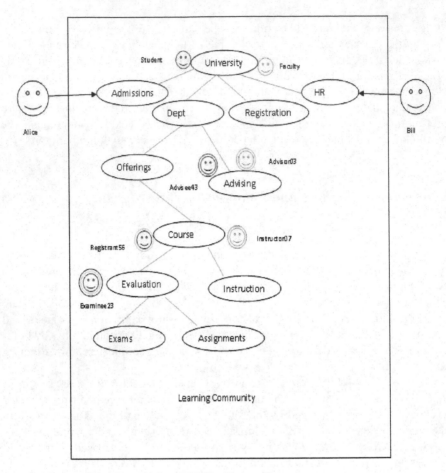

Fig. 4 Role-based Identities of Alice and Bill at Various Contexts

tionship afresh even with the previous partner expiring their previous uni-directional identifier and disassociating disclosed information from their new identity.

Temporal Aspect of Role and Relationship based Identity: Each role and relationship has some type of temporal aspect. After a certain amount of time, a role or a relationship-based identity and corresponding identifier become irrelevant to the context. For example, once a student graduates, their role as a student or their relationship with the housing authority becomes irrelevant. If the above role or relationship-based identity outlives an individual's studentship, it may jeopardize privacy for either that individual or other participants.

Expiration of Context: In an e-learning setting, every context has a purpose. A context may recursively spawn a finer grained context, which contributes to the purpose of their parent context. Once a purpose is achieved, the relevant context winds itself to its parent context. Any information disclosed for the purpose of the defunct context has to be made irrelevant for any other purpose. However, anything achieved in the defunct context that contributes to its parent context are attached to the participant's assumed role in the parent context.

Disclosure/ Obligation Management: To resolve foul acting, an actor in guarantor role may need to access the disclosed information of a participant. For the sake of transparency, a suspect should be allowed to observe the usage of their disclosed information. An obligation management tool for the guarantor and a disclosure management tool for the participants could help in this regard. Besides, for every possible context, usage guidelines for the disclosed information have to be developed and information receiver should be obligated to follow the guidelines. An information receiver needs to meet various obligations depending on many contexts, and an information giver needs to keep track of information shared with various parties.

Once the underlying purpose is achieved, the respective context or identity is no longer in use leaving no reason for misrepresentation. Once a context ends, information released in that context (under a role or a relationship-based identity) will be archived for a certain amount of time under its parent context for various needs (e.g. user modeling with mutual consent, resolving any complaint, etc.). For any archived information, the information archivist has an obligation regarding information retention or usage. As a context ends, the performance of an identity under that context may be propagated back to its parent context resulting in a backward propagation of values (reputation) from the innermost context to the outermost context. For example, in the outermost context, a person becomes a student for the purpose of attaining a degree. In the innermost context the student is evaluated in an assignment of a course, the student's mark in that assignment is propagated to its parent context of the course and the course grade is eventually propagated backwards to the outermost context contributing to achieving their degree.

Sanction against Foul Acting: Even though participants can disassociate themselves from their role or relationship based identities, they ought to be barred from doing so in case of any questionable action, while an investigation is launched by a participant holding a role with guarantor privileges. The roles perceived as holding the responsibility of a public trustee by other roles (e.g. an instructor in a course) are granted guarantor privilege. As part of a sanction, a participant found guilty of foul acting may be given identity imprisonment. By demonstrating satisfactory conduct, the participant can get digital forgiveness.

Identity Imprisonment: During communication between two actors, as soon as one senses some foul acting by the other, he/she could have the guarantor lock the identifier of the bad actor. In the locking process, complaints against the bad actor are filed to the guarantor of the respective context, and in response, the bad actor's activities are being monitored. Additionally, the bad actor will be restricted to change their existing identifier unless the bad actor is acquitted from complaints, or they have earned good reputation over a period of time. The victim may disown any information disclosed to the bad actor by choosing an omni-directional (indistinguishable) role based identity. Since the victim of the bad acting can identify and reject the bad actor, restricting the change of identifier is a sanction to the bad actor without revealing their true identity. In this way, the penalty for bad action is being condemned to an identity that cannot be shed.

354 M. Anwar et al.

Digital Forgiveness: On the other hand, by self-correcting and displaying good behaviour over a period of time, the bad actor can have the guarantor unlock their identifier with the bad reputation marker and let them choose a new identifier to be free of their haunting past. Once an actor is allowed to disown their guilt-ridden identity, they are forgiven from their committed bad acting. Other participants will no longer be able to identify the participant who has acted foul towards them in the past.

For example, a marker suspects the act of cheating by a student Alice during the marking of assignment1. The marker locks this identifier (i.e. Alice) and thereby reports to the guarantor of this context (i.e. the instructor) about the questionable act. Upon investigation, the instructor may lock the Alice identity for next two assignments that allows the marker to monitor Alice very closely for any further act of cheating. As Alice demonstrates integrity in the next two assignments, the instructor will unlock the Alice identity and allow the participant to assume a new identity. As a result, the participant of Alice identity will not be a victim of prejudice from the marker.

3.3 Worked Examples

In Table 1, we demonstrate the process of role and relationship-based identity management in the iHelp Discussion Forum, which acts as an online forum for students at the University of Saskatchewan to converse asynchronously with one another, with subject matter experts, and with their instructors. For example, as shown in Figure 4, upon logging on to the discussion forum page, a user with the pseudonym learner007 selects CMPT111 context to participate in the CMPT111 forum. As a result, an action menu followed by a list of posting threads for CMPT111 forum shows up on the upper right frame of the page. Then, learner007 may select an appropriate Action from the menu to start a new thread or to reply to an existing thread.

4 RELATED WORKS

In computer science, privacy is addressed from the perspectives of many areas from access control to data integrity to identity management [9]. Goffman's observations set the stage to think about privacy in terms of identity. He states that individuals reveal and conceal information selectively to maintain context-specific identity and social relationship [7]. Demchak and Fenstermacher note that privacy is directly related to the knowledge of identity [6]. A similar notion of privacy is manifested in the work of both Samarati and Sweeney [8, 9]. A general doctrine of their work is to release all the information, but to do so such that the identities of the people who are the subjects of the data (or other sensitive properties found in the data) are

Table 1 Role and Relationship Based Identity Management

Tasks	Processes
Context Constructions	Based on various purposes for discussions, various contexts are enumerated (e.g. University, CMPT, etc.; see oval 1 of Figure 6). Each context is created with a time-to-live time stamp to indicate an end after fulfilling its purpose.
Role-based Identity Constructions	Based on a user's relevance to a context and their expected activities in the context, each user account is granted various potential roles and a default pseudonym (e.g. academic11, learner002, etc.; see oval 2 of Figure 6) per role in various contexts.
Relationship-based Identity Constructions	A user in a given context may requisition for a relationship-based identity for a relationship type permitted for the assumed role (e.g. one-to-one student-teacher relationship) from the system. The system provides a default pseudonym (e.g. Bill; see oval 3 of Figure 6).
Identity Awareness	Each user sees a side-ways contextual identity tree (see Figure 4 & Figure 6) upon logging on to the system. Before submission of a message, a user sees the preview of their message, underpinning context, assumed role, and pseudonym.
Identity Assumptions	Upon a single sign-on, a user may choose a context, role, or relationship node (by left clicking on the node) from the contextual identity tree to participate in a respective capacity under a respective context. A user may right click in a pseudonym of a role in a context and choose from the lists of sub-contexts to use the same identity in the sub-context; see oval 4 of Figure 6).
Identity Expirations	A role- or a relationship- based identity and its associated postings are expunged from the system at the end of its owner context (the context for which the identity is created). If a role-based identity is used at any of the inner contexts of its owner context, the identity and the associated postings are expunged from only that inner context at its end. A user may shed any of their role- or relationship-based identity at anytime unless the identity is locked (see Identity Locking task). For that matter, the user may request the system to remove any message posted under their disowned identity.
Identity Locking	The user of a locked identity is barred from changing their pseudonym, and the user is not allowed to construct a new identity in the same context. For example, when a student with Student11 pseudonym is sanctioned for bad acting in a CMPT250 course forum, that student is locked in their Student11 pseudonym.
Digital Forgiveness	When a bad actor is forgiven, they are allowed to change their pseudonym associated with the foul acting or to create a new identity. When a bad actor is forgiven, they are allowed to change their pseudonym associated with the foul acting or to create a new identity.

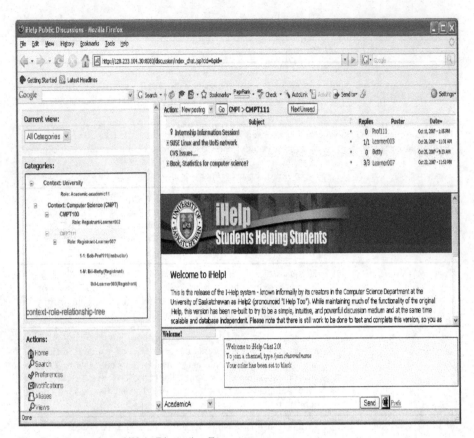

Fig. 5 A Screenshot of iHelp Discussion Forum

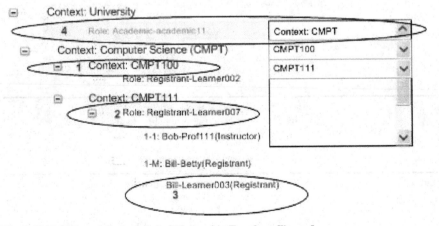

Fig. 6 Explanation of Context-Role-Relationship Tree from Figure 5

protected. In the similar notion, we view that a learner's or a teacher's privacy is their capacity to control the disclosure and usage of their identity information.

Our role- and relationship-based identity approach is inspired by digital identity management approaches appear in the literature [3]. An identity management system helps users to select among the anonymous, pseudonymous, or identified interactions and help them maintain the underlying identity. However, users need to understand context to select and maintain context-specific identities and social relationships. In the real world, our body conveys part of our identities by projecting information about ourselves [5]. In the disembodied online world, we lack adequate contextual cues to understand contexts. Besides, information can proliferate in lighting speed making it hard to understand the true nature of our audience. In the real world, our identity becomes irrelevant or unimportant in most part (except for very few purposes like legacy) with the passing away of our body. However, once an identity is disclosed, it may live in the online space forever. Therefore, an identity management system should facilitate understanding of contexts, crafting of contextual and temporal identities, expiring of identities, and ensuring accountability to help us properly control our identity and thereby preserve privacy.

5 CONCLUSION AND FUTURE WORK

The broad acceptance and adoption of e-learning amplifies the issues of privacy. Unlike the majority of the privacy-related research in the e-learning domain that aims at addressing only learners' privacy, we feel the need for a privacy-enhanced environment to support privacy for all the participants of e-learning. In that vein, we investigated the identity management approach to build a privacy-enhanced e-learning environment. We have identified the following inadequacies of identity management approaches that have appeared in the literature in addressing privacy: a) the notion of context is ambiguous and it is onus of users to understand the context; b) a partial identity of a user does not carry a temporal aspect; c) there is no expiring or reconstructing of a partial identity; and d) balancing of privacy and accountability are not addressed. Focusing on the above mentioned inadequacies, we present a role and relationship-based identity management approach in building a privacy-enhanced e-learning environment.

An important contribution of this work is that it creates a generalizable approach to data expiration. Personal or confidential information that is associated with a pseudonymous individual in a relationship-based identity context becomes disconnected from the person when the context expires. Thus the data itself, even if saved or retained, is disconnected from any individual and thus becomes useless for anyone trying to misuse (or re-use) personal information.

This paper introduces the notion of role- and relationship- based identity management by focusing on the e-learning domain. Since e-learning is an application area that comprises many scenarios, which are common in the digital world, this approach can naturally be adapted into other domains. Once the role hierarchy of a domain is defined and types of relationships among roles are classified, this model can be applied to that domain to allow participants to construct role and relationship-based identities for purpose-based well-defined contexts. We are in the process of building prototypes of a more general role and relationship-based identity management system. We will verify our prototype with user studies.

References

1. Anwar, M., Greer, J., and Brooks, C.: Privacy Enhanced Personalization in E-learning. In Proceedings of the 2006 International Conference on Privacy, Security, and Trust (PST2006), Markham, Ontario, Canada (2006)
2. Borcea, K., Donker, H., Franz, E., Pfitzmann, A., and Wahrig, H.: Towards. Privacy-Aware Elearning. In: G. Danezis, and D. Martin (eds.) Lecture Notes in Computer Science, pp. 167–178. Springer, Heidelberg (2005)
3. Camenisch, J., Shelat, A., Sommer, D., Fischer-Hübner, M. H. S., Krasemann, H., Lacoste, G., Leenes, R., & et al.: Privacy and Identity Management for Everyone. In Proceedings of the workshop on Digital identity management, Fairfax, VA, USA (2005)
4. Cavoukian, A. and Hamilton, T. J.: Privacy Payoff: How Successful Businesses Build Customer Trust. McGraw-Hill Ryerson, (2002)
5. Davis, F.: Fashion, Culture and Identity. University of Chicago Press, Chicago, IL (1992)
6. Demchak, C. C. and Fenstermacher, K. D.: Balancing security and privacy in the information and terrorism age: distinguishing behavior from identity institutionally and technologically. The Forum, 2(2), Article 6, (2004)
7. Goffman, E.: The Presentation of Self in Everyday Life. Doubleday, New York, NY (1959)
8. Samarati, P.: Protecting respondents' identities in microdata release. IEEE Transactions on Knowledge and Data Engineering, 13(6), 1010-1027 (2001)
9. Sweeney, L.: k-Anonymity: A Model for Protecting Privacy. International Journal of Uncertainty, Fuzziness and Knowledge-Based Systems, 10(5), 557–570 (2002)
10. Westin, A. F.: Privacy and Freedom. Atheneum, New York, NY (1967)

Using Rummble as a Personalised Travel Guide

Clive J. Cox

Abstract Rummble Ltd (www.rummble.com) is an online mobile local content provider that gives users access to trusted spatially-located content via the web and mobile. Rummble brands itself as a *"Personalised travel guide written by your friends"*. Users sign up and build a social network. They upload reviews of places they have visited and provide ratings for them. The service carries out a trust network analysis on each person's friends network and determines the individually most trusted people in their network. The service can then determine the likelihood a user will enjoy visiting a particular place by combining the trust (and ratings) for each person who has reviewed the place in question. For example, a user visiting the Barri-Gotic in Barcelona can immediately find via their mobile phone bars and restaurants they might like which have been reviewed by trusted people from their friends network and rated highly.

1 Demonstration Overview

The demonstration will show both the web and mobile interfaces provided by the service. The web service provides the usual selection of social networking tools: mail, blogs, photo upload, message board. There is functionality related to the mobile domain, SMS sending, control of who can send the user SMSs and when. Also, there is functionality related to spatial content: the user can specify their future trips and find out who will be in the same location and they can say where and when they will be periodically each day (e.g., office, home).

The core of the web service is the Rummble Explorer which allows users to explore via a Google maps mashup locations and find content that has been entered by members of their social network. This content can be filtered by tags and distance inside the social network and most pertinently by the trust the user has in the

Clive J. Cox
Rummble.com, Cambridge, England e-mail: clive.cox@rummble.com

Please use the following format when citing this chapter:

Cox, C. J., 2008, in IFIP International Federation for Information Processing, Volume 263; *Trust Management II*, Yücel Karabulut, John Mitchell, Peter Herrmann, Christian Damsgaard Jensen; (Boston: Springer), pp. 359–362.

content. Fig.1 shows a view of Barcelona with one "Rummble" for Cafe Schilling highlighted, showing its trust.

Fig. 1 Trust for a Cafe in Barcelona

The trust for the content is derived from the user's trust of the three people who reviewed Cafe Schilling and the rating is an expected rating derived from this trust and the ratings given by the three users showing what the system's present guess is for what the user's rating would be if they visited the cafe and rated it.

The user can then drill down into the actual review for Cafe Schilling and read the individual reviews and ratings and see the indivudal trust they have for each reviewer, as shown in Fig.2.

In order to lessen the possibility of information overload the Rummble Explorer can show only the content that the service believes the user might enjoy. This ability which is of even greater importance in mobile environments is available on the mobile Java application that Rummble provides. The demonstration will show this application in use. The mobile application is a rich client which provides functionality to:

1. Set your location via a map, GPS, or place name anywhere in the world.
2. Browse via a map the Rummble content and upload new content.

Fig. 2 Reviews for Cafe Schilling

3. Chat to Rummble users and on external IM networks (e.g., Yahoo, MSN, IRC etc.)

Fig.3 shows the mobile application showing the places it recommends for the part of Barcelona displayed on the map. As with the web application the user can read the indivudal reviews for the place in question and see their trust for each reviewer. By utilizing filtering based on the trust network analysis the user can be provided with a smaller and hopefully more appropriate selection of content which will allow them to quickly find places of interest while on the move with their mobile.

2 Conclusion

The recommendations provided by Rummble are based on private and transitive trust between users, and thereby provide a highly personalised service. Rummble harnesses social networks together with the Internet and mobile networks to assist

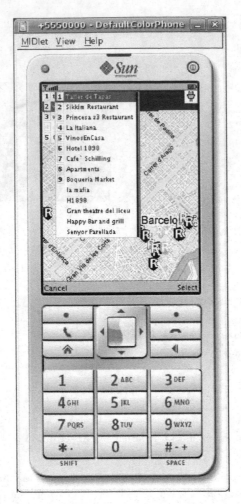

Fig. 3 Recommendations on the mobile application

people in finding places and selecting services that they will find interesting, useful and enjoyable.

An Inline Monitoring System for .NET Mobile Devices*

Nicola Dragoni, Fabio Massacci and Katsiaryna Naliuka

Abstract Users of mobile devices are increasingly requesting a controlled way to exit from the sandboxing model in order to exploit the full computational power of the device. Porting in-line security monitors to mobile devices requires to solve both theoretical and practical challenges. Current security monitors provided solutions only for the desktop and either monitor a single instance of an application. In this demonstration we show an inline monitoring system for .NET mobile devices developed in the context of the EU-FP6-IST-STREP-S3MS project[2]. The demonstration consists of two different demos with real mobile devices, highlighting the usage model and the main features of the system.

1 Usage Model

The goal of the inline monitoring system ([1] for details) is to give to the user the opportunity of downloading a completely untrusted program on its mobile device and then to run it safely. The inline monitoring system is used to enforce the user policies in a reliable and autonomous way. Obviously, in order to control the execution of the program the monitor needs to be notified about the relevant actions of the program. At first we could rewrite the entire virtual machine but this would require Microsoft or Sun preliminary agreement, and this effort alone would dwarf any technical difficulty. In-line monitors [2, 3, 4] looked more promising.

For this reason, we offer the possibility to rewrite the downloaded program inserting (*in-lining*) hooks that notify the monitor before and after each security-relevant

Nicola Dragoni and Fabio Massacci and Katsiaryna Naliuka
DISI - University of Trento, Via Sommarive 14, POVO (TN) - Italy, I-38100. e-mail: name.surname@disi.unitn.it

* Research partly supported by the projects EU-FP6-IST-STREP-S3MS, EU-FP6-IP-SENSORIA, EU-FP7-IP-MASTER.

[2] http://www.s3ms.org

Please use the following format when citing this chapter:

Dragoni, N., Massacci, F. and Naliuka, K., 2008, in IFIP International Federation for Information Processing, Volume 263; *Trust Management II*; Yücel Karabulut, John Mitchell, Peter Herrmann, Christian Damsgaard Jensen; (Boston: Springer), pp. 363–366.

event. The in-lining is performed directly on the device, so that we do not need to rely on any third party for that. As the result of the in-lining each security-relevant method is executed only if it has been allowed by the policy.

Example 1. Figure 1(a) shows two HTC P3600 smartphones playing chess by sending each other SMSs. The smartphone on the left has no monitoring framework installed, so the game is allowed to send as many SMSs as it will. The monitoring system of the phone on the right detected that the user-defined limit of the sent messages was exceeded. For this reason the game is terminated through the security exception.

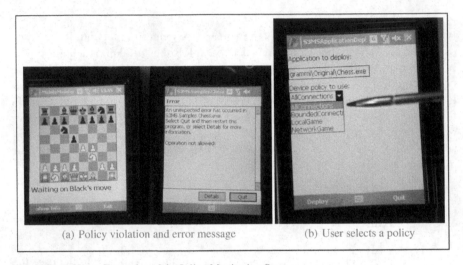

(a) Policy violation and error message   (b) User selects a policy

Fig. 1 Basic Usage Examples of the Inline Monitoring System

While the in-lining of the downloaded programs is performed on-device, the policies need to be managed off-line. The security policies are written in our policy language 2D-LTL and then automatically converted in the form suitable for monitoring. This representation of the policy is deployed to the device, where it is used by the in-liner to extract the method calls that are relevant to the policy and by the monitor itself.

As writing the policies in the logic-based language is likely to appear to complex for an average user, this task might be undertaken by the mobile service provider as the added-value service. At the end of the day the user simply selects the "right" policy from a pull-down menu (See Fig. 1(b)).

Example 2. Fig. 1(b) shows how a user of HTC P3600 might choose between four pre-set policies allowing any kind of connections, a bounded number of connections (max SMS sent and max MB downloaded), some access to GPRS or a purely local game where no connection is allowed.

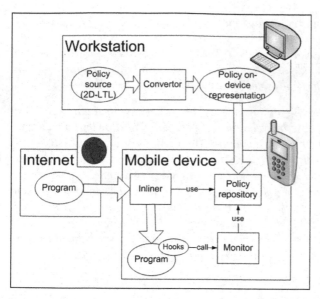

Fig. 2 Usage Model

Summing up Fig. 2 show our basic usage model that is further described below.

Scenario 1 *The user designs his security policies or, if he or she is not competent enough, picks the predefined one from the operator. The policy is formalized in the logical language 2D-LTL, which is described below. Then the policies are automatically compiled in the form suitable for the runtime monitoring. The compiled policies are deployed at the device. When the application is downloaded and installed at the device it might be in-lined with any of the user policies. After the user selects the policy the application is rewritten and the calls to the monitor are inserted before and after each call to the method mentioned in the policy. Then when the application is run the monitor checks whether its execution satisfies the policy, and is the violation is detected a security exception is raised in the application. If the application does not handle the security exceptions then it terminates. Otherwise if the developers took the security exceptions into consideration the application may be able to proceed (or at least to terminate gracefully, notifying the user about the situation). But in any case the execution that violates the policy will not be possible.*

2 Demonstration Description

The demonstration of the inline monitoring system consists of the following two demos.

Demo 1 *Bob and Anna want to play with a m-MMPORG game using their HTC P3600 smart phones. After they have downloaded the game on their devices, they* *select the same policy and they start to play. Unfortunately, Anna downloaded a malicious version of the mobile game: in the background it tries to connect to the remote server and to download tons of data. Thanks to the inline monitoring system the "good" version downloaded by Bob works properly and the malicious version downloaded by Anna crashes and is not allowed to execute.*

Demo 2 *Now Bob wants to play a downloaded chess game with Anna. As shown in Figure 1(b) he might choose between four pre-set policies allowing any kind of connections, a bounded number of connections (max SMS sent and max MB downloaded), some access to GPRS or a purely local game where no connection is allowed. He chooses the second policy and he runs the mobile chess application. Figure 1(a) shows the two HTC P3600 smart phones playing chess by sending each other SMSs. The smart phone of Anna (on the left) has no monitoring framework installed, so the game is allowed to send as many SMSs as it will. The monitoring system of the phone of Bob (on the right) detected that the user-defined limit of the sent messages was exceeded. For this reason the game is terminated through a security exception.*

References

1. Massacci, F., Naliuka, K.: Beyond Sandboxing: an Effective In-line Monitoring System for Mobile Code. Available at: http://www.ing.unitn.it/~massacci/mass-nali-08-implementation.pdf.
2. Erlingsson, U., Schneider, F. B.: IRM Enforcement of Java Stack Inspection. In Proceedings of SSP-00, Washington, DC, USA, 2000.
3. Erlingsson, U.: The Inlined Reference Monitor Approach to Security Policy Enforcement. Department of Computer Science, Cornell University, Technical Report 2003-1916, 2003.
4. Hamlen, K.W., Morrisett, G., Schneider, F.B.: Certified In-lined Reference Monitoring on .NET. In Proceedings of PLAS '06, Ottawa, Ontario, Canada, ACM Press, 2006.

STORE - Stochastic Reputation Service for Virtual Organisations

Jochen Haller

Abstract Virtual Organizations (VOs) are an emerging business model in today's Internet economy. Increased specialization and focusing on an organization's core competencies requires such novel models to address business opportunities. In a VO, a set of sovereign, geographically dispersed organizations temporarily pool their resources to jointly address a business opportunity. The decision making process determining which potential partners are invited to join the VO is crucial with respect to entire VO's success. A reputation system can provide additional decision support besides the a priori knowledge about potential partners. To achieve this in this demonstrator, reputation, an objective trust measure, is aggregated from multiple independent trust sources that inherently characterize an organization's reliability. To allow for the desired predictions of an organization's future performance, a stochastic modeling approach is chosen. This demonstrator presents a research prototype of the full Reputation Service for VOs including a web based User Interface.

1 Introduction

Virtual Organisations (VOs) are an emerging business model in application domains with a high demand for cross-domain collaborative business processing. Increased collaboration among frequently changing, previously unknown business partners and focusing on an organisation's core competencies requires such novel models to address busi-ness opportunities. A VO is defined as a set of sovereign, geographically dispersed organisations that temporarily pool their resources to jointly address a business opportunity one organisation alone is not able to master [1]. This demonstrator consists of the Web

SAP Research, e-mail: jochen.haller@sap.com

Please use the following format when citing this chapter:

Haller, J., 2008, in IFIP International Federation for Information Processing, Volume 263; *Trust Management II*, Yücel Karabulut, John Mitchell, Peter Herrmann, Christian Damsgaard Jensen; (Boston: Springer), pp. 367–370.

Service based STORE reputation service [2] that delivers reputation based decision support for a business partner selection to an organization playing the role of a VO manager. The VO manager is tasked, among other duties, with the VO formation by identifying and inviting trusted business partners.

2 Description

The STORE research prototype, more concretely the service provider implementation, consists of three types of Axis Web Services[1], deployed in a Tomcat Web Container. Figure 1 depicts the services and their interactions which are described bottom-up in the following paragraph:

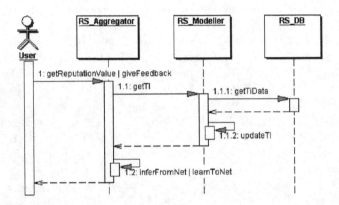

Fig. 1 Service Interaction Sequence Diagram

An organisation's (the trustee) reputation is based on so-called Trust Indicators (TIs), observable properties characterising the organisation's trusting behaviour. The database Web Service (RS_DB) collects the observed data for each TI which can then be retrieved by the TI Modelling Web Service (RS_Modeller). The latter service models each TI, according to a TI taxonomy, with probability density functions. Each TI is modeled in the taxonomy with individual attributes. These attributes entail a name, unique identifier, time interval in which period new data can be observed, a distribution assumption, etc. Delivery delay for instance is assumed to be exponentially distributed, since a trustworthy organisation is characterised by decreasing probabilities the higher a delay in days becomes. New data for this TI can be typically observed on a daily basis. Instead of a direct density estimation, a more robust posterior distribution $P(\theta|X)$ is calculated according to the Bayes Theorem.

[1] http://ws.apache.org/axis/

$$P(\theta|X) = \frac{P(X|\theta)P(\theta)}{\sum_S P(X|\theta)P(\theta)}$$

Newly observed data θ is hereby entering the equation as the emprirical distribution $P(\theta)$. The distribution assumption, denoting how a particular TI is expected to evolve, shapes the likelihood distribution $P(X|\theta)$. The latter also takes an organisation's past behaviour in form of historic data X into account. The denominator normalises the posterior distribution over a discretised time axis with states S.

The demonstrator implements the five TIs Cash Flow Quote, Country Bond Spread Index, Employee Fluctuation Rate, Delivery Delay and System Downtime with data fitting a large Brasilian company from the manufacturing industry. The third Aggregation Web Service (RS_Aggregator) infers an organisation's reputation value from the set of its characterising TI's posterior distributions[2] using a Bayes Network (BN). A BN can be represented by a directed, acyclic graph, where each node holds a random variable with a conditional probability depending on its parents. The tree topology used in this demonstrator aggregates the TI posterior densities as evidence (leaf) nodes and the expectation value of root node's density delivers the reputation value.

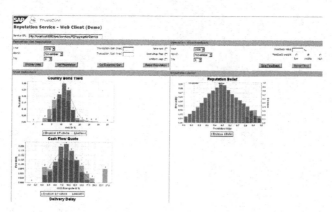

Fig. 2 Servlet User Interface (UI)

A VO Manager's representative (the trustor) who is interested in a potential VO member's reputation accesses the STORE service through a servlet generated UI using a standard Web Browser (Figure 2). A feedback mechanism to rate a selected VO member after conducted collaboration is also available.

---

[2] http://plato.stanford.edu/entries/bayes-theorem/

References

1. T.J. Strader, F. Lin, and M.J. Shaw. Information structure for electronic virtual organization management. *Decision Support Systems*, pages 75–94, 1998.
2. Till J. Winkler, Jochen Haller, Henner Gimpel, and Christof Weinhardt. Trust indicator modeling for a reputation service in Virtual Organisations. *The 15th European Conference on Information Systems (ECIS)*, 2007.

Author Index